CRITICAL ESSAYS: 1944 - 1996

Classic Anthropology

John W. Bennett

with contributions
by Leo A. Despres
and Michio Nagai

Transaction Publishers
New Brunswick (U.S.A.) and London (U.K.)

Library of Congress Catalog Number: 97–45618
ISBN: 1–56000–333–2
Printed in the United States of America

Library of Congress Cataloging-in-Publication Data
Bennett, John William, 1915–
Classic anthropology : critical essays, 1944–1996 / John W. Bennett with contributions by Leo A. Despres and Michio Nagai.
p. cm.
Includes bibliographical references and index.
1. Anthropology. I. Despres, Leo A. II. Nagai, Michio. III. Title.
GN25.B46 1998
301—dc21 97–45618
CIP

I would like to dedicate this book to the memory of the three Classic anthropologists whose work had the most influence on my early thinking and research:

Robert Redfield

W. Lloyd Warner

Clyde Kluckhohn

Contents

Tables and Figures

Preface

In 1994 I thought it was about time to compile a bibliography of my writings, and in the course of that effort I reread a number of my earliest articles and essays on sociocultural anthropology, plus various associated correspondence and notes. I was struck by the fact that some of the pieces fell into a rough developmental sequence from the early 1920s to the 1950s—not that I was actually writing in the 1920s—but beginning in the early 1940s I produced a number of essays about theories and methods covering a time period from the 1910s to the 1950s. This gave me an idea: if I could supplement these older pieces with additional essays I would have a kind of personal intellectual history of the era. And the dates I eventually selected—from 1915 to 1955—seemed to cover the period of classic efflorescence of anthropology in the twentieth century. Why not give it a name? The term "Classic anthropology era" came to mind, since much of the work produced during that period seems to be regarded as the most typical or perhaps the finest the discipline ever produced. The nature of the previously published pieces established the approach of the book: it could not be a formal history of the era and its works, on the order of Lowie's 1937 masterpiece, nor a blockbuster compendium like Harris's 1968 volume. It would have to consist of a series of analytical essays on particularly important works and ideas that shaped the intellectual outlook of the era—or at least, *my* outlook.

Now, the trouble with a collection of essays is the difficulty of maintaining continuity and thematic integrity. In order to assist the reader in his effort to find some unity, I supply the following comments: first, the essays contain a running commentary on the concept of culture—that concept which represents the dominant idea in Classic anthropology—at least in the United States. I develop two principal criticisms: first, the concept always seemed to me to have little relevance as a tool for explaining the world around us. For example, in my chapter 14 on "populist" anthropology, each author of the three books discussed, after pages of archaeology and ethnology, winds up with devastating criticisms of contemporary society and world affairs—hardly a word of which can be traced back to the anthropological concepts or research described earlier. It was also my early conviction that the anthropologists of the era never fully understood the consequences of using a second-order abstraction—a collective noun—to explain or interpret the nature of human behavior.

Second, anthropology during this era was dependent on data from tribal societies—that is, relatively isolated "folk" cultures, mostly removed from modern urban-industrial civilization, although influenced by it. This specialized data inhibited the discipline's ability to comprehend the nature of modern culture as it had began in the eighteenth century in Europe. But at the same time, anthropologists insisted on interpreting modern life as if their specialized concepts and data had prepared them for the task!

Third, some of my essays comment on the moral ambiguity of anthropology's attempt to report on and understand people who were actually vulnerable to exploitation—and possibly even made so by the reportage produced by ethnologists. Correlated is the peculiar resistance shown by academic anthropologists to applied social science (see chapter 12). I suspect this was due not only to scholarly arrogance, but also to a fear that such work might expose the moral shortcomings of the discipline. And these, of course, also were related to the prevailing relativism of anthropology's methodological and theoretical posture.

Finally—the very format, a collection of essays—can convey the episodic character of anthropology's intellectual organization. That is, it can be argued that discrete "essays" on interesting and important topics actually is anthropology's essence—then and now. I do not think that this is necessarily a bad thing: it results in constant exploratory novelty, and eclectic interpretation. In several of the older essays, I have included supplements which report on correspondence with critics, and which update some of the research.

I wanted the topics and people reviewed in the essays to represent dominating methods and themes of the discipline, and this, on the whole, meant social and cultural anthropology. As a matter of fact, the Classic era was sociocultural anthropology's greatest episode: bioanthropology, linguistics, and other subfields were in the shade—

and archaeologists strove mightily to be included in the sociocultural category.

Among the topics I have neglected is economic and ecological anthropology. This worried me because the most productive phase of my career was spent researching and theorizing in these fields. However, I had already produced collections of my papers and other writings in the econological field: my *Ecological Transition* (1976) and *Human Ecology as Human Behavior* (1993–96). In addition, I felt that the most important piece of writing produced in the field during the Classic era was Julian Steward's 1936 essay on the ecology and social organization of hunting bands—this essay was not only vital to econological anthropology, but influenced other aspects of Classic-era theory. However, anthropologists did not become aware of the full relevance of Steward's piece until the very end of the era or in the succeeding post-Classic period. As for myself, I first read it in the last years of the 1950s but did not really begin to use it until the mid-1960s.

I have included Americanist archaeology in the book (chapter 11) because it played a special role in my intellectual upbringing, and also because a remarkable efflorescence of archaeological theory based on cultural anthropology occurred during the Classic era. I selected Walter Taylor's 1948 book, *A Study of Archaeology*, to represent the ferment that American archaeology went through during the 1930s and 1940s, and also because I have always felt that Taylor's book was in some respects a neglected masterpiece.

I consider that the only significant multidisciplinary field to include academic sociocultural anthropology as a participant during the Classic era was psychological anthropology, or "culture and personality" as was the dominant expression. I have included an extended essay dealing with various aspects of the interface.

Chapter 8 deals with social organization—particularly kinship—the only chapter to concern itself with the sociological side of the discipline. The chapter also includes a sideline critique of structural-functional method and theory.

I have included a separate chapter on Benedict and Mead—the "famous lady anthropologists," as the public and the media called them in the 1940s and 1950s—because of their distinctive public renown—something no other anthropologist had or has attained. Benedict's *Patterns of Culture* (1934) was the most widely disseminated serious work produced by an anthropologist then and since, and it created an interpretive wing of anthropological effort and thought which continues to inform both the profession and the public. Margaret Mead personified anthropology to two generations of scholars and professionals in all fields of science, not just anthropology, and especially to the public: she was, in her biographer's phrase, a "citizen-philosopher," and no anthropologist before or since can be said to have truly fulfilled this role. Moreover, Mead always tried to use anthropological knowledge in her diagnoses and recommendations for dealing with the problems of modern civilization—something few other anthropologists did.

Although I was originally trained in Classic anthropology, my long-term interests took a divergent path, and I really cannot claim to be an authentic survivor of the era. At Beloit College in the 1930s I more or less specialized in southwestern archaeology, but also took extensive course work in history and the social sciences. At Chicago, under the influence of its broad multidisciplinary training, and the excitement of World War II, I moved into the study of contemporary communities and institutions, and aside from intermittent occasional excursions into ethnological theory and Midwestern archaeology, I spent much of my career outside the inner circles of the discipline. But I have somehow retained my curiosity about the era and a desire to interpret it. I have never been satisfied with most histories of anthropology, which strike me as rather pedantic, with too many names and dates and references to writings, and with a tendency to overestimate or underestimate the significance of certain materials. Biographies of major figures of the era show a tendency to exaggerate his or her influence on minds both within and outside of the discipline. While I have read most of these biographies (and a few autobiographies) I have used little material from them.

I have dedicated the book to three Classic anthropologists whose work influenced mine. Robert Redfield taught me the history of anthropology from his unique viewpoint, distinguishing historical from scientific approaches, and his concept of the "folk society" shaped my first research project and theoretical writings. W. Lloyd Warner introduced me to comparative sociocultural anthropology—his famous "Comparative Institutions" course at Chicago demonstrated the ways that anthropological ideas could be used to deal with issues in contemporary society. Clyde Kluckhohn, at long distance, was my chief source for interdisciplinary methodology, as well as the systematic theoretical approaches of social science and psychology.[1]

In the last analysis, the main problem in writing about the history of anthropology is the lack of a clear-cut central problem or substantive issue in the discipline. One can write a history of geology or astronomy and find it is a continuously unfolding story of discovery: fact based on fact; concept based on concept. Among the social sciences, the institutional fields—economics, political science, and to some extent sociology—have something of this unfoldingness since their subject matters are reasonably consistent and explicit. But anthropology, while presumably investigating culture as a central substantive entity has, by and large, recorded endless diversity and change, and these mainly in an archaic branch of humanity. Exceptions can be found for archaeology, for the process of material evolution and the general drift toward increasing complexity in all aspects of human affairs—themes which the social evolutionist theorists of the nineteenth century pushed to the limit. Unfortunately defective data and methodology discredited their approach, and although there have been efforts to revive it, it has never regained its prestige. And, in any event, modern global social and cultural historians like Fernand Braudel, Samuel Huntington, and Felipe Fernandez-Arnesto have concretized many of the themes.

Eight of the essays in the book were published before 1995—the oldest in 1944, and these older rather formal and didactic pieces reflect a prevailing acceptance of the Classic era and its central themes although they are not devoid of critical comment. The more recent essays, and especially those written for the volume in the 1990s, have a more informal style and are more analytic and objective in their views of the Classic era. I have avoided major rewriting and revising of the older pieces, because I want the reader to view them as more or less *vernacular expressions of Classic anthropology and its critical fringe*. The earlier items are usually more fully documented, and contain more in the way of period jargon. Most were written for periodicals whose editors insisted on ornamentation. As one ages, confidence in one's own ideas and exposition should increase, and respect for academic pomposities and rhetoric should lessen. I have analyzed and critiqued the material on its own terms, on the whole, and avoided the use of concepts and approaches of the 1980s and 1990s.

A Note on Style

The older essays in this collection presented a problem insofar as they used the present tense to refer to the authors and the ideas. I preserved most of these since I wanted to use the older pieces as exemplars of the dialog and semantics of Classic anthropology. In addition, the present tense is used in some cases as the "literary present"; that is, "as Jones states in his book...." In most cases I converted these present tenses to past, especially if the author cited or quoted was no longer professionally active. And where present tenses and other statements might lead to a false impression of where I stand on certain issues, I have inserted dates or appropriate comments in brackets.

Acknowledgements

George Crothers did yeoman service on secretarial assistance and word processing service. He also performed bibliographic research and basic background research for several chapters, especially chapter 11. Patty Jo Watson and David Browman advised on professional backgrounds and theoretical matters relating to chapter 11. Robert Sussman helped with interpretive problems relating to human evolution and the image of man in anthropology. Richard Fox provided encouraging support for chapter 15. All of these people read portions of the manuscript and supplied useful comments. Additional word processing service was provided by Deborah Rekase.

Notes

1. Although I have generally avoided references to my own career, I feel that in addition to the three persons to whom the book is dedicated, I should mention two additional names: James B. Griffin was my mentor for my brief archaeological career, although he was employed by the University of Michigan. He escorted me on several field trips and also provided me with a fount of insights and information on the prehistoric cultures of the United States. Herbert Passin, recently of Columbia University, was a close friend and colleague during graduate study days, and he was, I think, instrumental in inducting me into sociocultural anthropology, and into the applied anthropological work associated with World War II.

Literature Cited

Benedict, Ruth. 1934. *Patterns of Culture*. Boston: Houghton Mifflin.

Bennett, John W. 1976. *The Ecological Transition: Cultural Anthropology and Human Adaptation*. London: Pergamon.

———. 1993–96. *Human Ecology As Human Behavior: Essays in Environmental and Development Anthropology*. Expanded edition published 1996. New Brunswick, NJ: Transaction Publishers.

Harris, Marvin. 1968. *The Rise of Anthropological Theory*. New York: Thomas Y. Crowell.

Lowie, Robert H. 1937. *The History of Ethnological Theory*. New York: Farrar & Rinehart.

Steward, Julian H. 1936. "The Economic and Social Basis of Primitive Bands," in *Essays in Honor of A. L. Kroeber*, edited by R. H. Lowie. Berkeley: University of California Press.

Taylor, Walter W. 1948. *A Study of Archaeology*. Originally published as "Memoir no. 69," American Anthropological Association. Reprinted privately in 1964 by W.W. Taylor. Reprinted by Southern Illinois University Press, Carbondale, in 1967 and 1983.

1

Classic Anthropology: An Introduction

Introduction

In using a term like "Classic anthropology" I am aware of the risks of introducing yet another term with which to pigeonhole a complex and diverse scholarly field. Lowie (1937) focused on schools of thought and their adherents, and Harris, on the whole, did likewise (1968). Stocking (1987) invented "Victorian anthropology," which includes a major subtype: evolutionary anthropology. And then there is "Boasian anthropology" or "historical particularism." Penniman (1965) offered four main periods for the modern era, beginning in the late nineteenth century: convergence, construction, critical, and convergence and consolidation. Murray Leaf (1979) divided all Gaul into monistic and dualistic. My Classic era is clearly retrospective: I am looking back on something I experienced as a student and an entering professional, and, on the whole, I admire it and view it with a certain nostalgia. For like all "classic" phenomena—scholarly or automotive—it has a certain integrity.

I suggest that the Classic era had its decisive intellectual beginning in the 1910s, when the implications of Franz Boas's ideas about Culture led his students to strike out in novel theoretical directions, and continental ideas about Society began surfacing in Britain. It is not hard to argue that Kroeber's (1917) "Superorganic" paper, however controversial, represents a trendsetting piece of writing for the entire Classic era, or certainly in the United States. For ethnology, I nominate Malinowski's (1916–48) "Baloma" monograph as the beginning of systematic thinking about the relationship of tribal people to their social milieux (chapter 7). Margaret Mead and Ruth Bunzel, in their 1960 blockbuster anthology, *The Golden Age of American Anthropology*, gave part 5 of their book the title "Classical Period in American Anthropology, 1900–1920." However, much of their period would really fall into what I would call the pre-Classic era. Mead and Bunzel were concerned with the origins and development of *American* anthropology, and while my essays do tend to focus on the American scene, this is so mainly because of the enormous output of material. In addition, Mead and Bunzel were not trying to trace the conceptual or methodological development of the field—they were mainly concerned with the Americanists's preoccupation with the Native American cultures.

However, Bunzel, in her introduction to the final section of the book, noted that "Around 1920 anthropology began to change. There was a completion and a new beginning—or perhaps several new beginnings, for a crossroads had been reached" (Mead and Bunzell 1960: 574). She states that the "sense of urgency" among the Americans to study and record the ethnography of the Native American groups had given way to a desire to study customs as phenomena in their own right—not merely in a context of particular ethnographic description. The "museum-type" problems of origins and distribution of cultural traits, which dominated the period from 1900, were replaced by an interest in culture change; the role of the individual in culture, including the issues raised by the increasing popularity of psychoanalysis; the nature of values; and a growing awareness that anthropology had a role to play in the diagnosis of problems of modern life. But Bunzel said nothing about functionalism, social-structuralism, the nature of ritual and magic, and other theoretical concerns emerging in European and American anthropology. Nineteen hundred and twenty also could be taken as the date the Americans began to find that other national anthropologies were transcending the purely descriptive ethnological undertaking, influenced by sociology, economics, and other social fields. Thus, one prime characteristic of the Classic era was a convergence of anthropological interests on an international scale.

My terminal date for the Classic era is the mid-1950s, although many developments characteristic of the Classic persisted into later decades. The International Symposium on Anthropology sponsored by the Wenner-Gren Foundation in 1952 was the major milestone: the names of three American anthropologists stand out in the organization of the Symposium and its aftermath: Alfred Kroeber, Clyde Kluckhohn, and Sol Tax. Kroeber and Kluckhohn were largely responsible for the proceedings volumes, *Anthropology Today* (Kroeber 1953) and *An Appraisal of Anthropology Today* (International Symposium on Anthropology 1952); and Tax was a principal figure in the publication of the *Yearbook of Anthropology* (one issue only, in 1955). In the following year, Tax edited a partial republication of the *Yearbook* under the title *Current Anthropology*, and this can be taken as one event in the origin of the now "world journal of anthropology," under the *Current Anthropology* title. The plans for the journal were announced in 1957, but the first issue did not appear until 1960.

In other words, the Classic era entered its terminal phase with the publication in the mid-1950s of a series of syntheses and procedural documents which announced that anthropology was to be viewed henceforth as an organized multidiscipline on a worldwide basis. The mid-1950s witnessed not only the inauguration of new ideas and subject matter, but also a revival or reassessment of older anthropological interests. The atmosphere is suggested by a brief comment I wrote for the first issue of *Current Anthropology* (1960: 1) in response to a flyer sent out by Tax prior to the editorial work on the issue:

> [Suggest] dealing with the revival of certain older ideas and approaches—e.g., evolutionism; environmentalism; biological basis of behavior. In my opinion, one of the most significant aspects of contemporary anthropology, at least its historical aspect, is precisely this revival of nineteenth- and early-twentieth-century approaches and problems—to create, perhaps, the new "general anthropology." I would think of the task,...as a contribution to the history of current anthropology.

Sub-eras of the Classic can be chronological or topical. Emphasizing American developments, in some of the essays I will attempt a three-way chronological-topical classification: an "early Classic," which is more or less equivalent to the historical anthropology of the 1920s; the "middle Classic," or the systematic ethnology of the 1930s; and the "late Classic," or the functionalist anthropology of the 1940s.

Please do not take these classifications and period datings too seriously. They are tags, simplifying complicated trends, and it should be remembered that ideas do not always conform to time periods: new ones usually have remote antecedents, and outworn notions can echo down the corridors of thought forever. Certainly this is the case with my pre-Classic era: the anthropology of the latter half of the nineteenth century and the first decade of the twentieth century. During the Boas revolution of the early Classic era this period was identified as the heyday of Evolutionary Theory. However, nearly every major approach which characterized the emerging Classic era had a predecessor of sorts in the pre-Classic: statistical analysis (e.g., Tylor 1888); proto-functionalist explanation (Henry Maine 1861); historical reconstruction (Pitt Rivers 1906); literary analysis (Gomme 1968); cultural psychology (Brinton 1902); and so on. It is true that most problems of the pre-Classic seemed to center around origins and stages of development, but the substantive topics and methods were diverse. Can we say the same for the way the Classic era prefigures and is carried forward in the post-Classic era? I am not sure: we are too close to the contemporary highly diverse developments.

In any event, something very important happened as a result of World War II: the transformation of the isolated, culturally integral tribal society. These people became citizens of new nations, and their cultures tend to become badges of social and political identity rather than expressions of innate ethnicity. This dual development pulled the rug out from under the themes and schemes of Classic anthropology. Not that it matters, particularly. Anthropology, in its new institutional guises (medical, educational, economic, etc.)—and its adventures in the field of literary analysis—seems to flourish despite the transient ambiguity of its central subject matter and theory. But one thing is certain: sociocultural anthropology in the 1990s does not command the attention from scholars in other fields that it did, say, in the late 1930s and 1940s, when it was producing reams of fascinating new data (although other subdivisions of the discipline continue to command attention, particularly human paleontology, precisely because it provides new information and insights on human origins and culture).

The Idea of Relativism

As I define it, most of the Classic era is contained in the period between the two World Wars: a crucial era in modern history since it marked the beginning of the contemporary age of sophisticated technology, advanced communication, and cultural pluralism—and, above all, the dawning of the age of relativism—which we may define as the acceptance by scholars of all forms of human existence and all ideas as more or less equally valid and worthy of serious consideration—at least at the moment of encounter. Relativism also means the objectification of all elements of human existence—anything becomes available for examination. Conventional or traditional values and judgments of validity are (theoretically) discarded as criteria.

As a general idea, relativism in its various forms (see Hatch 1983 for a list and definitions) was an inevitable product of the explosion of scholarship and scientific knowledge beginning in the late seventeenth century and continuing down into the nineteenth. The underlying issue was the refutation of Christian or other deterministic ideas about the superiority of particular versions of humanity, made necessary by the accumulating information on tribal peoples and Oriental civilizations. Although the doctrines of superiority of Western and/or industrial civilization persisted, special explanations were invented to rationalize the new knowledge of cultural diversity (which inclined toward relativism) with the residual beliefs about human dominance or the superiority of Western thought and research. The history of the era is really a kind of eat-your-cake-and-have-it-too. Darwinian knowledge demonstrated the membership of *Homo sapiens* in the animal kingdom, but it also could be used to demonstrate the superiority of Man over animals, or even, as in "social Darwinism," the superiority of Western man over all other populations.

Relativism also had a specialized significance in ethnographic investigation: a necessary methodological attitude. For an accurate or objective report on the way of life of an alien culture, it was necessary to eliminate all prejudice based on one's own ways and view the culture in a sympathetic but neutral manner. This neutrality, of course, could easily make its transition to affection: "my tribe" or "my culture" was heard in the corridors during meetings and conventions. And the technique also was carried into a general philosophy: all cultures were equal: equally good, equally valid—but paradoxically, "mine" was the best of all!

Value-neutrality (however quixotic) also fitted the dominantly secular spirit of the scientific and scholarly professions. Anthropology was one of the most aggressively secular of these fields because of its necessary methodological relativism and also because it was the heir of the nineteenth century victors in the battle of science versus religion, fought especially over the Darwinian concept of the descent of man. Anthropologists during the Classic era prided themselves on not being churchgoing creatures, and on their skepticism concerning all matters of supernatural belief—again, a useful attitude if one was to study all religions equally objectively. Of course, and again paradoxically, ethnologists could develop an emotional and even intellectual fascination with a "native religion" they had studied.

The Between-the-World-Wars was also an age of accelerated social and political change, but this was hardly represented in anthropology. If anything, anthropology was the one social study that seemed in its research to ignore the revolutionary developments triggered by world wars, revolution, and associated political upheavals. The French revolution and related national revolutions of the late eighteenth and early nineteenth centuries produced the first prototypes of social science, and some of these, like the great communitarian experiments, the anti-slavery activities, and of course the writings of Karl Marx, brought early social science close to the revolutionary political temper of the period. Anthropology did eventually produce its "Applied" version in the middle Classic (chapter 12), but the field was professionalized and academic—as compared to some of the "defense of native races" advocacies of the nineteenth century.

Relativism and Idealization of the "Folk"

Several things converged in the early and middle Classic era: first, ethnologists fell in love—so to speak—with their data, or the sources of the data: the little tribal or peasant communities they studied intensively and whose cultures they endeavored to record and memorialize (see chapter 2, where I call them "stories"). Second, eventually the doctrine of cultural relativity was translated into a doctrine of humanitarian liberalism, featuring an ideology of tolerance and respect for all human groups—and especially the exotic, strange, even the terrifying. Third, ideas in the larger intellectual domain began to have their effects; in particular, the American idealization of the rural, the agrarian kingdom where people usually worked too hard to indulge in serious struggle, and where children were taught to be sober and upright human beings. Related was the theme that Robert Redfield abstracted from Ferdinand Tönnies and other social philosophers: the notion of the *Gemeinschaft*, or "folk society," as Redfield (1940) translated it, giving it sociological-anthropological resonance. The concept listed a series of criteria in the left-hand column, emphasizing cultural homogeneity and interpersonal harmony and integrity, while in the right-hand column were the "urban" traits of disharmony, integrity, and so on (see chapter 4).

These attitudes added up to what can be called, following Robert Edgerton (1992), the "idealization of the folk." Edgerton called the "folk society" version a "community-lost theory," referring to the nostalgic idea that with the spread of urban industrializatism, the beauty and peacefulness of rural life was disappearing. That is, a kind of Golden Age notion to set against the secularized Progress theory of the urbanists. Thus, without fully realizing it, some anthropologists were lining up with a modern version of the Golden Age—or at least an anti-modern position, with the "folk" or at least tribal societies, representing a valuable and vanishing way of life. Aspects of this attitude persist into the 1990s, in the form of advocacy movements like Cultural Survival, which preach the need to preserve diversity and novelty in World Culture—just as the environmentalists seek to save the diversity of habitat and biome. Relativism had preached that humans—"culture*s*"—can do no wrong, and that exotic diversity is the salvation of human Culture.

One important consequence of this combination of relativism plus a special nostalgia for non-urban society and culture was an apparent neglect of what I have called the "dark side" (Bennett 1995) of human existence. This is a rather quixotic situation, since while ethnologists were in fact researching societies like Dobu (Fortune 1932) with their aggression, deceit, and cruelty, these phenomena tended to be played down, or at least blurred in a romantic fog based on the distance that ethnographic portraits of the exotic tended to have during the Classic era.[1] After all, the observed hate and violence was not ours, but someone else's, and at a long distance, and also—and this was probably crucial—being performed by unsophisticated primitives who could not be expected to know any better. I doubt if any of these conventional rationalizations were conscious—but I believe they were there nonetheless. To a degree, at least, they were part of the worldview of Chicago graduate students in the late 1930s and early 1940s. At the same time we were unable to admit that these rationalizations were really part of a fundamental moral ambiguity of anthropology's posture vis-à-vis the dependent colonial peoples who constituted the major source of data for the discipline.

The Spirit of Classic Anthropology

Pick a year in the late 1940s, and let us attend the American Anthropological Association (AAA) annual meeting. Total attendance is about 350 persons. It is either wartime or just after, and the total membership of the discipline in those years was around 2,000. The meetings I attended as a graduate student were small, and the "greats" were there and actually presented papers. Graduate student papers were rare, presented under the explicit sponsorship of a professional person, or confined to odd-hour sessions as fillers. Arguments between some of the "greats" were expected: I recall one vigorous floor argument between Herskovits and Malinowski (probably at an Evanston session of the AAA annual meeting in the Chicago area in 1939) over the issue of historicism versus functionalism, which was my introduction to the inherent tension between the "British" and the "American" brands of anthropology. (In my remembered opinion, neither of the great men won the argument, which we regarded as a form of theater.)

In those years, and resuming in the 1950s, after the war, anthropologists saw themselves as cocks of the walk; superior in all ways to dull, dry sociologists, and certainly far more vital than the method-obsessed psychologists. In an invitational paper given at a psychology meeting by Clyde Kluckhohn, and later published in the *American Psychologist* (1948), he noted that ". . . those few anthropologists who seriously concerned themselves with the matter at all, the academic psychology of the first third of this century seemed to be preoccupied mainly with investigating trivial problems by increasingly refined methods" (Kluckhohn 1948: 439). I believe that such anthropological arrogance was based mainly on the fact that the ethnologists were producing startling new information about human behavior in exotic settings, while sociologists and psychologists were stuck in the same old civilizational ruts.

While I was delighted to belong to the more vibrant discipline, I also appreciated the need for the prosaic "social sciences," and studied them as part of the University of Chicago multidisciplinary approach. I understood that sociology was "dull" because it was concerned with our own overly familiar—but vital—society, and in addition had responsibilities in the humdrum field of everyday "social problems." Psychology was attractive despite its picayune methodologizing because it told me things about human behavior I needed to know, even if I could not easily apply this knowledge to the particular problems that anthropology was concerned with at the time. The time did come, however, during World War II and its immediate aftermath, when I had to use my sociology and psychology to solve problems relating to the war and its effects—among others: public attitudes and changes in community social and economic life as a result of Japan Occupation reforms (Bennett and Ishino 1963); and attitudes and psychosocial adjustment problems of foreign students (Bennett et al. 1958).

Disciplinary arrogance aside, anthropology, like all professional scholarly fields, developed its own ideology and apologetics. The Classic era was, above all, a period of *academic* ascendancy, when anthropologists began coming out of the museums and institutes and teaching the knowledge of the field to young people and the public (chapter 14 deals with this "populist" function). Teaching requires a formal presentation of a discipline, and that requires a definition and defense of the discipline (anthropology was now *called* a "discipline"—whereas for much of the pre-Classic it was an occupation, an intellectual hobby, a way to have adventure, or some kind of moral pursuit).

However, from the mid-nineteenth century on, anthropological studies were conceived on the scientific model—although the precise meaning of the scientific component varied by field and over time. For much of the nineteenth and early twentieth century—my pre-Classic era—"science" was conceived mainly as a taxonomic or descriptive field. It was this view of anthropological science that the young Franz Boas brought into the United States and began teaching at Columbia University in the last decade of the century. This conception of science required the systematic collection and ordering of information on physique, words, and customs—and this classificatory effort characterized most of pre-Classic anthropology.

A change in this approach emerged in the late 1930s (what can be called the middle Classic) coincident with the rise of disciplinary social and psychological science. These fields were by their subject matter required to do more than describe and classify. They were dealing with phenomena which commanded public interest in social forces and causes. As soon as anthropologists began trying to answer "why" questions about behavior and ideas, they were propelled into a different brand of "science," and by the late 1930s some had come to believe that it might not be science at all, but some form of expressive endeavor. Benedict's *Patterns of Culture* was the most dramatic instance of this awareness of a new domain (Caffrey 1989: 215–7). The "art versus science" issue became a topic of regular disciplinary discussion (e.g., Redfield's piece in *Anthropology Today* [Kroeber ed. 1953: 728–38]). By this time, the label was "Science and the Humanities." Boas had begun moving in the direction of psychological analysis early on, and while Kroeber allowed that human mentality does lie at the basis of culture, on the whole he stuck to the natural-history conception of culture-as-a-thing-in-itself (chapter 10).

By the late 1980s, cultural anthropology had moved aggressively in the direction of literary themes and methods, with one wing denying that sociocultural anthropology was a science, and asserting that its subjective, even mystical approach nevertheless was capable of meaningful statements about the human reality—you do not need science if you have insight. Echoes of C. P. Snow's (1959) "two cultures" manifesto of the 1950s resounded in AAA conference halls. The arguments drifted into a dichotomy: anthropology was either a science or not one (e.g., Plattner 1997, which contains a useful summary of the 1990s situation). Dichotomizing seems of little value when it is really a matter of different kinds of data, and equally valid views—just as I, in chapters 2 and 3 (written a decade or so apart), managed to espouse both points of view without being fully conscious of their contradiction.

Similar bouts with identity and conceptual definitions have taken place in all the social sciences. By the 1970s sociology began to move back into social history; political science on the other hand—at least one branch—moved toward statistical or "hard science" analysis. Psychiatry became less of a social or humanistic field and more of a hard medical therapeutic routine. The art versus science dialog in the last analysis is not so much a matter of opinion or values but rather the nature of the data one acquires by whatever type of scholarship one uses, and what can be done with such data. Some fields become more "scientific," others more humanistic. Anthropology swings back and forth because its data include both subjective and objective components.

Classic anthropology had a variety of ideological and moralistic undercurrents, despite the prevailing relativism. Curtis Hinsley (1981: 20–22) emphasizes the moral background to nineteenth-century anthropology, or at least the American proto-anthropological efforts of the first half of the century, whose practitioners were concerned with helping the American Indians reach some sort of equilibrium; or with optimistic evolutionary ideas about human welfare and the improvement of the human race. But this was an implicit or major concern—the larger ideological position featured the notion—which carried into the twentieth century and characterized Classic anthropology—that human dominance of the Earth was on the whole a good thing: progress and the triumph of the species. There were, of course, undertones of dissent over some of Man's habits and proclivities, like war, but most aspects of human "Culture or Civilization," in Tylor's phrase, were viewed uncritically as examples of human accomplishment.

This value attitude was perhaps the ultimate source of the idea of cultural relativity, thus sterilizing the discipline and removing the moral sense which had been at least marginally evident earlier. As noted previously, aspects of the "dark side" of human existence were placed in a category of "value-laden" issues, and anthropologists were not really supposed to deal with them except descriptively, neutrally. Some of the "postmodern," "literary," or "deconstructionist" anthropologists, while guilty of a good deal of fanciful and convoluted rhetoric, nevertheless are to be congratulated as sometimes attempting to handle such problems.

The amorality and secular relativism of Classic anthropology—at least with respect to some issues—was responsible for another major characteristic of the discipline: its quixotic attitude toward colonial regimes. The tribal societies which formed the dominant body of data for the field were subject to the overlordship of industrial nations, but the nature of the rule was not, except in a few isolated cases, the topic of anthropological analysis. The middle Classic—late 1930s and the early 1940s—did see the rise of "acculturation" research and theory, but this was based on a rather neutral analysis of "culture change" and mostly avoided detailed or critical reference to the policies and procedures of political administrations. Anthropology in its Classic era depended on the continued existence of tribal peoples and the continued free access of ethnologists to them, and any attempt to attack the powers that controlled the colonies would endanger this.

Still another major characteristic of the Classic era was its theoretical and topical diversity. This, of course, was inevitable given its central concept: Culture—which included just about every manifestation of human thought and action since, and including, the Paleolithic. Culture was not a unifying concept, like the cell was for biology, but a synthetic label for a heterogeneous, changing entity. Therefore ways of interpreting this smorgasbord were equally various, since subject matter is king in all the fields dealing with humans. In 1992 Fredrik Barth wrote a rather sour piece in which he noted that the anthropologists have used such a variety of approaches that it is simply hard to conceive of them as belonging to the same discipline. He pleads for "more determined models and theories" (Barth 1992: 69) lest the discipline fall apart. This centrifugal tendency in anthropology has been noted since the 1920s, and yet somehow the field hangs together (and will—so long as universities provide a haven). My own view is that extreme diversity is an inevitable consequence of the epistemology of the discipline and cannot be changed—only constantly reviewed and regularly deplored. Clifford Geertz also deplores: in a 1995 book he announced the reduction and decline of the discipline—or at least the cultural sector, which he had dominated intellectually for years.

I believe that some of my essays also demonstrate still another characteristic: the peculiar asymmetry of Classic anthropological theory, that is, brilliant descriptive analyses of specialized segments of social behavior—for example, varieties of kinship structure, or ritualized role relationships—interpreted with a rather elementary central theory. On the other hand, sociology during the same period had a strong central theory of Society, in which macrolevel phenomena like stratification could provide answers to questions concerning micro-level segments. Anthropologists in the Classic era tried very hard to find such useful explanatory principles in the culture concept, but somehow this effort did not bear much fruit. The best they could do was a series of largely eclectic protocols like diffusion or acculturation. However, when Gregory Bateson (1936) began to use an interpersonal-dynamics version of structural-functionalism as a theoretical basis for interpretation, something new was at hand. Concepts like his "schismogenesis," with its linkage of social behavior to human thought processes, could have been the foundation of a different, multidisciplinary anthropological theory (chapter 9). But the major figures in charge of Classic anthropology found it difficult to understand a behavioral or sociopsychological level of analysis, and Bateson's seminal conceptualizing on how adaptive aspects of human behavior could be translated into traditional culture was not really followed up.

The Concept of Culture

So we come to the prime characteristic of the Classic era: its exposition of the culture concept (some would call it an "invention" of the anthropological discipline). As we shall note in later chapters, there was nothing particularly new about this idea: beginning in the Enlightenment, scholars had been aware that a collective term expressing the distinctive behavior of the species was necessary in order to describe crucial differences and similarities among humans. Anthropologists carried the idea to an extreme: postulating that humans had created something new in the world: an entity, a phenomenon outside the biological substratum which made Man fundamentally different—superior—to all other forms of life.

The result was to assimilate just about everything behavioral into the concept of culture—to paraphrase Alfred North Whitehead, culture became an "undifferentiated absolute." Edward Sapir, who displayed more sophistication about concepts and concept-formation than most of his contemporaries, got caught in typical Classic confusion in lectures which were chapters for his never-to-be-formally-published book, *The Psychology of Culture* (Sapir 1994). Sapir's basic view of culture at the ethnographic level was behavioral-interactionist: *culture* is not what people react to, but rather, *other people*, so that the real stuff of everyday life is "interpersonal relations" (a term Sapir borrowed from the psychiatrist Harry Stack Sullivan who had popularized it). And in such relations, "culture" can emerge as the remembered patterns of behavior which solve problems, define reality, and so forth. Fine, but on the other hand, in the first chapter (really a transcript of a lecture) of the putative book, Sapir takes the standard textbook approach of culture as an undifferentiated totality—without explaining that the concept is heuristic and can serve various purposes. He defines culture as, variously, significant symbols; repetitive behaviors; or "an ad hoc term for those aspects of experience that do in a sense transcend the individual and to which we can attribute an historical and geographical continuity" (Sapir 1994: 41–2). Or, culture can be any behavior which is "not psychologically necessary"; or, culture is any behavior that can be "historized" (ibid.: 36); or culture is "all those aspects of human life that are socially inherited" (ibid.: 34–5). And so on.

In any event, I have dealt with Classic anthropology's concept of culture in several chapters[2]—although the topic is approached quite differently in each. In chapter 2 I touch on the humanistic and "literary" aspects of culture; while in chapter 3, I expound on the social science concept of culture as an analytical abstraction made from observations of behavior. These chapters represent the two sides of a controversy which has dominated anthropology since the Classic era. Chapters 10 and 11 are devoted to A. L. Kroeber's and Walter Taylor's "searches" for the meaning and definition of culture.

These chapters certainly illustrate what I believe to be the underlying semantic dilemma of Classic anthropology: once you assert that Culture exists, you must define it, but when you define it, you imply—or actually assert—that an "analytical abstraction" has reality—and then you are in the soup, so to speak. You can find yourself assigning causal significance to Culture when, at the same time, the "culture" itself is created by the behavior you are attempting to explain.

Classic-era anthropologists also were reluctant to make important choices or distinctions between the mental or behavioral phenomena they perceived to be culture. Attitudes, values, ideology, prejudice, discrimination, customs, habits, images, illusions, and so on were sometimes mentioned in specific contexts, and a few of them developed into significant sub-disciplinary fields. However, anthropologists seemed to insist on unique labels for familiar phenomena. This happened to concepts like *ethos*, which represented on the whole what was more familiarly called *ideology* by historians. "Ideology" is an extremely useful term and concept, well-established in the general literature, and by inventing jargon terms like "ethos" or "configuration," Classic anthropologists gave the impression that they had discovered something new. But by performing such terminological neologistics they made it difficult to establish meaningful intellectual linkages with other disciplines concerned with human behavior and its historical changes.

Another characteristic of the Classic idea of culture was the increasing focus on localism and diversity—a direct result of preoccupation with what Walter Taylor called the "partitive" aspect of the concept: that is, *cultures*. This was characteristic of other branches of the discipline—recall that in the first half of the nineteenth century, under the aegis of Christian ideas about the brotherhood of man, the human species was conceived as a unity, and the racial differences were believed to be unimportant.[3] By the end of the century, the doctrine of separate races had begun to take hold, and became stronger in the first half of the twentieth century—until its ideological counterpart, the doctrine of racism or superior-inferior races, began to have undesirable political and social consequences, and research began to focus on basic similarities among species rather than differences—something that had been assumed by scholars like James C. Prichard in the first half of the nineteenth century.

Similarly, in much of the nineteenth century, human Culture was seen as a universal, and the background ideology was "the psychic unity of Man." As the culture concept began to take hold, and especially in the United States, this universalist doctrine was submerged by the emphasis on diverse cultures and in general, a celebration of differences between human groups. This led Classic anthropology away from the growing realization by scientists in other fields that the human species was in danger of fouling its own nest, and dissolving into endless wars between uncompromising local populations and political units. By the 1990s, ecological anthropologists like Emilio Moran began to advocate a return to "global" concerns, but this will be difficult since the entire discipline has for so many years based its theory on the defense of the local and the diverse.

The emphasis on culture*s*—as over against Culture as a human universal—had a profound effect on the methodology of ethnological research and interpretation. It focussed attention on the need to explain *specific* behavioral sequences and styles—rather than human experience in general. The larger aim was not completely forgotten—the titles of some of the great textbooks of the period—Linton's *Study of Man*; Herskovits's *Man and His Works*—exemplified the desire to make statements appropriate for all circumstances. (Kroeber, however, called his text simply *Anthropology*—thus avoiding commitment as to its civilizational scope). However, the ethnological literature consisted almost entirely of reports on specific communities and cultures, so whatever general statements might be made had to be based on conclusions reached in these specific studies. Comparative research, with attempts to generalize from comparisons of a series of similar or different cultures, was somehow difficult to achieve, and in addition, had a negative reputation based on the fact that the anthropology of the late nineteenth and early twentieth centuries had used this technique. Frazer and scholars like him were in dubious repute—even worse, they were considered old hat.

Another consequence of the preoccupation with the diverse forms of localized existence is found in the idea of the *exotic* which permeated ethnology. The chief accomplishment of the discipline was felt to be its "discovery" of exotic ideas and customs. Certainly anthropology's popularity with the reading public was based on this (see chapter 14 on "populist" anthropology). At the University of Chicago in the late 1930s, we graduate students called it the "They do it different in Pago Pago" doctrine. But this attitude contributed to the divorcement of anthropology from the "real world" and from the recurrent evil and perversity in the human condition. And another problem with the idea of the "exotic" is that once you have exposed it, it is no longer exotic; indeed, you discover that it is really all around you. Unilineal kinship tendencies, strange rituals in which the sexes exchange clothes; marital customs where the father-in-law may initiate the bride into sex; and so on, all turned out to have their virtual counterparts or their hushed-up versions in modern society.

However, for some reason Classic anthropologists avoided serious analysis of contemporary culture. Linton's famous essay about the "100 percent American" (Linton 1936: 326–7) or Horace Miner's "Nacirema" piece (Miner 1956) were tours de force—something to captivate students, but were not scientific anthropology. And when anthropologists like Margaret Mead did take the topic of "our own culture" seriously, she tried to visualize it in terms of the assumptions anthropologists held about tribal culture: integrated, patterned, with a generalized, basic core or ethos. On the whole, inside anthropology, the concentration on exotic tribal culture had created an attitude toward modern life as trivial, routine, humdrum, unworthy of serious inquiry, and, after all, secular, commonsensical, and devoid of exotic phenomena demanding unusual treatment. There were no problems of origin—everyone knew where the customs came from—*if* they really were "customs." And it was always changing, so there were no imposing traditions to worry about. But culture was everywhere, and the distinctive processes and forms associated with the culture of tribals was the model. Only the content was assumed to vary. The possibility that what anthropologists were calling "culture" was in reality a special behavioral property of relatively isolated, small-population societies was not seriously considered. Culture was culture: there was no possibility of more culture or less culture.

The distinction between Culture as a universal, and culture*s* as existing entities was intersected by the distinction between Culture as a creation of human behavior, and culture*s* as the causes of behavior in specific real-life situations—that is, Culture-as-result versus Culture-as-cause. This vital distinction was frequently confused in Classic anthropology. I can recall one of Margaret Mead's most familiar gestures: in a conference of, say psychologists, she would rise from her chair, or bend over the table menacingly, and heckle the speaker for generalizing about some form of behavior when he was really describing a particular culturally induced response. And then she might continue the attack with a statement like, "culture is always present in every human situation." She was usually right about the first point—that a particular behavior was indeed created or caused by socialization in a particular culture; but often wrong about the second point—culture is not necessarily present everywhere. The concept was a sponge—Classic anthropologists simply had great difficulty distinguishing culture from behavior.

As previously suggested, much of the difficulty with the culture concept derived from the use of a collective or synthetic noun to describe a dynamic human and historical process. "Culture" was a term used to refer to various changing aspects of human behavior and interhuman relationships—which then was consolidated into a label for what was seen as a uniquely human capacity or essence. And this, of course, is the essence of *reification*—and while reification is a useful mental device, it always creates difficulties when you try to use it as a basis for explanation. Classic anthropologists were perennially caught in the Kroeberian dilemma (chapter 10): the acknowledgement of culture as a product of the human mind, but then to treat it as though it was a separate property of Nature.

And this in turn required—as already suggested—a set of characteristics or criteria defining culture. These categories (the famous "universal pattern" was an example) then became ordained criteria for culture, and these functioned as a limiting or constrained agenda for research. When later Classic anthropologists like Benedict or Mead began to experiment with ideas and processes outside these constraining categories, they turned to Freud or Marx or derivatives of these—rather than to ethnic cultures or people themselves. Only a few Classic anthropologists, like Edward Sapir or Gregory Bateson, sought to find meaning in behavior outside of, or at least in addition to, received theories.

The reification of the culture concept not only inhibited the examination of behavior in its own terms, but also forced anthropologists into ambiguous conceptions of history. They could not even agree on a simple definition of the term "history," as witness the famous opaque interchange between Boas and Kroeber (Kroeber 1935; Boas 1936). "History" in the Early Classic era meant tribal origins, virtually devoid of any context of national or continental human history. "Primitive culture" lacked history by definition, and contact and interaction with Euro-Americans was put in a separate processual, but not historical context.

In general, history was the one field where anthropologists missed the boat, judging by the success of recent historical research and writing on "cultural studies" and the treatment of civilization as entities. Historians—Samuel Huntington in particular (1996)—have come to see culture—religion, lifestyle—as crucial in the relations of nations, social segments of nations, and whole civilizations. This is precisely what anthropology could have done if it had preserved and developed the universalist ideas prevalent in the nineteenth- century discipline. It would also have given anthropology a useful image or a model of complex society—something it has not been able to develop. This failure is the most negative aspect of the Classic-era heritage.

Still, the greats of the early and middle Classic era included a number of European-trained scholars who most certainly had read general history, and who from time to time displayed this knowledge - although rarely in their ethnological work. Paul Radin, a literary and historical scholar once complained to me of the ahistorical atmosphere of the Department of Anthropology at the University of California at Berkeley where he spent most of his career. One of his temporary retirement posts was at Kenyon College, and he would come down to Columbus, Ohio, and look me up and ask for help in learning the maze of multilevel passages in Long's College Book Company, a rabbit-warren of used professional books, including much history and social science.) He said on one of these excursions that he was planning to spend the rest of his life reading nothing but history, since he felt that anthropology had ceased to produce anything of interest.

The Classic concept of culture was one of those ideas which is only partially amenable to scientific treatment. That is, while portions of the attributed contents of the concept—material objects, for example—can be examined "scientifically," other portions, like various aspects of human thought and behavior, are fundamentally fluid, dynamic, and historical. They are facets of the changing attitudes and activities of humans. Still, "culture exists" in the sense that it forms a background for human learning and experience—part of the milieu that people function within.

But when both sides—the scientific and the humanistic—are included in the concept, "culture" is extremely resistant to general theorizing. There are too many variable and unpredictable factors and outcomes. Basically, the nonmaterial side of the concept culture is what humans remember about their experiences in a social environment, and to attribute substantive quality to the described remembrances will always be productive of ambiguity and argument—not to mention overgeneralization.

Man and Other Animals: Dualisms

Well, it is not exactly news that Classic anthropology was wrapped around the concept of Culture and culture*s*. The decisive promotion of these concepts is usually attributed to Franz Boas (e.g., Sussman 1995: 2) insofar as he removed the Germanic humanistic ideals and made Culture a human universal property, and one that *distinguishes humans from all other animals*. This idea was given its earliest and most eloquent phrasing by A. L. Kroeber. And the phrase, "The Boasians" found frequently in histories of anthropology, refers to the cadre of students and followers of Boas, all of whom espoused, with varying nuances, the notion that Culture was the chief characteristic of *Homo sapiens*, and that culture*s* were the proof of the pudding; that is, that human groups are differentiated not by biological traits, but by socially derived habits and ideas. Man adapts by modifying behavior, not by modifying his physique and physiology.

This doctrine is not only the basis of Classic anthropology, but is the foundation of "cultural anthropology"—a term which includes ethnology, and also (usually) "social anthropology," although in some respects social anthropology was conceived as a separate field and domain (chapters 3 and 4 explore aspects of the distinction). And Classic anthropology developed a series of paired concepts or dualisms which to some extent are still operative in the epistemology of the general discipline. The important ones are:

- Culture and cultures;
- Culture and Society (or "the cultural"; "the social");

- Human and Animal (natures, behavior, etc.);
- Tool-making and Not-Tool-making—but perhaps Tool-*Using*;
- Cognitive thought and Instinctive thought; and then the old classic, not so obvious in anthropology, but nevertheless prone to enter the discussion,
- Good and Evil

Confrontations among these concepts generated controversies. There was the question of whether animals, and especially the Great Apes, could be said to have culture, or at least some traces of its existence (or could they have a soul; or consciousness; reason; etc.). In his paper, "Pre-Human Cultural Beginnings" (1928), Kroeber suggested that the rudiments or bases for cultural behavior might be visible in various primates, but only Man had the full-blown article. The discussions centered around the question of tool-making and tool-using: as time passed, the *use* of sticks and stones by other primates, birds and some other animals came to be recognized, but this fell short of true human behavior; hence, it could be held that these animals lacked culture. Some might say that the difference between humans and (other) animals may be "only a matter of degree," but others might reply, "but the extent of the difference is so great that for all practical or theoretical purposes, non-human tool behavior can be ignored." (Since we now have observed chimps and even birds actually making simple tools; many other species using tools, and various animals and birds capable of building complex structures, further modifications of the traditional concepts are in order.)

If moral values were brought into the discussion, then other aspects of the animal-human dualism appeared. If one's image of human was benign—man as one of the angels—then there was an inclination to deny man-animal characteristics, and to emphasize the uniqueness of culture, and so forth. Or if human violence, deceit, etc., was the topic, then "man's animal nature" entered the dialog.

And of course primate fossil evidence figured in the arguments, especially with reference to the Piltdown fossil (the original report: Dawson and Woodward 1913). If a human with a more or less fully developed brain—cranium—could also display the jaw of an ape, then clearly the issue of human versus animal was confused. It was impossible to credit the significance of fossil finds like Australopithecus, with his small brain but upright posture. The exposure of the Piltdown cranium-jaw combination as a fake, and the jaw an ape's, liberated

Sherry Washburn and others (Weiner et al. 1953; Washburn, ed. 1963; Spencer 1990) to focus on a variety of important physical steps in hominid evolution: brains, teeth, hands, upright posture. But then sociobiology, a product of the early post-Classic, revived the question of animal-human continuities by attributing behavioral and adaptive mechanisms found in animals to the human species as an all or none proposition. Man as animal, again.

These arguments derived from dualistic and polar conceptualizing. Either-or; black or white. But there is more to it than just logical confusion or exaggeration, since the shadings in physique and behavior among the various primate species, and between any one of them and other non-primate animals, really exist, however minuscule they might be. The cognitive pressure to make a firm commitment on one side or the other is what creates the controversies. Is a gorilla "like" man? or a man "like" gorilla—or are they both a chessboard, but the gorilla plays checkers while men play chess?[4]

Throughout the Classic era, attempts were made to achieve syntheses of these various opposing or complementary concepts. Kroeber insisted on the process of evolution as a way of visualizing both biological and cultural history with the same set of concepts—but still insisting on the fundamental separateness of the phenomena—an approach, with modern refinements, which was redeveloped by the social psychologist Donald T. Campbell (1975) in the 1970s. The unity in the joint system is thus viewed as methodological, processual; not ontological. Teilhard de Chardin (1965) called the process *hominization*; that is, the entire world, including animals, geology, etc., is absorbed into the human sphere (chapter 15).

So anthropology persists in evolving an "image of Man" out of ingredients from its biological, archaeological, and ethnological domains. But the "image" remains elusive and dialectical: the opposing dualisms swing back and forth as scholars choose their reference points. Culture is both unique to man but significant aspects of it can appear among animals. Man—like all self-directed organisms—is *both* good and evil, by turns; man, in fact, is a behaviorally multipotential organism—morally, he is both angel and devil; taxonomically, both animal and human.

In retrospect, Classic anthropology was remarkably self-contained. Preoccupied with tribal societies and their cultures, and concerned with museum displays, field work, and the accumulation of descriptive materials on changing tribal societies, anthropologists exhibited little knowledge of other disciplines. The significance of certain borrowings from sociology and other fields that characterized what I call the middle and late Classic eras represented the beginnings of a breakout from the cocoon. Anthropologists became aware that the field simply did not provide sufficient intellectual material for truly indigenous theory—except in a few more or less specialized domains like kinship and religious phenomena. Significant ideas were borrowed from related disciplines, especially psychology, sociology, and economics, and this established a kind of borrowing habit which has come to characterize the post-Classic period in the form of the "institutional anthropologies" which at the moment of writing bid fair to become the core of the discipline for the future. They really represent the only way the discipline—or subdiscipline of sociocultural anthropology—can modernize.

Aftermath

Now—if there were pre-Classic and Classic eras, there must be a post-Classic. In general, the anthropology of the period subsequent to the mid-1950s has continued to be characterized by diversity of topics and concepts, the inevitable result of the fact that culture is an empirical diversity. However, the early post-Classic period was marked by two contrasting developments: an *in*volutionary period stretching into the 1960s which featured an attempted revival of *e*volutionary anthropology and other pre-Classic and early Classic themes; and the emergence of a politically critical anthropology in the 1960s and 1970s, engendered by an awareness of the famous Classic-era contradiction: specialization in tribal culture combined with neglect of the issues created by colonial domination. Some of the essays in this book (chapters 4 and 12, especially) pertain to issues that transcend the Classic and extend into this later period of contrast and rebellion. In one sense the period represented the coming-of-age of a politicized anthropology; the emergence of anthropology into modern world society. And this, of course, had its inevitable reaction in the 1970s in the form of symbolist and literary anthropology—the Geertzian Revolution, as someone has called it.

Notes

1. With the rise of deconstructionist methods in cultural anthropology, plus the politicization of some aspects of ethnology since the 1970s, the pursuit of "dark side" phenomena by anthropologists has certainly increased. In recent years, no less than two monographs—one by Nancy Scheper-Hughes (1992), the other by Daniel Touro Linger (1993) on everyday violence in Brazil have appeared. But neither author attempts a moral critique: Scheper-Hughes is preoccupied mainly with her own reactions and interpretations, as based on her personal experiences while doing the fieldwork; Linger is concerned mainly with a straightforward functional analysis of Brazilian carnival behavior and its proclivity to induce violence between participants (see Bennett 1995 for reviews). The issue of deceit has been recently handled by F. G. Bailey (1991).
2. After all, this only mirrors Classic anthropology's obsession with the concept. Melville J. Herskovits's text, *Man and His Works* (1948) has 642 pages, and so far as I can tell, the word "culture" appears on every full page of text.
3. In 1949 sociologist Melvin Tumin and I published an introductory sociology textbook based mainly on structural-functional theory, expressing the then-current synthesis of functionalist anthropology and sociology, featured in the Parsons-Kluckhohn et al. interdisciplinary ventures. The book became a best-seller, but one thing led to another and Tumin and I never issued a revised edition (which would have had to, in any case, renounce structural-functionalism or at least introduce tiresome discussions of the emerging criticism of the approach). In the course of writing the book we had many discussions on the differences and similarities of sociology and anthropology—aside, of course, from the obvious one of industrial society versus tribal. We noted that both of the two fields at various periods believed in the existence of human universals—e.g., the "psychic unity" of the nineteenth century proto-anthropology and sociology; "cultural universals" of 1920s anthropology; or the Parsonsian universals of the 1940s. We also noted that the Parsons approach, which we used in the book (Bennett and Tumin 1949: 168) probably had its principal modern origin in the writings of Bronislaw Malinowski, an anthropologist! But then coming into the 1930s, anthropologists lost sight of human universals—or ignored the obvious biological (mammalian) universals—and started talking about culture*s* in their endless diversity. By the 1980s Culture, as a universal property, was back on the anthropological venue in a disguised form as rhetoric and symbolism.
4. I am indebted to Robert Sussman for the chessboard analogy.

Literature Cited

Bailey, F. G. 1991. *The Prevalence of Deceit.* Ithaca, NY: Cornell University Press.

Barth, Fredrik. 1992. *Social/Cultural Anthropology.* Wenner-Gren Foundation for Anthropological Research Report for 1990 and 1991. Fiftieth anniversary issue. New York.

Bateson, Gregory. 1936. *Naven: A Survey of the Problems Suggested by a Composite Picture of the Culture of a New Guinea Tribe Drawn from Three Points of View.* London: Cambridge University Press.

Bennett, John W. 1995. "Walks on the Dark Side: 'Sick Societies,' Interpersonal Violence, and Anthropology's Love Affair with the Folk Society." *Reviews in Anthropology* 24: 145–58.

Bennett, John W. and Iwao Ishino. 1963. *Paternalism in the Japanese Economy: Anthropological Studies of Oyabun-Kobun Patterns.* Minneapolis: University of Minnesota Press.

Bennett, John W., Herbert Passin, and Robert K. McKnight. 1958. *In Search of Identity: The Japanese Overseas Scholar in America and Japan.* Minneapolis: University of Minnesota Press.

Bennett, John W. and Melvin Tumin. 1948. *Social Life: Structure and Function.* New York: Knopf.

Boas, Franz. 1936. "History and Science in Anthropology: A Reply." *Race, Language and Culture*, pp. 243–59. New York: Macmillan.

Brinton, Daniel G. 1902. *The Basis of Social Relations: A Study in Ethnic Psychology.* New York: G.P. Putnam's Sons.

Caffrey, Margaret M. 1989. *Ruth Benedict: Stranger in This Land.* Austin, TX: University of Texas Press.

Campbell, Donald T. 1975. "On the Conflicts between Biological and Social Evolution and between Psychology and Moral Tradition." *American Psychologist* 30: 1103–26.

Dawson, C. and A. S. Woodward. 1913. "On the Discovery of a Paleolithic Human Skull and Mandible in a Flint-bearing Gravel overlying the Wealden (Hastings Beds) at Piltdown, Fletching, Sussex." *Quarterly Journal of the Geological Society* 69: 117–44.

Edgerton, Robert B. 1992. *Sick Societies: Challenging the Myth of Primitive Societies.* New York: Free Press.

Fortune, Reo F. [1932] 1962. *Sorcerers of Dobu: Social Anthropology of the Dobu Islanders.* Rev. ed. London: Routledge.

Geertz, Clifford. 1995. *After the Fact: Two Countries, Four Decades, One Anthropologist.* Cambridge, MA: Harvard University Press.

Gomme, G. L. [1908] 1968. *Folklore as an Historical Science.* Reprint. Detroit: Singing Tree Press.

Harris, Marvin. 1968. *The Rise of Anthropological Theory.* New York: Thomas Y. Crowell.

Hatch, Elvin. 1983. *Culture and Morality: The Relativity of Values in Anthropology.* New York: Columbia University Press.

Herskovits, Melville J. 1948. *Man and his Works: The Science of Cultural Anthropology.* New York: Alfred A. Knopf.

Hinsley, Curtis M., Jr. 1981. *Savages and Scientists: The Smithsonian Institution and the Development of American Anthropology, 1846–1910.* Washington, DC: Smithsonian Institution Press.

Huntington, Samuel P. 1996. *The Clash of Civilizations and the Remaking of World Order.* New York: Simon & Schuster.

International Symposium on Anthropology. 1953. *An Appraisal of Anthropology Today.* Edited by Sol Tax, et al. Chicago: University of Chicago Press.

Kluckhohn, Clyde. 1948. "An Anthropologist Looks at Psychology." *The American Psychologist* 3: 439–42.

Kroeber, A. L. 1917. "The Superorganic." *American Anthropologist* 19: 163–213.

———. 1928. "Sub-Human Culture Beginnings." *Quarterly Review of Biology* 3.

———. 1935. "History and Science in Anthropology." *American Anthropologist* 37: 539–69.

———, ed. 1953. *Anthropology Today: An Encyclopedic Inventory*. Chicago: University of Chicago Press.

Leaf, Murray J. 1979. *Man, Mind and Science: A History of Anthropology*. New York: Columbia University Press.

Linger, Daniel Touro. 1993. *Dangerous Encounters: Meanings of Violence in a Brazilian City*. Stanford: Stanford University Press.

Linton, Ralph. 1936. "Diffusion." In *The Study of Man: An Introduction*, pp. 324–46. New York: D. Appleton-Century.

Lowie, Robert H. 1937. *The History of Ethnological Theory*. New York: Farrar & Rinehart.

Maine, Henry S. 1861. *Ancient Law, Its Connection with the Early History of Society and its Relation to Modern Ideas* (First edition; many subsequent editions; latest reprint by Dorset Press). London: John Murray.

Malinowski, Bronislaw. 1916–48. "Baloma: The Spirits of the Dead in the Trobriand Islands." In *Magic, Science and Religion and Other Essays*, pp. 125–227. Selected and with an introduction by Robert Redfield. Glencoe, IL: The Free Press.

Mead, Margaret and Ruth Bunzel, eds. 1960. *The Golden Age of American Anthropology*. New York: Braziller.

Miner, Horace. 1956. "Body Ritual among the Nacirema." *American Anthropologist* 58: 503–7.

Penniman, T. K. [1935] 1965. *A Hundred Years of Anthropology*. 3d ed. London: Gerald Duckworth & Co.

Pitt-Rivers, A. H. Lane Fox. 1906. *The Evolution of Culture and Other Essays*. Edited by John L. Myres. Oxford: Clarendon Press.

Plattner, Stuart. 1997. "Scientific Anthropology at the National Science Foundation" in *Anthropology between Science and the Humanities*, in press, edited by Chris Furlow. Altimira Press.

Redfield, Robert. 1940. "The Folk Society and Culture." *American Journal of Sociology* 45: 731–42.

Sapir, Edward. 1994. *The Psychology of Culture: A Course of Lectures*. Reconstructed and edited by Judith T. Irvine. Berlin: Mouton de Gruyter.

Scheper-Hughes, Nancy. 1992. *Death without Weeping: The Violence of Everyday Life in Brazil*. Berkeley, CA: University of California Press.

Snow, C. P. 1959. *The Two Cultures and the Scientific Revolution*. Cambridge: University Press.

Spencer, F. 1990. *Piltdown: A Scientific Forgery*. London: Oxford University Press.

Stocking, George W. 1987. *Victorian Anthropology*. New York: Free Press.

Sussman, Robert W. 1995. "The Nature of Human Universals." *Reviews in Anthropology* 24: 1–11.

Teilhard de Chardin, Pierre. 1965. *The Appearance of Man*. Translated by J. M. Cohen. New York: Harper & Row.

Tylor, Edward B. 1888. "On a Method of Investigating the Development of Institutions, Applied to Laws of Marriage and Descent." *Journal of the Anthropological Institute* 18: 245–72.

Washburn, Sherry L., ed. 1963. *Classification and Human Evolution*. Chicago: Aldine.

Weiner, J. S., F. P. Oakley, and W. E. Le Gros Clark. 1953. "The Solution of the Piltdown Problem." *Bulletin of the British Museum of Natural History* 2: 141–6.

Introductory Note to Chapters 2 and 3

We have to begin somewhere. I scanned the raw material available and finally closed on the paper reproduced as chapter 2. It seemed to me to express the mood of the period (the late Classic and the transition to post-Classic era) rather well, and contains references to some of the methodological and philosophical issues developed in other chapters. As noted in chapter 1, it defines that half of the dualism concerning the culture concept in Classic anthropology, which views culture in humanistic terms; with chapter 3 giving the other half—the analytic and scientific. Now, chapter 3 was written at the close of a decade or more of interdisciplinary and applied social research in various places and on various topics, and as the essay makes clear, traditional culture-bound theories were inadequate to the task. However, chapter 2 actually was written a decade *later*, following my first year of field research in the northern Great Plains—where I focused on the behavior and patterns and values of North American post-frontier communities. This type of work obviously could benefit from "traditional culture-bound" or humanistic approaches. In other words, the duality of anthropological approaches to culture is usually shaped by the subject matters. The reader will note the similarity of some of the arguments in chapter 2 to late-Classic and post-Classic discussions in cultural anthropology, such as skepticism over the ability or even desirability of anthropologists to adhere to scientific canons of objectivity and detachment. The most important idea in the essay is the characterization of some of the great ethnological monographs as creating "stories" and "myths" about tribal society and culture which continue to exist in the literature even though the way of life of the original group is drastically altered by time and modernization.

2

Myth, Theory, and Value in Cultural Anthropology

I.

This essay is based on the following assumption: since the social sciences have a reflexive character (subject is also object), they will contain perspectives which can give meaning and direction to research as well as distort research results when used without awareness. Since the human reality is always in large part a mental interpretation or construction of empirical existence, social science must utilize such perspectives in order to provide an understanding of the data. Social facts do not speak for themselves; or only to a limited extent. This situation creates recurrent methodological and epistemological problems for the social sciences which are not subject to permanent solution, but must be continuously debated. In light of the comprehensive objective of anthropology to reveal the variety and depth of human existence, it should be clear that disciplined subjective interpretation always will be a part of the methodology.

I shall discuss the following aspects of this situation: the descriptive element in cultural anthropology which permits the ready conversion of data into "stories" which in turn can become converted into myths and images of man (hence suggesting some of the reasons for

---

Originally written in 1963 and published in 1964 with the same title as a contributed chapter to the book, *Fact and Theory in Social Science*, edited by Earl W. Count and Gordon T. Bowles (Syracuse University Press), and presented to Professor Douglas Haring as a *Festschrift*. The paper has undergone stylistic editing. Some later comments on its argument appear in the epilogue to chapter 3.

anthropology's relative popularity with the general reader); the relationship of these "mythic" qualities of anthropological research to theory construction and the notion of "a culture"; and the role of anthropology in the formation of values and social objectives, and the effect of the rise of scientific method upon this function.

II.

When we compare sociology with cultural anthropology from the standpoint of their public image, it is possible to say that of the two, sociology has acquired greater acceptance as a source of means for achieving social ends, while cultural anthropology has captured the greater popular interest. The sociologist is sometimes painted as a routine fact-gatherer or a jargoneer who obscures the familiar facts of everyday life with complicated and repetitive language. The anthropologist, deserving or not, seems to attract more glamour: he is seen as an intriguing, eccentric figure who is able to enjoy exotic experiences. His work, odd as it is, carries a special type of prestige not usually accorded to the sociologist, based on the fact that the anthropologist has the unique authority of "he who was there," while the sociologist is merely in our midst.

However, the sociologist is listened to more often than the anthropologist when specific problems or reforms of contemporary social life are concerned. More sociologists than anthropologists appear before congressional committees and are more frequently found in jobs in applied fields. The sociologist, though lacking in glamour and a certain prestige, nevertheless is "in"; he is well on his way to becoming an accepted functionary.

It is likely that the anthropologist *qua* anthropologist will never attain acceptance of this kind. If he works consistently within modern society he runs considerable risk of being assimilated into the sociologist's role. If he continues to work abroad, or on problems of historical reconstruction, he will retain his glamour but will not achieve much recognition as a formulator of answers to pressing social problems. He will be read, and probably ever more widely, but not for the specific advice he may have to offer. At the same time, the popularity of anthropology seems to grow if we may take as one index the fact that more and more paperbound books in the field flow from the presses. A recent [1963] count made by the writer of such books in anthropology and in peripheral fields such as Old World prehistory stopped at a conservative sixty-two; for sociology and its peripheries, twenty. Newspapers readily print accounts of anthropological discoveries and findings; magazines of mass circulation, like *Life*, feature "The Story of Man." Clearly anthropology has captured a share of the popular interest—or at least it has found acceptance as a fascinating subject [see chapter 14 on "populist anthropology"]. The names of the great anthropologists seem more widely known than those of the sociologists, and most of those sociologists who have received popular recognition equal to that of certain anthropologists couch their knowledge in evocative, discursive form more similar to anthropological writings than sociological.

On the whole, Classic anthropologists conceive of their field as a science while acknowledging an affinity to the humanities in the form of historical interests and in the creative activity of field work. In spite of this, criteria for evaluation of anthropological writings were [and are] mostly scientific. That is, they concern the verification of factual data and the relationship of fact to theory or generalization. Of course, anthropologists seem less consciously preoccupied with methodology than sociologists, who have made too much of it; but on the whole, the anthropologist resembles the sociologist in his quest for scientific accuracy and reproducibility. In the face of this dominant concern for the rigor and dispassion of science, it is necessary to ask why anthropology has continued to retain a popular side. This is to be found, I believe, in the *narrative* quality of anthropology: its "story" or its ease of conversion into stories.

Of course, narrative is not the only factor; plain facts and even theories can become topics of general public interest. Certainly the physical and earth sciences have disseminated their factual and theoretical knowledge successfully in recent years [1950s and 1960s]. However, the public, as a general rule, is not interested in either the fact or theory of science, but rather in the "story." Among the human studies, only those theories which, like the Freudian, appear to provide large, resounding explanations of complex happenings have attracted much popular attention. Most theories of sociology and some fields of social anthropology are neither appealing nor comprehensible to the general public because they are not susceptible to narrative treatment.

The "story" of a scientific field consists of its knowledge put into the form of a dramatic narrative: the "romance of archaeology"; the growth of the solar system; "disease detectives"; the adventures of Genghis Khan; life in the South Seas. A. J. Liebling's "The Jollity Building" (1937–42) is a good example of a straightforward piece of contemporary ethnography put in the form of a descriptive narrative, and the writings of Kurt Wolff [Bennett 1992] are even better examples. In such pieces the emphasis is placed on a series of events or at least *probable* events considered either diachronically or synchronically and prepared mainly for impact on the reader's imagination. These "stories" can be based on fact or completely imaginary, but if the latter, they must at least be in the realm of the possible. Immanuel Velikofsky's pure cosmological fantasies are not in the category; Fred Hoyle's imaginative but putative universes are (Velikofsky 1950, 1952, 1955; Hoyle 1955, 1956, 1957).

When we allow putative actuality in our category, according to contemporary thinking the work immediately escapes the classification of science and becomes literature—literature which is acknowledged to be close to science and scholarship but which is nevertheless not admitted into the inner circle. It is, in fact, regarded as popularization, more or less accurate, honest, or reputable. This is the essence of the media which command public attention: while they are either based on fact or true to a set of possible facts, it is not the unvarnished factual element in them which is dominant in the public's interest, but rather the intrinsic narrative. Likewise for theory: the public is interested not in theory as such, but as the cement or the continuity of the story, it will find acceptance. Theories do not interest the public unless they are already proven; that is, as a revelation of the relationships and meanings of facts and events, in which case they are no longer theories but simply the plot of a narrative.

Stories told over and over again sooner or later become a part of the imagination of the readers. In the process of retelling and of later analytic commentary the stories acquire embellishments or at least a constellation of meanings which begin to carry implications for many contexts of history and social life. These meanings will tend to revolve around the original intentions of the authors, but frequently they go beyond these into the realm of social mythology—which becomes as fundamental to interpretations made by intellectuals as to the everyday thinking and conversation of the average man. Myths are more than folklore; they help to define the meaning of life and the goals of society, the ideals and the norms of a culture. In this way they begin to approach a definition of the human reality as opposed to mere existence.

Science, as one of the important activities of our age, has contributed its share to the making of social myths. Certainly evolutionary science has done this. I am not certain whether sociocultural evolution [its attempted revival in the 1950s was still attracting attention in the 1960s] is pure fancy, historical fact, or reasoned interpretation, but it most certainly has become a mythic account of the nature of modern society in the guise of "progress" and all this implies. The ideas of "lower" and "higher" culture are part of the everyday judgments of men in all walks of life; these judgments are constantly acted upon, used as rationalizations and explanations. Another example may be found in Marx's doctrine of class structure: the layer-cake image of three basic class divisions dominates the conceptions of society held in the civilized world, "free" and totalitarian. These are true myths; that they also have a basis in social and historical fact only confirms their importance, their approximation to reality as the age defines it.

To illustrate the points of the preceding discussion I have included sociological materials as well as anthropological. However, while sociological knowledge has come to play a role in the making of social mythology, anthropology and its narrative still figures more importantly in the public imagination. I believe that the underlying reason for the narrative quality of anthropological knowledge lies in the character of its method. The anthropologist goes into the field to exotic places and actually *experiences* his data. The sociologist of course does field work in our own society, and insofar as he does, he is likely to capture some of the same kind of interest—witness the work of David Riesman (1950) and William H. Whyte (1956). But it is hard to equal the peculiar attraction of a field with a tradition of travel and exploration, and in this the anthropologist has the upper hand. The point is that the anthropologist writes ultimately about his personal experiences and the reader is there with him in imagination; the interest is vicarious, not purely intellectual or analytical. The anthropologist is not just a scientist in the public view but is a particular individual, a romantic hero. Note, for example, the character of the anthropologist in J.P. Marquand's novel, *Point of No Return* (1949): a unique personality with uniquely disreputable dress different from and apart from all other characters in the book [the character was actually based on W. Lloyd Warner, who was doing his Yankee City (Newbury Port,

MA) community study at the time the novel was in progress, i.e., Warner 1963]. The fact that the portrait is rather unfavorable and is based on a particular living anthropologist is beside the point. It is a matter of doubt as to whether any novelist would ever portray a sociologist with these distinctive characteristics.

The anthropologist's writings are predominantly descriptive. They represent compilations of information on something that was and is: the so-called ethnographic present. Whatever its scientific disadvantages, this concept has held a fascination not equalled by the detached, abstract, matter-of-fact analyses of the sociologist or the sociological anthropologist. This is because it tells a concrete story about a concrete reality—or at least seems to. In this sense, the "ethnographic present" is openly mythic, and at least partly fictional. The information offered in the purely scientific treatises of the anthropologist may not interest the public, but these same facts are readily translatable into "stories" about places, people, and happenings, and it is these stories, as I have already remarked, that command popular interest.

Another way of putting this is to call it the anthropologist's *style*—his mode of presenting himself and his data. In the writings of the great anthropologists one may find a personal touch which is often lacking in the other social sciences. The anthropologist may not always use the personal pronoun, but it is implicit in all that he writes, since, as I have said, "he was there." [Elsewhere in this book I call it the "virtuoso" attitude.] There is a sense of drama in his work, whether he features it or not—a feeling of discovery, revelation, and uniqueness. The concrete case study—the specialty of the anthropologist—can be offered on a platter, so to speak, as the experience and observations of a unique individual, a person who has done something no one else has been privileged to do.

This style of work has had its effect, in the most prominent instances, on the personalities, public and private, of the great anthropologists themselves: many anthropologists are colorful and somewhat deviant individuals who seek out anthropology as a haven. At the same time, the field creates a role which can or must be lived out: the more conformist individual may find himself taking on some of the characteristics associated with the role in an effort to identify with the professional personality type. However, this pleasant deviance of the anthropologist should not be overstressed, since as the field comes of age a more sober professionalism is evident. Still, conventions of anthropologists are notoriously livelier than those of sociologists, and I am sure that a study of anthropological careers would reveal substantial differences in background and outlook from those of sociologists.

Those anthropologists who, because of their personal flair, their ability to tell stories or provide materials easily convertible into stories, or their ability to convey the sense of an important personal experience, a human reality, include the persons often regarded as the "great anthropologists"—Frazer, Hooton, V. Gordon Childe, Malinowski, Linton, Mead, and Benedict come to mind immediately. These have not all had the same success in terms of purely popular interest, but most certainly their work has had a mythic significance in the culture of the modern world. They have contributed to what H.G. Wells, in *The Croquet Player* (1937), called "breaking the frame of the present." Wells meant that anthropological knowledge, along with that of geology and paleontology, had destroyed the old Western image of man as recent, omnipotent, or divine and substituted a view of man as varied, ancient, and dependent upon a complex environment. The discovery of human fossils meant that man must join the animal kingdom; the availability of prehistory required an understanding of present events as intimately dependent upon ancient prototypes; and the revelation of nonliterate cultures meant that history was not contained entirely in the experiences of the West and possibly China but must be written with the whole world in view. Thus the old parochial myths of Western man had to be revised in the light of anthropological knowledge and new myths substituted. The groundwork for these had been laid in the democratic revolution and anthropology and geology themselves were among the products of these revolutions.

III.

It is necessary to distinguish several phases in the creation of these myths. The phases are roughly equivalent to the theoretical development of anthropology as Alexander Goldenweiser saw it in numerous essays (1931, 1933, 1937) [that is, the pre-Classic through the Classic eras]. The doctrine of progress and evolutionary thought, in general, represented the first or optimistic stage in which the older myths of Western invincibility were retained but the newer knowledge contained within them. This was done via the familiar doctrine of progress which, of course, had non-anthropological origins. Man was presented as a conquering hero who had worked his way up out of slavery to the natural environment toward a high objective—the aristocratic industrial civilization of the nineteenth century. The existence of diverse brands of humanity was now recognized, as was the historical depth of the adventure, but all non-Western and earlier stages were seen as somehow inferior, inadequate, or *unrealized* versions of man. These generalizations of the mythic content of nineteenth-century anthropology are probably unrepresentative of the writings of their authors, but I am not talking about the scientific content per se; rather, the interpretations and popularizations made of the writings. At the same time, such interpretations are not entirely ad hoc; they represent a fair reading of the latent themes and central attitudes of these works. Fact, theory, and myth are inextricably interwoven in nineteenth-century—and twentieth- century—science.

Thus, it is difficult to say without careful investigation precisely how much influence the anthropological writings had on the myths or to what extent the myths were larger creations which determined the course of anthropological theorizing. I cannot answer such questions here; I can only point to the fact that anthropological studies succeeded in combining the older parochial myths of Western uniqueness and superiority with the newer knowledge of human variability and history, and that insofar as they did, they played an important role in nineteenth century social ideology. As we look back upon this work, we are likely to see it as much in the context of social ideology as in the role of the foundation of anthropological science.

The second stage of anthropological mythmaking or (myth-joining) was characterized by an interest in the details and variety of human phenomena, with little regard for large historical generalizations. The ideological content of this work was manifest in its relativistic emphasis on the autonomy or integrity of the unique culture. The strong emphasis on this doctrine in American anthropology, and its lesser significance in Europe, exemplifies its ideological character. Margaret Mead has recently noted Boas's preoccupation with the dignity and freedom of the individual which was transferred in some of his students to the notion of the integrity of cultures. In these ideas it is now relatively easy to trace the social issues of an industrializing, urbanizing America with its injustices, minority difficulties, and increasing problem of the role of the individual. These issues have by no means withered, and of course the myths abetted by the second stage of anthropological science survive. However, anthropology has its own scholarly dynamic, and at this time interests are no longer concentrated upon depiction and relativism.

In this third and contemporary stage of anthropological thought [that is, as of 1963] there is a return to evolutionary approaches in that man is treated once more as a single species about which to generalize. At the same time, the unique details of distinctive cultural adaptations are taken into account and built into the problem. It is too soon to predict the mythic significance of this, but perhaps certain outlines may be visible. Recall that the second-stage answer to the growing problem of the survival of the individual in the mass society was simply to reaffirm individualistic autonomy and independence. However, this answer is no longer relevant, since the simple assertion of individual freedom becomes a hollow slogan in the midst of great pressures and needs for channeling and directing behavior of increasingly large numbers of people. Consequently the myths of the future, like sociologist William H. Whyte's "social ethic," (1956: 6ff.) may come to stress the adjustment of groups of individuals to the demands of the environment, natural and social. This will be the case on a worldwide basis, on the ground of a common world culture; and the sense of the unique, individual culture may be lost. Self-fulfillment may be played down in favor of conformism. Such themes are visible in contemporary [1960s] anthropological thought, and I believe it to be the general direction of social ideology as well.

It is important to note that whether anthropology is concerned with the sweep of human history, man as a species, or with the individual and the unique culture, the level at which generalizations are pitched is peculiarly susceptible to mythic construction. *Man* and *Culture* have a universalist resonance not as apparent for Group and Society and other terms important to the sociologist. These latter suggest mundane, contemporary phenomena; while the anthropological terms have a timeless connotation. Of course, sociological and anthropological ideas have mingled often enough in the recent history of Western thought, but they also seem to speak to different intellectual and ideological traditions. The anthropologist talks to the philosophers of history and culture and the humanists in general; while the sociologist speaks more often to the administrator, planner, social engineer and statistician. It is noteworthy that the applied anthropologists, who frequently associate with administrators and planners, have created a good deal of unease in anthropological circles and have never been fully accepted by the profession [see discussion in chapter 12]. This division does not appear to be so marked for the applied wings of sociology and psychology, although some tension between theoretical and practical interests exists in all fields.

I have said that the mythic quality of anthropological materials lies in their strongly descriptive character, which makes them susceptible to conversion into "stories," which in turn become part of the belief system and reality definition of the times. Progress, stages of development, racial inequality, racial equality, cultural variability and integrity, and human social adjustment are all catchwords expressing these myths; ethnological compilations and studies as well as paleontological and archaeological research all contributed to their formation. The factual quality of the research materials was undeniable, but it should be apparent that the basic ideas were themselves difficult to prove. Developmental states and cultural uniqueness were perhaps among the more obviously ideological, as subsequent critiques have claimed. In both cases we have ideas great in potency but extremely difficult to prove; in both cases these ideas were taken uncritically and for granted in their heyday. The evolutionists never conclusively demonstrated the existence of stages; the relativists never conclusively demonstrated the uniqueness or autonomy of cultures.

IV.

Within the profession the researches of great anthropologists have played a role not entirely different from that of myths. These researches, in the first place, succeeded in pushing anthropological ideas in certain directions from which they rarely depart. Bronislaw Malinowski's attempted refutation or qualification of Freud's Oedipus situation is such a case: his finding that in the Trobriands the affective relationship supposed to exist between son and father was transferred to uncle and nephew has been used as validation of the principle of cultural variability and the relativity of generalization and social laws (Malinowski 1927, 1929). Leslie Spier's demonstration of pottery seriation became a basic postulate of the relationship between time and the artifact; in larger terms, a proof of the *geological* aspect of the human adventure (Spier 1917). Ruth Benedict's *Patterns of Culture* (1934) lives on as an assertion of the reality of cultural uniqueness, even in the midst of the most strenuous revisions of her ideas. Robert Redfield's Yucatecan continuum of change remains a basic postulate in the theory of change and development in spite of its situational specificity and conceptual ambiguities. Margaret Mead's studies of adolescence lie at the basis of our view of the individual and his milieu, even though many of her findings have been challenged and revised. [As they were, in spades, in 1983, with Derek Freeman's polemic.] Clyde Kluckhohn's (1944) interpretations of Navaho witchcraft as a form of socially approved redirection of hostility clinched an argument in the social and psychological sciences and exists today in dozens of versions [see chapter 9].

We may consider these theoretical perspectives as myths to the extent that they represent highly probable, meaningful, but nevertheless not entirely demonstrable generalizations about human experience. Each, or at least some, have been based upon unique researches—often studies of a single people; and it is hazardous in the extreme to generalize about a species as variable in behavior as man from a single case. A variety of defenses have been made of this anthropological propensity to generalize from very small numbers of cases, and many of the arguments are sound; but the fact remains that scientifically it is a tricky business. The plausibility of such generalizations cannot possibly derive from the representativeness of the case, since frequently this is totally unknown. Instead, it is based upon the human plausibility of the case as a whole; that is, it has the comprehensiveness of a long novel but is told with the veracity of a competent witness. It is believable simply because of the large amount of detail presented by the anthropologist and the authority with which he presents it. Somehow this creates an atmosphere of conviction which tends to convert the particular existential case into a symbol or symptom of human reality, and it is this which begins to take on another characteristic of myth, in this case, the myth of "culture."

The Trobriand islanders have found their way into countless literary and scientific documents in person and in disguise, as testimony of the human condition. What relationship these mythic Trobriand natives may bear to the living creatures observed by Malinowski, or, indeed, to the people of the contemporary archipelago, no one knows. Malinowski in a sense *created* a culture or a people in the course of many volumes of reportage; they continue to be recreated by the reader and by those who mine the volumes for exemplary materials. The

Trobrianders—a small, insignificant pocket of humanity, doomed to eternal obscurity and anonymity until Bronislaw Malinowski happened to find them, now elevated to a major intellectual myth of the Western world—are a people no scholar will ever forget, no librarian ever pass over, no social science graduate student ever ignore. From time to time it will be necessary to review current interpretations of Trobriand culture and the causes it has been made to serve, by rereading Malinowski's volumes. I have little doubt that the Trobrianders as portrayed in recent commentaries are by no means identical with Malinowski's originals.

The myth of Pueblo culture was built up in the years after the publication of Benedict's *Patterns*, reinforced by a number of American anthropologists. Fortunately for anthropological science this romantic myth was given an antidote beginning with Li An Che and continuing down through hardheaded ethnologists like Dorothy Eggan [see chapter 6 for the whole story]. Yet the original myth survives in some social science circles and in the arts-and-crafts tourist domain of Southwestern culture—the myth of those inscrutable, pacific, superhuman Pueblo Indians, mysteriously resisting contamination, efficiently socializing their young, and magnificently preserving the ancient arts and ceremonies.

Wherever we find a major ethnological compilation on a particular people, there we shall also find the makings of myth and legend: the conversion of that people into a special Personage or Culture which lives in the "ethnographic present" and which becomes a type case of the human variation—the inexhaustible novelty of man's behavior and relations with Nature. One curious aspect of this is that while anthropologists are known to the public as being responsible for our knowledge of these primitive cultures and are viewed as eccentric romantics therefore, the emphasis *within* anthropology has shifted away from ethnological depiction toward a social science preoccupation with problems, not peoples. The authors of the contents of most anthropological journals strike a sharp contrast with the public image of the anthropologist as the romantic mythmaker and intrepid and tantalizingly eccentric explorer.

Aside from the conversion of ethnological writings into semi-mythological constructions of cultures by the readers, the ethnologist in the grand tradition engaged in something related to mythmaking when he created his narrative. The literal rendering of tribal culture is an impossible task: even the most attenuated culture possesses a complexity far beyond the capacity or the patience of any ethnologist to record in detail. Such literal recording of the ongoing stuff of everyday existence was never the primary goal of ethnology; rather, the objective was the construction of a typical slice of life. The temporal ordering of events was telescoped in order to present this typical portrait in brief compass and within the attention span of the reader. Moreover, no ethnologist ever knew all there was to know about a tribal culture any more than any of us ever can know all there is to know of any human situation, however familiar it may be. The ethnologist was always required to fill in the gaps, to reconstruct situations with a disciplined use of the imagination. This technique is akin to that of the writer of responsible fiction, and numerous anthropologists, Redfield and Benedict in particular, have seen a humanities component in anthropology as a result. The meta-anthropological wing, as represented, say, by the work of Edmund Carpenter (1956), is an established though not especially prominent contemporary development. David Bidney (1953) has written on some of its philosophical, that is, value-*creating*, implications.

V.

In earlier passages I have commented upon the role of anthropological knowledge vis-à-vis social ideology, remarking that as often as not, the major theories of anthropology have followed ideological currents of the age. In this concluding section I shall consider the question of the extent to which anthropology should explore or recommend desirable social objectives.

This is, of course, the most difficult issue of all, since in the development of Western thought, a clear, possibly irrevocable separation between science and philosophy has occurred. If science essays to recommend or discover social goals, it is accused of abandoning its objectivity; even more, the view is held sometimes that values have nothing to do with fact and therefore philosophers are better off if they remain ignorant of science. Who steps into the breach? Most often, it is the pragmatists—the politicians and social administrators who set objectives by fiat or piecemeal decision, while the scientists and philosophers sit on the sidelines, shackled by their own views on the negative relationship of truth to action.

But if, as I have suggested, a science creates myths willy-nilly, even if they are not visible until the second generation, then it is clearly in the business of creating values, and this should be explicitly recognized. Some of the myths fostered by anthropology in the first three decades of this century—individual integrity and autonomy and cultural relativity—retain their nobility but are no longer completely serviceable in the face of new social problems and cultural forces. Needed now are new images and myths which, as Paul Goodman, a novelist, recently pointed out in a brilliant series of articles in *Commentary* (reprinted in Goodman 1962), dignify work and give the individual a sense of accomplishment in the routine tasks of industrial civilization. Such images cannot be constructed ad hoc; man's rational control of society has not reached and probably never will reach the point where he is able to inject value vitamins at will. However, this does not absolve the anthropologist from the responsibility of thinking about the problem and studying it with all his skill and intelligence. Further diagnosis is needed—searching inquiry into the existence and reality of contemporary man—before the power of mass society destroys the ability to think and to feel strongly about those important issues.

In addition to dignifying work, contemporary civilization with its rapidly growing population requires thinking on the subject of interindividual responsibility. The growth of cities, the institutionalization of the economy and of choice, clashes with the individualistic striving for autonomy and license, creating vast moral problems of delinquency, conformism, and neurosis. Here again anthropology has work to do. Franz Boas (1940) once wrote a remarkable essay on the different meanings given freedom in various societies which suggests possibilities for an anthropological study of the basis of personal-social responsibility. I do not mean "study" in the literal sense of acquirement of a $200,000 grant from a foundation. There is too much of this monetary substitute-for-thinking in the social sciences. I mean a general effort toward the development of a social conscience among anthropologists. They might well consider their role a privilege, not a right, and one that carries definite obligations to serve society by doing a little critical thinking about its ends and means.

The point is that the problems of our time are poorly served by concepts like "cultural patterns," "interaction," "culture process," and "social structure." These concepts have definite utility within the science, and I am not suggesting they be scrapped (as C. Wright Mills might do) simply because they have little relationship to the contemporary reality. However, they cannot interpret this reality because they are nonspecific, and the full meaning of contemporary human affairs will be found always in the specific situations. The mission of anthropology is not to write current history, of course, but its accumulated knowledge has much to say on the adaptive value of cultural traits and of course on the movements and directions of history, the major ideas and myths of the age. Above all, anthropology has research techniques which blend existential description with a search for reality—if you will, the "scientific" and the "spiritual" meaning of man.

Anthropologists at one time were voluble about these matters, pronouncing on the goals and meaning of civilization and the destiny and fulfillments of humanity. This was, in fact, the great age of evolutionary ideology, and while it was shown to have made grievous methodological and factual errors, who is to say that the myth of social evolution was wrong from the standpoint of its general civilizational results? It sustained colonialism and its evils, to be sure, but it also helped produce nineteenth-century-European scholarship. Evolutionary theory was one of the great civilizing forces, as Loren Eiseley has pointed out in various writings (1958, 1960).

With some important individual exceptions, modern anthropologists do not usually deliver themselves of interpretations of contemporary civilization—at least not at the level of the major myths. Possibly this is because anthropologists do not approve of the direction life has taken and refuse to justify it or explain it, and also because the nineteenth century anthropologists were apologists for the current order, and this got them into trouble. This is not, however, very convincing. In the first place, the nineteenth century anthropologists rarely *consciously* justified or defended something; that is, they were not propagandists in the cynical modern sense, but were *participants* in the age. In the second place, I am not asking that anthropologists *defend* anything, only that they intellectually analyze, criticize, and possibly rebuild. In the third place, the loss of a public voice by the contemporary anthropologist has gone hand in hand with the rise of scientific objectivity and relativism. This is a most desirable attitude when it comes to methodology, but it is a curse when it is misapplied, as it has been so widely, to the role of the scientist and his knowledge, in the public arena.

I suppose that anthropologists do not take active roles in the combative world of ideas because they are lost without their scientific orientation. Their science is highly generalized, and it says little about the nature of contemporary historical reality. In the mid-twentieth century, it is primarily physical scientists who speak out and (wholly justifiably, in my opinion) claim the authority of their profession in so speaking out. Surely anthropologists are aware of clear and present dangers in the drift of world society; yet there is no "Bulletin of Anthropological Scientists" to discuss these issues and their possible solutions [referring here to the "Bulletin of Atomic Scientists," which was very influential in the early 1960s]. Anthropologists write about American culture patterns and values; but which anthropologists have made trenchant analyses of the current state of public morality, the citizen's role in politics, the influence of mass media, the problems of the automobile age, and the drift and inevitability, the hopelessness and powerlessness of the affluent society?

Only a few relatively independent thinkers and writers who are not academically hog-tied, or who use their academic and professional connections largely as a point of departure, seem to be able to make the analyses of contemporary civilizations which the anthropologist has so signally failed to provide. Most of these men are to be found in the "policy sciences"—a mélange of sociology, administration, economics, and related fields which seems to have escaped the curse of "objectivity" and relativism for the time being. Of course there are anthropologists who have likewise: Redfield's moral sense and Mead's willingness to criticize modern culture come to mind immediately. On the whole it has been those anthropologists who in their writings are willing to go beyond empirical factitiousness toward the construction of reality and meaning who have spoken out.

It is, in fact, the persistent confusion of existence with reality which lies at the root of the problem. The majority of anthropologists, although much less aggressive about this than many psychologists and sociologists, are nevertheless positivists who deny or do not care whether there is any reality beyond the scope of their measuring instruments, even while their own methods plainly imply the opposite, as I have said earlier. The utmost integrity and dispassion must be utilized at the data-collecting stage; no one questions this. But there are tools for data collection, and above all for interpretation, which permit a mental grasp and penetration far beyond the recording of visual and numerical observations. The intellectual, moral, and even affective attempt to so penetrate is what I would regard as the search for the human reality, as over against mere existence. This reality can be constructed in various terms, but however it may be constructed, it is one route to an understanding of man in his moral as well as his naturalistic contexts. We should compliment anthropology on having made some recent attempts in this direction, but much remains to be done.

The effort called "applied anthropology" has sometimes been viewed as anthropology's contribution to the world of values and social action, but most applied anthropologists are not really concerned with these matters. "Application" has come to refer mainly to *employment* by government and industry and the research periphery cultivated in such employment. "Applied anthropology" does not signify "engaged anthropology;" the role is that of the detached student or the local employee, and has very little in common with the role of the social analyst, critic, or idea-creator. [Sol Tax's "action anthropology" was the exception to this statement—see chapter 12.] Applied anthropologists have been eager to serve the organizations of society and to put their technical knowledge to use in the service of such organizations, but they have not shown much interest in diagnosing problems or, above all, suggesting new directions. "Application" is a vague term; surely within its meaning should be that of exploring the contemporary condition of man and the changes, actual and desirable, in that condition.

The implications of these arguments need to be summarized. The acceptance of a scientific orientation by anthropology in the twentieth century seems to have militated against anthropology's willingness to swim in or against the tide of social ideology, and to make statements on the direction and meaning of this tide. This, in my opinion, is a real loss. Secondly, while anthropology has lost its high ideological relevance, it has acquired popularity and a myth-making function which I suppose is a gain. However, this gain is also, perhaps, anthropology's loss, since it might well contribute to the feeling of detachment from great events and ideas. A sense of purpose is lost, and the emphasis comes to be placed on the *content* of the field, rather than on its meaning for humanity. The fascinating qualities of anthropological subject matter form the basis of popular interest, and the anthropologist makes no great effort to insist on the meaning these discoveries may hold for the nature of man, history and civilizational growth and decline. And while problems dealing with these matters sometimes occupy his *professional* attention, even there the emphasis is not on their ideological and human significance but on disciplinary theories and concepts. Something has dropped out of anthropology: a middle ground of social awareness [by 1995 there were signs of a return engagement]. Possibly this is the distinctive *American* element or contribution to the field. Most of the nineteenth century figures who did have this awareness were European.

There will be numerous objections to these conclusions. The most familiar will concern itself with the demand that anthropologists, as scientists, not engage in the formation of empirically undemonstrable positions. I have not recommended this in such flat terms. I have said that the very function of anthropological science inescapably involves "myth" even while investigating and painstakingly recording social existence. Existence is empirical; reality, however, is constructed and thought through. The great anthropologists have been those who have gone beyond mere existence and tried to create the sense of a human moral reality. In spite of the innumerable methodological faults of the configurationists, they have been more successful at this task than the factitious social anthropologists. This, too, was Redfield's primary objective, and it was this that Oscar Lewis seems not to have grasped in his criticisms of Redfield's pioneer work on Tepoztlan (Redfield 1930; Lewis 1951). Without this struggle to convey a sense of the human reality, anthropological knowledge is largely paper and ink, at least insofar as its relevance to contemporary issues of man and society are concerned—and it is these issues with which I am concerned here.

Thus, the mythic quality of anthropological knowledge, in its various dimensions, presents a challenge to the dominant scientific orientation of the professional discipline. There is no question that the growing prestige of the social sciences has influenced the outlook of anthropologists to the extent that there is a desire to join forces with the empiricists and systemic theorists among the sociologists and psychologists: the "behavior science" movement is the apotheosis of the trend [or *was*, in the 1960s!—see chapter 3]. At the same time, the distinctive function of cultural anthropology remains the depictive and *interpretive* integration of masses of data on real human situations; without this, the field will be indistinguishable from certain branches of sociology and social psychology. And this technique inevitably retains myth-making qualities and moral responsibilities which should be acknowledged and not disguised. My own predilections have always been in the social science direction; but as a professional anthropologist I have been of two minds on this score and have endeavored to keep alive in my work the anthropological quality of imagination, of descriptive impact.

At the same time, the mythic qualities of anthropological knowledge create problems of methodology, and hence of truth, which cannot be ignored. There must be a constant, never-ending search for better techniques of rendering the actuality of social life in order to guard against the unconscious propagation of romantic error. The anthropologist, to an extent greater than any other "social scientist," relies upon *words* as a device for the recording and presentation of data, and words are notoriously deceptive. It is a testimonial to Malinowski's greatness that he was constantly preoccupied with this problem and strove to overcome the shortcomings inherent within it as well as to realize its vast communicative potentialities. I am saying that *the anthropologist must be, at least in part, a literary artist*; and if he abandons this goal for abstract or enumerative modes of presentation (however necessary these may be in dealing with data), he also abandons what is most unique in his professional heritage.

Literature Cited

Benedict, Ruth. 1934. *Patterns of Culture*. Boston: Houghton Mifflin.

Bennett, John W. 1992. "Surrendering to Loma and to Sociology and Trying to Catch Them: Some Recent Writings of Kurt H. Wolff." *Reviews in Anthropology* 21: 1–16.

Bidney, David. 1953. *Theoretical Anthropology*. New York: Columbia University Press.

Boas, Franz. 1940. "Liberty among Primitive People," in *Freedom, Its Meaning*, edited by Ruth N. Anshen, pp. 375–80. New York: Harcourt, Brace.

Carpenter, Edmund, ed. 1956. *Explorations: Studies in Culture and Communication*. Series began publication with Dec. 1953 issue. Toronto: University of Toronto.

Eiseley, Loren C. 1958. *Darwin's Century: Evolution and the Men Who Discovered It*. Garden City, NY: Doubleday.

———. 1960. *The Firmament of Time*. New York: Atheneum.

Freeman, Derek. 1983. *Margaret Mead and Samoa: The Making and Unmaking of an Anthropological Myth*. Cambridge, MA: Harvard University Press.

Goldenweiser, Alexander A. 1931. *Robots and Gods*. New York: Alfred A. Knopf.

———. 1933. *History, Psychology and Culture*. New York: Alfred A. Knopf.

———. 1937. *An Introduction to Primitive Culture*. New York: F. S. Crofts.

Goodman, Paul. 1962. *Utopian Essays and Practical Proposals*. New York: Random House.

Hoyle, Fred. 1955. *Frontiers of Astronomy*. New York: Harper & Bros.

———. 1956. *Man and Materialism*. New York: Harper & Bros.

———. 1957. *The Black Cloud*. New York: Harper & Bros.

Kluckhohn, Clyde. [1944] 1962. *Navaho Witchcraft*. Peabody Museum of Archaeology and Ethnology, Harvard University. Reprint. Boston, MA: Beacon Press.

Lewis, Oscar. 1951. *Life in a Mexican Village: Tepoztlan Restudied*. Urbana, IL: University of Illinois Press.

Liebling, A. J. 1937–42. "The Jollity Building," in *The Telephone Booth Indian*, edited by A. J. Liebling. New York: Doubleday Doran.

Malinowski, Bronislaw. 1927. *Sex and Repression in Savage Society*. New York: Harcourt, Brace.

———. 1929. *The Sexual Life of Savages in Northwestern Melanesia*. London: George Routledge.

Marquand, John P. 1949. *Point of No Return*. Boston: Little, Brown.

Redfield, Robert. 1930. *Tepoztlan: A Mexican Village*. Chicago: University of Chicago Press.

Riesman, David. 1950. *The Lonely Crowd: A Study of the Changing American Character*. New Haven, CT: Yale University Press.

Spier, Leslie. 1917. *An Outline for a Chronology of Zuni Ruins*. Anthropological Papers, American Museum of Natural History, vol. 17, part 3.

Velikofsky, Immanuel. 1950. *Worlds in Collision*. New York: Macmillan.

———. 1952. *Ages in Chaos*. New York: Doubleday.

———. 1955. *Earth in Upheaval*. New York: Doubleday.

Warner, W. Lloyd. [1941] 1963. *Yankee City*. Abridged edition of the Yankee City series, vol. 1, *The Social Life of a Modern Community*, by W. Lloyd Warner and Paul S. Lunt. New Haven: Yale University Press.

Wells, H. G. 1937. *The Croquet Player*. New York: Viking Press.

Whyte, William H. 1956. *The Organization Man*. New York: Simon and Schuster.

3

Interdisciplinary Research and the Concept of Culture

With an Epilogue concerning Chapters 2 and 3

Either we limit our studies to the kind of thing a single man can readily do, and work within the bounds of traditional disciplines, or we boldly try to understand society, and to that end use all the materials and techniques available. Before long those who choose the latter alternative—which, under the press of events, seems to be chosen for them . . . will use each other's materials and they will do what human limitations made necessary: work together on large projects, using their professional skills in common and educating each other.
—Ralph Gilbert Ross *(1952:28)*

Introduction

The purpose of this paper is to discuss some consequences which the growing movement for unity and cooperation among the social sciences has for anthropology. It is believed that participation in this movement has produced certain stresses in the intellectual relation-

---

First published in 1960 with the same title in the *American Anthropologist* vol. 56, pp. 169-79. The original draft was dated 1945 and this published version was completed in 1953, but a comparison of the two versions shows no significant differences. The text has been slightly edited for stylistic reasons. I have added an epilogue which to some extent is also an introductory statement to the paper. This epilogue might be read prior to reading the paper.

ships of anthropologists, as well as changes in the conceptual tools anthropologists must use in their work. Cultural anthropology alone is considered; a study of possible effects upon the other fields of modern anthropology is a task requiring separate treatment.

Most of the observations in this paper are based on the writer's own experiences in interdisciplinary research and teaching;[1] consequently the essay is in some respects a personal testament. However this may be, the purpose of the paper is not to advocate anthropology's participation in interdisciplinary studies, or to suggest that all the difficulties of our science may be cleared away by such participation. The question of the relationship of any one of the several sciences of man to a unified approach is a difficult one which cannot be handled in a brief paper. (For perceptive comments on interdisciplinary research see Darley 1951.)

Federation versus Integration

It may be surprising to some that the question of anthropology's relationship to interdisciplinary studies is to be raised at all, since one of the essential tenets of the anthropological faith has been a kind of interdisciplinary union of separate but converging studies of man—the famous and somewhat arrogant-sounding "study of man." This point therefore deserves preliminary comment.

The traditional anthropological conception of interdisciplinary effort meant—and for many, continues to mean—a simple federation or coexistence of classificatory groups of data relating to man. Traditional anthropological interdisciplinary research meant—for example—physical anthropology contributing the biological descriptions, linguistics the materials on speech, and ethnology the customary behavior data for a given group of humans. Experiments in integrative, explanatory research (beyond mere combinations of data)—for example, Boas's study of variation in head form in differing cultural and natural environments—did not progress, and in general anthropologists have done little work of this kind. Unification or rather federation was achieved primarily on the basis of classificatory and historical principles.[2] Thus research was collaborative but not integrative in the full sense, since an attempt to organize data around a definite and common conceptual scheme was lacking, and consequently explanatory linkages of various forms of data were not achieved. A federation of sciences based on such grounds perhaps can last only so long—allowing for certain social lags and sympathetic-traditional bonds—as a more comprehensive, synthetic, and rigorous approach, with willingness on the part of specialists to bury differences and make drastic conceptual concessions, is not in existence.

Interdisciplinary Research

In recent years [i.e., the 1940s and 1950s] the most striking characteristic of the arena of sciences dealing with human phenomena has been the tendency toward interdisciplinary attack on problems of common interest. The basic scientific objective is *explanation* rather than description, and an explanatory approach can yield interpretations with a high proportion of consensus among the participant scholars. Such consensus, and such interpretations, are made possible by the adoption of a *common conceptual scheme*, or some approximation thereof. This type of scientific activity, and the emerging conceptual scheme,[3] is referred to variously as "the multidimensional approach," "structural-functional analysis," "problem-oriented social science," "behavior science," "action theory," and the like, the choice of term depending upon which aspect of the general activity one wishes to utilize for the name, or which particular sciences—biology, psychology, sociology, and so forth—are included in the scheme.

Anthropologists have engaged this movement in varying ways. Culture and personality studies represent one of the earlier manifestations of the trend and, while these have recently been in the process of merging into the broader approach of which they were a forerunner, they continue to attract large numbers of young anthropologists. The "applied anthropology" movement has developed interdisciplinary tendencies of a diverse and often constructive variety. Other anthropologists, frequently isolated in small institutions or in "combined" departments with other social scientists, have undertaken joint research programs with representatives from other fields. Still other anthropologists are involved in new educational experiments, like the Harvard Department of Social Relations, where the avowed intent is to establish the behavior sciences on an integrated footing.

The approach is in part based on the need emerging during World War II for highly integrated information covering a large number of relevant variables. Cultural data alone, no more than sociological, psychological, political, or economic, were not sufficient to answer the needs for information and prediction that accompanied highly organized psychological, economic, political, and military warfare. Anthropology as traditionally developed could supply, for example, detailed comparative and descriptive data on exotic world areas or measurements for physiological reactions of pilots, but the extent to which anthropology contributed more depended, not on anthropology itself, but on *the affiliation of anthropologists with members of other disciplines, where teamwork was the rule.* If answers to questions which demand a careful explanatory accounting of the functions of a large assortment of variables are to be given, some sort of "uni-operational" conceptual scheme (a term used in a commentary in *Human Organization* in 1952), which permits the several sciences to equate observations and operations, must be utilized. And, in turn, a conceptual scheme of this kind visualizes the component sciences not as independent areas of knowledge but rather as groups of experts on specific phenomena, or variables, for example, cultural anthropologists on values, sociologists on roles and interaction, biologists on genes, psychologists on personality mechanisms, economists on a special institutional phase of cultural and social behavior, and so on.

Now, a research design of this type places certain demands upon those who participate within it. In the first place, it requires a multidimensional perspective toward problems of man—a perspective which automatically rejects reified and/or single-variable explanations of human phenomena. Second, it is methodologically eclectic as regards the collection of data on any variable, for example, data on group regularities or "culture" might be collected as well in laboratory situations or by attitude survey methods as in the fieldwork approach. Third, it requires very considerable methodological rigor, and more, transformability of the data of one variable into the others (leading again to a rejection of explanatory reification of any descriptive or phenomenological variable). Fourth, it is contemptuous of any discipline which makes heavy claims for its own uniqueness or completeness.

These features of interdisciplinary research seem to run counter to some current aspects of [Classic] anthropology. Insistence on "culture" as the master concept with both descriptive and explanatory power, rather large claims for anthropology's expertness and destiny, the insulation of many anthropologists from current methodologically complex aspects of social science, and certain other characteristics of our contemporary science are all somewhat awkward from the point of view of the interdisciplinary scientist. This might place the anthropologist working in these interdisciplinary projects in a peculiar position. On the one hand, he is called upon to adopt certain rules of the game (see above) and also to perform as a particular technical expert—as an expert on the patterned aspects of group behavior, for example (note we did not say "culture"!)—and in this role he is known as an "anthropologist." But on the other hand, his very participation, and presumed acceptance of the rules concerning research on multiple variables, requires that he often discard or revise some of the ideas common to the field of anthropology. And some of these ideas are those which have become expressive symbols of the solidarity of the company of anthropologists.

We will attempt to illustrate some of these points by a consideration of the concept of culture and its relation to interdisciplinary research.

The Concept of Culture

Two tendencies stand out in the development of the concept of culture. First, the concept clearly had the status of a "felt need," in that the great range of human variation emerging from research required description in its own terms, since it could not be understood by available biological and environmental concepts. Nor were purely individual behavioral traits adequate for group analysis and description. "Culture" emerged as a needed tool, and consequently it became convenient to regard any sector of human experience and its phenomena not readily explainable in other terms as a part of "culture." This led to a tendency to permit the culture concept to assume sponge-like qualities, soaking up whole batteries of analytically distinguishable factors—a process which often slips into reification.

The second major tendency in the emergence of a culture concept appeared in the interest of anthropologists in small, face-to-face communal groups. It was observed that such groups possessed a high quotient of shared norms of conduct, and this corpus of "integrated" and "homogeneous" learned behavior traits came to be designated as the "culture" of the group. Culture was thus identified with a holistic, tribal unity, and eventually this unity was assumed to be present in every human society. The possibility that different types of social groups and institutional systems—for example, a nation or corporation—might not possess such a homogenous collection of learned traits, for the reason that face-to-face relationships were not the predominant mode, was ignored or underplayed. Culture was culture—it was the same for all human groupings and it became a "level of reality," thus much more than a useful analytical abstraction.[4]

The idea that small, face-to-face groups possessed remarkably homogenous sets of learned behaviors dominated anthropology until the mid-1930s. The research on nonliterate groups had served to build up an image of culture which stressed homogeneity and integration, and had resulted in a relatively static concept. Since cultures were integrated, change came with difficulty, and then largely from outside forces which disturbed the integrity of the logically related structures. Hence the popularity of such concepts as "diffusion," "acculturation," and "borrowing"—these terms and many others all referring primarily to stimuli originating *outside* of the system under investigation. Deviant trends within the culture were studied, but often it was found these deviations could be subsumed under more complex statements of the holistic pattern itself, and thus they were minimized as an agent of change. Moreover, little attention was paid to such analytical dimensions as factional conflicts, economic relationships and goals, demographic pressures, and the like.

What this approach did was to restrain inquiries into subjects and problems which demanded analytical distinctions beyond the cultural. Yet, such inquiries inevitably appeared, and a series of compromise positions were worked out, appearing under the headings of functional theory, culture, and personality studies, "applied anthropology," British social anthropology, and the like—all becoming prominent in the late 1930s. Although these fields attempted analyses of social relationships, functional aspects of social life, institutional variation, and the importance of the personality variable or dimension, most of them continued to work with an implicit notion of "one tribe—one culture." Many of the theoretical difficulties of these fields may be traced to the fact that in solving problems of dynamics, they attempted to use descriptive-holistic concepts of culture, instead of tools with greater analytical power.

The "cultural variable" for the majority of anthropologists thus retained its status of an integrated whole characteristic of a society or group, and anthropological research, by and large, consisted of a search for the locus and changes of this tribal culture. This anthropological enterprise reached an extreme phase in the "national character" studies of World War II, when anthropologists actually attempted to isolate the ethos—the holistic face-to-face tribal culture—of great modern nations.[5]

Now, this general conception of culture does not do particular violence to the data of descriptive historical inquiries. If the problem is one of tracing the movement, in space and time, of abstracted items of behavior, whether they be sounds, potsherds, kinship terms, or religious beliefs, it is convenient to label these items as "belonging" to a particular "culture." The archaeologist who works with discrete sites or in "culture areas" demarcated by pottery styles, like the ethnologist who traces kinship customs from one tribe to another, can afford a phenomenological definition. It is actually the most convenient concept for his operations. He may push his theoretical considerations of this concept to extreme limits, but in the last analysis it remains a useful descriptive construction limited in explanatory power, and whatever connections or relatedness one observes between the patterns must remain purely *logical*—the logic of similarity and difference. Culture in this sense cannot "function," since function requires and introduces an entirely different set of analytical concepts. These are unnecessary in purely historical-descriptive inquiries.

Any anthropologist who participates in an interdisciplinary movement is likely to reject this descriptive-holistic or "phenomenological" version of the cultural variable. In the first place, he cannot afford to see all social scientific problems as problems of culture because he discovers that a whole range of problems require finer discriminations. If he studies social relationships in modern society and its institutions, as he is likely to do currently, he soon discovers that he cannot assume that his subjects are simple bearers of culture who are learning and interacting in the face-to-face group atmosphere. The more differentiated and impersonal structure of institutional systems of complex societies cannot be analyzed *initially* with the concept of culture pattern of learned behavior traits—other than in the most generalized and impressionistic manner. The anthropologist instead discovers a need for refined versions of certain familiar tools: studies must be made of the *roles* typical of a *system of social relationships*, the *values* and *norms* associated with these roles, the *expectations* of behavior brought to the situation by the individual actors, their *needs* and *motivations*, and, finally, the varying dimensions of the "situation" itself. Anthropologists are not unfamiliar with these analytical variables, but in the great body of cultural anthropological research, they often have been obscured by the emphasis on culture.[6]

Actually, an analysis which seeks systematic knowledge of these variables in their interactive context often requires a kind of cultivated ignorance of "culture." That is, the question of what, if any, shared and transmitted patterns may exist is a question which need not be assumed at the outset to be relevant. In many studies, the meaning and relevance of this question, if it *is* regarded as part of the investigation, emerges only after analysis of the data. Culture patterns thus may become one of the products of this type of study, but it is not inevitable that they do so. It may be that the particular structure of relationships under examination does not partake significantly of "cultural" description.

In the second place, the interdisciplinary cultural anthropologist observes that culture *as such* is a purely descriptive concept, and that in order to be included as a variable in any investigation of interaction or social relationships it must be translated into terms which are meaningful as factors in behavior, or in social action. *It is not enough to say that "culture" is at work; one must specify exactly how and in what locus*. The "culture" becomes transformed into concepts such as "value orientation," "norms," "expectations," "means" and "ends," and "group atmosphere." These terms represent differing functions of systems of patterned regularities in behavior; they play definite and differing roles in the response of individual to individual; and they fulfill varying missions in the total analytical process. Thus "culture" can "explain" human phenomena only when it is seen as part of a system of relationships between people. It is their *response to* and use of the "patterns" that is of moment.

This leads to a third consideration. In dynamic interdisciplinary research the cultural anthropologist not only breaks "culture" down into a series of analytical variables, or operational concepts (and also stresses new variables which are not "cultural," e,g,, "social relationship"), but *he also becomes critical of the holistic notion of "one tribe – one culture."* He substitutes—if he uses "culture" at all—what might be called a systemic or institutionally varying definition of the cultural variable. He simply observes that in the process of interaction in any concrete system of social relationships, certain traits come to be patterned, or regularized. These systems of patterns, or institutions, must be isolated as the meaningful factors or sets of factors in their concrete, and varying, situations. There is no commitment to the size or duration of the human group with the "culture"; it is simply the pattern-construct aspect of any interactive process: in most cases, values or norms.

If the anthropologist understands these procedures—and he must in order to be a fully cooperative team member—he will likely reject, in whole or in part, certain aspects of the traditional [i.e., "Classic"] approach to culture. In particular, he is likely to be skeptical of tendencies toward explanatory reification, mechanical historical "culture theory," and tribal holistic concepts. His "skepticism" does not necessarily mean "disbelief," for he recognizes the legitimate roles these concepts may play at their own levels.[7] But he becomes, through his experience, a different kind of anthropologist—one who often finds little in common with, say, historical anthropology.

The Emergence of an Analytical Scheme

The foregoing remarks have summarized consequences for the concept of culture deriving from certain contemporary movements in the social sciences. The same process may be viewed also as the culmination of certain long-range trends in cultural anthropology itself—this was anticipated in previous paragraphs where developments in cultural anthropology demanding analytical distinctions beyond the simpler "cultural" ones available were cited. Further discussion of this matter will conclude this paper.

It was remarked previously that in some sense the emphasis on "culture" in anthropology has often operated to obscure or rub out analytical distinctions which permit finer discrimination between the variables and phenomena of human social life and behavior. A convenient example is probably found in the temporary submergence in the early years of the century of inquiries into kinship—a study which demands fine *systematic* distinctions between status position, role, norms of conduct, and the like—after Morgan's and Rivers's pioneer efforts. This temporary subsidence followed the rise to popularity of the culture concept and, for at least a decade or more, interest in large and voluminous concepts like "universal pattern" and "diffusion" obscured the analytical efforts of British scholars like Radcliffe-Brown, who have been concerned with people in interaction rather than with holistic abstractions.

It is my conviction [in, of course, the 1950s] that cultural anthropologists have been insufficiently aware of the tendencies in their own ranks toward the emergence of an analytical scheme which is potentially equipped to supplement the abstractive scheme of culture constructs. Malinowski's work in retrospect would appear to mark some sort of turning point in cultural anthropological studies, in that the concept of "function"—because it poses a dynamic rather than a descriptive static question—requires an analytical scheme above and beyond "culture." This became apparent in Malinowski's early works, yet at the time Malinowski never seemed fully aware of the implications of his own doubts concerning the standard cultural interpretations of the period. His generally superorganicist or "American" article on "Culture" in the *Encyclopedia of the Social Sciences* is sufficient evidence of this.

One of the earliest expositions of an analytical scheme in Malinowski's writings appears in the closing pages of "Baloma" (1916–48) [see chapter 7]. He begins his concluding discussion by requiring that the "social dimension" of a belief be explored, over and above the mere recording of the versions of the belief current in the group. That is, he is saying that the belief has several dimensions of variation in addition to the standard-group-typical-descriptive pattern version, which the anthropologist of those days was likely to collect to the exclusion of anything else. In the subsequent pages this "social dimension" emerges: (1) the belief will vary in terms of the various *social institutions* in which it plays a role; (2) it will vary according to the way it is involved in the *emotional behavior of individuals*; (3) it will vary according to *individual cognitive* and *imaginative manipulation*; and (4) it will vary according to the different *statuses* and *roles* of individuals who use it as a *means to an end* in social action. The terms in italics are the writer's; Malinowski was not constructing an analytic conceptual scheme but simply describing the "social dimension" of supernatural belief. Yet these are the terms now applied to the variables he perceived.[8]

In later years contributions like Bateson's *Naven* (1936) and, still later, Kluckhohn's *Navaho Witchcraft* (1944) [see chapters 7 and 9], were credited with the exploration of analytical variables, while the purely descriptive cultural studies gradually become a kind of pedestrian background for cultural anthropology. The Bateson contribution was principally in the direction of an exploration of the significance of social role as a channelizer and selector of behavior, and the Kluckhohn offering stressed the ways men redirect hostile behavior and assuage anxiety. It is true that both researchers utilized cultural concepts and showed general concern with the configurated aspects of behavior. However, the important contributions were not to culture *qua* culture, but to other analytical dimensions of social behavior. Or, saying it another way, phenomena which had been grouped by other anthropologists into an undifferentiated culture construct, were factored out into relevant behavioral variables [i.e., "functionalism"]. And, by so doing, an explanatory dimension to "cultural" research was added.

Thus there has been a tendency in cultural anthropology, for at least three decades, to recognize and develop an analytical scheme which would rise beyond the boundaries of the culture concept, and would permit explanatory solutions to problems of social behavior and interaction among humans. However, while this has been under way, the purely culturological approach has reached a peak of development in research like the national character studies of Mead and others.

However, as Kluckhohn and others have suggested, analytical schemes are required whether the ultimate goal of analysis is some sort of picture of a whole culture, or whether more segmental objectives are present. The culture concept and its descriptive subsidiaries—"pattern," "trait," and the like—are simply insufficient in themselves, or in elaboration at their own level, to provide the discriminatory power needed in the analysis of human interaction. An approach which gets down to the "sense data," as it were, of human relationships is required, and anthropology, along with other social sciences, has been in the process of developing concepts needed in such an approach.[9]

However this may be, cultural anthropologists should be willing to recognize that sociology and social psychology have probably accomplished much more along these lines, and that anthropology must be ready, in the coming decade, to learn a great deal from these sister sciences. The anthropological demonstration of the variability of human customs, and its total historical perspective on man's accomplishments, are fundamental in the social sciences and constitute anthropology's major and signal contributions, but they are a lesson and a body of knowledge which by themselves are not sufficient to solve problems of finer grain. To do this, anthropology must be willing to borrow concepts from neighboring fields (see Beals 1951).

As such borrowing—which is really coexperimentation with other social sciences on the utility of concepts and factorable expressions of human social behavior—takes place, one will see the gradual emergence of an interdisciplinary conceptual scheme and research program in which cultural anthropology will have a role to play. Precisely what that role may consist of is not entirely clear at present, although Parsons's suggestion of anthropology's responsibility for the further clarification of culture concepts and their relation to analytical concepts is an interesting one (Parsons 1949: 40). Along with this may go some reasoned tempering of anthropology's rather grandiloquent claim that it represents the only self-contained science of man. This claim may be coming to sound slightly hollow in the ears of those persons who have been sold a large package only to find that, while it contains brilliant oddments, it is somewhat lacking in the precision and conceptual equipment necessary for the solution of contemporary problems of importance in the social sciences.

Epilogue, 1995

This essay raised hackles in the profession—some echelons of which wrote me off as a practicing anthropologist. The applied and social-anthropological branches, however, liked what I wrote. A.L. Kroeber wrote the following (dated 13 May 1954):

> Like all your other articles, the one in the present *Anthropologist* intrigues and interests me enormously. I suppose you and I are about as far apart in our basic slants as we can be. Perhaps it is a matter of temperament. I am all in favor of a greater anthropology with the concept of culture as its spearhead. Am I doing you an injustice if I construe you as wanting culture kept in its place, and that you would feel happier with a little anthropology in a large social science?

At the time, this is certainly what I had in mind. In any case, the paper represents an apotheosis of the late-1930s–1940s period of cross-disciplinary fertilization that produced applied anthropology, the wartime studies of military social organization, attitude surveys on the home front as well as in conquered or "liberated" territories, and so on. My general attitude seems to be a kind of benevolent arrogance—note the remarkable phrase, " . . . purely descriptive cultural studies gradually become a kind of pedestrian background for cultural anthropology."

The term "interdisciplinary research" was in vogue at the time, but by the late 1950s the terms, "multidisciplinary," or "cross-disciplinary," came to be preferred. (I do use "multidimensional" in the paper as a synonym for "interdisciplinary," but later it developed a different resonance.) The point was that after years of experience, it became clear that actual interdisciplinary activity was extremely difficult, since the separate disciplines had enormous difficulties translating their concepts and theories—and even data—into each other's terms. The Harvard Social Relations Department was the grand experiment of interdisciplinary optimism, based on Talcott Parsons's "theory of action" (e.g., Parsons and Shils 1951). This entity produced some remarkable statements of social and cultural theory from a "structuralist-functionalist" perspective, and a few research projects, but on the whole more effort was probably expended on the effort to explore the rhetoric of disciplinary synthesis than actual synthetic research. And its life was short—the disciplinary departments eventually prevailed.

The paper seems to come down on the side of social anthropology and against cultural—although I do not believe I intended this quite in the way it reads. Social anthropology received approving remarks because it was possessed of a *de facto* "analytical scheme": status, role, etc., and the approval given to Linton's *Study of Man* was likewise based on his chapters dealing with these analytical concepts. This theme seems to me now to be the real meaning of the paper, and also, the one I would cheerfully continue to support. The culture concept was simply not capable, by itself, or with the purely descriptive concepts used in the 1930s and 1940s, to handle the interpersonal behavioral dynamics of social life. At the same time, I was skeptical of the distinction between "social" and "cultural" (as I said in other papers and in chapters of this book), and so I remain.

The obvious antidote to this piece is, of course, the essay reproduced as chapter 1 of this book. In that essay I seem to take the position that anthropology is a more or less humanistic concept, not really fully subject to scientific objectivity. In other words, t*he defects of the purely cultural approach, as defined in the present chapter, become inevitable and probably desirable features in the discussion in chapter 1.* I suggested in the Prologue that the basis of the difference is probably methodological and topical. And so the confrontation persists: the issue will never be resolved. Both humanistic, evocative ambiguity and sharply definable, analytic precision have places in the anthropological undertaking. Which approach is dominant depends largely on the subject matter. Certainly you need evocation for writing about feelings and values and precise categories for data on behavior of people in contexts of status and role. But both approaches need something of both if you want a full, detailed account of a social situation or process.

I also received an indignant letter from Geoffrey Gorer concerning note number six, where I take his work in reference to the reform program of the Japan Occupation to task. He protested that I misinterpreted the concept of "whole culture." That is, in the rhetoric of the Mead-Benedict et al. group, "whole culture" referred to the core ethos or value system of the culture, and not, as I interpreted it, to simply *everything* in the sociocultural system. That is, I took the term too literally. I expect I did. But if "ethos" or whatever was meant, then the terminology used by these people should have been more explicit. The trouble with so much of the purely culture-oriented research and theory of the early-middle Classic was its lack of conceptual clarity, or its failure to come out flat-footed and say that anthropology was a humanistic undertaking and there was no point in trying to present it in "scientific" rhetoric. Margaret Mead was particularly at fault: she would vacillate between encomiums for the "science" of culture and of anthropology, and eloquent disquisitions on the humanistic aspects of the discipline and of culture.

Another theme in the paper which I did not develop fully or clearly concerns the "cultivated ignorance of culture" phrase. This referred to the fact that before one could really comprehend "patterns" or values or meanings in a cultural situation it would be necessary to apply a standard conceptual scheme in order to have at least a trial framework of categories into which to put the data—concepts like "status" being an example. Well and good—I stand by this, of course, but on the other hand, it is apparent that the whole process is complex. A lot depends on the nature of the categories and patterns one seeks: it may be necessary, especially in cases where the worker is already highly knowledgeable about the general culture, to start with the patterns and then work back into the structural frame of the system of social relations.

I note also that this essay contains a statement of the "theoretical poverty" of anthropological "schools" like functionalism (note 9). I repeat this theme in chapter 7 of the present book. I was trying to say that the value of functionalism—or "structural-functionalism"—was not as explanatory theory, but as the source of an "analytical scheme" useful for sorting and handling data, and as a step toward interdisciplinary synthesis. From another point of view, thus, "functionalism," or the "analytical scheme" I advocate, *is in itself the meaning and nature of culture and social organization.* (There is, in the last analysis, no easy way out of the conceptual labyrinth created by the social sciences in the past fifty years. One does one's best, and actually all approaches will bear some fruit.)

I think the paragraph that begins, "If some features of . . . " contains a succinct statement of the implications these social-based approaches had for Classic-era anthropology. The incompatibilities were serious and it is understandable that the discipline began fragmenting into something like Snow's "two cultures" (1959). And this division continues to exist in the 1990s. On the other hand, the differences to some extent are more logical and rhetorical then actual, because when anthropologists of whatever persuasion get to work on particular problems or situations they manage to cooperate fairly well at the conceptual and data levels. The amount of actual synthesis varies depending on the topic and problem. The famous Harvard Values Project (Vogt and Albert 1966) is a case in point: this was conceived as a classic example of the kind of "interdisciplinary" work defined in the essay. A team of anthropologists, sociologists, psychologists, and philosophers was assembled, financed, and sent into the field to study a selection of Southwestern communities and societies. Some of the products displayed multidisciplinary synthesis; others were strictly disciplinary. The overall results, in other words, were mixed. The project used a generalized functionalist "analytical scheme," based on Harvard Social Relations theory and this certainly provided an organizing frame, but since most of the concepts, particularly that of "value", had been defined prior to the research, little that was novel or fresh emerged—at least on the meaning and nature of the concept of "value."

This essay provides another glimpse of my attachment to the work of Clyde Kluckhohn. Kluckhohn attracted me because he managed to retain an anthropological identity but at the same time participate extensively in the interdisciplinary approach; indeed, he was one of the authors and upholders of "analytical schemes." He accepted Culture as one of the three major sectors of human reality in the Parsons scheme: the others were Society and Personality.

In the last analysis, while my optimism in the closing paragraph as to the increasing dominance of the approach in the anthropological discipline is not warranted, the approach certainly has not disappeared. In fact it remains as a major alternative. What I did not see (although I seem to have paradoxically anticipated it, *vide* chapter 1) is that it was one alternative, not the entirety of inquiry into the nature of human affairs.

Notes to the Original Paper

1. Beginning in 1941, with a study of food habits and social structure in a rural community, in collaboration with sociologists and dietary experts; then to experiments in graduate teaching with sociologists and psychologists; next, in field research in Japan with sociologists and psychologists; and currently, in studies of personal-social adjustment of Japanese students, done with sociologists, and clinical and social psychologists.
2. For the documents bearing on the recent Wenner-Gren conference the notion of anthropology as "an integrated Study of Man," or "synthetic science" is cited repeatedly (e.g., see Kroeber 1952, and Lowie in International Symposium on Anthropology 1953: 67). Others participating in the conference observed that precisely the opposite is the case: that anthropology is a collection of subjects selected on commonsense grounds without any important agreement at the conceptual level; that is, the federative rather than the integrative character of anthropology (see Straus, ibid.: 153).
3. Lest there be some misunderstanding concerning the relationship of research to common conceptual schemes, the following must be said: The intention or desire to do interdisciplinary research is not sufficient in itself to insure success. Success, measured by the ability of the research team to transform its problems and its data into mutually comprehensible categories, requires some type of conceptual scheme, or body of concepts, which transcend the phenomenological boundaries of the special disciplines involved. The conduct of the research therefore simultaneously becomes a *search* for a scheme, and the progressive *evolution* of such a scheme. In some cases existing schemes may be taken over more or less intact—but in such instances they usually become revised in the process of research. Consequently it becomes possible to speak of "common conceptual schemes" both as desiderata of true interdisciplinary research, and, at one and the same time, as products of that research.
4. See Steward (1951) for additional comments on these issues. Note also Redfield's earlier decision to confine "culture" to the homogenous folk society and exclude it from the urban (Redfield 1941). Related comments have been made by Hart (1951).
5. Some thoughtful evaluations of the attempts at constructing national character have recently appeared (see Mead 1950 and Benedict 1946b), but in both of these papers the concept of whole cultures and its status as the goal of research is not questioned, though modified to some extent. All of these wartime studies were designed with practical ends: by knowing the enemy's culture one is better able to devise weapons of psychological warfare. Thus Gorer (e.g., see his comment in

Mead 1950: 95) recommended that the Japanese "way of life" and the Emperor not be attacked in propaganda, this recommendation being "based on an understanding of the *whole* Japanese culture." Gorer really means the particular expressive-symbolic aspects of Japanese culture that he studied. If he had really studied the "whole" culture, he would have discovered the existence of liberal, universalistic, democratic elements of considerable historical depth which were crying for change in the whole Japanese system. Politically it might have been more expedient to strengthen the hand of these elements; because by maintaining the policy of "revere the Emperor" and the Japanese "way of life" the Allies preserved the value orientations and social relationship system which in Japan and elsewhere tends to be defeative of democratic change. Of course, the mistake lay in maintaining the policy into the Occupation—yet, the initial choice of the policy made this continuity inevitable. Gorer might have considered the Japanese *political* institutional culture—the attempt to deal with the "whole culture" simply meant an inability to discriminate between the differing functional significance of various institutional segments and analytical variables. In a like manner, the defects and distortions of Japanese social life in Benedict's brilliant monograph, *Chrysanthemum and the Sword* (1946a), are due precisely to the lack of critical discrimination among the profoundly varying status groupings, roles, and institutional patterns in Japanese society.

6. The assortment of analytical variables noted in this paragraph consists, of course, of those most suitable for the analysis of institutional variation and change at the societal level. A problem which required a multidimensional approach to, say, personality development would be structured differently and contain certain additional or different variables. (See Tolman, "A Model for the Personality System," in Parsons and Shils 1951.)
7. This point should be emphasized, lest it be thought that the matters discussed in this paper constitute an argument against the use of "culture" in any and all contexts. The importance and value of the concept in historical descriptive studies is not questioned. But the concept in that form is felt to be inadequate for studies of human interaction or institutional variation.
8. Among numerous examples of contemporary schemes, see Parsons and Shils 1951, part 1; Bennett and Tumin 1948, part 2; Davis 1949, part 1. A related scheme is presented by Nadel (1951), which is interesting in that it is offered as social anthropological theory, but is acknowledgeably based on structural functional sociology and interdisciplinary behavior science formulations. Linton's *Study of Man* (1936) has probably enjoyed its long and deserved popularity primarily because of its analytical contributions, like the distinction between ascribed and achieved status, and status and role.
9. One important implication of this concerns the theoretical poverty of the well-known anthropological "schools," like historicism or simple functionalism. From the point of view developed in this paper, these schools are not theoretical positions, but rather *aspects* from which one approaches empirical data (i.e., from the standpoint of time series; in terms of unique qualities; with respect to interconnectedness of elements, and so forth). What these schools have lacked is a theory of social behavior which can provide chains of testable hypotheses. Note how an exception to the rule provides such hypotheses: *Navaho Witchcraft*. Since its publication a whole series of coordinated researches on witchcraft have been set in motion. The point is that a theory of social behavior requires an analytical scheme; an analytical scheme requires a precise, not a vague, definition or rather denotation of the status of the culture construct. It is the writer's feeling that

sooner or later, this question of the denotation of culture is going to have to be answered by anthropology, if it is to survive as a field of study. (See Barnett's *Innovation* [1953] for one suggestive answer.)

Literature Cited

Barnett, H. G. 1953. *Innovation: The Basis of Cultural Change.* New York: McGraw-Hill.

Bateson, Gregory. 1936. *Naven: A Survey of the Problems Suggested by a Composite Picture of the Culture of a New Guinea Tribe Drawn from Three Points of View.* London: Cambridge University Press.

Beals, Ralph L. 1951. "Urbanism, Urbanization, and Acculturation." *American Anthropologist* 53: 1–10.

Benedict, Ruth. 1946a. *Chrysanthemum and the Sword.* Boston: Houghton-Mifflin.

———. 1946b. "The Study of Culture Patterns in European Nations." *Transactions of the New York Academy of Sciences* 2(8): 274–79.

Bennett, J. W. and M. Tumin. 1948. *Social Life: Structure and Function.* New York: Knopf.

Darley, John G. 1951. "Five Years of Social Science Research: Retrospect and Prospect," in *Groups, Leadership, and Men*, edited by H. Guetzkow. Carnegie Press.

Davis, Kingsley. 1949. *Human Society.* New York: Macmillan.

Hart, C. W. M. 1951. "Review of *Sociologie et anthropologie* by Marcel Mauss." *American Sociological Review* 16: 405–406.

International Symposium on Anthropology. 1953. *An Appraisal of Anthropology Today*, edited by Sol Tax et al. Chicago: University of Chicago Press.

Kluckhohn, Clyde. [1944] 1962. *Navaho Witchcraft.* Papers of the Peabody Museum of American Archaeology and Ethnology, vol. 22, no. 2, Harvard University. Reprinted with an introduction by T. Parsons and E.Z. Vogt. Boston: Beacon Press.

Kroeber, A. L. 1952. "International Symposium on Anthropology: Origin and Aims." *News Bulletin, American Anthropological Association* 4(2).

Linton, Ralph. 1936. *The Study of Man: An Introduction.* New York: Appleton Century.

Malinowski, Bronislaw. 1916–48. "Baloma: The Spirits of the Dead in the

Trobriand Islands." In *Magic, Science and Religion and Other Essays*, pp. 125–227. Selected and with an introduction by Robert Redfield. Glencoe, IL: The Free Press.

Mead, Margaret. 1950. "The Comparative Study of Cultures and the Purposive Cultivation of Democratic Values." *Perspectives on a Troubled Decade 1939–1949*, Conference on Science, Philosophy and Religion, Tenth Symposium. New York: Harper.

Nadel, S. F. 1951. *The Foundations of Social Anthropology.* Glencoe, IL: The Free Press.

Parsons, Talcott. 1949. "The Present Position and Prospects of Systematic Theory in Sociology." *Essays in Sociological Theory, Pure and Applied.* Glencoe, IL : The Free Press.

Parsons, Talcott and E. A. Shils, eds. 1951. *Toward a General Theory of Action.* Cambridge, MA: Harvard University Press.

Redfield, Robert. 1941. *The Folk Culture of Yucatan.* Chicago: University of Chicago Press.

Ross, Ralph G. 1952. "Elites and the Methodology of Politics." *Public Opinion Quarterly* 16: 27–32.

Snow, C. P. 1959. *The Two Cultures and the Scientific Revolution*. Cambridge, MA: University Press.

Steward, Julian H. 1951. "Levels of Sociocultural Integration: An Operational Concept." *Southwestern Journal of Anthropology* 7: 374–90.

Vogt, Evon Z. and Ethel M. Albert. 1966. *Rimrock: A Study of Values in Five Cultures*. Cambridge, MA: Harvard University Press.

4

The Micro-Macro Nexus in Classic and Post-Classic Anthropology

Introduction

The purpose of this paper is to consider the articulation of small and large social systems as an issue in the history of anthropological ideas. This includes anthropology's increasing concern with the historical present, as well as implications for theories of anthropology and kindred disciplines. I assume that anthropology will continue to join with other social disciplines in dealing with the problems of world social transition. However one may define micro-macro articulation, it certainly refers to a set of social problems which anthropologists cannot solve alone.

For historical purposes, I have found it useful to condense the many available topics into just three general ones: (1) "micro" and "macro" phenomena defined as different types of community, society, or culture; (2) "micro" and "macro" as referring to interactive processes of

---

Originally written in 1984 and published in 1985 as "The Micro-Macro Nexus: Typology, Process, and System" as a chapter in the book *Micro and Macro Levels of Analysis in Anthropology*, edited by R. Dewalt and P. J. Pelto. Academic Press, New York. This essay originally was scheduled for reprinting as a chapter in my *Human Ecology as Human Behavior* volume (1993-96), but was excluded because of its emphasis on the history of anthropological ideas. The latter half of the essay deals with the contemporary world situation and how anthropologists might confront it, and this distinguishes it from other chapters in the present volume which focus on methods and concepts rather than historical events. However, chapter 12 also deals with application, so this chapter is a kind of companion. The paper also shows how in one context the ideas of the Classic era have influenced the post-Classic.

change, involving diffusion, influence, and defensive adaptation; and (3) the question of broader systemic convergence in world society—how small-scale social phenomena, and/or local communities, are being incorporated into ever-larger systems of action and control. I shall confine the analysis to general or theoretical issues.

The phrase, "micro-macro" refers to at least two different things: first, the size or magnitude of the social forms and processes: "micro" in this sense means "small-scale," and "macro," "large-scale." Second, the phrase may refer to "local" social forms as contrasted to "external" forms which may intervene or influence the local. Logically, this duality creates a fourfold table: one may have "small" forms with highly "local" peculiarities, but, also: "local" forms which are duplicates of the "large" and "external" forms; and so on. The term, "microcosm," refers to a small-scale phenomenon which contains all or most characteristics of the macrocosm.

My choice of the word "nexus" in the title refers to an emphasis on process. The main task is to determine how the micro—or local—forms interact with the macro—or external—forms: how people solve their problems in a milieu of relationships and adaptive coping. Thus, the "micro-macro" issue is a basic issue in human history; and along with environmental problems, it is an opportunity for anthropology to make a significant contribution to public policies and affairs.

Historical Background

Although "applied anthropology" had its inception in the "native races" protection issue in England in the 1840s and 1850s (Reining 1962); and in the Amerind problem of the 1880s and the formation of the Bureau of American Ethnology as a shield against mistreatment of the tribes (Hinsley 1979), the full implications of the historical progression toward incorporation of indigenes in larger social systems did not become manifest until the 1950s. The liquidation of the colonial empires subsequent to World War II meant that the national state became the dominant political frame of tribal societies. For the first time, anthropologists were required to take the nation as a system into full account; its demands on tribal populations and communities were insistent; political freedom meant conformity to formal law and regulation; the District Commissioner was replaced by the national bureaucracy.

Before this happened the "micro-macro" issue for anthropology was largely one of defending tribal communities against unfeeling interventions of colonial power. This meant, for example, the need to explicate the rationality and morality of tribal modes of punishment of wrongdoers in the face of insistence by administrators on adherence to Euro-American legal and moral constructs. On the other hand, such issues were not felt to be important by rural sociologists and anthropologists working in European and North American *rural* society; the local-external relationships there were usually visualized as "normal": rural communities were seen as normal components of the total society, conducting their affairs in full awareness of their role and position in the nation. *Nation* was an accomplished fact; not a problem of social emergence. Change was part of "progress"; it was accepted as normal—though often unsettling—by the rural population.

Classic anthropologists eventually assimilated modern rural society into the concept of "complex society," and this was contrasted to tribal and peasant-folk communities, conceived as homogeneous, non-institutionalized entities. Thus the anthropological image of the world down to about 1960 was one-sided: the possibility of the existence of a *general* or "cross-cultural" process of micro versus macro, local versus external, was not seriously entertained. Awareness of such a process would emerge only when tribal or peasant communities were subjected to intervention by bureaucracies or governments whose centers of power were located at a distance from the communities' territories.

After World War II the inauguration of new national states in former colonies required a new view of the social process: the national state came to be seen as an institution which generated problems of local-external interaction in communities everywhere, not only in the so-called underdeveloped countries. Thus, Vidich and Bensman, in their 1960 book on a small town and its rural hinterland in New York State, made a strong case for the way the larger national society impinged on the culture and economic welfare of the community to its detriment. My mid-career paper (Bennett 1967) on macro/micro relationships in a post-frontier agrarian region in Canada was in one sense an answer to Vidich and Bensman's conclusions. In that paper I sought to show that for better or for worse, the residents of the rural region had forged their own institutions in the context of local-external interactions, and therefore found it possible to obtain the rewards and resources they needed—as well as having to forego certain things as a result of surveillance by external agencies.

Since the 1960s, anthropologists have tended to conceptualize the macro/micro process as general and pervasive, applicable to all societies and all national state systems. Most of the work has, of course, taken place in the developing countries; anthropological studies in Western rural societies are really only getting under way. Some of the specific cases, however are currently receiving close attention; an example is the "family farm" issue in North America (e.g., Williams 1981; and Bennett 1982). Much of this increasing anthropological work on rural communities is informed by the idea that social life and production in smaller units is—or can be—more effective and rewarding than life in communities with industrialized agriculture (Walter Goldschmidt's 1947 book, *As You Sow*, was the pioneer statement). The same issue is important for new programs in Third World rural development: both the World Bank and the U.S. Agency for International Development showed interest by the 1980s in traditional modes of production and community organization as a substitute for the scientized and technologized modes of production promoted by earlier development programs.

Returning to the issue of the national state as the key social frame in the modern world, the basic question was whether the state was the best means of organizing indigenous government and production in former tribal-peasant populations under colonial control. Obviously regional federations and production systems would have been more efficient and perhaps less abusive of traditional ways. However, the adoption of the national state model was politically and perhaps economically inevitable, given the fact that most of the leaders of the new nations had been educated in Europe or North America and trained in the doctrine and practice of state politics and autonomy. The structure of the international market economy also required independent national governing bodies as the responsible organs for control of funds and execution of development projects. However, the shift to national states meant that the world came to be populated by dozens of new nations differing greatly in resource potential and in their capacity to make their own decisions, introducing new dimensions of inequality and political instability. It was this choice of the independent state as the model for the post-colonial world that was and is mainly responsible for the difficulties and tensions of development—granted that residues of "imperialism" and exploitation play their role as well (for examples of studies by anthropologists, see Richard Adams 1970 for Central America; and Beck 1985 for the Middle East).

However, to identify the contemporary micro/macro issue as generated exclusively by the transition from colony to new nation is historically short-sighted. As Lloyd Fallers observed in his 1974 book on the nation-state, with reference to the East African situation:

> This does not mean that the microcosmic, everyday lives of contemporary East Africans are for the most part still conditioned by precolonial ethnic cultures and social solidarities alone, nor is their more self-conscious political behavior. That ethnic *Gemeinschaften* remain needs no emphasis, but the new states are not simply arenas for raw ethnic competition and conflict, as news reports might sometimes lead one to believe. For one thing, the precolonial societies of the region were never as discrete as would be suggested by the lines anthropologists are accustomed to draw on "tribal" maps. There were "international" political systems in East Africa before the coming of Arabs and Europeans and there were much cultural interchange. The image of Africa as a stagnant region is now recognized for what it is: a product of Western ignorance and prejudice. The "dark continent" has in fact been the scene of vast population movements, of the rise and fall of countless empires. (Fallers 1974: 35)

Fallers goes on to sketch the complex reality of East African politics and culture: the interaction within regional social systems; the multilingual accommodations; the crosscutting loyalties and allegiances; the constant interplay of local communities and larger political systems. These phenomena were neglected by anthropologists for years, as Fallers implies in the quotation. This was due probably to sociological and political ignorance—as Fallers seemed to imply; and also to the focus on discrete tribal entities induced by ethnological theory; or by the conformity to colonial concepts and restrictions. In my own case, I can recall from my graduate school days that the complex local-external relationships were acknowledged by professors, but were considered to be the subject matter of "history" or "sociology," not anthropology. Anthropology concerned culture—that is, *ethnicity*—the purer the better, although Robert Redfield (1955) seemed to disagree: for him, the basic anthropological unit of analysis was not "a culture," but "the little community," a particular physical and institutional frame for human existence. The importance of the distinction was lost to Redfield's American contemporaries, and probably was not fully appreciated by Redfield himself.

The Problems

Thus, as tribal and peasant communities began publicly and officially merging into national populations, anthropologists came to discover what historians and sociologists had known for a long time: that the social forms of most small communities were not created *in situ*, but had evolved in complex relationship with the institutions of larger societies. This is a theme that emerged first in the "peasant studies" of the 1950s (Redfield 1956; Wolf 1957). As this awareness developed, anthropologists began changing their fundamental image of humanity: instead of an exclusive preoccupation with a patchwork of single communal entities, they began to perceive a world of interactive communication with localities and social units of indefinite boundedness.

The issue took a tripartite form. The first was an old one: the purely descriptive differences between small, relatively isolated network-type communities on the one hand, and large, multi-institutional, multigroup societies on the other. This typological problem had its roots in an old tradition of European folk sociology which had always enjoyed some influence in anthropology—the dichotomy of the *Gemeinschaft* and *Gesellschaft*. The second issue concerned the nature of the relationships of *local* groups and communities to the *external* institutional and organizational apparatus of government, economic markets, and political movements (this is where peasantry became crucial). This problem concerned social dynamics and process, not typology. The third issue concerned the nature of large suprasystems: the way the local and the external combined to make up single large interactive entities; for example, the nation.

These distinctions also clarify relationships between the various social disciplines. Sociology is the study of the supra-systems as wholes; rural sociology (and some types of agricultural economics) focus on the study of the local systems in contact and interaction with external entities and the nation; general or macroeconomics resembles sociology insofar as it posits the existence of large economic systems as wholes that pervade everything else; political science has branches in both camps: studies of local politics and national political systems and movements. Cultural anthropology (ethnology) was preoccupied with the descriptive typological differences between small (local) and large (cosmopolitan) societies. All of these fields are of course patchworks of specialized inquiries that contain differing empirical emphases on small and large systems. Their *theories* however, remain based in the dominant interests as noted above. That is, sociological theory is "macro" on the whole; its difficulties often stem from the misapplication of societal-level theory to local social groupings. Cultural anthropology, although beginning to do research on larger systems, historically operated with theories derived from the study of small, low-energy societies with a high degree of isolation. But there are few or no anthropological studies of large systems as wholes, although a handful of classic works came close; (e.g., studies of large African tribal nations like Herskovits's *Dahomey* [1938]; Leach's book on Burmese tribal politics [1954]; or Fallers's book quoted previously. A. L. Kroeber was interested in civilizations, but his emphasis was on aesthetic and ideational aspects. These productions, however, did not spawn a general anthropology of large politico-economic systems. What general theory pertaining to such systems exists in anthropology—e.g., social stratification—is, on the whole, derived from other disciplines.

The question, of course, in everyone's mind is whether there can be any such thing as a distinctively *anthropological* theory of large systems. That is, are the existing theories derived from sociology, economics, and political science the only possible theories? There simply has not been sufficient work by anthropologists to justify a detailed appraisal of theoretical trends. Even "urban anthropology," which is an attempt to look at large social systems, has been mainly concerned with urban subcultures or lifestyle groupings [that is, at the time of writing]. This is useful work insofar as it shows that sociologists have missed a lot, but on the other hand, some of the classic studies of this kind, like Whyte's *Street Corner Society* (1943), were produced by sociologists.

The point is that the paradigms employed by anthropologists from the late nineteenth through most of the twentieth century were derived from the study of relatively small, isolated social groups. The concept of culture was almost entirely derived from a contemplation of shared mental products and customs in such societies, and the prestige of the culture concept was derived from ethnographies like Malinowski's on the Trobriands, or Margaret Mead's Pacific Island studies. The facts and speculations introduced in these productions captivated the intellect of anthropologists as well as other social scientists for two generations, and helped create "schools" like "functionalism," "British structuralism," or "culture and personality." Thus, movement toward a wider compendium of social facts from a larger sample of human societies was delayed.

This meant that since anthropology started its empirical investigations lower in the levels of social experience than sociology, its theoretical corpus also terminated at a low point. Sociology, often showing willingness to engage in participant observation at microlevels (following anthropology's lead, in other words), has always been interested in the theoretical relevance of such studies for higher levels of societal generalization. Anthropology, however, simply lacks a block of *indigenous* theory dealing with the most general issues of macrosocial functioning. It must borrow such theoretical propositions or concerns from sociology, economics, political science, social psychology and related subfields, and this borrowing habit creates a series of "institutional anthropologies" [see chapter 12].

Early Research on Civilization Configurations

I deal with A. L. Kroeber's work on this topic in a separate essay (chapter 10), so I can be brief. In the literature on the micro-macro issues I surveyed for this paper, I found few references to the fact that Kroeber had spent the final decade or so of his career trying to deal with the largest possible social systems: entire civilizations and institutional parts of these civilizations. The reason for the neglect was not due only to a lack of interest in Kroeber's work, but also that he was not really concerned with the problem of how large-scale civilizational systems affected local or small-scale phenomena.

More significant in the latter context was the Redfield-Singer "little tradition – big tradition" approach (Redfield 1955; Singer 1958). This was an attempt, basically, to bring anthropological ideas to bear on the problem of articulation of major universal religions or belief systems like Islam, with local social systems and the way of life of communities. The effort was mainly empirical—a series of research papers and monographs ensued, but it did not establish general theory or a permanent subfield in anthropology. We shall discuss some of its technical aspects later. Classic-era anthropologists perceived the work as "history," not anthropology, since it appeared in the heyday of the Classic-theory efflorescence on tribal culture and social organization. Another problem with the material produced was its abstruse subject matter. Certainly the basic problem of big-little tradition was relevant to economic and social development processes which had become a major concern of public policy and international social life at the time. However, Redfield, Singer, and others participating in the approach were concerned with scholarly matters like the meaning of religion in peasant societies, the symbols and values of Oriental religions, and the like. I have always felt that the good work of this University of Chicago group—if it had been the source of a continuing disciplinary effort—would have permitted anthropology to make a major contribution to world history and also to help modernize and broaden the discipline's subject matter.

Micro-Macro As Descriptive Typology: Folk and Urban

Now to return to the problem of how to describe the differences between the small, interactive-network communities and large, pluralistic—usually national—societies. As already noted, this effort was influenced by the dichotomous typology that developed in German social scholarship influenced by the romantic tradition. Ferdinand Tönnies's *Gemeinschaft* was the type of the folk community and its presumably socially, emotionally satisfying total environment; *Gesellschaft* was the open, accessible, impersonal system of large communities (Tönnies 1940). Sir Henry Maine's sequence from status to contract was another version (1861); Durkheim's mechanical-organic still another (Simpson 1933); and a general synthesis was attempted by Howard Becker, who used *sacred* and *secular* to denote the grand types (1950). Robert Redfield's *folk-urban* dichotomy (1947) was the only full-fledged anthropological version of the tradition. It was closely related to the German sources, via the sociologist Robert Park. All of these dichotomies produced valuable descriptive distinctions, but were of little use in analyzing empirical social situations. The typologies were largely devoid of a concept of system or process: societies were viewed as collections of traits and tendencies, not a matter of the continuous adaptive struggles that characterize all human communities, large and small. Thus, social process and locus were not important in this tradition.

At a more empirical level, anthropologists always distinguished between bands and villages, towns and cities; this was seen as part of the historical transition from nomadic food-collecting to settled agricultural societies, with the concomitant increase in population. V. Gordon

Childe's various "revolutions" (food-producing; urban; industrial) represented one of the most popular versions (1942). Empirically based, Childe's temporal typological constructs had a background in European scholarship, and of course in the nineteenth-century Danish and continental archaeological tradition. One of the most useful systematizations of the village-cosmopolitan transition was contributed by Alfred Weber (Eckert 1970), whose distinction between *culture* and *civilization* was sometimes used by Redfield in his class lectures to clarify what he meant by "culture." In this conception, culture is a quality which can vary quantitatively; that is, some societies have more culture than others. Thus "culture" is represented with a *Gemeinschaftliche* intimacy and interactiveness. Civilization, on the other hand, is represented by literacy, institutions, and contractual relations. Redfield's version was ultimately expressed in the "little tradition–big tradition" concepts mentioned previously; this preserved the Weberian notion of culture, but it anthropologized civilization by acknowledging that these entities, and especially the ancient Oriental versions, also had culture (e.g., universalistic religions like Hinduism). Perhaps the key underlying concept is *consensus*. Societies with culture have a high quotient of agreement as to what constitutes the traditions and lifeways—even granting the existence of variant patterns. The agreement is manifested by universal religious beliefs; formal institutions, patriotism, and so forth. Their fabric, however, is characterized by a variety of often incompatible subcultures based on social stratification and other structural differentiations.

Running through these typological theories was an unstated *preference* for the folk way of life as a more humane, satisfying form of human existence. Alienation and despair were inevitable in the urban and industrial macrosocial systems, and problems of deviance and inequality become acute. Such ideas were congenial to anthropologists who were eager to uphold the folk way of life since it was their trade specialization. However, in the late 1940s and 1950s a tougher breed of ethnologists pointed out that tribal and peasant societies actually were rife with hostility, gossip, and the suppression of individual tendencies. The controversy over Pueblo culture, started by Benedict's benign characterization of the culture in her *Patterns of Culture* (1934), marks the beginnings of this awareness in the 1940s (chapter 8).

Thus, an intellectual paradox appeared: while the typologies had broad historical and descriptive validity, the closer one got to the real life of folk societies, the less "folk" they seemed to be. Or put analytically, the typologies were of little use for handling human behavior in concrete social settings. If betrayal, hostility, deviance, alienation, impersonality, and the like were typological qualities of the *Gesellschaft*, then what were they doing in folk societies?

Further ambiguity in the typologies concerned population and territorial size. Were the "micro" types concerned with small populations and territories and the "macro" with the large? And if macro concepts meant institutions and organizations without definite geographical or territorial boundaries, then was the distinction really a matter of the local community versus the diffuse external system? Implicit in the Redfield-Singer distinction between big and little traditions was the notion that the local communities replicated the big traditions, making them true *microcosms* of the civilizational society or macrocosm. This meant that it was necessary to distinguish between culture and society (Miner 1955). The typological folk society may differ profoundly from the social system of the urban, but the folk might well assimilate the cultural lifeways of the urban, while preserving or generating its own unique, naive cultural patterns. In anthropology the dominant issue was the status of the *tribe* as a basic unit of demographic, economic, political, and cultural analysis. Doubts about the validity of the tribal unit began surfacing in the 1940s, and flowered in the 1950s, exemplified by Edmund Leach's examination of Burmese hill tribes as political fictions (1954). The issue did not become a source of theoretical reformulation until Fredrik Barth's book on ethnic boundaries and cultures appeared at the end of the 1960s (Barth 1969). For generations the folk world was believed to be divided into distinct tribal entities with their own language, cultures, politics, and so on. This partly fictional paradigm was probably supported mainly by the work of the Americans who found this kind of multidimensional correlation reasonably accurate in many regions of the New World. But in other parts of the world, especially Africa, tribes were ambiguous due to indigenous military conquest and the existence of quasi-feudal political systems. The collapse of the colonial empires in the 1940s revealed these tendencies. Many "tribes" began to cultivate their identity as a rationale for asserting their control over weaker and less aggressive neighbors. A tribe, in other words, had to be viewed less as a linguistic or cultural entity and more as a self-conscious political faction or gang.

As this new status emerged, tribes also entered the historical present, often in the guise of "peasants." It is likely that the persistence of typologies in anthropology was in part due to the fact that anthropologists studied people without histories—written or articulate histories, that is (see Wolf 1982). Lacking a sense of historical unfolding of institutions and customs, one can only formulate types of cultures, kinship systems, artifact styles, etiquette, and brands of magic and ritual. Peasants lack history; hence a concern for the type, "peasant" as contrasted to "farmer;" American Indians lacked history, hence a concern for the "tribe" as a type, or the tribal cultures as unique. The case of the Amerinds is especially significant. Anthropologists were aware for years that these people were in fact accumulating a history, as the reservations evolved and the relationships with governments and citizen reform organizations developed. But this history was written on the whole by non-anthropologists. (Noteworthy exceptions are Joseph Jorgenson's 1978 monograph on Amerinds as part of the political and economic institutional structure of American society; and Brian Fagan's (1984) history of Old World–New World interaction.) In any case, tribes are becoming "historical" all over the world and anthropologists are responding to the challenge.

Along with nationalization came urbanization. This process also presented a severe challenge to anthropologists because they had no theory of urbanization other than the archaeological (e.g., R. Mc. Adams 1966). Even more disturbing was the fact that the cities of the Third World began filling up with "folk" people; that is, detribalized persons and peasants (Roberts 1978). Once again the social phenomena began outstripping the typologies. Peasants had their problems in cities, but they also on occasion showed remarkable adaptability, forging far-flung networks of mutual support between village and city, and establishing poverty as a way of life (Whitten 1969). Peasant status, for a decade the subject of typological debate (e.g., Redfield 1956) gradually evolved into studies of adaptive processes (e.g., Halperin and Dow 1977).

Talcott Parsons in his *The Social System* (1951), shifted the basis of classification from types of whole societies, cultures, or communities to social interaction processes, using the structure-function dichotomy as the key to the analysis of process. The structural component referred to frameworks of social relationships that persisted because they performed important functions in everyday life and in the congeries of tasks and goals called institutions. The dominant emphasis in the scheme was analytical description, and application of the concepts to real cases produced portrayals of equilibrium-seeking social systems. The incapacity of the scheme to deal with change formed the basis of the extensive critiques of Parsons appearing in the 1950s and 1960s.

The most enduring aspect of his scheme, however, were the "pattern variables." These conceptual pairs, designating characteristics of social action in any and all societies, have proven continuously useful as tools of descriptive analysis. And it is these variables which came to serve as a replacement for the folk-urban categories. The original versions appear in *The Social System* (Parsons 1951:67, emphasis added):

1. The Gratification-Discipline Dilemma
   Affectivity versus Affective Neutrality
2. The Private versus Collective Interest Dilemma
   Self-Orientation versus Collectivity-Orientation
3. The Choice between Types of Value-Orientation Standard
   Universalism versus Particularism
4. The Choice Between "Modalities" of the Social Object
   Achievement versus Ascription
5. The Definition of the Scope of Interest in the Object
   Specificity versus Diffuseness

Parsons saw these five pattern variables as more than mere tags for dominant "dilemmas," "choices," or "definitions" of social action. He recognized that they could become cultural descriptions insofar as there existed an "element of consistency of pattern which must run throughout a system of value-orientations in a cultural tradition" (ibid.: 67). And it was this potential for cultural description and analysis that attracted Clyde Kluckhohn to the scheme (Kluckhohn 1951). In later pages (Parsons 1951: 102–5) Parsons showed how the pattern variables combine and crosscut each other to form major vectors of social behavior and values (see table 4.1): Universalism-Particularism are combined with Achievement-Ascription to create a fourfold table defining "major value-orientations" for a specimen social system of culture. The illustration is useful because the two pattern variable sets represent ideas important in both sociology and anthropology. "Achievement" and "ascription" appear in Ralph Linton's *Study of Man* (1936); the universalism-particularism set owes much to the contract versus status dichotomy that goes back to Sir Henry Maine. Some of Redfield's folk-urban criteria parallel many of the pattern variables. Max Weber dealt with most of the variables in his many works on historical sociology, and one of his conceptual pairs—traditional versus rational-legal—constitutes a sixth pattern variable set if one wishes to add it to Parsons's list (see Bendix 1960, chapter 12)

Anthropologists familiar with the Redfieldian version of *Gemeinschaft-Gesellschaft* typology could identify the universalistic and achievement variables with the "urban" pole; and the particularistic-ascription with the "folk." However, such premature segregations gave way immediately to the recognition that all societies have all four pattern variables, with variable tendencies or emphases in one direction or another. Thus, the institutions associated with large, pluralistic societies will have characteristic forms of universalism (for example), which would not be present in smaller, more uniform social systems. Universalism becomes necessary when the population is large, with diverse subcultures and obedience. Unless people are treated alike—

TABLE 4.1
Types of Combination of Value-Orientation Components to Create Major Social Value Orientations

	Universalism	**Particularism**
	A.	**B.**
Achievement	Expectation of active achievements in accord with universalized standards and generalized rules relative to other actors.	Expectation of active achievements relative to and/or on behalf of the particular relational context in which the actor is involved.
	C.	**D.**
Ascription	Expectation of orienation of action to a universalistic norm defined either as an ideal state or as embodied in the status-structure of the existing society	Expectation of orientation of action to an ascribed status within a given relational context.

Based on Parsons (1951: 102).

given similar opportunities—inequality can lead to anomie and social revolt. Obviously the political orientation is an important mediating variable: democratic institutions or ideology create a stronger mandate for universalistic prescriptions. Still, beyond and beneath the level of public institutions, particularism flourishes in the complex societies wherever local social systems with relatively small populations must allocate resources in accordance with traditional status and social rewards (e.g., Bennett 1982, matrix table, p.209).

The Parsonsian pattern variables became a permanent part of social science. Their utility for descriptive analysis has been demonstrated and they have entered into the frames of reference of most sociocultural anthropologists. Only economics, which possesses its own scheme-of-action pattern analysis based on the theory of utility-maximization and rational choice, has not really effectively incorporated them.

In general, as societies develop into large systems, their members must learn to deal with bureaucracies and their universalistic regulations. Affectively neutral attitudes may characterize the association of strangers. Interplay develops between self-oriented desires and collective needs for order. There appears a greater need to achieve one's position in life rather than to rely on birth status. And highly specific definitions of the situation, especially in occupations requiring efficient performance in impersonal organizations, become typical. These tendencies are those associated with what is called "modernization," which is largely a matter of the spread of the patterns of the Euro-North American urban-industrial social systems across the world. It can be assumed that rudimentary forms of these patterns were present as well in ancient urban civilizations. Abstract types are only a first approximation of difference and similarity; they must eventually give way to historical concreteness.

Micro-Macro as Local-External Relations

Thus, the major contemporary world social issues concern change-processes. These contain issues of ideology and nostalgia. They concern human rights, the rewards to be found in cultural diversity versus global cultural uniformity in the urban-industrial order, and of the loss of community freedom in the process of political centralization. How can local peoples preserve the freedom to make their own decisions, and at the same time how can communities provide reasonable freedom for their own members, in a world of increasing pressure to produce at higher levels of efficiency and output?

The first necessity in pursuing the problem of influence and change is to specify particular loci of the community. The relationships between small-scale–large-scale phenomena, and local and external, in North America will be different than those in India—even though historically, India may be moving in a generalized European-North American institutional direction as her national government consolidates its control over localities. Concreteness is thus the order of the day. An ethnology of the change process must locate its units of observation and analysis in real times, places, and institutions. Attention is paid both to social structure and to cultural traditions and styles, because these often vary independently in change processes.

The second requirement of an inquiry into micro-macro, local-external change relationships is to specify the nature of geographical and social space. For example, in a typical North American rural context, the local community may be seen to exist within the following "spheres":

1. The *migration sphere*, or the geographical spread of persons who formerly lived in the community. This will produce dispersal of kin, friendship, vacations, occupation, subscriptions to media, or travel. Indices of cosmopolitanism may be constructed from these descriptive data.
2. The *resource allocation sphere*, or the loci of the power to assign rights to key resources to community members, including bureaus that control government land, credit, water rights, or taxation. The larger the community, the more responsible resource agencies located in the community; the more remote the community, the fewer and farther these may be.
3. The *marketing sphere*. If the community is agrarian, its products may be distributed world wide. The income of the community is derived from the entire geographical area in which its products are distributed. This can include local garden products, manufactured items serving the locality or nation, or cash crops sent overseas. Both local or external agencies may perform the distribution functions.
4. the *local shopping sphere*. Commodities for production and consumer goods may be acquired locally or at a distance, depending on transportation facilities and cost. The automobile has, of course, widened this sphere greatly, but changing costs of operation and the condition of the local and national economy will tend to make the sphere contract and expand.
5. The *kinship and friendship sphere*. Aside from migration of community

members, people will move within the region for marriage, visiting relatives, helping with chores, and so on.

These five spheres are by no means the only ways to map the geographical and social space, but they are among the most important ones—for example—for a North American agricultural community. Each sphere will produce a map of movement, social connections, and need-satisfaction. The boundaries of the community will thus be flexible, depending on the particular function observed and the time of the observation. The mapping of spheres is not merely a matter of analyzing the external relationships, but also serves to demarcate the internal territorial and time-distance relationships; for instance, resource allocation may be a matter of ties to the capitals of the state-provincial or federal governments, while marital ties may serve to designate mainly internal spatial networks. The methods followed in this type of analysis are, of course, the familiar ones developed by cultural and economic geographers, although anthropologists are likely to introduce special techniques reflecting their disciplinary interests. For example, mapping of kinship connections within the region may be done so as to show any tendencies toward preferential mating or biases in the line of descent (see Smith 1976 for an anthropological introduction to location analysis; and Whitten and Wolfe 1973 for a discussion of network analysis).

The selection of the "spheres" concept to delineate key micro-macro issues of the North American rural community is influenced by the distinctive settlement pattern of this part of the world—the so-called open-country neighborhood system in which agricultural producers live apart, on their own acres. Their services are provided by specialized village and town centers, whose populations are, in the main, composed of tradesmen and specialists (and recently, substantial numbers of retired country people). If we turn to the European scene, the foci of analysis are likely to differ. Ronald Frankenberg's studies of British rural communities of varying sizes is an example (1966). Here the village or town is the unit of settlement; farmers live in the settlements and move out to their fields, or the individual farmsteads are clustered into somewhat spread-out communities. In this situation, the interest shifts from geographical spheres of interaction to social role relationships. Frankenberg carried out part of his analysis in typological terms, but with an awareness of process. In fact, his approach was a synthesis of the Redfieldian folk-urban model with a conception of role relationships: in rural society, the *number* of roles, when compared with urban society, tends to be *small*. But the *patterning* of these roles is *complex*:

> Rural social life is built up out of a relatively small number of role relationships—which are arranged with great fluidity into varied patterns. Urban life makes up for the loss of these by a large number of role relationships and their formalization. (Frankenberg 1966: 283)

Similarly, the "social fields" in rural society tend to be composed of a small number of persons, while in urban society the "number of people met by an individual . . . may be large" (Frankenberg 1966: 287). While these generalizations do not escape the artificiality of polar types, they do include social interaction, and hence have greater utility in analyzing influence and change.

But village, community, or kin group are by no means the only frames of human existence. There are also the large nation-tribe, as found in southwest Asia and parts of Africa; or the regional cooperative resource networks, uniting many villages in water schemes, as in southeast Asia; or the sectarian agricultural communes in North America and Europe. These and other settlement types and institutional forms will have their own distinctive relationships with the nation-state government and its demands for support. Nowhere is the relationship an easy one, and it cannot be expected to improve in Third World settings where tribes or communities remain more persuasive frames of identity than shifting national governments. The transition from medieval to modern Europe involved the conquest of the feudal nobility by the state; the conquest of much of Africa and Asia involves the conquest of tribal and village solidarity and autonomy by the militarized post-colonial state. Farmer and ethnic revolts increasingly simmer in the background.

Viewing human aggregates in the context of centralized state government, then, requires a very different approach from the Classic era ethnological study of the single demographic and/or settlement unit, bounded by the tribal hunting grounds, or the village and its fields. Some recognition of the flexibility of boundaries was always available, because even the most isolated societies had a nested set of territories for different functions—some of them shared with other demographic, community, and social units. The research focus, however, was usually on the physical fact of a breeding population inhabiting a particular settlement space. This focus tended to exclude the wider ties and functions. The band or village was the main unit of analysis, its "culture" the prime target of research.

For example, Julian Steward (1956) did not succeed in rendering the complexity of modern Puerto Rican society in his study of a series of separate village communities, each with a different economic pursuit. The fact that the separate communities were really parts of a larger whole—the functionally interdependent political economy of the island-nation—somehow escaped the Steward research program and vitiated many of its conclusions. There was no theory of larger systems. More generally, Steward's approach to cultural ecology lacked a clear conception of system, hence no way of determining the roles of particular parts of that system. His approach was traditional: to find the causes—especially ecological—of particular social forms, not to portray the dynamic adaptive reality of a social system.

The dynamism of these interactive systems also means that the anthropologist must find a basis for generalization other than the goal of presenting a static, one-time portrait of an operating culture. These traditional objectives of Classic anthropology were suited to isolated communities that changed slowly. In the modern world of national governments and market systems, the chief components are in constant motion. Hence one cannot produce a forever-portrait of a modern community; it becomes a study of one community at one particular moment. There will need to be reasons for studying the society at a particular point in time, and these "reasons" define the problems to be solved.

The second main requirement in studying the micro-macro relational nexus is to ascertain the major quantitative and qualitative dimensions of exchange. That is, what is the net outflow and inflow of goods, services, people, energy, products? Who has the power to change and direct these flows? I am not necessarily speaking here of some abstruse quantitative energy-calculus—the data can be collected with any degree of detail the researcher selects, depending on the demands exercised by the problem. To deal with exchanges it is usually necessary to be concerned with models of behavior that derive from disciplines other than anthropology, in particular, economics, and some branches of social psychology. These models make certain assumptions for the purposes of analysis that have been a source of disagreement among anthropologists, since they tend to assume an element of rational choice and preference: people *are* motivated, at least in part, by the need to increase gain or profit, whether this is expressed in monetary or in qualitative terms, like status. To achieve such ends, people must make trade-offs between quantities of desired goods. If one wishes a lot of love, one may have to take less of material achievement. In a folk world, goods, commodities, and relationships might have been finite (a "zero-sum game"), and the means for providing them limited (Foster 1965), but in the expanding world of the nation, there are no such constants. The promises of the state to its citizens, however, tend to be larger than the market will bear; thus poverty emerges, and people who existed with few possessions or power will now desire more of both. The external exchanges thus generate new internal exchanges, and the relationships among community members are irrevocably changed, because needs, values, and ideologies are altered.

These processes are all accompanied by values. In the 1970s and 1980s, as anthropologists participated in research on aspiration, poverty, development, and the power interplays of communities and external organizations, they inevitably assimilated value orientations from political commentary. During the early 1970s, for example, the writings of Andre Gunder Frank (1969) were particularly influential. In such interpretations, the relationship between micro and macro is defined as one of exploitation, or as a prolongation of imperialist domination into the post-colonial world of new nations. While analytical neutrality continues to have its virtues, the possibilities of combining or alternating ideological frames with dispassionate ones are considerable; the individual worker must make his own synthesis.

A third requirement for the anthropological study of the interplay and change arising from micro-macro relationships concerns the need for an adaptational frame of reference. This refers to the ways the local populations have found to manipulate the external forces and agencies—and, of course, vice versa. Although the external bureaucratic systems usually have more power to enforce their demands (whether in the benevolent interests of the communities, or against them), the local people are never devoid of capacity to modify the demands or blunt the forces of compulsion. A case of significant proportions has occurred repeatedly in African and Latin American countries in the 1970s and 1980s as the new national governments sought to keep food prices low so that the urban masses could buy it, and thus avoid food riots. The farmers, however, ignored government pleas and modest incentives to increase production for markets because they considered that prices were too low. Instead, the farmers reduced crop and livestock offtake, focussing their efforts on production for their own use, and for local and regional markets. What can governments do—shoot the farmers, tax them, construct government farms and ranches? All methods have been tried, but none work very well, or for long, and the situation is an example of the importance of economic markets in development and, simultaneously, of the considerable power residing in the hands of the *campesiños* who alone have the capacity to produce food (Wolf 1969).

Similarly, the vulnerability of the industrial nations to energy sources, like oil, has also revealed the existence of impressive sources of power in the raw-materials-producing nations even granted the fact that the industrial nations may continue to operate as "imperialist" extractors of natural substances for the benefit of their own populations and profiteers. Clearly, the world is moving toward a complex system of interdependency which will make simplistic ideological perspectives useless for analytical purposes. Anthropologists must be sensitive to these growing complexities of the adaptive world system. A field of defensive strategy analysis is emerging in development anthropology as a result, and "cultural survival" movements are flourishing.

Of equal, and perhaps even greater importance, is the growing disparity in wealth and power in the developing countries. It is now clear that economic development—which in almost all cases has meant an accommodation of the new national economies to the world market system—increases disparities in income. This is linked to a sharpening of individual differences in talent and capital (social and financial), and increasing social differentiation based on the ability to seize opportunity. Mexican *ejidos* have tended to fall under the control of the most energetic and capable members; coffee-producing farmers in East Africa have tended to exclude their land-poor neighbors and even kinfolks from membership in the profitable cooperatives; rural families with members living and working in cities can set up networks of influence and exchange which give them an advantage over families without such connections; migratory pastoralists who make the transition to a form of ranching, and buy trucks, make deals with peasant farmers for forage, and so expel their smaller-herd-owning relatives and tribal members off the range. The examples are legion. The failure of development initiatives to distribute economic benefits evenly is one of the great failures of the "development decades" since World War II. In general, the more interactive the relationships between the local social units and the national institutions, the greater the tendency toward increasing inequality of goods and opportunity. Accordingly, some societies change rapidly, keeping their traditions; others do not change at all, and their traditions wither under the influence of the New Poverty. "Culture patterns" give way to ethnic identity-seeking, localism to nationalism. The analysis of such processes is becoming the anthropology of the future.

The Nature of Micro-Macro Suprasystems

And so we approach the third problem—the nature of the very large systems of interdependency and feedback that are coming to characterize the world society. The current literature contains a number of attempts to model world systems, some of them containing definite ideological orientations, and therefore actually critical documents (e.g., Wallerstein 1974 on "capitalism"). The technical understanding of the emerging suprasystems is one thing; the direction the process of emergence *should* take is quite another.

A major theoretical issue concerns the applicability of systems theory to social phenomena. A radical negative position would hold that societies are historically evolving and living organisms with sentient properties, and thus systems theory, which was devised originally for analyzing the properties of mechanical and physical power phenomena, cannot handle the dynamic qualities of the social process. A compromise position acknowledges the unique properties of social phenomena, but recognizes that systems theory and concepts may be useful n particular cases for understanding the nature of change and interdependency. "Social systems" became an acceptable buzzword. The best appraisal of the issue in the 1960–1980s was Walter Buckley's 1967 book on the applicability of theoretical systems analysis to sociological analysis. "Adaptive system" is the term he used to refer in general to social systems, implying by this a process of communication and adjustment that constantly modifies the relationships among the various components, while at the same time preserving certain process mechanics. This accords well with traditional anthropological ideas of the resistance of microcultural and social phenomena to transformations of macrostructure—a situation commonly encountered in the change processes associated with economic and social development in the Third World, as well as in such distinctive microsocial cases as the Hutterian Brethren of North America.

To theorize about large systems in terms of their abstract properties is one of two ways to conceive of the social magnitudes and processes involved. The second is to view suprasystems as Immanuel Wallerstein does, as concrete historical entities, held together by ideologies, economics, and politico-military force, as conditioned by population magnitudes. Size of systems in this second perspective is then measured not so much by social space or complexity, but by geographical space and the exercise of economic and political power, sorted out by advantage and opportunity into "cores" and "peripheries." The essential criterion of a suprasystem, then, would be certain broad patterns of conforming behavior over large geographical areas, this conformity conferring some sort of advantage on certain groups in large, well-endowed populations. One gets very close to Marxian concepts here. In a sense, Fernand Braudel (1981), Wallerstein, and some others in this school were modernizing and certainly broadening Marx. Above all, they opened up the doctrine to accept sources of dominance, or dominant thematic content other than "capitalism" or economic phenomena exclusively. For Wallerstein, however, economics did play a crucial role, and it is fair to say that economic institutions may constitute the most effective means of forging what he called a "world system."

The unity of the two approaches—the analytic-abstract (AA) and the historical-concrete (HC) approaches to suprasystem theory—can be seen when a particular problem is researched. The current best example of a world suprasystem is the international market economy, also called the "capitalist system." This market system—again setting aside the ideological strictures from the left for purposes of discussion—can function without necessarily resorting to major politico-military measures to force nations and societies to surrender their political autonomy. "Co-optation" is used in place of or in preference to force. That is, the term "empire," in its old sense of an existing monopoly of force over a large geographical territory including many sociopolitical entities, has not been essential to the existence of the market system. In fact, the present world has more politically independent entities than ever before. The market system seems to have acted as one of the liberating forces, helping to dissolve the old colonial empires.

One can resort to AA principles to help explain this HC situation. Systems theory crossed with adaptational theory holds that systems are built up of component subsystems that interact with each other on the basis of mutual advantage. Such advantage, of course, is a dynamic process and the balance constantly shifts. When it turns against the advantage of one of the component subsystems, adaptive manipulation or countervailing force is exerted. For example, by borrowing *very* large sums of capital from government and private sources in the First World, Third World countries do not merely accumulate debts, they come to own the banks, so to speak. Foreclosure is impossible, because it would be equivalent to bankrupting the lending sources. At the sociopolitical level, one perceives constant shifting of alliances in order to exert leverage. The contemporary Middle East is an excellent example. By such combinations, countervailing power is exerted in order to permit the suprasystem processes to function. In terms of this essay, the microsocial entities combine, separate, and combine again in order to defend their interests and perpetuate or redress the shifting balance of advantage. The "independence" of nations is thus relative to their power positions.

The sociological tradition was focussed largely on the question of social class. Tribes, cultures, and communities were seen as secondary in importance. The social class, defined as a group of people with similar opportunities or deprivations, was considered to be the basic social unit of analysis for large systems. *This distinction between autonomous, culturally or geographically based social units on the one hand, and politico-economic advantage-deprivation groups on the other, constitutes the basic cleavage between the traditional ethnological and the traditional sociological-political approach in the social sciences.* The resolutions of the theoretical and methodological problems arising from this distinction were impossible so long as the issue was conceived as purely theoretical. History was the only final court of appeal. Considering the problem from the HC "world systems" approach—the course of recent history up to the 1990s, was characterized by the progressive emergence in all countries of class phenomena as increasingly assertive over against culture, ethnicity, and geography [in the 1990s, culture appears to be gaining as the crucial factor]. At any rate, class or culture aside, increasing numbers of people in all countries seek advantage on the basis of their relationship to the political economy. Some peasants in Latin America and Africa move rapidly into cash-crop production; they are willing to surrender their isolation and some of their cultural distinction in order to achieve a favorable place in the market system. On the North American continent, the best example is Quebec. This is the "world system" in operation.

However, suprasystems theory can be neglectful of the physical aspects of world processes. Population, food production and consumption, land degradation, environmental poisons, and the like have their own rhythms, and these appear to be increasing, often at an exponential rate. While the world suprasystem tends to fluctuate on the basis of adaptive power principles, the ecosystem appears to be running down. Malthusian processes operate in complex ways—not necessarily on the basis of some simple ratio of population magnitudes to available resources, but as an equation with flexible terms. It is *population size* plus *effective demand* plus the *scientific capacity to enhance*, as well as exploit, *resources*.

More useful, though less intellectually intriguing, is the synthesis of both sociological and ecological data for significant subsistence economies associated with particular world regions and biomes. I have suggested the term *socionatural systems* for these entities (Bennett 1981, 1993–96). A study by an anthropologist makes an interesting empirical attempt to analyze one, the Mormon frontier in Arizona (Abruzzi 1981). A socionatural system brings together the relevant physical resources, social resources, technology, and human needs and wants into a system of production. These systems are defined not by some environmental value, but by human purposes. This may be a fatal flaw. However, if the concept of sustained resource yield can be introduced as a check against resource abuse, this defect can be handled. The difficulty is that all such control systems are referred ultimately to human demands that are virtually unchallengeable in most political systems, democratic or authoritarian.

Put another way, the world ecosystem (including humans of course) cannot seem to be brought under control because the micro-units or subsystems seek to maximize gain and gratification, and as the world fills up, this can be done only at the expense of other subsystems. Frequently, however, means are found through science and technology to modify impacts or make a given quantity of resources yield at a higher rate or level. This fluctuation in the Malthusian equation, while productive of human need-want gratification, also makes planning and control of resource use-abuse extremely difficult. Thus, controls are decisively exerted over the process only when crises of one kind or another emerge, and present human needs are jeopardized. Meanwhile, the thinking public tends to be whipsawed between prophets of Malthusian doom like Paul Ehrlich (Ehrlich and Ehrlich 1974), and prophets of cornucopian optimism like Julian Simon (1981).

Suprasystems are not confined to world systems. Reverting to AA-type theory, there are no absolute magnitudes for defining a system as big or little. This is a relative matter, depending on the data and the problem. It is here where anthropological issues become critical. The criticisms of ethnological work appearing during the ideological battles of the 1960s and early 1970s was mainly concerned with the traditional acceptance of the colonial framework of tribal life, and its almost total neglect in the ethnological reconstruction of tribal culture. That is, the "micro" entity, a tribal community, was presented devoid of its systematic interconnections with larger politico-economic systems control. This battle has largely been won by the critics, but their victory was not so much an ideological conquest as the result of inevitable historical changes. The liquidation of colonial empires after World War II virtually abolished the isolated tribal society and ethnologists really had no alternative but to broaden their scholarly horizons.

Anthropological cultural ecology may be used again as an illustration. In place of the classic monographs concerning single tribal or peasant communities, cultural ecologists are beginning to produce studies of traditionally based economic systems covering larger geographical areas, as these systems are being modified by increasing involvement of the economic and sociopolitical development nexus in market economies. If the single-community frame of reference is preserved, the locality is carefully selected as a type case of some larger systemic process. Robert Netting's (1981) book on a Swiss agricultural community is an interesting hybrid of the old and new. While a single community study, the presentation includes hard data on population and economic trends derived from large-system economic and historical documentation, so that the published monograph contains implications beyond the immediate confines of the village. That is, it is a study of how a central European society survives in an interconnected world.

When anthropologists use world-systems concepts in their research, the frame of reference changes radically from the community-centered approach. One starts with a large entity, defines it cross-culturally, then examines a particular local case to see how participation in the system has modified, benefited, or disadvantaged the local society. A case in point is the international cooperative movement. This "movement" is an organizational template originating in the Rochdale experiment in England in the late-nineteenth century (Worsley 1971). That is, while indigenous cooperation is as old as *Homo sapiens*, the modern institutionalized cooperative, found in all countries and introduced by European colonial regimes as well as the development agencies in the recent period, is a planned system of management and production that requires adaptation to local conditions (Bennett 1983).

The institutional cooperative contains a general ideology of mutual advantage derived from sharing scarce goods, thereby making them more readily available, or more equitably distributed. This ideology is, of course, usually modified in execution, and the cooperative organization can be adapted to agricultural societies with marked inequality of ownership of productive resources. Thus, the co-op does not necessarily solve structural problems. Indeed, like other development interventions, it may worsen them. For those groups who can benefit from cooperative organization, however, it produces distinct gains. Cooperative organization also contains strong universalistic, rational-legal, and functionally specific elements, requiring accurate record-keeping, appropriate distribution of surpluses, equitable distribution of necessary factors of production, and intelligent dealings with outside agents of the market system. On the other hand, because the cooperative is also a local organization, it also can serve to protect indigenous cultural patterns and values against invasion by alien perspectives and practices. Such processes constitute the focus of the growing anthropological interest in co-ops and "commons"-type resource management in developing countries (McCay and Acheson 1987). It constitutes a good example of the use of world-system constructs to guide anthropological research on micro-macro issues.

The Adaptational Nexus

An underlying question in this essay has been the value of the contribution anthropologists might make to the micro-macro problem, given the fact that much of the relevant theory has already been furnished by the institutional social sciences. Must anthropology simply borrow this theory? And if it does, can anthropology retain its professional distinctiveness? The question is meaningless on scientific grounds. If anthropology has nothing to offer beyond available sociological, political science or economic concepts, then so be it. Social theory, however, is not finite. It is an intellectual exercise that can be informed by many different insights and views of reality. Thus, anthropology's traditional focus on intimate social situations, and its emphasis on the mental life of people in communities, may provide valuable perspectives and concepts.

The most important of these insights concerns the adaptational nexus—how local people cope with external influences, and how they may strive to modify these forces in Third World countries. The rate of failure of development projects is substantial, and most of these failures can be attributed to the failure of planners and technical aid specialists to understand the full context of local responses to intervention. Economic thinking is based on assumptions of cross-cultural universality of certain reactions, like the desire for more return on one's labor. The possibility that this is not always appreciated or envisaged, or that local social arrangements might be jeopardized by its achievement, has been seriously neglected. Although the point is often understood by the development planners, they must officially ignore it because the plan, or the country's objectives, take precedence. Anthropologists have participated in research on the need for more local participation and autonomy in development planning (e.g., Ralston et al. 1981—a study commissioned by USAID).

Individual motives, or the motives of people in social systems, rarely conform to simple paradigms of social behavior. The tendency to assume they do is a proclivity of technical experts in urban-based institutions without first-hand knowledge of local communities and their cultures. Contributions to this problem have been made by development anthropologists, and these constitute one of the genuine achievements of applied anthropology—a contribution not fully appreciated by the academic fraternity [for further discussion, see chapter 12]. More often than not, however, these contributions have issued from critiques of the development process, rather than as products of participation by anthropologists in the projects. It has been difficult to incorporate anthropological work in development, largely for practical reasons. The amount of time required to perform an adequate anthropological study of local sociocultural conditions affecting project acceptance is often longer than the organizational time-frame of the project itself.

In addition to the study of sociocultural factors influencing project acceptance there is need for anthropological work on the problem of effective size or magnitude of productive processes. Attempts to merge local production systems in larger market-based entities, based on Euro-American models, have also not met with outstanding success, and development specialists have shown considerable interest in alternative arrangements that preserve the smaller, indigenous technology systems. These systems have proven to be remarkably efficient users of available physical and social resources, even though their productive magnitudes are not always in conformity with externally-set standards and goals. Anthropologists have done research on the technical dimensions of these local systems. "Cultural ecology" is giving way to more sophisticated studies of energy utilization and productive efficiency under substantively rational conditions.

Aside from these practical dimensions, the anthropological inquiry into micro-macro relationships has a scholarly importance. Rural sociology, which grew up under the aegis of the North American and European agricultural establishment, has never fully understood the need for an examination of the rich social matrix of local-external relationships in the developed societies, let alone the emerging national societies of the Third World. A new "rural anthropology" is needed and both sociologists and anthropologists can supply this need. There are some models. Bruno Benvenuti's (1962) study of rural life in the Netherlands is an outstanding exception to the rather perfunctory research carried on by most rural sociologists. Benvenuti's approach shows a profound appreciation of the cultural aspects of rural-urban interaction, and the influence of the market system. In broader perspective, S. H. Franklin's (1969) studies of European "peasantry" in transition to a new pan-European market agriculture illustrated the profitable results that can be obtained when one views the agriculturalist of a continent as intelligent beings who cope with changing macrosocial forces and are willing to make trade-offs with their own institutions in the process.

To an extent greater than any other modern anthropologist, Eric Wolf has explored the relevance of historical approaches. History was always an important mode of endeavor in cultural anthropology although the excessive empiricism of the "historical approach" of the Boasians, and the universalist generalizing of the Kroeberian school [chapter 10] prevented work on true history. The growing attention given historical writings by anthropologists is a good sign. In essence, this means the attempt to identify social and cultural forms in societies with recorded history and in societies "without history" (Wolf 1982). The influence of Fernand Braudel's work (1981) is crucial, because he offers a method of writing history at the level of cultural patterns, institutions, and everyday structures of life. Above all, it is in the anthropological analysis of recorded historical events that answers to some of the issues of microsocial and macrosocial interaction can be found.

Literature Cited

Abruzzi, W. 1981. Mormon Colonization of the Little Colorado River Basin. Unpublished Ph.D. diss. Department of Anthropology, State University of New York, Binghamton.

Adams, Richard N. 1970. *Crucifixion by Power: Essays in Guatemalan Social Structure*. Austin, TX: University of Texas Press.

Adams, Robert McM. 1966. *The Evolution of Urban Society: Early Mesopotamia and Pre-Hispanic Mexico*. Chicago: Aldine.

Barth, Fredrik. 1969. *Ethnic Groups and Boundaries: The Social Organization of Culture Difference*. London: George Allen & Unwin.

Beck, Lois. 1985. *The Quashqa'i Confederacy*. New Haven, CT: Yale University Press.

Becker, Howard. 1950. "Sacred and Secular Societies." *Social Forces* 28: 361–76.

Bendix, Reinhard. 1960. *Max Weber: An Intellectual Portrait*. New York: Doubleday & Company.

Benedict, Ruth. 1934. *Patterns of Culture*. Boston: Houghton Mifflin.

Bennett, John W. 1967. *Hutterian Brethren: The Agricultural Economy and Social Organization of a Communal People*. Stanford, CA: Stanford University Press.

———. 1981. "Social and Interdisciplinary Sciences in U.S. Man and the Biosphere Program," in *Social Sciences, Interdisciplinary Research and the U. S. Man and the Biosphere Program*. U.S. Man and the Biosphere, Department of State, Washington, DC.

———. 1982. *Of Time and the Enterprise: North American Family Farm Management in a Context of Resource Marginality*. Minneapolis, MN: University of Minnesota Press.

———. 1983. "Agricultural Cooperative in the Development Process: Perspectives from Social Science." *Studies in Comparative International Development* 18: 3–68.

———. [1993] 1996. *Human Ecology as Human Behavior: Essays in Environmental and Development Anthropology*. Expanded edition. New Brunswick, NJ: Transaction Publishers.

Benvenuti, Bruno. 1962. *Farming in Cultural Change*. Assen, Netherlands: Van Gorcum.

Braudel, Fernand. 1981. *The Structures of Everyday Life: Civilization and Capitalism: Fifteenth-Eighteenth Century.* New York: Harper & Row.
Buckley, Walter. 1967. *Sociology and Modern Systems Theory.* Englewood Cliffs, NJ: Prentice-Hall.
Childe, V. Gordon. 1942. *What Happened in History.* Harmondsworth: Penguin.
Eckert, Roland. 1970. *Kultur, zivilization, und gesellschaft: die Geschichts-theorie Alfred Webers, seine studie zur geschichte der deutschen soziologie.* Tubingen: J.C.B. Mohr.
Ehrlich, Paul R. and Anne H. Ehrlich. 1974. *The End of Affluence: A Blue-Print for Your Future.* New York: Ballantine.
Fagan, Brian M. 1984. *Clash of Cultures.* New York: W. H. Freeman.
Fallers, Lloyd A. 1974. *The Social Anthropology of the Nation-State.* Chicago: Aldine Publishing.
Foster, George. 1965. "Peasant Society and the Image of Limited Good." *American Anthropologist* 67: 293–315.
Frank, Andre Gunder. 1969. *Capitalism and Underdevelopment in Latin America.*" New York: Monthly Review.
Frankenberg, Ronald. 1966. *Communities in Britain.* Harmondsworth: Penguin.
Franklin, S. H. 1969. *The European Peasantry: The Final Stage.* London: Methuen.
Goldschmidt, Walter. 1947. *As You Sow.* New York: Harcourt Brace.
Halperin, Rhoda and James Dow. 1977. *Peasant Livelihood.* New York: St. Martin's.
Herskovits, Melville J. 1983. *Dahomey* (2 vols). New York: J.J. Augustin.
Hinsley, Curtis M., Jr. 1979. "Anthropology as Science and Politics: Dilemmas of the Bureau of American Ethnology, 1879–1904," in *The Uses of Anthropology*, edited by W. Goldschmidt. Special Publication no. 11, American Anthropological Association, Washington, DC.
Jorgenson, Joseph G. 1978. "A Century of Political Economic Effects on American Indian Society, 1880–1980." *Journal of Ethnic Studies* 6: 1–82.
Kluckhohn, Clyde. 1951. "Values and Value-Orientations in the Theory of Action," in *Toward a General Theory of Action,* edited by T. Parsons and E. Shils. Cambridge, MA: Harvard University Press.
Leach, Edmund R. 1954. *Political Systems of Highland Burma.* Boston: Beacon.
Linton, Ralph. 1936. *The Study of Man: An Introduction.* New York: Appleton Century.
Maine, Henry S. 1861. *Ancient Law, Its Connection with the Early History of Society and Its Relation to Modern Ideas* (1st ed.; many subsequent editions; latest reprint by Dorset Press). London: John Murray.
McCay, Bonnie J. and James M. Acheson. 1987. *The Question of the Commons: The Culture and Ecology of Communal Resources.* Tucson, AZ: University of Arizona Press.
Miner, Horace. 1955. "The Folk-Urban Continuum," in *The Language of Social Research*, edited by P.F. Lazarsfeld and M. Rosenberg. Glencoe, IL: The Free Press.
Netting, Robert Mc. 1981. *Balancing on an Alp: Ecological Change and Continuity in a Swiss Mountain Village.* New York: Cambridge University Press.
Parsons, Talcott. 1951. *The Social System.* Glencoe, IL: The Free Press.
Ralston, Lenore, James Anderson, and Elizabeth Colson. 1981. *Voluntary Efforts in Decentralized Management.* Institute of International Studies, University of California, Berkeley.
Redfield, Robert. 1947. "The Folk Society." *American Journal of Sociology* 52: 293–308.
———. 1955. *The Little Community: Viewpoints for the Study of a Human Whole.* Chicago: University of Chicago Press.

———. 1956. *Peasant Society and Culture: An Anthropological Approach to Civilization.* Chicago: University of Chicago Press.
Reining, Conrad. 1962. "A Lost Period in Applied Anthropology." *American Anthropologist* 64: 593–600.
Roberts, Bryan. 1978. *Cities of Peasants: The Political Economy of Urbanization in the Third World.* London: Edward Arnold.
Simon, Julian L. 1981. *The Ultimate Resource.* Princeton, NJ: Princeton University Press.
Simpson, George. 1933. *Émile Durkheim on the Division of Labor in Society.* New York: MacMillan.
Singer, Milton. 1958. "Traditional India: Structure and Change." *Journal of American Folklore* 71.
Smith, Carol A., ed. 1976. *Regional Analysis* (2 vols.). New York: Academic Press.
Steward, Julian H. 1956. *The People of Puerto Rico.* Champaign, IL: University of Illinois Press.
Tönnies, Ferdinand. 1940. *Fundamental Concepts of Sociology: Gemeinschaft und Gesellschaft.* Translated by Charles Loomis. New York: American Book.
Vidich, Arthur J. and Joseph Bensman. 1960. *Small Town in Mass Society: Class, Power, and Religion in a Rural Community.* Garden City, NY: Doubleday & Company.
Wallerstein, Immanuel. 1974. *The Modern World System: I: Capitalist Agriculture and the Origin of the European World Economy.* New York: Academic Press.
Whitten, Norman. 1969. "Strategies of Adaptive Mobility in the Columbian-Ecuadorian Littoral." *American Anthropologist* 71: 238–42.
Whitten, Norman and A. Wolfe. 1973. "Network Analysis," in *Handbook of Social and Cultural Anthropology*, edited by J. Honigmann.
Whyte, William F. 1943. *Street Corner Society.* Chicago: University of Chicago Press.
Williams, Anne S. 1981. "Industrialized Agriculture and the Small-Scale Farmer." *Human Organization* 40: 306–12.
Wolf, Eric R. 1957. "Closed Corporate Peasant Communities in Mesoamerica and Java." *Southwestern Journal of Anthropology* 13: 1–18.
———. 1969. *Peasant Wars of the Twentieth Century.* New York: Harper & Row.
———. 1982. *Europe and the People without History.* Berkeley: University of California Press.
Worsley, Peter, ed. 1971. *Two Blades of Grass: Cooperatives in Agricultural Modernization.* Manchester: Manchester University Press.

5

The Plains Indian Sun Dance: Leslie Spier's Historical Reconstruction, and Functionalist Research by Others

With a Supplement: A Review of Subsequent Researches on the Sun Dance

Introduction

A variety of approaches evolved within the framework of the Boas tradition, from analytic quantification to subjective interpretations of cultural wholes. The essential quality of this body of materials has not been that of a school with unified methodology and common goals, but rather as Lowie and Kroeber pointed out long ago, a series of offshoots all more or less illustrative of some particular facet of the Boas training. The wide scope of Boas's interests and his catholicity of theory, were productive of a variety of fruitful approaches to the study of Man and Culture.

Originally written in 1943 and published in 1944 as "The Development of Ethnological Theory as Illustrated by Studies of the Plains Sun Dance," *American Anthropologist*, vol. 46, pp. 162-81. This version has been stylistically edited. The original source of the paper was a Research Paper for the doctoral degree program at the University of Chicago in 1943. In the 1960s it was included in the Bobbs-Merrill Reprint Series in the Social Sciences, and in translated form in symposia produced in Japan and Germany. Through the years I made some effort to keep abreast of the ethnological literature on the Sun Dance, and in 1973 I asked students in a graduate seminar to help me update the discussion of the later treatments of the Dance. This permitted me to draft a memorandum, most of which appears here for the first time as a Supplement to the chapter. The history of anthropological research on the Plains Sun Dance is a mirror of the development of early Classic era historical analysis into several "schools": functionalist, psychological, structural, and others.

It does not necessarily follow, however, that consistent tendencies cannot be found in Boas's own anthropological literature. Throughout his contributions there was constant attention to the requirements of empirical research and the necessity for sound and exhaustive treatment of masses of carefully organized detail, with restricted generalization from such data. Although Boas's early interests in the physical sciences may have been atypical for the period (Kroeber 1943:7), this insistence upon the close relationship of theory to fact can be viewed as an essentially nineteenth century empiricistic outlook.

This methodological rule was transmitted to Boas's students with extraordinary success during the formative years of American anthropology. In this period the necessity for recapturing the Indian past was uppermost; the problems lay primarily in the data-securing field, and not in pure theory. Combined with this feature was the basically polemic approach to nineteenth century evolutionism, an attitude that resulted in probably healthy reaction against sweeping generalization, and introduced the analysis of cultural units with a wealth of descriptive detail.

From the combination of these three factors—a methodological principle, the American demand for descriptive data, and the desire for systematic studies of cultural microcosms—emerged the "historical" school of the second and third decades of the century. This group of investigators was interested in tracing the development of American Indian cultures and tribal groups. Their methods had little to do with academic historical research,[1] but were based upon the close-range empirical techniques developed by Boas in his studies of art forms and mythology.

Many critical essays dealing with this phase of anthropological research are available, but a consideration of its place in the changing currents of research through the years is lacking. In this paper I shall study an initially reconstructionist treatment of a single cultural phenomenon—the Sun Dance ceremonial of the Plains Indians—and its transformation into functional and other approaches, from 1920 to the present [that is, 1944; and beyond, in the Supplement]. As a recurrent topic of anthropological research, it has portrayed the vicissitudes and steady growth of ethnological theory.

Contributions on the Sun Dance

The Spier Analysis

Following the publication of Lowie's study of Plains Indian societies (1916), the next large body of data awaiting analysis was the series of monographs on the Sun Dance, dating back to Alice Fletcher's (1883) account of the ceremony for the Oglala and culminating in Dorsey's (1903) monumental description of the Arapaho dance. This latter monograph had stimulated a number of other accounts that appeared as a programmatic series by the American Museum, and by 1921, Spier's monograph.

The methods used by Lowie had set the style: analytical-descriptive studies of trait diffusion in order to trace the historical development of a culture complex or series of complexes. Spier therefore stated,

> It is the aim of the present study to reconstruct the history of the sun dance and to investigate the character of the factors that determine its development. (Spier 1921: 453)

His objective was thus clearly two-sided: an historical reconstruction plus a consideration of the formal-functional elements of the ceremonial in order to understand the processes by which it took hold in the various tribes. References to Spier's paper in contemporary works usually characterize the method as "historical"; actually the distribution-reconstruction study was only one theme of the paper. As Spier stated,

> The character of transmission has been such as to produce a greater uniformity throughout the area in the distribution of regalia and behavior than of the ideas . . . associated with them. The corollary of this is that tribal individuality has been expressed principally in pattern concepts of organization and motivation . . . it follows that the determinants must be sought in the conditions under which incorporation proceeds. (ibid.: 453)

Although the approach was broader than a mere trait-distributional study, as the passage indicated, the problem was formulated with the terminology and objectives of the period, namely,

> The Problem presented . . . is essentially historical: to trace the relations between the various sun dance ceremonies. This should provide some notion of tribal reactions to the diffusion of a ceremonial complex. (ibid.: 460)

For this general purpose,[2] Spier had available a number of accounts of the tribal ceremony, varying from the detailed, 338–page volume by Dorsey (1903) for the Arapaho to a three-page account of the Sisseton Dakota ceremony by Skinner (1914). Most of the data were concerned with the procedure, structure, and regalia of the dance, a preliminary study of which convinced Spier that various performers of the dance were remarkably similar. He therefore isolated some fourteen traits which were common to all tribes, not using these in his analysis. He also omitted from comparison details of the ceremony that were wholly unique for individual tribes. His analytic discussion of these, however, in the later chapters on "Organization" and "Diffusion," bolstered the distributional conclusions.

A critical study of the universals showed marked uniformity throughout the area, but at the same time a greater development and elaboration of them among the Arapaho and Cheyenne. The distribution of Spier's listed traits showed much the same thing—again reinforcing his conclusions.

When he reconsidered his distribution tables with certain conclusions already indicated as a result of intense study of the universals and uniques, Spier was struck by their essential agreement, in spite of the fact " . . . that complexes, such as the buffalo hunt, are given no more weight than such minor traits as the finger plume" (Spier 1921: 477).

Even the non-comparability of source material could be resolved by the cross-check afforded by these interlocking reconstructions, for

> no more striking example of difference in reporting could be found than between the single inadequate account of the Gros Ventre and the half dozen representing the Blackfoot ceremony, yet both score alike in coincidences with the three central tribes. (ibid.: 478)[3]

The final results of this study convinced Spier that the majority of elaborated traits were held by the tribes in the geographical center of distribution(really the southwest corner of the Plains area, but culturally central) with the complex decreasing as the borders of the Plains were approached. The whole range of the less-important traits showed a widespread and somewhat random distribution, but no matter which group of tribes shared a particular trait, one or more members of the "central" group shared it as well.

At this point Spier confessed that

> two equally plausible reasons might be advanced to account for these conditions: either these minor rites were diffused from different parts of the Plains or from the central group. (ibid.: 479)

The answer to this problem was obtained by the analysis of the organization and the nature of certain specific elaborations, rather than through the doctrinaire medium of trait-distribution.

The foregoing brief description indicates the broad outlines of Spier's method, which although historical in orientation, nevertheless contained important functional elements. Underlying this procedure can be seen a number of basic premises that we shall present not to criticize Spier as an anthropologist, but rather to characterize ethnological theory of the period.

Criteria for Historicity

Eclectic as his methods were, Spier defined the problem as "essentially historical"; his objective to "trace relations," and by so doing, to reveal and analyze differences in form and function in terms of the cultural differences in the various tribal recipients of the traits. This view is to be regarded as fundamental in the ethnology of the 1920s: *historical relations are basic to an understanding of cultural differentiation.* Or rephrased in contemporary [1940s] terminology: phenomena with a common origin subsequently separated in space (and time), tend to develop formal and functional differentiation. And further, if two sets of phenomena, widely separated in space, show significant formal and/or functional similarity, it can be assumed that they have a common origin.

Spier found this view somewhat inadequate. We find him observing the remarkable formal homogeneity but functional inconsistency of the dance from tribe to tribe, and trying to explain this puzzling feature by analyzing organizational and causational factors in detail. His results validated the historical-distributional outline, but he was nevertheless led to plead for more detailed studies of cultural "variability," and more concrete isolation of certain vague concepts of the period.

It follows that Spier's criteria for formal similarity are important for an understanding of his conclusions. Here we find some variation according to the type of investigation under way. For trait distributions the criteria are less rigid, thus:

> The semi-roofed type is used by Oglala and Ponca, although the Ponca structure is little more than an encircling wall of boughs. (ibid.: 470)

Here the rather ambiguous concept of "semi-roof" is utilized as sufficient to establish a tentative historical connection. And again:

> It is reasonable to assume that the bower built over the altar by the Southern Cheyenne . . . is simply the same screen [found in Arapaho, Kiowa, etc.] extending around three sides of the altar. (ibid.: 472).

Conscious of the unweighted character of these traits in the distributional phase of his study, Spier checked them by a careful analysis of other features. In organizational data his criteria for similarity were more carefully worked out, and were also regarded by him as more reliable. Thus after his lengthy discussion of the leadership principle, he concludes,

> I think we can be certain that the former is the older, because of their respective distribution and because the individual organization appears again as the basic element in the fraternity. (ibid.: 489)

Thus priority is established by (1) distribution of traits, and (2) formal elaboration, which in principle is later than simpler elements. An additional example:

> It may be that we have in skin and bundle a disintegrated image, or that the two used together finally coalesced in an image. (ibid.: 468)

Again formal complexity is used for defining the type of connection. The factor of functional nonconformity as governing the receptivity of a particular culture element was not considered here, although Spier discusses it fully in other contexts. For distributional purposes he holds to the facts of presence and absence.

Criteria for Diffusion and Independent Invention

Fundamental in this context is the feeling that Spier regarded the Sun Dance as a patchwork of essentially discrete elements thrown together by a series of historical accidents. This is the obvious interpretation of such statements as:

> These considerations suggest the sun dance is a synthetic product. (ibid.: 460)

> The particular collocation of culture elements found in each sun dance is the product of a long series of historic events. (ibid.: 521)

Wissler's popularization of the Sun Dance data in his many accounts of Plains culture starting in 1902 (e.g., Wissler 1912) and references in Lowie's *Primitive Society* (1920) are perhaps responsible for Spier's emphasis on this: that a discovery of these "collocations" will allow him to achieve final verification of his historical reconstruction. These processes of change and selection are viewed as individualistic:

> Two stages are involved in these processes; first, the appropriation of the novel trait by the individual, and then its socialization, its acceptance by the group. . . . I do not mean to imply that novelties are not sharply limited by their acceptance or rejection at the hands of the group, but that modifications are demonstrably the product of individual activity. (Spier 1921: 511–3)

The phrasing of the problem in these terms really obscures the underlying approach, which is essentially sociological. Although the individual may have provided the impulse in a specific contact situation, Spier makes clear the subsequent incorporation of the trait is a "group phenomenon." He discusses the masochistic ("torture") complex in terms of its modification by the "group," or "tribe" as a whole. Spier desires to give us more than a mere statement of the facts of intertribal history, because,

> A history in this form would give no insight into the processes that shape a particular cultural form . . . so long as we present a series of stages statically conceived we fail to make clear in what way a particular trait acquires its peculiar character. The data on the sun dance are far from adequate to permit the full delineation of these developmental processes. The desideratum is a more precise knowledge of the function of the innovating individual, of his cultural equipment, the character of his milieu, and the extent of his contribution; that is, information of the type presented by Radin [1914] in his "Sketch of the Peyote Cult of the Winnebago." (Spier 1921: 522)[4]

In final appraisal, we should perhaps recall that although Spier went much farther than a mere historical study, the problem and initial methodology were certainly couched in historical (i.e., empirical) terms. Spier's extra-historical accomplishments are demonstrated not so much in his conclusions but rather in his promises and expectancies. He desires more information on "processes" of diffusion and assimilation—he seems aware of the need for definitions of these concepts, and feels that if they are forthcoming, we will know more about not only the history of traits, but also the functional processes that bring them into being. Later, Spier (1929, 1936), disavowed his reconstructionist and distributional approach in no uncertain terms, but it would appear that he had begun to feel the same way in 1921. The emphasis in the Sun Dance paper actually seems away from historical reconstruction and toward the more or less functional analysis of organization, mythology, and processes of diffusion and modification.

Subsequent Contributions: 1921–44

Following the publication of the Sun Dance paper in the American Museum series, interest was directed toward the general problem of culture history and quantitative representation of distributional data. The former received the greatest attention, perhaps since it had its roots deep in the earlier museum classifications of Indian culture, and because Wissler had already developed his approach along these lines. The Sun Dance material was received as confirmation of this general view.

In 1926 Clark Wissler (1926: 88ff.) used Spier's incidental remark concerning the center-to-margins distribution of the ceremony as an aspect of his validation of the age- and culture-area system. The Plains became a static, timeless, descriptively analytic entity for Wissler by which he could demonstrate these highly—really overly refined concepts.

This same current carried Roland Dixon into a critical attack on of the age-area concept in 1928 (Dixon 1928: 167–81), in his effort to define alternative principles of trait and trait-complex diffusion. Presenting a series of tribal distribution maps, with the number of traits of the ceremony marked in each tribal area, he showed the "falsity" of Wissler's theory.

> It is evident that the plotting of the actual distribution does not reveal an orderly, concentric, and definitely zoned diffusion. (Dixon 1928: 171)

The difficulty with both these attempts to use the Sun Dance for special purposes (as Kroeber once observed) is that they classed a highly complex ceremony with such simple elements as arrow-releases and moccasins, in the assumption that both obey similar laws of movement. Areal distribution, with its graphically appealing maps and numbers, made the spacio-temporal process of cultural transmission seem a neat, orderly affair. The maps in the publications conceal the vagaries of tribal movement and migration: Dixon shows the Ute in one spot and considers them marginal, arguing that they show a high development of traits, and therefore the "center" must be devalued at the expense of the "margins." Actually the Ute were moving constantly during this entire period, and could have picked up a heterogeneous assortment of traits from nearly all the northwestern tribes.

Kroeber voiced most of these objections to the culture-area concept in 1929, and used the Sun Dance data to show their oversimplified nature. He pointed out that Spier was trying to ascertain the *actual* historical picture—to determine if diffusion of the ceremonial corresponded to actual knowledge of tribal movements, and not to develop pseudo-laws of cultural transmission. On the other hand, I think that Spier was really interested in the type of situation later called *acculturation*: the way in which traits are received and modified by another culture under certain conditions of contact. If the Sun Dance and arrow-releases did show a comparable areal picture, and therefore gave analogous results for the theoretician, "the *meaning* of these results must be different" (Kroeber 1929: 258).

While this ethnological controversy was in progress, Forrest Clements and others were reviving the long-dormant quantitative method of trait-list analysis and attempting its application to actual cultural situations for which the data were relatively complete. This work began in 1926 (Clements et al. 1926), continued sporadically through 1931, and in 1932 the first culture-element study issued from the California press to definitively establish the revived technique.

Clements (1931) actually used Spier's distributional tables to test the value of a four-cell analysis on cultural data. Using the coefficient of correlation (R) and the coefficient of association (Q), he showed a complex and somewhat distorted picture that nevertheless, to him, seemed to substantiate Spier's results. He discussed the factor of known tribal movements and tried to minimize their apparent contradiction of his conclusions, more or less evading the issue by concluding that:

> What we have here then is not the orthodox picture of a culture area with successive waves of diffusion from a single center, but rather a number of points of origin scattered over the whole Plains area, each with its own zone of influence gradually merging into the neighboring zones. (Clements 1931: 226–7)

The following year, Driver and Kroeber (1932) published their pioneer "culture element" study, in which, along with Polynesian and Northwest Coast material, there appeared still another analysis of the Sun Dance data. Again using Spier's traits, they used a series of proportion formulae to check tribal possession of traits against each other. Their results showed the error of Clements' method, and also confirmed Spier's conclusions. This attempt was partly inspired by Spier's well-known retraction of the value of his study, calling it "meaningless and unnecessary" (Spier 1929).

The reasons for Spier's growing distrust may have lain in the popularization of his study by Wissler and Dixon, and the subsequent doubt which greeted mention of the culture-area and age-area hypotheses. In addition, it was becoming evident that the abstraction of cultural elements for purposes of compiling trait lists was a more intricate problem than first thought, a factor which Spier emphasized in his Yale publication on Southwestern tribes (Spier 1936).

This position apparently developed before 1929, while Spier was engaged in field work with the Gila Yumans. This study, when compared to the distributional method used in the Havasupai paper, convinced him that detailed analysis of specific cultural features, with an eye to meaning and function, contributed more towards establishing historical relationships than trait-distributional tables.

Driver and Kroeber "... prefer to believe that Spier is a better culture historian than he wants to admit" (1932: 234), on the basis of their statistical reanalysis. In addition, it would appear that Spier actually used a precursor of the same method in the Sun Dance study that he later applied to the Lower Colorado and Gila Yuman relationships: namely, descriptive analysis of certain behavioral features. As noted, the distributional chapter in the Sun Dance paper is only one of several techniques used to arrive at a historical outline.

References to the Sun Dance since 1932 [that is, up to 1943] have shown a consistent tendency to emphasize the functional nature and theoretical aspects of the dance rather than its history. Thus Ralph Linton (1936: 405) used it as an example of how form can remain fairly constant while meaning, use, and function vary according to the culture receiving the complex. Ruth Benedict (1938) had a similar interest, showing how the ceremony varies in reason for performance in each tribe, but has remarkable homogeneity in detail of outward form. Spier observed this also, but did not develop this point because his objectives were mainly historical.

Kroeber (1939, actually written in 1935–36) displayed a similar preoccupation with function, but also adhered to the older tradition in that he commented upon more recent data on tribal distribution which might modify Spier's conclusions. He further commented upon how such a complex ceremony could develop in a relatively short time, explaining this (as Spier did) by the fact that most of the elements of the ceremony were old cultural forms simply adapted to new uses and functions. Both Benedict and Kroeber note the general "instability" of Plains culture as explanatory of the intense elaboration of ceremony and social institutions in the area as a whole.

A step beyond this position was made by Marvin Opler (1941) and E. A. Hoebel (1941). The former analyzed the Ute Sun Dance as a borrowed ritual, peculiarly and dynamically integrated within Ute ceremonialism and basic logics. Briefly,

> . . . the Ute never borrowed the sun dance of the Plains at all. Rather, they seized upon its existence, hastening to reinterpret it in the light of their own religious experience. (Opler 1941: 571)

Here the fact of diffusion is merely the basis for an analysis that penetrates into the fundamental cultural processes conditioning the modification of the ritual. Opler specifically stated that an examination of the rite "must throw light upon the integration of the (Ute) religion and upon its distinctive features" (1941: 571). The dance was used as data corroborative of a particular series of hypotheses about Ute culture, not as material descriptively analyzed for its own sake. Further, as in all ethnological papers of the contemporary period [that is, the 1940s], a thread of generalization ran throughout the piece. One receives the impression that Opler's conclusions were thrown out challengingly as general propositions about all cultures of this particular type. He concludes, for example, with the statement that the dance emphasizes those features of Ute culture which operate as consolidating factors in the face of over powering acculturative influences.

> In this sense, the ritual becomes the instructive symbol of vitality of primitive culture fighting for existence in the midst of modern civilization. (Opler 1941: 572)

Hoebel (1941), in a briefer note, showed a similar interest in that he placed the Comanche Sun Dance within a general matrix of messianic revivalism in Indian culture. Again, the dance data are used as a *point of departure* for developing special problems of cultural dynamics; not as subject matter in themselves.

Some new data was offered on the occurrence of the dance in other groups. Linton's (1935) account of the Comanche ceremony shed light on the southern extension of the dance and on the character of a ritual apparently borrowed from a series of scattered sources. Interesting parallels appear in a comparison with other Basin tribes. It is significant that although Linton's interest was primarily historical, he did not feel required to make a detailed trait-analysis of distribution, instead relying upon a careful discussional analysis of relations.

Lowie (1924) and especially Opler's (1941) paper provided relatively detailed accounts of the Ute dance, over and above Spier's 1921 summary. These later data were particularly interesting for the linkage with the Ute dream-complex. Opler made clear the profound functional differences between the Ute dance and the Arapaho, Cheyenne, et al., varieties; it was quite definitely a ritual of solidarity marking the temporary Spring establishment of the camp and the resumed social activities, rather than a fulfillment of a vow or an individual request for supernatural help.

A summary of these observations is in order. The original analytic emphasis was placed upon a reconstruction of the distributional history of the ceremony—its movement from tribe to tribe, and probable origin. This approach was featured in some of the most dogmatic utterances of the historical-distributional school in the 1920s. In Spier's study, however, lay the seeds for later methodological trends: functional analyses of the variability of elements in different tribes. Through the years, this phase was taken up by the functionalist wing of American anthropology and used to illustrate various theoretical points relating to primitive ceremonials and the diffusion of culture. This trend culminated in the consideration of the dance as illustrative data for specific problems of cultural dynamics. In the other direction, the dance was utilized by adherents of the new school of quantifiers of culture-element data, and subjected to statistical analysis. This trend showed within itself an increasing sophistication and attention to the formulation of problems.

The Concept of "Trait"

The Cultural Trait List As a Clue to History

It is not the purpose of this essay to deal comparatively with the various historical reconstructions of the Sun Dance. Our primary interest is with the methodology or theory typical of the periods in which the analyses and reanalyses were made. Consideration of this problem should lead us to the theory of the trait and the trait-list as a technique for historical reconstruction. In accomplishing this, we shall deal with certain historical conclusions secondarily as part of our investigation of the trait-analysis method.

Spier summarized his trait tables in a chart showing the number of traits held in common between each tribe. He arranged this chart in approximate geographical order, with the northern marginal tribes at the far right and lower edges, the southern marginals at the left hand and upper edges. This created a heavy grouping in the center of the chart, where the Gros Ventre, Arapaho, Cheyenne, Oglala, and Ponca groups were placed. It was this suggestive arrangement which caused his optimism in spite of the unequal nature of his sources, since he was able to observe that despite the differences in reporting, the distribution was symmetrical.

The distribution of these traits convinced him that the origin of the ceremony lay with the Arapaho and Cheyenne, and that subsequent diffusion could be reduced to a series of problems in local differentiation and borrowing. Certain systematic resemblances could be noted: alignments of tribes in terms of specific traits, such as the actions at the fall of the tree, counting coup, and so on.

It is often assumed that this trait-analysis established the history of the ceremony, but as we indicated in part 1, the geographical distributional study must be regarded as merely one research technique among several. After the traits-in-common groupings had demonstrated a relationship that could be interpreted either way, Spier tried to reconstruct the history of certain specific features, in order to discover the true course of diffusion.

For example, he discussed the self-torture feature in detail, concluding that it is a secondary element of the dance, and because of its distribution and intensified form in a particular area, that it originated in the Village tribes. If torture is a secondary element, then the original nucleus of the dance, as shown by a close analysis, is the trait of erecting a pole in an enclosure as a dance arena. But even the pole idea is an old Plains custom, appearing in various ceremonies of the Omaha, Osage, Pawnee, and other tribes. Then,

> But so much for the original form. While the Oglala are probably eliminated from the group of originators of the dance, they may still be said to constitute, with the Arapaho and Cheyenne, the center of diffusion. But inasmuch as the Oglala place their emphasis on torture while the majority of the tribes do not, the ceremonies of the latter would seem to have had common origin with those of the Arapaho and Cheyenne. (Spier 1921: 494–5)

The other arguments rest upon more or less equivalent documentary and logistic proof, and lead toward the ultimate conclusion that the Arapaho-Cheyenne nucleus originated the dance, with a slight priority in favor of the Arapaho, since the Cheyenne ceremony has Oglala features. Analysis of the antiquity of the entire complex placed it as late eighteenth century, and if this was correct, the Cheyenne must have been in the Plains, with a Plains-type culture, during the latter half of the 1700s.

Materials on the Cheyenne published subsequent to Spier's analysis, however, would suggest that the tribe entered the Plains circa 1800 or later.[5] If these more recent conclusions are correct, it seems doubtful that the Cheyenne could have played a major role in the origination of the dance, although they may well have assisted in its later elaboration. Spier felt that the Arikara-Hidatsa ceremony was probably derived from the Arapaho-Cheyenne type, with the Village tribes then forming the basis for a secondary diffusion to Blackfoot and Crow. However, the early association of at least a portion of the Cheyenne-Sutaio with the Arikara renders it more than possible they may have picked up some form of the embryonic dance from them.

The methodological significance of this revision—if revision it is—lies in the implication that a full contingent of elaborated traits need not automatically indicate origins. With a common language the Cheyenne could very quickly take the dance from the Arapaho and then help develop it, having derived the preliminary stimulus from the Arikara. These remarks need not materially revise Spier's conclusions, since the Arapaho could still be sovereign, but they do throw some doubt on the trait-distributional method as a clue to history. Spier rightly observed that the documentary evidence for Cheyenne-Arapaho contact was almost nonexistent, and so lacking the data on the Cheyenne entry into the Plains, he fell back upon the traits alone. This procedure resulted in somewhat dubious conclusions. [And Spier himself seems to have become aware of this, judging by his later disavowals of reconstructionist methodology.]

Another instance of possible nonconformity between history and trait-distribution can be seen in Spier's interpretation of the Arapaho-Gros Ventre relationship. On the basis of numbers of traits he gave priority to the Arapaho. It is known that the Gros Ventre (Atsina) were late offshoots of the Arapaho, and considered themselves as such. Thus the question of priority has little meaning here; actually the dance was a common complex, with areal separation being responsible for minor differences. Trait variances indicate merely this spacio-temporal break, and not an historical-directional relation. It is known, for example, that the Blackfoot transferred the dance to the Sarsi, which the trait lists do tend to confirm, and on the surface of things, the "same" situation holds for the Gros Ventre-Arapaho. Actually the *meaning* of these two sets of trait differences is quite different; in one case, genuine diffusion, in the other, splitting of a single complex.

Driver and Kroeber reworked Spier's data with a refined statistical technique which seemed to confirm Spier's conclusions. Most significant in their analysis was the fact that the secondary diffusions also indicated their primary relationships; thus the Blackfoot traits bear primary relationships to the Arapaho, but also indicate their dependence on the Gros Ventre, from whom they actually acquired the ceremony. The most important difference in the Driver-Kroeber conclusions was the failure to establish the Village tribes as an important secondary center of diffusion. This demonstration was accomplished by Spier not by trait-distribution, but rather by documentary evidence and on the strength of the Village invention of the self-torture complex. Kroeber's Assiniboin-Cree association as a tertiary center derived from the Gros Ventre and Blackfoot was consequently broken up to compensate for the consideration of Hidatsa-Arikara as the main center for the northern area. Driver and Kroeber explain this by showing that the Village culture was in serious decline after 1800, when the data were obtained, and therefore trait analysis was hardly adequate. Spier, in the face of this difficulty, had used evidence other than trait-distribution.[6]

A third example of the distortion implicit in the trait-distributional criteria: Spier, after an extended analysis, found that in the Arapaho, the Sun Dance and age-societies had a close, interlocking coordination. This implied a long period of common growth. Since Lowie had shown that complex age-societies meant old age-societies, and since no other tribes had this close linkage of dance and society, Spier concluded that the Arapaho must be credited with the origin of the dance.

Alternative explanations are two: first, Driver and Kroeber emphasize the depth of cultural history in the Village tribes, showing that the Arapaho may have borrowed age-societies from them. These two factors might suggest that the Sun Dance may have originated in the Hidatsa-Arikara and then elaborated by the Arapaho after the Village tribes' decline (post-1800). The second alternative is that the age-society–Sun Dance coordination could be regarded as a particular functional adjustment in Arapaho culture, of the same order as the shaman-Sun Dance integration among the Ute. Logically there is no more reason to assign the Sun Dance to the Arapaho on the basis of the age-society tie, than there would be to call the Ute the originators on the grounds that the shaman feature represents the first step in elaboration of the dance from an individualistic beginning.[7]

The Concept of "Trait"

Let us pass now to an examination of the logic and rhetoric of trait construction.

For experimental purposes I made a trait-analysis of the Comanche Sun Dance, using Linton's data. Of the total forty-eight possible traits, only nineteen could be considered true analogues to Spier's traits. Furthermore, striking resemblances to the Ute dance were apparent, but being of a generalized character (e.g., shaman-control) could not be counted as specific traits. The problem of congruity was insurmountable in many cases; the Ute trait at times representing greater or lesser complexity than Spier traits; in other cases, the functional significance varied.

If such difficulties were true of the Ute experiment, it would follow that Spier experienced similar difficulties. This problem becomes important when we recall that some of the re-analyses accepted Spier traits at face value. Therefore, the Spier traits were checked against the original data. Space permits only a single example:

> "Center Pole Activities"
> "Shouting"
> "Counting coup"
>
> *Hidatsa* (Lowie 1921: 425)
>
> After he had three times pretended to do this, the other man actually struck the log. Then they all shouted, "We have killed our enemy!"

It happens that the other tribes count coup on the tree, thus symbolizing victory. The Hidatsa custom expresses a similar idea, but the trait list distinguishes between "Shouting" and "Counting coup," and credits the Hidatsa with only the former.

> *Arapaho* (Dorsey 1903: 84)
>
> As the tree fell with a crash toward the north, all gave a wild shout, rushed up, touching the stump (thus counting coup), and rubbing their arms and breasts. . .

Spier records only "Counting coup" for the Arapaho, however, this suggests the division between counting-coup and shouting was more or less arbitrary, "Shouting" being selected only when information on the other was nonspecific.

At both levels of operation, Spier's traits are noncomparable entities: (1) the procedure of selection and compilation involved combining notes on specific activity with generalized references; vague suggestions of procedure with fully developed routine; inverted and other wise distorted activity with standard practices; (2) the procedure of comparison involved the consideration of elements of behavior, attitudes, regalia, et al., as all of equal weight and comparability.

Spier was fully aware of the second difficulty. He does not, however, give explicit information on the first; namely, how he made his choices of traits. That this was a careful one is evident, but its irrevocable subjectivity is equally apparent.[8] Many alternative groupings could be made: the single entry, "Procession," for instance, could be broken into three traits based upon type of assembly, activities during the march, and type of leader. The ritual preparation before the dance, such as fasting, bathing, and so on, could be included in the list.

In Spier's judgment the extreme variety in meaning and organization of the dance offered sharp contrast to the relatively formal stability. His trait lists showed the latter; his descriptive analysis discussion the former. However, his trait lists might have expressed some of the functional variability also, had they been differently constructed.

The difficulty of evaluating the Driver-Kroeber and Clements reanalyses lies in the fact that they merely used Spier-determined traits and handled them statistically. It is not particularly surprising that the use of statistics on a well-assembled trait list yielded results similar to Spier's inspectional and arithmetical analysis.

In the light of recent developments [1940s] in culture element studies, statistical analysts are fully aware of such problems. Driver's (1938) work has focussed attention upon the variability of all factors; Kroeber (1940) has shown the consequences of a personal bias in collecting data.

The underlying problem concerns the quest for the "unit of culture," the irreducible minimum which is the goal of the quantitative student. There exists a growing recognition of the methodological impossibility of determining such an absolute unit, since functional theory is based on the idea of the interdependence of cultural phenomena at all levels. In this view the trait becomes an abstraction having no value other than the immediate one placed upon it by the user.[9] Irreducibility depends on the context: a trait can be minimal for one system, overly complex for another. In historical reconstruction, method must be adjusted to goal. At what level must traits be abstracted to serve the problem in view?

This is a difficult problem when documentary materials are meager. Spier, unable to eliminate this difficulty, divided his study into a trait-distributional study and a functional analysis. The former was composed of arbitrarily segregated units, and had little interconnection with the analytic discussion.

The significant difference in Spier's later approach in his 1936 monograph on Gila River tribes lies in the fact that the trait list is utilized as a convenient graphic summary of cultural resemblances—an appendix to a discussional historical reconstruction. In 1921, the trait list was a vehicle of the reconstruction itself.

These remarks suggest another problem: could the Sun Dance itself, as a complex, really be considered a unit? While the details of form remained fairly uniform from tribe to tribe, the function of the ceremony varied considerably. The answer depends upon particular objectives. If engaged in tracing the movement of a series of elements through space and time, the ceremonial can be arbitrarily defined as a unit.

If, however, attention is focussed upon the contribution of the ceremony to the total cultural matrix of which it is a part, each sun dance must be considered as a unique problem. Classification, although necessary here as in historical inquiry, becomes quite different: traits are grouped in terms of functional relationship instead of formal similarity. This underlines one major difference in anthropological theory of the 1920s and the 1940s.

As Opler's and Hoebel's contributions showed, problems become manifold when the ceremony is handled in the later manner. These may be typical: did small bands usually develop group ceremonies, for purposes of reaffirming group solidarity? Was the shamanistic feature of the Comanche and Ute dances evidence of contact and diffusion or is it a result of parallelism? Cultural-ecological determinism?[10]

If, for example, the first question could be answered in the affirmative, one would have a cogent argument for the unitary character of the dance, and thus incidentally support historical premises.[11]

It will now be clear to what extent Spier's use of "functional" analysis both resembled and differed from the current [1940s] approaches. Whereas 1940s ethnology often combines history and function in the same analysis, methods in the 1920s made a careful distinction. The sense of problem differed: functional analysis was considered as a prop for historical reconstruction; by the 1940s the two represented a merged field of inquiry.

Even when engaged in strict historical research, the ethnologist cannot ignore change and development in the functional process. For example, the relationship of the Sun Dance to certain annual ceremonies typical of marginal Plains and Prairie tribes involved dynamic questions of cultural contact and interaction. Spier gave a few clues, relegated to footnotes, but no systematic analysis was made.

There are other problems concerning the degree of separation possible to make between a ceremony and underlying cultural patterns. Sun Dance varied according to the particular use a tribe made of its features within the traditional framework of the culture. For example, if the Sun Dance was considered a part of, and classed with, the general pattern of bundle ceremonies in the Blackfoot, could it be taken as equivalent to the shamanistic ceremony of the Ute?[12]

Benedict's emphasis upon instability and individualistic patterning of Plains culture bears on such questions; a case study of Sun Dance homogeneity in separate tribes could contribute valuable evidence for her thesis. What of the comparative stability of the Plains and Pueblo Indians? If the horse played such a large role in the rapid diffusion of the Sun Dance, spreading it throughout a tremendous geographical area and into diverse tribal groups, is not this uniformity as "stable" as the repressed Appolonians of the mesas?

Historical reconstruction in the light of these remarks emerges in its proper place as an adjunct to a general investigation of culture as a body of phenomena susceptible of analysis with the methods of science.[13] For the purposes of constructing causal relations and general uniformities, no single set of techniques can be used to the exclusion of others. Function must be reinforced by history, and vice versa; the particular problem at hand determines the emphasis.

The evolution of this viewpoint prompts the observation that perhaps the most fortunate aspect of the Boas tradition was its inner eclecticism, fostering as it did many independent and enthusiastically experimental approaches to the study of culture. In the course of years these distinct tendencies are blending both in their sense of problem (which is fundamental) and methodological orientation; the rigid exclusivism and polemic controversy are instead subordinated to mutual inquiry and comparative study.

Supplement: A Review of Subsequent Researches on the Sun Dance[14] (A 1973 Seminar Report)

The seminar which produced this material focussed on studies of the Sun Dance which appeared in the 1950–1970s period after the original paper was written, plus one or two used in the original paper deserving of extended comment. These later studies display a variety of theoretical approaches—functional, psychological, structural, and modified historical developmental.

My examination of Linton's 1935 paper on the Comanche Dance did not adequately represent his contribution. He was the first post-Spier student of the Dance to explicitly view it from attitudinal and functional perspectives. Showing no particular interest in how the Comanche received it, or in the form of the Dance as related to other tribal ceremonials, he singled out particular features and attributed them to Comanche attitudes and interests. For example, he noted that the Comanche did not consider the healing element in the Dance as significant—in contrast to other tribes—since healing was a standard feature in all Comanche ceremonials. He noted that the Comanche did not perform the Dance consistently and regularly, and many features of their Dance lacked the elaborate rituals found in other groups.

Later, in 1943, Linton published his treatise on "nativistic movements," one of the first attempts to develop a theoretical understanding of changing cultural behavior in relation to contemporary historical developments. He did not refer specifically to the Sun Dance in this context, but other writers—like Anthony Wallace, David Aberle, and Joseph Jorgensen (in his Sun Dance monograph to be considered in a moment)—did so. In general, Linton's 1935 paper appears to be the first major post-Spier contribution to the Sun Dance literature which *consciously* used approaches other than the historical and diffusionist themes.

In 1948 Fred Voget signed on with his study of "Individual Motivation in the Diffusion of the Wind River Sun Dance to the Crow," and continued the approach in a 1950 paper on "A Shoshone Innovator." This material sharpened the psychological theme implicit in the earlier Linton piece. Voget was concerned with the actual persons involved in the transmission process, as the following passage documents:

> . . . the three Crow leaders, Big-Day, Hill, and Old-Coyote, reveal that both cultural and individual factors were operative in their attitudes toward and participation in the Sundance. Each shared the following: (1) a dissatisfaction with the general cultural situation; (2) a reorientation of their values around the native culture and specifically in native religious expressions; (3) life crisis which demanded solution and for which they turned to a nativistic religious expression, and (4) a progressive reinforcement which confirmed them in the native direction which they had taken. (Voget 1948:646)

Voget was not concerned with the specific form the Dance took in Shoshone and Crow societies—only with the motivations and cultural backgrounds of the actual people involved in the process. It should be noted that Spier advocated such individualistic studies of the transmission process as noted in the quotation from Spier (1921: 522; see p. 164 of this chapter). Thus Voget's piece illustrates the growing lack of interest in culture seen as collections of traits and their movement in time and space. These later topics are taken as givens in the later studies, and the emphasis shifted to psychological and social functioning, in order to evolve an explanatory theory of group ceremonial activity.

Anthony Wallace's 1956 study, "Revitalization Movements," a direct descendent of Linton's "Nativistic" paper, went further in analyzing the various forms of these group responses to colonialism, enslavement, and rapid cultural change. Wallace did not actually include the Sun Dance in his classification, however, since the original Dance as practiced in the Plains was not really a "revitalization" response to change and domination, but rather a socially integrating ceremonial devised by nomadic people for reestablishing social contact at regular intervals. However, the resumption of performances of the Sun Dance when the Government withdrew its ban on the ceremonial, could be viewed as a change in the function of the Dance toward nativism and revitalization. As a matter of fact, this proposition is implied or accepted in most of the later writings on the Dance: Hoebel's 1941 paper on the "Comanche Dance and the Messianic Outbreak of 1873" is a case in point. Jones (1955: 256), in a study of the Northern Ute, attributed the dance to the "frustrations inherent in an acculturative situation." Similar findings were noted for the Arapaho by Hultkranz (1952). And by 1956, Voget summarized these various studies attributing the Dance to some kind of revivalism, using the term "reformative nativism" to emphasize its highly conscious, political nature as contrasted with "passive nativism" (Vogt 1956: 250).

Demitri Shimkin (1953) studied the ceremonial as practiced by the Wind River Shoshone, including a return to a Spier-type historical reconstruction, involving the breakdown of Dance data into a series of traits. However, this history and formal analysis was of secondary importance for Shimkin, since he was mainly interested in the psychological and social functions of the ceremonial. Using a number of techniques, including Rorschach tests given to participants, he established ways in which the Dance was integrated with social structure and cultural times. A background issue was the substitution of the Ghost Dance for the Sun Dance in tribes like the Ute (using Morris Opler's 1941 paper), and its retention among the Wind River Shoshone in spite of similar forces in the latter which might have led to the substitution. Shimkin concluded that where the Sun Dance was closely integrated into the existing social structure and sociopsychology, it appeared to be more easily surrendered, whereas more loosely organized forms of the Dance, like the Wind River version, could be retained. The conclusion appears to reverse the long-held doctrine in ethnology to the effect that the *more integrated* a culture complex may be, the *less likely* it would be to disappear under external pressures. Perhaps, but as the late Classic and post-Classic anthropologists eventually came to discover, especially via acculturation studies, anything is possible in culture change because people are capable of thinking and doing anything.

We come then to Joseph Jorgensen's 1972 book, "The Sun Dance Religion" in which he used the Dance topic as part of his version of the radical or critical phase of post-Classic anthropology. For Jorgensen placed the Dance squarely in the context of the exploitative processes of "American capitalist democracy," and the political domination and subsequent deprivation of the Indian groups by the United States. But his analysis was by no means a naive left-leaning tract, since his anthropological frame of reference was based on David Aberle's excursus on the Linton, Wallace, et al. "nativistic revival" concept (Aberle 1966). He located the roles of the Dance in various tribes in terms of the history of the groups' relationships to the majority society, and used Aberle's typology of "transformative" and "redemptive" movements to describe the reactions.

In essence, Jorgensen's problem was to explain the *persistence* of the Dance into the contemporary era—not its history and diffusion, nor (primarily) its function and psychology. His initial answers were elementary: the ceremonial's "beauty" (that is, its rhythms, costumes, movements, etc.) and its functions in the service of anxiety alleviation—"personal redemption." He also used some 365 variables, including many of the Spier items, to compare the Dance on different reservations, finding that the social structure of the reservation community and the general economic situation was influential in shaping the particular form of the Dance and the development or diminution of particular components. He found that the particular relationship of the reservation community to the Government and the immediate external environment were not as significant as internal structural elements in shaping the form of the Dance. Jorgensen's analysis is ingenious and complex, and not entirely convincing, but it does show how an explicit use of moral and political values can illuminate a scholarly approach to a familiar topic. He concluded that the Sun Dance helped Indians "cope with life," so in the last analysis he lined up with the studies of Voget and others interested in the sociopsychological dimensions of the ceremonial. And Jorgensen's use of trait analysis was not designed to show historical movement, but rather to discover how sociopolitical and economic factors could influence the form and functions of the Dance in particular communities.

These later writings are all characterized by lack of concern for cultural tradition or "custom" in the sense that the dance is perceived as a form of human behavior responding to objective circumstances, and how traditional forms of behavior can alter their meaning and function with historical change. Thus the Sun Dance made its way from the early Classic historicism and empiricism of Spier, to the dynamic sociopsychological functionalism of the later Classic and finally, politically critical post-Classic anthropology. Origin of the Dance remains a problem, but it is no longer defined historically and geographically, but in sociological or sociopsychological terms. The meaning of the ceremonial as perceived by the participants is seen to be of greater moment than the vicissitudes of particular cultural traits.

Notes to the Original Paper

1. The term "history" meant only general development and origins, not the exhaustive analysis of social, economic, and political structure through time. [Spier performed another classic experiment in historical reconstruction, namely his "Chronology of Zuñi Ruins" (1917), done on the basis of seriation studies of Zuñi potsherds. This study is one of the two or three most influential methodological pieces in the history of American archaeology.]
2. Compare with the goals of contemporary [1940s] acculturation studies as illustrative of the constant factors in the American ethnological tradition: " . . . the possible relationships to be discerned between the selection of traits under the various types of contacts leading to acculturation, and the situations in which acculturation may occur" (Herskovits 1938:133).
3. This would, however, be expected regardless of the fullness of the accounts, since in the light of more recent knowledge the Gros Ventre must be regarded as late offshoots of the Arapaho. The underlying technical problem—how to define the unit for analysis—is recurrent in ethnology. Goldenweiser (1940: 469) notes that Tylor in 1888 and Hobhouse et al., in 1930 encountered the problem in the form of their unit, a "tribe," for statistical analysis. A trait was uncritically counted twice if it appeared in contiguous tribes. Similar logical difficulties inhere in the configurationist approach: What are the boundaries of the configuration—is it an overall ethos or specific core behavior? Does the configuration delimit the culture, or vice versa? To test the configuration empirically, what units must we use? The problem is also highly important in archaeological analysis. A systematic methodological investigation of it as it appears in various anthropological approaches would be immensely valuable.
4. In this passage Spier also cited, as bad examples, the works of Gabriel Tarde (1903) and Alfred Vierkandt (1908), nineteenth-century anthropologists who used stage theory to explain resemblances in social institutions. This is Spier's one contribution in the monograph to the "Boasian" critique of evolutionary anthropology. [This is a 1995 revision of the original footnote.]
5. Grinnell (1923) collected much documentary evidence to show the Cheyenne left a Minnesota-North Dakota homeland around 1800, proceeding into the Plains in

small groups, some remaining as farmers well after this date. These later groups finally reunited with their nomadic kinsmen, the Sutaio, west of the Missouri in the Black Hills. These later groups supposedly received the Sun Dance from the Sutaio, the latter getting the ceremony from the Arapaho or Kiowa. Strong (1940) excavated a well-authenticated Cheyenne village site near the Minnesota border in South Dakota, which indicates the Cheyenne were farmers well after 1750, living in permanent villages with palisades. Kroeber (1939: 81) also felt that the Cheyenne could not have become true Plains Indians "until well into the nineteenth century." Swanton's (1930) work on tribal movements emphasized the lateness of the Cheyenne entry.

6. A procedure often ignored by others. Compare P. Kirchoff's (1943: especially pp. 100–7) oversimplified use of traits and trait lists in developing sweeping historical and cultural relationships.
7. It is understood, however, that Spier was on firm ground in his isolation of the Arapaho. The age-society feature was only one of several elements of proof. It is interesting to note that Linton used logic very similar to Spier's in his brief analysis of the Comanche dance (Linton 1935). He felt that since the dance contained many variable elements and alternative rituals, the Comanche "had not had the Sun Dance long enough to establish an integrated pattern" (Linton 1935: 427). However, he showed that the dance was under complete control of the shaman, who arranged all details and whose word was law on the sequence of events. The possibility of variability being a result of such individual control rather than short duration should at least be considered.
8. These general criticisms can be levelled at any use of ethnological data for trait lists. Unless statistically and self-consciously controlled, they represent inherent defects. We should distinguish here between these basic difficulties and those features of Spier's analysis which were largely a product of the period. Examples of the first are: circumstances determining the selection by a culture of a particular trait are complex and usually lost to the observer; stability of trait elements must be determined, since alteration or loss of traits may affect history; time-differentials distort the picture, since not all traits travel at equal speeds; the use of abstract concepts as traits is a dangerous procedure (cf. Spier's trait, "individual initiative"); the problem of "similar" traits rests ultimately on careful analysis and logic, not positive proof. Such difficulties are as common in the 1940s as they were in the 1920s. As an example of the second category, we may note Spier's trait, "semi-roofed lodge." Here Spier counted any structure even vaguely approaching this norm as similar to all others, on the basis of the principle of formal similarity as expressing historical relations. This was a fundamental credo of the time.
9. Cf. Linton (1936: 397–400). Also W. Z. Park (1938: esp. p. 158). Park felt "Certainly the only unitary nature possessed by culture elements comes from the actual . . . history." Archaeologist were concerned with problems of trait theory and construction before ethnologists encountered the issues. Among famous instances where trait analysis and typology became a controversial issue there is the case of Caribbean and Floridian archaeology, as Cornelius Osgood and Irving Rouse developed it. [For a discussion of the case and its problems, see Siegel (1996: 682).] Therefore, what kinds of problems require what kinds of procedures involving culture categorization?
10. These considerations suggest that contemporary ethnology [1940s] has not fully explored the theoretical significance of its materials. Advanced as the Benedict, Opler, et al., interpretations may be, much more could be done. What is needed is

clearer recognition of the conceptual unity of all culture for purposes of solving general problems. Interest in the peculiar character of atomistic cultural groupings must be subordinated to the formulation of more general propositions relating to structure and process.

11. Lesser's (1933) study of the Pawnee Ghost Dance hand game developed this point. The revival of the bundles, which played so large a role in the spread of the Dance, was an historically certain fact; the hand game as studied through its historical changes threw much light on the meaning of its function in the tribal culture as a whole.
12. Linton, for instance, emphasized the variability of the Comanche dance. If several observances of the ceremony were analyzed separately, it is possible that historical relationships might be revised: the semi-roofed lodge dance might be linked to the Dakota, the roofed type to the Arapaho.
13. The legitimate heir of historical reconstruction can be found today in Americanist archaeology rather than ethnology [e.g., chapter 11]. The entire historical school represented only one phase of the Boas tradition: the intensely empiricistic. Boas's own dissatisfaction with reconstruction called attention to his underlying preoccupation with process. In later years the processual trend dominated in ethnology, while the empirical, trail-element interest drifted into archaeology on one hand, and the mathematical refinement of the California studies on the other. But the old interest in classification is better preserved in archaeology than in Western trait-element studies; the trials, methods, and controversies of archaeology are more reminiscent of historical ethnology than are the culture-element studies of today [1940s].
14. Particularly helpful students in the seminar in which these later contributions were examined included Nanetee Rochberg and Elaine Sawyer.

Literature Cited in Original Paper and Supplement

Aberle, David F. 1966. *The Peyote Religion among the Navaho.* Chicago: Aldine.

Benedict, Ruth. 1938. "Religion," in *General Anthropology*, edited by F. Boas, pp. 627–65. Boston: D.C. Heath.

Clements, Forrest E. 1931. "Plains Indian Tribal Correlations with Sun Dance Data." *American Anthropologist* 33: 216–27.

Clements, Forrest E., Sara M. Schenck and T. K. Brown. 1926. "Plains Indian Tribal Correlations with Sun Dance Data." *American Anthropologist* 28: 585–604.

Dixon, Roland B. 1928. *The Building of Cultures.* New York: Charles Scribner's Sons.

Dorsey, George A. 1903. *The Arapaho Sun Dance.* Field Columbian Museum, Anthropological Series, vol. 4, Chicago.

Driver, Harold E. 1938. *The Reliability of Culture Element Data.* Culture Element Studies 8, University of California.

Driver, Harold E. and A. L. Kroeber. 1932. *Quantitative Expression of Cultural Relationships.* University of California Publication in Anthropology and Ethnology, vol. 31, no. 4.

Fletcher, Alice C. 1883. *The Sun Dance of the Ogalalla Sioux.* Proceedings, American Association for the Advancement of Science, 1982, pp. 580–4.

Goldenweiser, Alexander A. 1940. "Leading Contributions of Anthropology to Social Theory," in *Contemporary Social Theory*, edited by H.E. Barnes, H. Becker, and F.B. Becker, pp. 433–90. New York: Russell & Russell.

Grinnell, George B. 1923. *The Cheyenne Indians, Their History and Ways of Life*. New Haven, CT: Yale University Press.

Herskovits, Melville J. 1938. *Acculturation: The Study of Culture Contact*. New York: J.J. Augustin.

Hobhouse, Leonard T., Gerald C. Wheeler, and Morris Ginsberg. 1930. *The Material Culture and Social Institutions of the Simpler Peoples: An Essay in Correlation*. London: Chapman & Hall. The introduction and chapters 1 and 2 originally appeared in *Sociological Review* (1914): 289–99.

Hoebel, E. Adamson. 1941. "The Comanche Sun Dance and Messianic Outbreak of 1873." *American Anthropologist* 43: 301–3.

Hultkrantz, Ake. 1952. "Some Notes on the Arapaho Sun Dance." *Ethnos* 1: 24–38.

Jones, John A. 1955. *The Sun Dance of the Northern Ute*. Bulletin of the Bureau of American Ethnology, anthropological paper 137, pp. 203–64.

Jorgensen, Joseph G. 1972. *The Sun Dance Religion: Power for the Powerless*. Chicago: University of Chicago Press.

Kirchoff, Paul. 1943. "Mesoamerica." *Acta Americana* 1: 92–107.

Kroeber, A. L. 1929. "The Culture Area-Age Area Concepts of Clark Wissler," in *Methods in Social Science*, edited by S.A. Rice, pp. 258.

———. 1939. *Cultural and Natural Areas of Native North America*. University of California Publications in Anthropology and Ethnology, vol. 38.

———. 1940. "Statistical Classification." *American Antiquity* 6: 29–44.

——-. 1943. "Franz Boas: The Man," in *Franz Boas, 1858–1942*, by A.L. Kroeber et al. Memoirs of the American Anthropological Association, No. 61.

Lesser, Alexander. 1933. *The Pawnee Ghost Dance Hand Game: A Study of Cultural Change*. New York: Columbia University Press.

Linton, Ralph. 1935. "The Comanche Sun Dance." *American Anthropologist* 37: 420–8.

———. 1936. *The Study of Man: An Introduction*. New York: Appleton Century.

———. 1943. "Nativistic movements." *American Anthropologist* 45: 230–40.

Lowie, Robert H. 1916. *Plains Indian Age-Societies: Historical and Comparative Summary*. Anthropological Papers of the American Museum of Natural History, vol. 11, part 13.

———. 1920. *Primitive Society*. New York: Boni and Liveright.

———. 1921. *Sun Dance of the Shoshoni, Ute, and Hidatsa*. Anthropological Papers of the American Museum of Natural History, vol. 16, part 5.

———. 1924. *Notes on Shoshonean Ethnography*. Anthropological Papers of the American Museum of Natural History, vol. 20, part 3.

Opler, Marvin K. 1941. "The Integration of the Sun Dance in Ute Religion." *American Anthropologist* 43: 550–72.

Park, W. Z. 1938. *Shamanism in Western North America*. Northwestern Studies in the Social Sciences, no. 2.

Radin, Paul. 1914. "A Sketch of the Peyote Cult of the Winnebago: A Study in Borrowing." *Journal of Religious Psychology* 3:1–22.

Shimkin, Demitri B. 1953. *The Wind River Shoshone Sun Dance*. Bulletin of the Bureau of American Ethnology 151, anthropological paper 41: 397–484.

Siegel, Peter E. 1996. "An Interview with Irving Rouse." *Current Anthropology* 37: 671–88.

Skinner, Alanson. 1914. *Political and Ceremonial Organization of the Plains-Ojibway*. Anthropological Papers of the American Museum of Natural History, vol. 11, part 5, New York.

Spier, Leslie. 1917. "An Outline for a Chronology of Zuñi Ruins," in *Anthropological Papers of the American Museum of Natural History*, vol. 18, pp. 207–332.

———. 1921. "The Sun Dance of the Plains Indians: Its Development and Diffusion." *Anthropological Papers of the American Museum of Natural History*, vol. 16, part 7.

———. 1929. "Problems Arising from the Cultural Position of the Havasupai." *American Anthropologist* 31: 213–22.

———. 1936. *Cultural Relations of the Gila River and Lower Colorado Tribes*. Yale Publications in Anthropology, no. 3, New Haven.

Strong, William D. 1940. *The Northern Great Plains*. Smithsonian Miscellaneous Collection, vol. 100.

Swanton, John R. 1930. "Some Neglected Data Bearing on Cheyenne, Chippewa, and Dakota History." *American Anthropologist* 32: 156–60.

Tarde, Gabriel. 1903. *The Laws of Imitation*, translated by Elsie Clews Parson. New York.

Tylor, Edward B. 1888. "On a Method of Investigating the Development of Institutions, Applied to Laws of Marriage and Descent." *Journal of the Anthropological Institute* 18: 245–72.

Vierkandt, Alfred. 1908. *Die Stetigkeit im Kulturwandel*. Leipzig.

Voget, Fred W. 1948. "Individual Motivation in the Diffusion of the Wind River Shoshone Sundance to the Crow Indians." *American Anthropologist* 50: 634–46.

———. 1950. "A Shoshone Innovator." *American Anthropologist* 52: 53–63.

———. 1956. "The American Indian in Transition: Reformation and Accommodation." *American Anthropologist* 58: 249–63.

Wallace, Anthony F. C. 1956. "Revitalization Movements." *American Anthropologist* 58: 264–281.

Wissler, Clark. 1912. *Societies and Ceremonial Associations in the Oglala Division of the Teton-Dakota*. Anthropological Papers of the American Museum of Natural History, vol. 11, part 4, New York.

———. 1926. *The Relation of Nature to Man in Aboriginal America*. New York: Oxford University Press.

6

Interpretations of Pueblo Indian Culture by Laura Thompson, Esther Goldfrank, Dorothy Eggan, and Others

With Two Supplements:

1. Letters Received after Publication of the Article

2. A Review of Subsequent Studies of Pueblo Culture and Behavior

Introduction

Intensive research upon the same nonliterate people by a several ethnologists usually generates controversy and disagreement over the nature of fundamental institutions and cultural expressions. Things

---

Originally written in 1945 and published in 1946 as "The Interpretation of Pueblo Culture: A Question of Values." *Southwestern Journal of Anthropology*, vol. 2, pp. 361-74. Also published in the Bobbs-Merrill Reprint Series in the Social Sciences in the 1960s. The text features the language and preoccupations of anthropology and related disciplines in the 1940s. I have revised the original text stylistically, and added two Supplements, the first on comments on the paper received shortly after it was published, most of them dealing with theoretical issues, particularly epistemology. The second Supplement is similar to the one for the previous chapter on the Sun Dance: it contains an update to 1975 on published researches on Pueblo culture, and how they dealt with some of the issues I discussed in the 1946 paper. In general, I feel that the paper anticipated many criticisms of Classic era ethnological research emerging after World War II. As a matter of fact, the self-critical methodological attitude I used here is one of the marker traits of the post-Classic. The subtitle ("A Question of Values") seems to have been a shocker for the correspondents summarized in supplement 1. That value judgements and preference could influence anthropological interpretation was more or less taken for granted by everyone, but in those days you simply did not say so in public, or publish formal inquiries into the process.

which are accepted verbatim about groups reported on by single field workers are subjected to considerable scrutiny and argument when the subject is opened up to additional members of the profession.

Studies of Pueblo Indians—especially the Hopi and Zuñi—are instances of the operation of this rule. There are controversies of long-standing over the definitions and composition of lineages, clans, and phratries; certain types of marriage, particularly cross-cousin marriage, have been extensively debated; and the kinship system has furnished considerable fuel for the argument over the relationship of terminology and social features. Usually such disputes are highly technical and concern only the inner circle of specialists. In most cases they have no great significance for wider philosophical and theoretical issues in social science.

A controversy over somewhat different issues and having significance for broader problems will be discussed in this paper. In a series of publications appearing during the past few years [i.e., 1940s] two principal interpretations of the basic dynamics of Pueblo[1] society and culture have emerged. These two interpretations have appeared not so much as explicit theoretical positions, but more as implicit viewpoints within the matrix of methodological and empirical research on Pueblo communities.

As with other controversies, the respective adherents imply, if not openly claim, that their respective interpretations are more correct or fundamental. There is little or no argument over or challenging of particular facts, since in most cases the various parties work with similar or even the same data. Hence the disagreement is one of interpretation of facts rather than over contradictory sets of facts.

The two perspectives are not to be viewed as polarities in diametric opposition. As we shall find there is cooperation in research and interchange of concepts and conclusions and in many cases the differences are not clear-cut. Yet there are differences, and none of the ethnologists concerned have yet answered the following questions: Can the two interpretations be held simultaneously, or are they inherently contradictory; and, are the differences a result of choice of problem, choice of fact, or of differing values held by the respective workers?

In the background of the controversy are appraisals of Benedict's interpretation of Pueblo culture as "Apollonian." These critiques did not necessarily deny the truth of her characterization, but rather pointed out that there was another side to the story and that her method contained unacknowledged value orientations (e.g., An-che 1937). In his criticism of Benedict's analysis of Pueblo leadership; Li An-che also, for the same reasons, criticized Kroeber's analysis of Pueblo men's attitudes toward houses. In a sense this older phase of the difference in perspective goes to the heart of the problem; namely, if interpretations of the same facts differ, is this not at least in part a consequence of differing values?

The Two Viewpoints

I wish now to present, by paraphrasing, the two viewpoints. The first view: Pueblo culture and society are integrated to an unusual degree, all sectors being bound together by a consistent, harmonious set of values, which pervade and homogenize the categories of world view, ritual, art, social organization, economic activity, and social control (Thompson 1945 is an expression of this perspective; and her paper will be used as the conceptual model in most of the discussion). Humans are believed to have the ability to act freely and voluntarily in ordering their own affairs and fitting them into an harmonious universe. The outcome tends to be virtually a fulfillment of the ideal-typical nonliterate, homogeneous, "sacred" society and culture. Associated with this integrated configuration is an ideal personality type which features the virtues of gentleness, non-aggression, cooperation, modesty, tranquility, and so on.

In some publications, this ideal pattern was presented as the "real," that is, it is presented as lived up to more often than it is not (e.g., Benedict 1934, she would now [1940s] recognize other possibilities, of course). In other writings the correct estimation of the ideal patterning is acknowledged, but qualifying materials from "real" patterns are added (e.g., An-che 1937; Eggan 1943). In still others, the ideal pattern was described as an ideal without explicit information as to its "real" manifestations or its consequences in other contexts of the society and culture (e.g., Thompson 1945).

The second view: Pueblo society and culture are marked by considerable covert tension, suspicion, anxiety, hostility, fear, and ambition (see Goldfrank 1945 for a 1940s exposition). Children, despite a relatively permissive, gentle, and frictionless early training, are later coerced subtly and, from an American humanitarian viewpoint, brutally into behaving according to Pueblo norms. The ideals of free democratic election and expression are conspicuously lacking in Pueblo society, with authority in the hands of the group and chiefs, the latter formerly holding the power of life and death over his "subjects." Individual tendencies are suppressed. Witchcraft is covert, but highly developed.[2]

Like the first, this view is usually qualified in one way or another, and as I have noted, is not necessarily in conflict at all points with the first (e.g., Thompson and Joseph 1944; Goldfrank 1945; where elements of both views are represented, though not clearly presented in relation to each other). What is apparent, however, is a tendency among the workers on one side to avoid the conclusions and implications of the other. I believe, therefore, that the differences in interpretation, plus the relative avoidance by each of the views of the other, are evidence of a genuine difference in outlook and are not simply the result of conscious, objective choice of problem. I mean here that research may have been directed and influenced in part by personal-cultural tendencies which differed among the respective workers.

I want to take up first the question of values or preferences represented in the two interpretations. I acknowledge a certain amount of uncertainty and inconclusiveness of the imputations, but I also believe that an inquiry of this sort—however preliminary—will have its value in stimulating further inquiry into the meaning of cultural analysis in the larger culture of which it is a part.

The first view may be seen in a context of theory basic to much of anthropology, which lays stress upon the organic wholeness of nonliterate life in contrast to the heterogeneity and diffuseness of modern civilization. One may trace this emphasis from the earliest American ethnological writings to the various manifestations of the configurational approach, and to Redfield's formal theory of the "folk society." This general viewpoint is in part an expectable outgrowth of the anthropological preoccupation with nonliterate communities; in part traceable to certain perspectives in the culture of American social science [for additional discussion, see references to "the love affair with the folk," in Edgerton 1992; Bennett 1995].

In the latter case I refer to a general critical attitude of the social scientist toward the heterogeneity of modern life, and a fairly clear attitude toward the organic character of nonliterate life as preferable.[3] Some direct statements of this value position can be found;[4] in other cases, one must perceive it more by the frequency of the choice and emphasis on problems which deal with it (e.g., Speck 1935). In this paper, I wish to make the imputation by studying the rhetorical atmosphere. For example:

> Thus the Hopi have extended their harmonious, organic view of the universe logically and aesthetically through the world of nature and also through the world of man at both the personal and the social levels. Combining acute observation and induction with deduction and intuition, they have worked the flux of experience with its multitudinous, apparently unrelated details into a world view which is a notable achievement not only in pragmatic utility, but also in logic and aesthetics. . . . Under relentless environmental pressures the Hopi has become a specialist in the arts of logical thinking, logical living, and logical character building . . . he even grows corn with the consummate skill of the artist . . . (Thompson 1945: 552; see also Benedict 1934: 116–9; and others)

The choice of such words and phrases as "harmonious," "acute," "notable achievement," "logical," and "consummate skill" in this passage is, I think, fairly good evidence of the possibility that the author *approves* of the Hopi configuration. There is nothing to be condemned in such approval—one only asks perhaps for a more conscious recognition on the writer's part of her values, plus some thought as to their probable influences on her analyses.

As to what such influences might be, we can consider the following passage:

> Actually the Hopi Way . . . sets up ideal conditions (in terms of external and internal pressures toward a single goal) for the development of an integrated system of social control, which functions effectively with a minimum of physical coercion, by fostering its internalization within the individual in the form of a superego or conscience consistent with the social goal. (Thompson 1945: 546)

There are two things of importance here: (1) the statement that the Hopi configuration is imposed "with a minimum of physical coercion"; and (2) a generalized swallowing-down and obfuscation of the imposition of group will and authority upon the individual—"external and internal pressures," "fostering its internalization," "conscience consistent with the social goal," and so on. These can be viewed as circumlocutions of what adherents of the other approach would call "authority" and "totalitarianism."

Now my preliminary conclusion is as follows: In this first, or "organic" theory of Pueblo culture, there is an implicit value orientation toward integrated, conformist group life. At least in the case of the writer used as an example (Thompson), it appears possible that this preference-position is inarticulate and may influence her conclusions in such a way as to obscure certain features of the Hopi social system and culture.

The second, or "repression" theory of Pueblo culture stresses the very features which the "organic" viewpoint elides or ignores. In regard to "physical coercion," Goldfrank emphasizes the severe physical and mental tortures of Hopi child initiation and socialization (Goldfrank 1945: 525–32; see also Eggan 1943: 360, 369–70; An-che 1937: 69–72), including descriptions of the horror and rigor of these rites. To these are added a multitude of subtle techniques for coercing the child into the norms. Whereas Thompson views Hopi participation in work as an example of "harmonious" and spontaneous cooperative attitudes toward fulfillment of the universal plan of Nature (Thompson 1945: 541, 546), Goldfrank states,

> Large-scale cooperation deriving primarily from the needs of irrigation is therefore vitally important to the life and well-being of the Pueblo community. It is no spontaneous expression of goodwill or sociability. What may seem "voluntary" to some is the end of a long process of conditioning, often persuasive, but frequently harsh, that commences in infancy and continues throughout adulthood. (Goldfrank 1945: 519; see also An-che 1937: 69–72; Dennis 1940)

It is possible that the two views we are examining are not necessarily contradictory, but simply emphasize different aspects of Pueblo culture. However, the situation is made more complex by the fact that not only is there a difference in emphasis, but that certain value orientations seem to have intruded which influence the respective arguments in different directions. Thus, one cannot really know for sure what the selections of particular social facts to characterize "Pueblo culture" are based on.

While the "organic" approach tends to show a preference for homogeneous nonliterate culture, the "repressed" theory has a fairly clear bias in the direction of egalitarian democracy and spontaneous or non-neurotic behavior. There tends to be a rejection of the hyperpersonalized, inverted, "thick" atmosphere of the small, homogeneous society, in favor of the greater individuation and accessibility of urban life. The preference is not nearly as evident as the other orientation—at least it is not so in the published literature. But observe this conclusion from Goldfrank's paper:

> It is, then, the "deeply disciplined" man, both at Hopi and at Zuñi, who is so desired and so necessary to the proper function of the community. Emotional restraint, reserve, avoidance, or the need to reject is the price he pays for achieving his society's social ideal. (1945: 535)

Note the phrase, "the price he pays"—in other words, to become an ideal Hopi a man must repress his spontaneity, originality, enthusiasm, outgoingness, individualism, and so on, and become neurotic.[5] Clearly this is not a desirable situation in the eyes of the libertarian American anthropologist, who may have had his or her experience with our own forms of coercion and who may be in process of rebellion against them.

I think something of this sort lay beneath Li An-che's observation of Bunzel's (1932) remark to the effect that Zuñi prayer is "not a spontaneous outpouring of the heart. It is rather the repetition of a fixed formula" (An-che 1937: 64). Li comments, "why . . . should 'spontaneous outpouring' . . . be . . . antithetical . . . to 'repetition'?" In Bunzel's case I think there may have been a tendency to follow a typical American value pattern which approves spontaneity, sincerity, originality and condemns rote repetitions as insincere, shallow, etc. But as Li points out, from a scientific standpoint it was not a question of the *form of prayer*, but rather the kind of cultural framework within which "feelings" take place. Bunzel unconsciously, and perhaps in a typically American-liberal way identified "feeling" with "form."

Differences between the two points of view are also evident in the question of "environmental pressures." Both sides recognize the tremendous environmental difficulties faced by the Hopi, and the "successful" adjustments made to them. Thompson emphasizes man's "positive measure of control over the universe . . . the external world of nature" (1945: 541); "nature-man balance" (1945: 548); and the fact that "under relentless environmental pressure" the Hopi have become "specialists in logic," "artists," "experts" (1945: 552), and so on.

Whether Goldfrank, Eggan, and others would grant all this I do not know, but what is apparent from their writings is an entirely different emphasis on the environmental question. Dorothy Eggan described the forbidding desert environment as productive of an attitude which I believe can be called "defeatist" (in Western culture); namely,

> Of course, these sedentary people . . . worked out a religion designed to control the unappeasable elements.[6] But even this prop became a boomerang since their be-

> liefs held no promise of virtue through suffering; rather *all* distress was equated with human failure, the consequences of "bad hearts." (Eggan 1943: 359)

Goldfrank goes even further, interpreting the religious pattern as a special response to agricultural needs; but even more significantly, the drastic Pueblo techniques for molding personality into "yielding" forms are seen as a result of the necessity to "achieve the cooperation necessary for a functioning irrigated agriculture" (Goldfrank 1945:527).

From Thompson, Joseph, and some others we get a picture of Pueblo environmental adjustment as a kind of glorious fulfillment of a unique world view, a master-plan. From Goldfrank and others, the adjustment is seen as a difficult, harsh adaptive experience, determinative of those phases of Pueblo culture and society which seem repressive and authoritarian.

By way of final illustration:

The book, *The Hopi Way*, may be used as illustration of what can be interpreted either as an ambivalence on the whole question or as merely a less definite specimen of the organic viewpoint. On the matter of tribal initiation, Thompson-Joseph cite the whipping and its severity as a flat statement of fact; then explain,

> This ceremony, in which the Mother Kachina may be interpreted from one point of view as symbolizing the mother . . . illustrates dramatically the complementary functions of the maternal and paternal kin in steering the child along the road of life. . . . And finally, through the discipliners' castigating of one another, it shows that the adult pattern of social control is not one in which one group, namely the children, terminate it, but one in which each adult individual is expected to exercise a certain amount of control over the others. (Thompson and Joseph 1944: 56)

In other words, the whipping is seen here as an incidental means to an end. There is nothing about the coercive severity of the means, yet the means are taken account of.

In a chapter on "Hopi Hostility" written by Alice Joseph, we find an account of certain hostile behavior patterns; but consider the following:

> To put it briefly, among the Hopi, not only work and spiritual activities, but even the emotional attachments to the various members of the group, father and mother included, seem to be consciously and practically under the direct, regulating influence of the society. (Thompson and Joseph 1944: 122)

This seems a curious method of avoiding a direct statement of coercion. What, one might ask, is "society" other than those individuals who insist on obedience and order? The author seems to be saying, "Yes, there is hostility, but look how well it is controlled by society." Hostility becomes a kind of regrettable psychological artifact.

The feeling of ambivalence is strengthened by the passage which follows the above:

> The child who does not submit and tries to form deeper attachments of his own choice will most likely run the risk of finding himself without response from the object of his unruly affection. Repeated disappointments of this sort will usually lead to abandonment first of the open manifestations of such emotions, then of further attempts to establish new attachments. (Thompson and Joseph 1944: 122)

This flat statement of a pattern which we might well call "cruel frustration" contrasts oddly with the almost laudatory descriptions of the "well-balanced and resilient character of the social structure . . . well integrated control system" (Thompson and Joseph 1944: 128).

In short one can find elements of both points of view scattered throughout *The Hopi Way*, and this reader must confess that he had difficulty seeing how the two can fit together. Stated flatly as they are, they simply do not mix. [That is, Thompson and Joseph make no effort of synthesizing the apparent opposites with a coherent multidimensional or multipotential theory of behavior.]

I believe it is fairly clear, therefore, that over and above the objective choice of problem and method, there is some evidence of attitudes of approach ("organic" theory) and avoidance ("repressed" theory)[7] toward Pueblo culture. In cases of mixture or ambivalence, separate components of the two viewpoints stand out in an unassimilated mixture, or that the whole complex is not presented.

The Issues

Now, precisely what are the issues at stake in regard to the interpretation of Pueblo culture?

Lacking close familiarity with Pueblo research [I visited Pueblo communities a total of five times over the years], it is very difficult for me to assess the various specimens from the standpoint of excellence of field work and general scientific operations. As far as I know, the workers on both sides of the question are careful students of culture; they hold respectable jobs, have had considerable field experience, and are accepted within the academic fraternity as active professional anthropologists.

Their work on Pueblo culture, we have every reason to believe, has been done with due respect for basic rules of scientific method for the collection of data, and it is also highly probable that the actual field data collected by all would represent a highly homogeneous mass. This homogeneity would also hold true for the broadest generalizations and interpretations—re social organization, technology, ritual forms, ideologies, and so on.

In other words, it is difficult to explain the difference in viewpoint from the standpoint of "good" and "bad" ethnology.

If, however, we attempt to appraise not the data and collection of data, but rather the suggestions as to conceptual tools for manipulation of the data, a somewhat different picture appears.

The "organic" approach can be charged with the following:

1. The sin of omission of certain important sets of data, especially those having to do with the severity and authoritarianism of Pueblo socialization processes. The "organic" point of view tends to avoid the apparent fact that the unique Pueblo homogeneity arises in a severe conflict process which is drastically suppressed, and from this standpoint I think we must award laurels to the "repressed" school for facing the reality of the situation and seeing the process as well as the end product.

2. An unconscious tendency to distort or misrepresent some facets of the Pueblo configuration. As Titiev[8] notes:

> Dr. Thompson, for instance, exhibits an unfortunate tendency to distort various items taken from the literature. A girlish pursuit game, somewhat comparable to following-the-leader, is magnified (p. 58) into a faithful portrayal of "the guidance role of the mother and the difficult and centripetal life course of the Hopi girl . . . " Moreover, in an effort to stress the cohesiveness of Hopi society, Dr. Thompson omits all but a casual reference to the split of 1906 that tore Oraibi to bits . . . etc. (Titiev 1946)

3. A tendency to make personal or subjective interpretations. The extreme configurationist approach, which the "organic" approach represents, tends to assume the validity and demonstrability of its concepts and then use them on specific sets of data in an effort to reveal the "inner meaning" of these data. Thompson does not tell us what "logico-aesthetic integration" *is*, or where it fits into a general corpus of culture theory, or why she chose it as a major conceptual tool.

Lacking the documentation of a *Balinese Character*, or the careful conceptual manipulation of a *Navaho Witchcraft*, a configurationist approach must inevitably slip into impressionism.

What I am saying here is that all things considered, one is more likely to have scientific faith in the viewpoint which tries to see the whole picture and evaluate its various parts [i.e., a generalized functionalist view]. But this is by no means the whole story. For beyond the issue of scientific completeness and validity lies a further question.

Let us assume that some of the difference in viewpoint stems from the fact that the respective authors have not published all their data or analyses of it, and that therefore if the "organic" group were to let us in on all their materials, their interpretation would not differ significantly from the other approach. Even if this were so—and I doubt it—it would be equally evident that the respective authors *choose* certain aspects of their data and conclusions for immediate publication. And further, the general controversy—if it can be called such—has been in progress for some years. Surely in this time the various differences would have been resolved if it were merely a matter of unequal publication.

The differences in viewpoint, therefore, cannot be explained entirely either on the basis of scientific goodness or badness, nor on the basis of publication differentials. Underneath both of these factors lies what I have already suggested may be a genuine difference in value orientation and outlook in the feelings about, the interpretations of, Pueblo society and culture in the light of the values in American culture brought to the scientific situation by anthropologist.

For even if the methodological defects in the current "organic" approach were corrected, this group would still place most of its emphasis upon the pervasive organic world view. There is nothing "wrong" about this—I am convinced that elements of this world view actually exist—just as I am also convinced that Pueblo society achieves a certain kind of homogeneity by repressive measures.

It is not so much a question of poor versus good anthropology, but rather a matter of the particular stress laid upon certain sets of facts—which facts could be identical for both sides—and the emphasis placed upon certain theoretical views of the materials. These, in turn, are bound up with the value question already discussed. This is really a very complex affair and the moral, if any, is that in cultural studies we can all be equally objective in the collection and ordering and interpretation of facts, but since social science is a part of our culture, research gets tangled in our attitudes toward the data. Why should Benedict, Thompson, et al., choose the organic emphasis, and why should Goldfrank, Eggan, et al. choose the repressive emphasis? This question quite transcends the fact that both groups of anthropologists may be equally reliable field workers and capable culture analysts.[9]

Inspecting the value question more closely, I think the issue can be resolved into one of means and ends. To Thompson's way of looking at things, the *end* is the most important and significant factor; the "end" in this case being the unique and rather remarkable Pueblo world view. To her this phenomenon has rare beauty and aesthetic appeal, and one receives the impression that the means of achieving this ideal really do not matter—at least she does not appear to be particularly concerned with them.

But to Goldfrank it is precisely the *means* that count—and this is her bias. She probably grants the organic, homogeneous, logico-aesthetic world view, and concerns herself almost entirely with the means for achieving this. Means, to her, are the important things; these are what the social scientist should study objectively, and compare to the *ends*—because no society ever had them one-to-one. One suspects a kind of critical realism here, which contrasts sharply with the impressionistic, evocative approach of the extreme configurationist school.[10]

Thompson and Goldfrank, then, clearly disagree over the respective values of means and ends, and this question goes beyond any issue of scientific methodology, referring ultimately to current overt and covert value conflicts in our culture at large. Scientific anthropology is thus implicated in an on-going process in our own culture, and from this level of observation, it is "non-objective" and "culturally determined."

I do not believe, therefore, that we can definitively answer the questions, Who is right? Which emphasis is preferable? Who will decide? A decision on the grounds of scientific method alone does not provide an answer as to the "why" of choice of the different value positions, and this is the more fundamental and far-reaching question. Neither is it possible to say that one side or the other is less influenced by values. Thompson seems to be more subjective and possibly less aware of the influences upon her work, but at the same time we can show that the value orientation is just as marked in Goldfrank's work, only it is different sort of value and one which happens to appeal strongly to the more literal-minded social scientist. A "repressed" approach could conceal and distort to the same degree as do some specimens of the current "organic" approach.

The answers to these various questions can only be given in tentative form. First, the *fact* of influence upon anthropological research by values and personal preferences should be recognized and extraverted. At the present time [1940s] we do not do so in sufficient degree. Secondly, as individual anthropologists we should be both more modest and more willing to think into and publish the implications and biases in our own analyses. I do not suggest an Olympian objectivity—only a serious concern with the problem. Third, we must be willing to turn to logical analysis to help decide the merits of such a case as the one reviewed in this paper.

What I mean in the last sentence is simply this: I do not believe that it is possible to decide, upon scientific grounds alone—that is, by repeated visits to Pueblo communities—whether it is more correct to emphasize organic wholeness or repression. The interpretation of Pueblo culture in these terms is a reflection of preference and value and I do not see how this can be eradicated or corrected by collecting more facts and making more interpretations. Therefore it becomes a problem for the sociologist of knowledge to deal with. He can, with greater detachment, make a reflexive analysis of the meaning of the respective interpretations in culture of which they are a part; he can seek out biases and stresses obviously not completely apparent to the researchers. There is no reason why they should be. If we were completely objective about our own writings we would never be able to write anything because we would be in a state of constant self-disagreement.

The case has something of a parallel in another major area of controversy in contemporary sociology and social anthropology: the question of whether African-Americans constitute a caste. [This was a major issue in the 1940s for both sociology and anthropology—see John Dollard 1957.] Here, as in the Pueblo case, there are conflicting viewpoints: Negroes form a caste and they do not. Both sides can present abundant documentation and "proof;" both sides betray conscious and unconscious value orientations. The matter cannot be decided entirely on the basis of whose facts are the better—for the simple reason that the controversy's major dimension is not scientific method but values.[11]

What is perhaps most interesting—and not a little amusing—is that these controversies, so plainly a matter of value and preference, endure as long as they do without some objective attempt to sit down and realistically arbitrate the matter. The Puebloists have been firing their respective interpretations back and forth for a decade, yet none have seen fit to dig into the semantic and ideological issues—at least in print. It is not, perhaps, an easy thing to do, since it requires a good deal of self-objectivity and humility. I do not pretend to be much more willing to go through that than the next fellow.

Supplement 1: Letters Received after Publication of the Article

Prologue, 1996

In the year or so following the publication of this essay, I received a number of letters from anthropologists and sociologists commenting on the issues raised, particularly the "sociology of knowledge" approach used or recommended. The paper was ahead of its time in the sense that the problems of bias and cultural determination of ethnological knowledge had not reached a point of clear articulation in the discipline. Anyway, in 1948 I worked up a follow-up piece on the contents of these letters, but was not able to have it typed formally and submitted for publication because at the time I was preparing to leave for an assignment overseas. I reproduce here the original draft virtually unchanged from the original. I have omitted some tendentious passages, changed verb tenses, and cleaned up the jargon. As usual I have also inserted a few contemporary comments in brackets. I offer it as a pioneer statement of the whole problem of reflexivity in anthropological research. The emphasis on the sociology of knowledge was the result of my close association with Kurt H. Wolff, who had just joined the staff of the Department of Sociology and Anthropology at Ohio State University. Both the paper and this commentary also feature the rhetoric of semantics and the philosophy of science popular in the late 1940s, and especially at the University of Chicago, where I had just finished my degree work.

* * *

One misapprehension which a number of my correspondents shared, and which is probably mainly my fault, is that I was mainly concerned with the question of "personal bias" in ethnological interpretation. This is true insofar as I dealt with the work of individual ethnologists. However, there is a much broader issue. The point is that all social-scientific work takes place in a sociocultural setting, and as such, one must expect that the work will reveal cultural interests, values, and the like. One can look at scientific work quite apart from the individuals who produce it, and still see it as a sociocultural manifestation. This is precisely what the sociologist of knowledge attempts to do.[12]

It is also possible to change the level of observation so as to take into account the personality of the individual scientist, and when this is done, one can expect to find personal influences in the research. My paper, however, had nothing whatever to do with this aspect of the problem. I was not particularly concerned about *who* was writing on Pueblo ethnology—only *what* had been written. It seemed to me that this "what" showed rather clearly the involvement of ethnological work in contemporary cultural trends and controversies—particularly issues of means and ends, and the problem of freedom and equality.

My correspondents were more interested in questions of personal involvement than in broader issues. Thus one writer emphasized that the chief exponents of both the "organic" and "repressed orientations were women, and this he seemed to feel was quite significant. It may be. However, one cannot easily impute a "feminine" influence in the materials studied without first investigating the social role of the female ethnologist both in the anthropological society and in the society at large [see chapter 13 for additional discussion].

What might such a role be? One can hypothesize that the woman scientist must compete in a predominantly male world, and that therefore it is necessary for her to be just so much better than the average male scientist. Then in anthropology, the woman may tend to adopt viewpoints and theories which are marked by their uniqueness and dramatic quality, which might help her to compete and to stand out from the rest. Or, one might inquire into the pre-anthropological background of female anthropologists. Is there a tendency for them to come into anthropology from fields—literature, psychology—characterized by their emphasis on insight and impression?

Gordon Willey wrote to expresses considerable interest in the personality factors which might lie at the root of the particular orientations studied in my paper. To quote his letter:

> I am anything but a psychologist, but I am inclined to wonder if the "organic" view, in this case, isn't interestingly symptomatic of the American Intellectual, particularly of the social sciences, of our time. Recruited from the middle class and the small town, he has usually spent years in conscious or unconscious revolt against their repressive mores. He becomes, or so he thinks, a "cosmopolitan," an "intellectual," a "sophisticate." Yet an ambivalent drive is there, too, for the old "thick" atmosphere of the womb-society of the small group which will protect him against the torturing complexities of modern urban life . . . .
>
> Your "repressive" (or "cynical," as some would say) point of view seems to me the outlook of the truly mature and world-wise, those who take a dim view of any "thought-control" manipulations designed to bring about a "logico-aesthetic" world view, a serene "world of eight corners," or a "Reich that will last a thousand years." Somewhere or sometime in the misery of the past they've been stung by that one before.

Willey's proposal introduces a complicating factor into the problem of determination, since it does not make the simple assumption that the organicist merely loves outright the small-group atmosphere, but may actually both love and reject it at the same time. Hence one can demonstrate sophistication by writing artistically and persuasively and at the same time indulge in sentimental attachment to the folk world.

But the hypothesis jumps with both feet into the middle of the affair. It cannot explain why the particular "organic" intellectual would leave the folk atmosphere in the first place. What sort of "drive" is operative here? *Why* would he feel a need to both reject and cling to the folk past?

Concerning Willey's second paragraph, I think it is misleading to equate the "repressive" approach with the "truly mature and world-wise." I do not think that the organicist is necessarily any less worldly-wise and mature than the repressivist. Both are really operating with references to an ideology. The attitudes differ, but whether they differ on the basis of some quality of superior wisdom or maturity is highly debatable. To adopt such a view would be to simply equate urban mass-democratic heterogeneity with some particular value concerning better wisdom and more mature experience. Urban life is a particular sociocultural environment which one has a right to prefer, but which as a scientist one must study without incorporating its characteristics as a value with which to interpret some other cultural style. As it happens there is evidence which suggests that the adherents of the "repressive" viewpoint are somewhat more careful as cultural analysts, but this is not a *necessary* situation, determined by the nature of their particular set of values. As I remark in the essay, "It is possible that a 'repressed' approach could conceal and distort to the same degree as do some specimens of the 'organic' approach."

Dorothy Eggan, in a thoughtful communication, provides some important questions on the approach of the sociology of knowledge, and in addition furnishes a kind of "interview" as suggested in my article, which outlines the motivational background of her own field work with the Hopi.

Eggan notes that the sociologist of knowledge (that is, anyone playing that role) which we call in to help us straighten out our perspectives ". . . will have *his* personal biases and culturally induced phobias . . . so that his analysis will have to be 'impersonally' analyzed, and on and on and on." This is the problem of the infinite regression in epistemological analysis. There is no pat answer; simply the one which points out that all knowledge is a process which is never realized in full; that man's knowledge of the world is always a matter of levels and approximations, containing the potentiality of being forever superseded. Theoretically, there is no limit to the number of "systems," meta-languages, meta-meta-languages, etc., with which we can describe phenomena, and which may supersede one another in "objectivity." This is not to say that any one of these systems or meta-languages is "better," only that it sees the phenomena (or knowledge) from a new perspective; that is, a perspective less-involved in the particular set of determining factors responsible for the phenomena under examination.[13]

Ideologies lie within ideologies, and the process of dissection is never at an end. The different stages of the process are meaningful in themselves; the fact of a regression does not refute the possibility for, nor the validity of, any one stage. Rather than a defect, the regression becomes a procedure. We only see it as an obstacle if we take a rationalistic "eighteenth century" point of view toward knowledge as being absolutely "right" or "wrong," or in terms of some final discovery of reality (see Wolff 1943; also endnote 13 on "imputation").

My paper, while cast on a higher level of observation than the research being analyzed since I used that research itself as data, is nevertheless on its own level presumably "determined," or "a part of" certain ongoing intellectual currents. Just what this might be is indicated later by Hugo Engelman's comments. Let us reserve the problem for the discussion of his contribution, and proceed with Eggan's observations.

Another and related point she raises is that the sociologist of knowledge is entangled in a problem of objectivity, in that he, in order to make his analysis, must select certain materials from the writings he analyzes, to use as evidence, imputation, or illustration. How can he be sure that he is not distorting and biasing the meaning of the original authors, by this process of selection? The answer is that he cannot be absolutely sure. Again, the knowledge gained by critical analysis is always a matter of approximation. It happens that in the area of scientific writing which involves "imputation" of meaning and significance in written productions we have especially acute problems of verifiability and probability stemming from cultural relativism. This is why Wolff has recommended that the sociology of knowledge requires an "empirical attitude" (research),[14] and why I suggested the need for interviews with the field workers.

There is buried in the above comments some important observations on the state of ethnology. If the sociologist of knowledge can serve ethnology at the level of value-analysis, it implies perhaps that there is something in contemporary ethnology which might be distinguished from strictly objective science. What might this be? It suggests to me that the attitude of *virtuosity* has characterized ethnology for a long time, and is a the root of much of the type of thinking examined in my previous article. This attitude involves a belief that ethnological field work is an art; that it is done differently by different workers, who become virtuosos and artists with the particular subject matter of their "tribe." It is true that much good ethnology has been done with this point of view, but the excellence of this work is not so much in the scientific direction as it is in the direction of free, aesthetic-intellectual originality [1996: a prophetic statement?]. With the ethnologist becoming a virtuoso, whose work cannot be challenged not only because no one else has been there, but also because he *is* a virtuoso and is not to be questioned, one might expect an important valuational element in his work. He observes the culture *through* his personalized attitudes (which are themselves likely to be a part of a subculture also) rather than *around* them. We do not object to this approach; only insist that it be distinguished from an approach which utilizes procedures based more closely upon empirical or "objective" science. We also request that the former approach accept its susceptibility to critiques of its "determination" by personal-cultural factors at a lower level than the level of empirical science.

As Dorothy Eggan also suggests, a trend toward collaborative and cooperative research in the social sciences and ethnology may eliminate virtuosity and correspondingly reduce the more obvious ideological features in ethnological interrelations. The "outstanding personality" is less likely to dominate the field and color the results; the interaction between the workers is on an intellectual level and the "tribe" is seen as a scientific problem demanding the formulation of hypotheses instead of mystic penetration into obscure and devious psychology. Personal biases are checked and rechecked, divergent opinions and ideologies come out in discussion, and the group may provide its own epistemological therapy. At least, such trends are possible with collaborative research, whereas they are not so to nearly the same extent in isolated research [1996: well—it is true that the Age of the Virtuoso is part—but whether the issues of bias have been met is another question]. It is probably also true that research of the cooperative type will, as time goes on, lead in the experimental direction and away from the highly interpretive-intellectual direction [1996: not-so-prophetic prediction!]. There is nothing culture-and-personality study needs half so much as the careful formulation of hypotheses, the performing of a few experiments in the field to test these hypotheses, and the measure of the phenomena the ethnologist so blithely assumes exists [see chapter 9 for further discussion].

There could be cause for regret at such developments, if one takes a predominantly romantic view of anthropological work. An important ideological element in anthropology stems from our field's association in the nineteenth century with German idealist philosophy and romanticized brands of Darwinism. "Primitive man" was viewed as new and unspoiled, and research on him took the form of "expeditions," a highly romantic form of travel deeply involved in "exploration," "penetration into the wilderness," "knowing Nature's true meaning," and the like. Such exploratory work was difficult and it took intrepid individuals to carry it out. Hence the Rivers, Malinowskis, and Cushings became virtuosos, "outstanding personalities": eccentric, didactic, colorful rovers whose word was law when it came to their "tribe." (I am not making light of their contributions—only trying to characterize the ideological atmosphere.) Much of this atmosphere clings to anthropology today [1948], and many of its bearers are living and active [1996: still true?].

Romantic currents not only manifested themselves in individuals but also more systematically in whole schools. Ruth Benedict, in *Patterns of Culture*, explicitly acknowledged the influence of Dilthey, whose works are probably the apotheosis of German romantic philosophy carried into social theory. The development of the *ethos* wing of modern functional-patternist anthropology [that is, the "late Classic"] has retained these strong romantic features, in the desire to "know" the innermost core of meaning, the pervading spirit of the group. Although the goals are usually cast in scientific language, they are fundamentally akin to such romantics as Wordsworth, who, in Alfred North Whitehead's phrase, was haunted by the "brooding presence" of Nature, who "*always grasps the whole of nature as involved in the tonality of the particular instance*" (Whitehead 1925: 121). A more concise description of the goals of ethos anthropology than the last quoted sentence could hardly be written. Merely substitute "culture" for "nature."

Eggan provides me with some valuable information upon another problem which I deliberately glossed over in my article, since it demands separate treatment. This is the problem of "neurotic behavior" as a classificatory device for describing Pueblo (and any other non-Western society) personality. She remarks that although she did not use the term herself in her paper (Eggan 1943), she has been quoted again and again as believing that the Hopi are neurotic. In part this was due to her use of the word "maladjustment," which she now feels was a mistake. She was really trying to say,

> that normal children adjust to their society's dictates, that most of us do not enjoy this adjustment and therefore use culturally allowed vents to relieve our frustration, that the Hopi do adjust to their cultural and environmental dictates and I suggested that one of their vents was gossip . . .

This type of behavior is no more "neurotic" than the behavior of an average individual in any society. Presumably because the Hopi do it, it becomes immediately suspect of strangeness and neuroticism. This introduces an ideological angle complementary to the types I distinguished: the "organic" and the "repressive," based on certain preferences for desirable ways of life. A third would be the case above, where for ideological reasons *all* "primitive" cultures are suspected of neurosis and abnormality. There is a trace of this theme in the Freudian and neo-Freudian approaches to nonliterate cultural analysis.

The preoccupation with clinical definitions created confusion in culture-and-personality ethnology, and it is time that the tendency be exposed. The clinic, with its interest in therapy and its concepts of normality has no place in a scientific analysis of behavior in a culture other than our own. Culturally bound concepts like neurosis merely introduce biases into the analysis. On the other hand, one can count on the fingers of one hand the monographs which have seriously tried to answer such questions as: From the *standpoint of the culture under examination*, what classifications of behavior can be made? What typical kinds of frustration are found in this society, and how do the people meet them? What attitudes are held toward homogeneity or heterogeneity of behavior, and how do these attitudes affect individuals who manifest that behavior? These may be difficult questions to answer, but no short cut can be found via the tortuous maze of "normality," "neurosis," and the like. Inevitably this route leads to the attempt to give scientific support to a particular concept of normality—an ambiguous procedure which may have its uses in political action (e.g., the AAA "Statement on Human Rights," *American Anthropologist* 1947), but is simply confusing intrascientifically (for a consideration of the problem see Green 1946, 1948).

A final comment from Eggan's paper before we go on to another correspondent:

> You are right about me at least, when you suggest that one may "like" a culture so well that one feels forced to struggle to be frank and objective, however well one may or may not succeed in it. The appeal of the country is very strong as is also the appeal of a culture where the "way" is so rigidly decided for the individual by the group. Who among us is not weary of the necessity to decide among the many "ways" available in our culture! But in the field or out I am always aware of this pull and when I am inclined to "envy Hopi peace" ("General Problem of Hopi Adjustment," p. 358) I am even more aware that all cultures have their stresses and I doubt deeply that *any* affords "psychic serenity." It is hard for me to believe that most people who have been inoculated with anthropology can fall very far into that trap. It is far easier for me to believe that our unconscious traps us many other ways when we present our material: approval of fellow workers, finding field data to bolster up preconceived theories, and just plain inability to see things in our data which are antithetical to our own personalities, are a few of them. . . . Yes, research gets tangled up with values as does our interpretation of events and people.

I am gratified to find corroboration of some of my guesses and imputations. However, I do not quite agree with Eggan that an "inoculation" with anthropology will eliminate these ideological factors. It may eliminate them on the level of "cultural bias," but as I have pointed out, there are various levels or contexts of ideological involvement in scholarly activity. One may see culture-pattern research as determined by the romantic tradition, and at the same time one can grant the objectivity of this research *within its own level.* Then there is the context of choice of problem. As I pointed out in the paper, a cultural interpretation may be quite objective, but the very choice of *emphasis*, which cannot be decided scientifically, comes from a particular set of preferences.

As for the other traps which Mrs. Eggan cites, I quite agree that all of these are operative. They provide us with another dimension of the social setting of science: the determination of written productions by status and prestige in the case of the individual scientist. The previous remarks on the "virtuoso" tradition are pertinent here. To discover this dimension of "social determination" (as contrasted to "ideological"), one would have to interview ethnologists.

Well, Sociologist Hugo Engelman wrote to say that I got involved in a contradictory and regressive situation when I assumed—as I seem to do in the paper—that sociocultural determination is entirely a matter of values. In order to make the kind of analysis that I did, It would not be possible to hold to the point of view that everything is value-determined, since that would make my analysis merely the expression of another value. But I attempted to transcend the ideological system and make a scientific or scholarly analysis. Engelman felt that social science is determined socioculturally on the highest level of complexity: the level of change from one system to another—since social science points out and analyzes on-going change. Now, value-determination is *intra*-systemic—inside a cultural system, and not involved in articulating on-going change from one system to another.

Further, according to Engelman, any language of analysis which uses motivational psychology (purposes, needs, drives, etc.) is value-determined, and therefore an ideology. Thus all motivational analyses are subject to ideological variation; there can be no consensus because of the value-determination. The number and kinds of motive are endless, and depend in part or whole upon one's ideology. The two viewpoints on Pueblo culture analyzed in my paper used motivational psychology, in that they conceived of society and culture as having purposes, needs, etc. However, they differed in their ideologies respecting the nature of these purposes and needs. Engelman would therefore class them as ideologies and not scientific theories. Engelman's points, while penetrating, are based on a highly schematized philosophical system and this commits him to rather rigid definitions.

What Engelman is doing is to attempt to escape from the regression-relativist difficulty discussed earlier. His solution to the problem has much in common with the second solution in endnote no. 14: The development of a new language of analysis which is not bound to the terms of the materials being analyzed. I suggested the use of a theoretical psychology or a "sociology of knowledge." Engelman suggests the substitution of "truly scientific for ideological concepts." While I agree that perhaps such a solution is ultimately desirable, it is an ambiguous task. Also, this criticism does not mar the particular contribution of my paper: the demonstration of ideological components in some ethnological research. I may have fallen into the trap of regression-relativism by implying that the "theories" analyzed were "value-determined," but I *did* show the possibility of these "theories" having ideological components. This part of my analysis stands.[15]

Dorothy Lee wrote me that [endnote 8; footnote 34, p. 370, in the original article] I indulge in the same sort of activity as did the targets of my criticism. She says,

> Did you analyze your own writing in the article? In the footnote . . . you speak of the terrifying and bewildering experiences, the terrifying noises. Whom do they terrify, horrify, and bewilder? And "the effect . . . can be imagined"—can it, really? My experience with other cultures has been that they always outrun my imagination.

She has me there. My phraseology most certainly betrays an unconscious desire to prove my point, plus the assumption that certain kinds of experiences have the same effects on members of other cultures as they do on ourselves. I would defend myself by saying that there is fair evidence to the effect that Pueblo initiation actually does have these consequences and will produce these emotional responses, although I should have put it that way instead of using "imagination." Anyway, the criticism bears out my remark [on p. 372, in the original 1946 article] concerning the fact that we can never be completely objective about our own writing. This, in turn, casts some doubt on the validity of Engelman's rather optimistic view that a "truly" scientific approach can be attained. Is not it always a question of limits, of incomplete realization?

A very good and very much down-to-earth ethnologist [whose name seems to have vanished from the manuscript: 1995] was content with commenting briefly and possibly with covert disgust that the "organic" people were all those who have never done long-term intensive resident study of Pueblo culture, thus implying that their particular viewpoint was merely the result of short-term study. Possibly, but I do not think that the whole matter can be so easily dismissed. If we see scientific activity as implicated in ongoing social and cultural patterns—whether we view this as value-determined or on a higher level, or both—we could not be satisfied with an explanation of these differences which sees them as the result of the amount of time spent in the field. The time factor could have consequences, but that still leaves the problem of why the *particular* interpretations were made. The time element does not explain the choice of particular value-orientations.

By way of conclusion, let us speculate on just what implications the case of Pueblo culture might hold for our knowledge of human behavior in general. Dorothy Eggan suggests the most important implication in her comment, " . . . *all* cultures have their stresses and I doubt deeply that *any* affords "psychic serenity." Instead of seeing "organic holism" or "repression" as single themes, making our choice according to our preference for a way of life, perhaps as scientists we might simply see that Pueblo culture offers an example of the fact that human adjustment is a difficult and complicated affair, and that punishment and reward, hostility and love, serenity and chaos, competition and cooperation, are inherent in every social system. Human behavior offers us a very broad and complex assortment of tendencies, which make the problem of adjustment difficult since the environment, in an animal with complex behavior, becomes correspondingly more complex. There is, in fact, no royal road, no utopian solution to the problems of social life; but neither is the outlook completely pessimistic. The Pueblo show us that considerable social order can be achieved through the strong channelization of behavior, and in the presence of a small population, but they also show us that this is achieved with the aid of a system of outlets for behavioral tendencies which are short-circuited in the process. All societies have similar structures; the differences appear in the particular behavioral tendencies selected for enlargement and diminution. If we wish to choose one structure over another, we have every right to do so; but as scientists let us attempt to make clear the grounds for the choice.

Supplement 2: A Review of Subsequent Studies of Pueblo Culture and Behavior

Prologue, 1996

In 1974 I enlisted the aid of a graduate seminar to help me analyze publications appearing subsequent to the publication of my 1946 paper. I was interested in seeing to what extent my arguments about value determination, etc., might have influenced subsequent writings. The following material was prepared from my class notes on the discussion and working papers, and written in 1975 but not previously published. I am especially indebted to Linda Barnes and Jill Brody, members of the seminar, for their insightful comments and analyses.

* * *

Interpreting Pueblo Culture (1975)

The exercise made it clear that the history of interpretations of Pueblo Indian cultural behavior had properties similar to those for the Sun Dance: changing emphases and topics in ethnology and cultural anthropology were mirrored in the literature. Studies of Pueblo Indians to date were reviewed by Edward Dozier in 1964 who noted that the original focus was depictive ethnography and a strong interest in historical origins; relations with nomadic Southwestern groups like the Navaho; and Pueblo kinship patterns. In the mid-1930s, under the influence of Benedict's *Patterns of Culture* interest developed in cultural and psychological themes. However, this changed toward acculturation and ecological problems by the 1970s. Functional analyses were not as prominent as in the case of the Sun Dance, since the emphases were on behavioral and valuational issues.

Now, my paper was not concerned with tracing this history and development of anthropological theory, but rather with an epistemological problem: how different understandings and interpretations of Pueblo behavior and culture might be explained by different values held by the ethnologists studying the communities. The two contrasting interpretations—"organic" and "repressive" were traced to the long tradition of idealization of tribal and "folk" societies; and to theories of neurosis and psychopathology in Western civilization. Certainly the literature examined on the whole bore out such conclusions, but although I do mention the issue, insufficient attention was given to the fact that the ethnographers on both sides sometimes acknowledged data which might argue against their own position. For example, Esther Goldfrank (1945) and Dorothy Eggan both noted the high degree of integration and consensus in Pueblo society, and on the other hand, Laura Thompson and Ruth Benedict both did comment on the whippings associated with certain Kachina ceremonials. A balanced interpretation of Pueblo society would recognize the obvious: that both "organic" and "repressive" elements existed in it, just as they do in all human societies. In the last analysis, the whole business of Pueblo cultural interpretations is really an example of the way preconceived concepts and theories might distort or constrain ethnographic interpretations. But as I suggested, the *choices* of particular concepts and theories might well be dictated by personal values.

In 1954 E. A. Hoebel in a review of theoretical contributions of Southwestern Indian studies, seemed to agree with my general argument, noting that the same ethnographic data could be interpreted differently. He believed that the organic-repressive confrontation might never have arisen without the stimulus of Ruth Benedict's portrait of the Pueblo as "Apollonian." Benedict insisted that one or two psychological factors could serve as organizing foci for whole-culture patterning. She did not note that this habit of characterizing human groups other than one's own on the basis of simplistic symbols or values is as old as the human species (e.g., see Harris 1968, who cites examples and criticizes the Benedictian patternist approach). Moreover, the source of the particular behavior—"Apollonian" in this case—is attributed to psychological elements, without sufficient regard for the social and physical environment in which the group may reside. In the Pueblo case, explanations of certain "Apollonian" traits like group-orientation and equanimity can be found in the small size of the communities, and the hard work required to live an agricultural existence in the middle of a desert. But this kind of social ecology also provides a fertile soil for the repressive, hostile elements noted by other ethnographers. [See chapter 13 for additional comments on Benedict.]

Now, our seminar group tried to find out what sources other than "values," or particular theoretical models or traditions might have been found. The search focussed first on the work of Laura Thompson, since among the various interpreters after Benedict her rendition of

Pueblo cultural behavior seemed the most extreme. In her several writings, she went overboard in her admiration for "wholeness" and "integration." We noted that much of her research had been sponsored by the Indian Education Research Project and was explicitly designed to diagnose the "Basic Personality Structure" of the Hopi [Kardiner 1956, see chapter 9]. This was another of those attempts to find an inner, unvarying core value-ethos-eidos-configuration or whatever—in the life of a designated group or society. The project used a series of psychological tests which contained an orientation toward integration or balance: for instance, it was assumed that the cradle-boards used in Pueblo child rearing would accustom the child to restrictions, and thus enhance feelings of security (e.g., Thompson and Joseph 1944: 51). And the Kachinas, although their stylized violent behavior was noted, were interpreted as a force contributing to restraint of behavior since the gods would punish. And so on. The conclusion of the 1944 study for the Project emphasized the high levels of conformity, etc. produced by Pueblo child rearing methods. In other words, Thompson's exaggerated respect for Hopi (Pueblo) inner order and integration was—at least to some extent—an artifact of the methods used in the key research project.

In any event, by the 1950s Thompson, perhaps as a result of my paper and related writings of others, had begun to soften her interpretations. In her 1950 book on the Hopi, with its significant title, *Culture in Crisis*, she acknowledged "errors and omissions" (1950: viii), but that they "will not affect substantially the primary thesis." And that they did not: the book continued to underline stability and conformity in Pueblo behavior.

Esther Goldfrank in her 1945 paper presented a dual image: she viewed the cradle-board issue, for example, in terms similar to Thompson and Joseph—but on the other hand, she recognized that the induced fear of the kachinas might encourage the child to accuse relatives and neighbors of witchcraft as a result of the disillusionment suffered when parents let the child know that the kachinas were these same people dressed up in funny costumes. On the whole, as I said in my paper, Goldfrank saw the Hopi in the rather dour terms. However, by 1948 she seemed to place more emphasis on peace and tranquility (Goldfrank 1948: 254)—another case of the combined image which became increasingly common as work on the Pueblos continued.

Florence Hawley Ellis, in a 1951 paper, returned to the theme of interpersonal aggression. The repression others had noted she attributed to extreme punitive measures the children were subjected to, and the tolerance on the part of parents of violent behavior among siblings, etc. She concluded that "The 'peaceful' pueblos became the more peaceful through socially channelizing and making use of the urge toward aggression" (Ellis 1951: 201). The argument in some sense combines the two perspectives: yes, there is a seamy side, but it produces peaceful results.

In 1956 Dorothy Eggan, still concerned about my arguments, reviewed her data and that of others with particular reference to fear. In effect she asked what functions or uses fear might have in the adult society. Her answers were expectable: it could be used to promote learning in childhood and it could be used to promote social and individual behavioral control. Hardly an unusual finding—no society on earth lacks such mechanisms in some form or other. In Eggan's, and in other writings of the period, it is beginning to appear as if the social behavior of tribal peoples is basically similar the world over, especially in these small populations and demographically dense communities;—or for that matter, in pockets in all societies of any size.

On the whole, Eggan's writings on the Pueblo cultural behavior problem were carefully thought through, and presented an attempt to avoid bias and simplistic theory. Her views had a functional or adaptational cast insofar as she presented the Hopi as people who survive under considerable stress and who require a carefully adjusted social system in order to keep going. For example, she analyzed gossip as a necessary device to keep the community in order, but at the evident cost of anxiety and cruelty to individuals (Eggan 1956: 364). The bitter with the better. The change from Eggan's 1943 piece to her 1956 article mirrors the intellectual progress of [Classic] cultural anthropology from simplistic psychological analysis to a more sophisticated, well-rounded functional social psychology which takes into account both the emotional problems of the individual and the group problems of order and survival.

The earlier position—*early* "culture and personality" anthropology—believed that by examining methods of infant and child rearing one could anticipate or predict adult behavior and cultural patterns. By the mid-1980s, this had begun to change toward greater respect for the adult behavioral world as a phenomenon with its own constraints and demands for adaptation, not necessarily based on childhood experience.

Reverting once more to the earlier, culture-and-personality context period of interpretation, there was R. Brandt's book, *Hopi Ethics* (1954), one of the contributions of the Harvard Values Project. Brandt used tests (in the mood of the period), in particular, the Psychological Contemporary Context Theory (PCCT), administered to a sample of adults and young people in a effort to show that people living like the Hopi would develop the kind of ethical norms and attitudes typical of the culture, as revealed by ethnographic studies. The theory of the study was based on the proposition of psychic determinism; that is, that the "culture" of any group (at least, a presumably integrated, socially continuous group) is equivalent to the statements the members give on a set of questions designed to elicit responses to critical and standardized life situations and interpersonal experiences (another version, perhaps, of Kardiner's thesis of the interpenetration of personality and culture—see chapter 9). But the responses to the PCCT did not stand alone; Brandt also used available "theorems" to explain the tabulated results: one relating to "rewards" and the other concerning "utility." The meaning of the first is obvious: a person will acquire or manifest a particular ethical-moral attitude or value if his use of it in behavior is rewarding. The "utility" theorem seems to be a negative corollary of the reward concept, insofar as Brandt believed that if individual Hopi had an unfavorable attitude toward certain acts and experience it was because their experience with the attitude and its correlated behavior was unfavorable. Brandt used the idea to explain Hopi attitudes toward hunger, rainfall, social dissension, and violence.

Brandt's methodological apparatus seemed both too complex and also too simple for explaining attitudes toward the obvious hardships and predictable problems of Hopi existence. But the critical mood created in reaction to simplistic culture-and-personality interpretations required "proof" of such inquiries into cultural behavior. In any case, Brandt's analysis did accept, without question, the dual or combined nature of Hopi culture: its harmony and conformity and its hostile tension and repressed frustrations. The duality approach was also evident in Alexander Leighton and John Adair's 1966 contribution to the Indian Education Project. They acknowledged the conformity, harmony, and cooperative elements in Pueblo (in this case, the Zuñi) life, but also, the "Dionysian" elements, including shame, gossip, witchcraft, and the like. Their principal critique concerned Benedict's portrait of Pueblo life as "Apollonian," which they felt was not necessarily wrong, but rather the result of the fact she was working with old data; that is, she gave a picture of Pueblo culture prior to extensive social change and acculturation. Leighton and Adair proposed that the "Dionysian" elements in the culture had been there all along, but were dominated or suppressed by the "Apollonian." In the acculturative situation, intensifying after Benedict's information had been collected, the "Dionysian" side of the culture emerged. The thesis is imaginative, and introduces the factor of change and response to external pressures, but on the whole seems somewhat forced or too neat. The approach continued to use static, literary concepts and ideal types, even though it did include an attempt to render them in behavioral and dynamic terms.

Work on Pueblo acculturation accelerated through the 1950s and into the 1960s. The tendency seen in the Leighton-Adair approach tended to dominate: that is, to attempt to account for the duality of the cultural behavior in terms of change and culture contact. That is, writers kept seeing both the "organic" and "repressive" elements in the culture—or more precisely, since the early 1930–1940s research tended to confirm the existence of these entities, it was incumbent on the later workers to account for them. The whole affair was not simply an example of the persistence of scholarly ideas, but was based on the peculiar situation of the Pueblos: societies who managed to resist incursions by outsiders and who clung to their traditional lifeways. This presented a distinctive problem for anthropologists, who felt required to explain why these people were so resistive to cultural change.

In the various acculturation-oriented studies, which became a dominant form after the mid-1950s, attention was paid to phenomena like the following: the role of ceremonial cycles as an integrative force; the fact that crucial aspects of Spanish culture were, in the first round of contact, similar to Pueblo patterns, and were incorporated into the system rather than resisted; the geographical remoteness of the Pueblos in the Southwestern desert, where American settlement was sparse and fleeting—until the 1950s, when serious cultural change began; and, of course, the Pueblo sociocultural system itself, having weathered the storms of change, had become evermore successful in resisting additional episodes. Two of the more insightful treatments of cultural conservatism in the Pueblos were Edward Dozier's and Edward Spicer's writings of the mid-1950s. Both workers viewed the conservatism process as one of "compartmentalization": which seems to mean that the Pueblo (like the Japanese or the Hutterites) had a sufficiently strong native tradition and social system (or isolation!) so that they could accept what traits from external sources they felt were compatible, and reject those they felt were hostile (e.g., Spicer 1954: 665). However, when the Pueblo communities were forced to accept foreign elements by punitive means (military in the case of the Spanish and administrative in the case of the Americans) they responded by adopting the traits but keeping them outside of the traditional cultural corpus. Dozier noted,

> These Pueblos accommodated by outwardly appearing to have accepted the imposed cultural patterns, but they continued to practice their own indigenous religion and customs behind closed doors . . . .(1964: 90)

However, some differences in the nature and degree of the resistive devices was noted among the various communities: Hopi and Zuñi were viewed as more resistive, due to their high degree of integration, while the eastern Pueblo communities, historically and geographically more accessible to both the Spanish and the Americans, were typical "compartmentalizing" societies.

J. Bodine in 1972 used quantitative methods in his acculturation research, in which he distinguished between various segments of the populations of the communities: resident, nonresident, degree of isolation, ceremonialism, and demographic nucleation. In other words, he came to see the Pueblo culture as entering a phase of differentiation due to the progressive impact and penetration of American ways, as the Southwest became increasingly settled. In 1971, J. Levy and S. Kunitz ended the reliance on the duality thesis of Pueblo culture, and pointed out that many of the previous researchers:

> tended to deny that tribal societies generated their own tensions, and consequently, their own social deviance. The first conceives of aboriginal society as free from social deviance until the coming of the White Man after which time social disintegration fostered higher levels of deviance among Indians than among Whites because traditional Indian cultures had not developed the institutions or the cultural concepts necessary to control deviant behavior. . . . (Levy and Kunitz 1971: 119)

In other words, the earlier conventional interpretations of change in Pueblo culture relied on external forces from "White" society, not recognizing that Pueblo social systems could themselves have been the source of conflict and deviance. In other words, the "organic" viewpoint would in this analysis be redefined as the "traditional culture" concept, and the "repressive" concept as behavior produced by foreign incursions. Levy and Kunitz, then, appear to prefer to see Pueblo society as a complex, self-generating system, with its own characteristics of inconsistency and contradiction.

Thus, as time passed, following the researches I used in my characterization of views of Pueblo cultural behavior in the 1940s, subsequent work by ethnologists suggests avoidance of preconceived explanations and value judgements, and a more eclectic and multidimensional view of Pueblo cultural behavior. Or, more generally, a growing understanding of the basic similarities and contradictory aspects of all human societies.

Notes

1. The literature actually covers only Hopi and Zuñi, but there are indications that the issues are relevant for the Eastern Pueblos also. I will not attempt to discriminate between Hopi and Zuñi, since the similarities are sufficient to permit generalizations at the level of this paper. I wish to disavow any implication that I am setting myself up as a Pueblo expert, since I am merely examining published materials from the standpoint of logical analysis. My actual acquaintance with the Pueblo Indians [in 1948] consists of three dance ceremonies at Hopi villages and two hours in Zuñi.
2. Titiev states that witchcraft lies at the bottom of much of what appears to be Apollonian behavior among the Hopi. Hopi men do not like to assume chieftainship for a particular ceremony which has been dropped from the calendar because "the Hopi believe that a forward or aggressive person is a witch" (1944: 106). See also Titiev 1942.
3. The emphasis also appears in the field of sociology, where a great many concepts like "social disorganization," "community," "social control," and so on have a basis in quasi-idealizations of rural society and culture.
4. E.g., Sapir 1924. See Tumin (1945) for an analysis of the value-orientation of Sapir's paper and the general problem it presents for cultural analysis. In a more general way, there is a large hint of the idea in the current stereotype of nonliterate cultures as "simpler" than modern civilizations and therefore so much easier to study and learn from. In the case of Southwestern ethnology, these tendencies may often assume a special form conditioned by the pervading sense of mystery and glamour of the country itself. A good deal of ethnology and archaeology in the Southwest has been done with a kind of eager reverence for turquoise, concho belts, Snake Dances, and distant desert vistas, and while this need not materially distort the scientific conclusions, it provides the worker with a favorable attitude toward whatever he may work with. This attitude is, I think, particularly noticeable in the Thompson (1945) paper cited frequently in this essay.
5. A parallel view is expressed by John Collier in his foreword to the Thompson-Joseph volume (*The Hopi Way*):

   The Hopi, thus making inner form and inner power of the limitations of their

> nature world, similarly have internalized their social limitations. The limitations are extremely severe. The Hopi have achieved peace, and not through policing but through the disciplines and the affirmations planted within each of their several souls. The achievement has been maintained across millennia and is maintained now. And the Hopi pay for their peace, severe payments. (Thompson and Joseph 1944: 9)

This statement illustrates in some respects the ambivalent viewpoint of the whole Thompson-Josephs volume—the goal, "peace," is exalted along with the worldview, but the price of this achievement is hinted as being a high one.

6. To Thompson, this is a feature of not very great importance in Pueblo religion. The fact that ritual "reaffirms symbolically the Hopi world view" (1945: 549), she appears to feel is of greater significance.
7. I am not so sure of this. It is quite possible that the adherents of the "repressed" approach are rejecting those features of Pueblo culture they emphasize simply because they like the rest of the culture so well that they wish to be "frank" and "objective" about the whole. To decide such questions one would need to interview the various anthropologists on both sides.
8. The failure to tell the whole story, and to avoid or distort certain features of it, is best represented in the initiations situation. A study of any of the various accounts of Hopi initiation ceremonies leaves no doubt of the traumatic effect they must have upon the domination and "rigid discipline" (Titiev 1944: 139) of elders, supernatural beings, and ghosts, who subject them to bewildering and terrifying experiences. On the night of the Kwan ceremony the entire village is shut off from the outer world, and the spirits of the dead, along with bands of Kwan and Horn men, race through the streets with horrifying noises. The effect of this "night of mystery and terror" (ibid.: 135) on the boys can be imagined—because of them everyone in the village becomes involved in this incredible and dangerous business. All of what happens in the kivas is not yet known but Titiev's remarks clearly indicate the strenuous psychological shock involved, with or without physical injury:

   > What befalls the initiates in the presence of this weird assembly of living Hopi, visibly "dead," and unseen spirits, no white man can tell with assurance; but from the general context I think we may reasonably conjecture that in some manner the novices are ceremonially "killed" . . . (ibid:. 136).

9. In a sense, this problem is part of the wider problem of "objective" as *versus* "cultural" approach in social scientific studies (cf. Wolff 1945). The chief characteristics of the latter as contrasted to the former are: an attempt at explicit, conscious recognition of the fact that all cultural studies proceed *through* rather than *around* the biases, values, and choices of subject of the researcher; and that scientific method is not a goal in itself but rather a technical problem. The approaches are by no means easy to distinguish; however, at the moment of writing [1946] I do feel that the "cultural" approach, being more willing to recognize the social matrix of scientific investigation, is thus more liable, other things being equal, to have somewhat more insight into questions of value. The "other things being equal" is important, however—the adoption of the "cultural" approach does not justify, as in the Thompson case, the ignoring of important methodological procedures and rigor. [I suspect this note is as relevant in 1996 as in 1946.]
10. Esther Goldfrank died in April 1997, as this chapter reached final form. Through the years I had a certain amount of friendly correspondence with her, and I admired her sensible approach to the Pueblo culture interpretation problem. She married her second husband, Karl Wittfogel, in 1940, and became involved in his

complicated relations with the House UnAmerican Activities Committee, and also American radicals and liberals. In the early 1950s his challenging thesis of "hydraulic societies" attracted considerable interest, and I invited him to speak in a graduate seminar of mine—knowing that this would receive unfavorable attention on the Ohio State campus. It did. However, we went through with it, since I felt that regardless of his political activities he should be treated as an important scholar. Esther was deeply grateful, and for the remainder of Wittfogel's life, she kept me informed of his work and professional difficulties, and from time to time asked for little favors—like letters of recommendation—to which I responded.

11. I am indebted to Kurt H. Wolff for suggesting the case of "caste."
12. For a survey of the problems and methods of the sociology of knowledge, the following are recommended: Mills 1939, 1940; Dahlke 1940; Degré 1943. The term, "sociology of knowledge" is unsatisfactory, and Kurt Wolff and I have proposed "sociology of intellectual behavior" as a replacement.
13. Actually two separate but related problems have been merged in the above paragraph. The problem of infinite regression is one, and the methodological tool of the meta-language is the other. The former concerns the continual transcendence of a given production of knowledge by higher levels of observation, which look down at the production and see it as ideologically "determined" or at least participative within an ideology. Theoretically this process of transcendence could go on indefinitely, each level of observation containing some ideological elements only visible from the next higher level. The second problem, the one of meta-language, is different in that it does not transcend the scientific operation itself, but remains within it. A "meta-language" is simply a logical system which includes within it other logical systems on a lower level of abstraction. Mathematics is thus in many respects a matrix of languages and meta-languages, various forms of calculus expressing more complex relations and explaining the less complex propositions of the algebra. Einsteinian mathematics was a meta-language to Newtonian mathematics.
14. Of course, these pat remarks pass over some difficult philosophical problems. For example, in social science we are not only involved in a semantic regression but also cultural relativism. This can be shown by contrasting psychology with culturology, as follows: In psychology the propositions and knowledge presumably refer to common-human characteristics, hence they refer to the scientist's behavior also. The problem is simply one of constructing various psychological meta-languages to attain ever more explanatory propositions of common-human behavior. This would amount to refining and purifying the knowledge of psychology, eliminating local variants of knowledge. In cultural science, however, the propositions and the knowledge refer not to common-human characteristics, but to *differences* in behavioral systems. Hence the propositions must be introduced as an additional variable; i.e., different scientists behave differently because they belong to different cultures. And further, the possibility becomes exceedingly difficult, since there is no common systemic background, only "different cultures." One of the problems which this raises is the one of imputation (also touched upon by Eggan—see later). I impute an ideological factor in a piece of research. Someone else, from a "different culture," and hence with an ideology different from mine, imputes a different ideology in the same piece of research. Not only, therefore, do we have the regression (hierarchies of ideologies), but we also have relativism (differences between observers in the ideologies seen and their own ideologies). There are several answers to the problem. One of them has been offered in the text, namely, that the regression (and the relativism) do not invalidate any given or

particular analysis. It is valid in its own culture and in its own hierarchical position. Another answer is to break out of the regression and the relativism with a new meta-language which does not use a theoretical psychology.

However, this is not so much a solution but rather a new type of analysis: for example, the ethnologist's research would be seen not as "ideologically determined" but as the product of certain drives in certain environmental presses. This would require fuller knowledge of the research and of the ethnologist as a person. A third possible solution to the problem is collaborative research, as defined in the essay. Much of the "ideological" aspect of contemporary ethnology is produced by the "virtuoso" tradition, and with a community of observers this feature would be considerably reduced or at least made apparent.

15. Certain difficulties with the phrase "value-determination" are semantic. The image called up by the phrase is asymmetric: something, a "value," acts forcefully upon another thing, an individual thinker; thus a cause-effect logic is introduced which in turn gets us involved in the regression-relativist problems discussed in this paper. Otto Neurath (1944) objects to the asymmetric character of many social scientific concepts, and in a discussion of the participation of social science in ongoing social life, he uses the phrase, "Systematized Transfer of Traditions" (1944: 38–41). Let us look at the phenomenon of "value-determination not as literally this, but as the passing of one system of idea patterns into other systems; e.g., the passing of political ideology into the behavior of scientists. This occurs according to various circumstances which will vary historically and will vary according to types of social relations and social roles. The scientist is not "determined," but simply participates in ideological patterns, due to various types of social relationships. These can be analyzed. Then we come to Engelman's position, that scientific behavior which is not participative in ideological patterns is quite possible. Once we talk about things determining other things, everything becomes determined, and we get involved in a vicious regression. If we avoid determination asymmetry, we see the possibility of nonparticipation in idea patterns, simply through the changing of social relations and the achievement of a higher level of perspective. Well and good. But this still leaves us with the problem of handling a certain type of behavior, namely, the eagerness-desirous-behavior of the scientist in promulgating an ideology mixed with scientific analysis. Is this behavior of the individual scientist "evidence" of some sort of "determination" of his behavior by something? What do we do with this level of analysis? From this argument it would appear that the semantic revision of the problem as suggested above is not a total revision, only another solution (number four—see endnote 13 for the other three) to the regression problem, and a solution handling some of the data but neglecting other.

Literature Cited in the Original Paper and the Supplements

American Anthropologist. 1947. "Statement on Human Rights." *American Anthropologist* 49: 539–43.

An-Che, Li. 1937. "Zuñi: Some Observations and Queries." *American Anthropologist* 39: 62–76.

Benedict, Ruth. 1934. *Patterns of Culture*. Boston: Houghton Mifflin.

Bennett, John W. 1995. "Walks on the Dark Side: 'Sick Societies,' Interpersonal Violence, and Anthropology's Love Affair with the Folk Society." *Reviews in Anthropology* 24: 145–58.

Bodine, J. 1972. "Acculturation Processes and Population Dynamics," in *New Perspectives on the Pueblos*, edited by A. Ortiz. Albuquerque: University of New Mexico Press.

Brandt, Richard B. 1954. *Hopi Ethics: A Theoretical Analysis*. Chicago: University of Chicago Press.

Bunzel, R. 1932. "Introduction to Zuñi Ceremonialism." Forty-seventh Annual Report, Bureau of American Ethnology, pp. 467–544.

Dahlke, H. Otto. 1940. "The Sociology of Knowledge," in *Contemporary Social Theory*, edited by H.E. Barnes, H. Becker, and F.B. Becker. New York: Appleton-Century.

Degré, Gerard L. 1943. *Society and Ideology: An Inquiry into the Sociology of Knowledge*. New York: Columbia University Press.

Dennis, Wayne. 1940. *The Hopi Child*. New York: Appleton-Century.

Dollard, John. [1937] 1957. *Caste and Class in a Southern Town*. 3d ed. Originally published for the Institute of Human Relations by Yale University Press, New Haven. Garden City, NY: Doubleday.

Dozier, E. 1964. "The Pueblo Indians of the Southwest." *Current Anthropology* 5: 79–97.

Edgerton, Robert B. 1992. *Sick Societies: Challenging the Myth of Primitive Societies*. New York: Free Press.

Eggan, Dorothy. 1943. "The General Problem of Hopi Adjustment." *American Anthropologist* 45: 357–73.

———. 1956. "Instruction and Affect in Hopi Cultural Continuity." *Southwestern Journal of Anthropology* 12: 347–70.

Ellis, Florence Hawley. 1951. "Patterns of Aggression and the War Cult in the Southwestern Pueblos." *Southwestern Journal of Anthropology* 7: 177–201.

Goldfrank, E. S. 1945. "Socialization, Personality, and the Structure of Pueblo Society." *American Anthropologist* 47: 516–39.

———. 1948. "The Impact of Situation and Personality on Four Hopi Emergence Myths." *Southwestern Journal of Anthropology* 4: 241–62.

Green, Arnold W. 1946. "Sociological Analysis of Horney and Fromm." *American Journal of Sociology* 51: 533–40.

———. 1948. "Culture, Normality and Personality Conflict." *American Anthropologist* 50: 225–37.

Harris, Marvin. 1968. *The Rise of Anthropological Theory*. New York: Thomas Y. Crowell.

Hoebel, E. 1954. "Major Contributions of Southwestern Studies to Anthropological Theory." *American Anthropologist* 56: 720–27.

Kardiner, Abram. 1956. *The Psychological Frontiers of Society*. New York: Columbia University Press.

Leighton, D. and J. Adair. 1966. *People of the Middle Place*. New Haven, CT: Human Relations Area File.

Levy, J. and S. Kunitz. 1971. "Indian Reservations, Anomie, and Social Pathologies." *Southwestern Journal of Anthropology* 27: 97–128.

Mills, C. Wright. 1939. "Language, Logic and Culture." *American Sociological Review* 4: 670–80.

———. 1940. "Methodological Consequences of the Sociology of Knowledge." *American Journal of Sociology* 46: 316–30.

Neurath, Otto. 1944. "Foundations of the Social Sciences." *Encyclopaedia of Unified Science*, vol. 2, no. 1. Chicago: University of Chicago Press.

Sapir, Edward. 1924. "Culture: Genuine and Spurious." *American Journal of Sociology* 29: 401–29.

Speck, Frank. 1935. *Naskapi: The Savage Hunters of the Labrador Peninsula.* Norman, OK: University of Oklahoma Press.

Spicer, Edward H. 1954. *Potam, a Yaqui Village in Sonora.* American Anthropological Association Memoir No. 77.

Thompson, Laura. 1945. "Logico-Aesthetic Integration in Hopi Culture." *American Anthropologist* 47: 540–53.

———. 1950. *Culture in Crisis: A Study of the Hopi Indians.* New York: Harper & Row.

Thompson, Laura and Alice Joseph. 1944. *The Hopi Way.* Chicago: University of Chicago Press.

Titiev, M. 1942. "Notes on Hopi Witchcraft." *Michigan Academy of Science, Arts, and Letters*, vol. 28, part 4.

———. 1944. *Old Oraibi: A Study of the Hopi Indians of Third Mesa.* Papers, Peabody Museum of American Archaeology and Ethnology, Harvard University, vol. 22.

———. 1946. "Review of 'The Hopi Way.'" *American Anthropologist* 48: 430–2.

Tumin, M. 1945. "Culture, Genuine and Spurious: A Re-evaluation." *American Sociological Review* 10: 200–7.

Whitehead, Alfred N. 1925. *Science and the Modern World.* New York: Macmillan.

Wolff, Kurt H. 1943. "The Sociology of Knowledge: Emphasis on an Empirical Attitude." *Philosophy of Science* 10: 104–23.

———. 1945. "A Methodological Note on the Empirical Establishment of Cultural Patterns." *American Sociological Review* 10: 176–84.

7

Early and Late Functional Analysis: Bronislaw Malinowski's *Baloma: Spirits of the Dead* and Clyde Kluckhohn's *Navaho Witchcraft*

With a Supplement: Some Subsequent Studies of Witchcraft with Special Reference to Attempts to Distinguish between Social, Cultural, and Psychological Phenomena

Introduction

The two monographs which constitute the core of this chapter are landmarks of ethnographic field method, since both authors found it possible to integrate a description of their field methods with the factual material obtained with these methods. Few Classic ethnographic monographs did this—the majority simply presented the material without detailed comments on how it was gathered, or how the field situation may have influenced the content. I consider that these two pieces which, despite differences, resemble one another in topic and approach, are among the finest examples of insightful field investigation produced in the Classic era. The two monographs are also fragments—though complete in themselves—of much larger and more extensive

---

The main part of this essay is based on lecture notes for part of a course in anthropological theory taught in the 1950s and 1960s. A brief Supplement considers witchcraft research in the late 1930s into the 1960s as a case study in the dialog between proponents of functionalist and culturalogical approaches. Both the main essay and the supplement were written in 1995.

ethnographic investigations of the peoples concerned. This gives assurance of validity since they are part of a known cultural context. In such full contexts, where the relationship of parts of a social system are more easily determined, functional analysis can attain maximum plausibility.

In the 1920s and 1930s anthropological functionalism was only one of several varieties. Versions of functionalism could be found in philosophy, sociology, physics, engineering, and architecture. Although French scholars played an important role in its development, particularly in sociology, American functionalism had strong indigenous roots in the pragmatic emphasis in U. S. philosophy and scholarship—often associated with the work of John Dewey—beginning in the late 1910s and evolving through the 1920s. Functionalism and pragmatism were "modern" expressions of the new age of rational science and value-free analysis. To anthropologists, with their anxiety over whether culture could be handled objectively, functionalism seemed to provide a solution. One could keep the parts of culture more or less intact, but determine what the parts signified for each other. Above all, it was not necessary to actually define the *whole* culture—something most anthropologists were beginning to suspect was impossible—since the meaning of significant parts could be revealed through functional analysis. And for many purposes this partial but detailed analysis was sufficient.

Actually functionalism as a means of interpreting reality is fundamentally simple: a matter of inquiring as to the relationship of something to neighboring things, and/or, what the 'something' means in larger contexts. The phrases, "X and Y are related through A;" and "X functions thus and so in relation to Y and A" are examples of functional logic. All functional inquiries can be subsumed in such propositions and their various permutations. This useful and indispensable, but everyday mental habit became, for a quarter-century, a major "school" of anthropological inquiry and interpretation.

And of course, it was nothing new in anthropology. As Marvin Harris noted (1968: 423), most major works of the Classic era used "functionalist" explanations whether this was acknowledged or not. Even the culture-pattern theorists were using functional analysis insofar as they attempted to show that certain ideas and values fitted particular personality or behavior patterns in the group. And we saw how functional interpretations of an implicit nature appeared in Spier's

Sun Dance (1921) monograph when he discovered that reconstructions of historical origin based on material properties and provenience were insufficient to trace movement and connections. One required data on meanings and uses. Ralph Linton in chapter 23 of *The Study of Man* (1936) managed to make distinctions between form, meaning, use, and function theoretically explicit. Professional historians from the nineteenth century routinely made functional analyses when they attempted to explain the significance of any social or political phenomenon, and a number of prominent scholars used a blend of historical and functional analysis which might have become the basis for a systematic sociocultural anthropology if its methodological implications had been appreciated. Sir Henry Maine was probably the most prominent and skilled of these writers, and his *Ancient Law* (1862) a monument of proto-scientific social anthropology.)[1].

Linton's presentation of form, meaning, use, and function extended the exposition of the commonsensical basis of these principles of interpretation. But Linton wanted to go further than simple commonsense notions: he tried to create precise definitions, e.g., "The *use* of any cultural element is an expression of its relations to things external to the socio-cultural configuration; its *function* is an expression of its relation to things within that configuration" (Linton 1936: 404). This sounds impressive, but just what is a "configuration?" How do you define it, and how do you know what is supposed to go into it?—by the uses and functions of things? Moreover, suppose a phenomenon has relations to things both outside and inside the "configuration"—are use and function then identical? And so on. The whole affair demonstrates the difficulties of trying to make analytically precise, interpretive concepts out of descriptive classifiers that vary in tense and reference—a crucial epistemological problem in Classic era anthropology. Linton himself made a related observation when he pointed out (ibid.: 407) that "function" is to some extent tautological (although Linton did not use the precise term) insofar as anything that is shared in a group is automatically functional. That is, no matter how people really feel about something and no matter whether they need it or not, if they know and accept or practice it, it is automatically "functional." So, everything has a function. Linton wanted to restrict the use of the term to, more or less, the Malinowskian sense of something which contributes to human needs (ibid.: 411–3)—although he backed off from offering this as a formal definition. Linton's chapter on "Function" has a somewhat tentative feeling, and he seems to have been aware of the slippery nature of these basically commonsensical terms.

Now, if the concepts—especially function—are indeed reflections of ordinary everyday logical thinking, then it follows that they can be combined with any other set of descriptive classifiers. Linton, for example, rejected the British social-structural emphasis on function and linked his concept of function to, of all things, traits and trait complexes; the early Classic era standard descriptive terms for cultural analysis: ". . . the trait complex is the most likely locus of function" (ibid.: 403). Radcliffe-Brown denied that function had anything whatever to do with "culture," and everything to do with "society;" and Malinowski located function in the context of human needs and institutions satisfying those needs (Malinowski 1944). The function concept became elaborated in anthropology through the 1930s and into the 1940s, as it picked up organismic analogies, biological ideas like homeostasis, and temporal versus non-temporal analysis.

The most important reason for the rapid rise of functional analysis during the early-middle Classic era was that it offered a discipline that was floundering in a mire of descriptive detail, a means of explaining the why and wherefore about cultural and social phenomena. The use of ideas about historical or geographical origins to explain the existence and meaning of culture and social organization, as well as developmental-stage theories of change, had been rejected by both the American and British anthropologists, for different but equally cogent reasons, and this instituted an implicit search for new explanatory principles. Malinowski found these principles in his own field work, and Radcliffe-Brown in the theoretical and philosophical scholarship of the French school of sociology organized by Émile Durkheim. The treatment of Malinowski and Radcliffe-Brown by Robert Lowie in chapters 12 and 13 of his 1937 book, *The History of Ethnological Theory*, remains one of the best, since while his chapters do not contain the cogent details of later critical analyses, they focus on the essential intellectual properties of the two approaches—Lowie noted, for example, that both anthropologists were uninterested in or were unable to accommodate data on historical change.

Later polemics and critiques of functional approaches seem to have focussed on three major issues: the first was the point just made, that functional analysis found historical inquiries—or more precisely, the use of past events to help explain the state and nature of present phenomena—difficult to handle. The second issue concerned the way function might be related to the degree of integrity of the group and its culture—or "solidarity" as some writers called it. A third issue was really a combination of the first two: the notion of feedback or "homeostasis," which referred to the fact that change in sociocultural entities tended to follow a cyclical path, from time to time returning to prior states as a result of changes feeding back into the system and causing conservative reaction. However, this theory of homeostatic change was never fully worked out—it was usually seen as a kind of conservative force in human affairs, and it assumed that social or cultural systems had some kind of innate stability or "equilibrium." Some analysts called this an "organismic analogy," which meant that the characterization resembled the empirical descriptions and theoretical generalizations about natural systems, like the reciprocal and permutating relationships of life forms in a pond or woodland. Certainly such feedback processes were present in social behavior and social systems, but they could not be relied on—they lacked the status of laws, and conservatism in human affairs existed for historical and ideological reasons, not as some kind of automatically operating process. If there is any such, it has to be expressed in something like "chaos" theory or "stochastic" processes.

As suggested earlier, the main problem with functionalism was not its ontological status (as a valid empirical proposition, social behavior *does* have functions), or its general utility as a mode of reasoning, or its historical myopia, but in the various trimmings it acquired in the course of its development and used by anthropologists from the late 1920s through the 1940s. The rejection of functional analysis in some quarters eventually became so vigorous (e.g., Gregg and Williams 1948) that the use of the term became virtually taboo, and by the 1990s one could find reasonable functional studies in which the author avoids or simply does not know about the ultimate source of the implicit concepts or mental devices used. For example, an ethnologist, Daniel Touro Linger (1993), makes a coherent multidimensional functional analysis of ceremonial patterns in Brazilian life but fails to identify the method used as functionalist.

In the late 1950s and early 1960s it became fashionable to use the term "synchronic" to identify an approach with ahistorical, atemporal dimensions; and "diachronic" to define approaches with historical change objectives and data. The critics of functionalism condemned it for lacking the capacity for or interest in diachronic analysis, in favor of an excessive synchronicity (late Classic anthropology loved such terms but who is to say they were any less pontifical than the literary jargon used by the postmodernists?) Marvin Harris was particularly concerned with this situation, and waxed indignant about the British study, *African Political Systems* (Fortes and Evans-Pritchard 1940), where explanations of particular political forms totally ignored historical causes, especially the way British local rule had modified and influenced native social organizations (Harris 1968:537–8). Synchronic analysis is fine where the historical background is known or can be assessed for its importance, but where the historical sources were ignored, the possibility of error was considerable. However, the synchronic failing was not really a defect of the functional idea—only a failure on the part of practitioners to do their homework. And this was acknowledged by such sensible Classic era ethnographic functionalists as Fred Eggan, Raymond Firth, and Edmund Leach.

The Monographs by Malinowski and Kluckhohn

Both monographs are concerned with the background problem of parts and wholes, and how this problem gave rise to or required a functionalist explanation. In both cases the writers chose exotic phenomena: belief in spirits of the dead and witchcraft. The phenomena loosely categorized as "religion," "magic," and "the supernatural" always fascinated anthropologists, especially because in the nineteenth century Christian dogmatists resisted the objective study of "religion," and therefore the right to study it objectively represented one of the salient aspects of the anthropological approach—something that set anthropologists apart from other students of humanity. The rationalists tended to see religion as an opiate, or more neutrally, as a source of social order, and felt it should be studied as such. On the other hand, religionists declared that religion was a revealed truth, sufficient unto itself without "scientific" or scholarly study. The battle was fought throughout the nineteenth century, and anthropologists and their predecessors played important roles in the struggle.

Throughout the Classic era, supernaturalist phenomena were classified as "primitive religion" (for a typical text, see Radin 1937), the term seemingly dissociating such phenomena from what were "true" religions like Christianity or Islam. At any rate, the religiosity of the nineteenth century had made objective analysis of the great universal faiths difficult; hence it was all right to study "primitive" phenomena, since they were not true or revealed. True or primitive, most Classic anthropologists visualized religion and magic as conferring a certain order and predictability—their "functions"—in tribal life. Robert Redfield seemed to consider religion as the moral force promoting community solidarity. However, neither Radin, Redfield, or other theorists really faced up to the disordering functions of religion and magic. Perhaps the only exception was the study of witchcraft, which for most of the Classic era was regarded as unsettling and disturbing—although as we shall see later, late-Classic students like Kluckhohn suspected that witchcraft might also have benign effects.

The two monographs to be considered are of similar length: a little over 200 pages—and both begin with a detailed description of the ethnographic phenomena researched, which is followed by interpretations and theoretical observations. And both include descriptions of the circumstances of interviewing and the implications of various types of rapport and approach for the validity and reliability of the data.

Malinowski's *Baloma* Monograph

This monograph is an extremely early Classic era production—written in 1914–15 and published in 1916 in the *Journal of the Royal Anthropological Institute*. It can be argued that Baloma is the first truly modern ethnological monograph, in the sense of its methodological self-consciousness. Malinowski ([1916] 1948: 214) did not stop at what he called "one-dimensional account" ethnography—that is, simply writing down what the informant told you and leaving it at that—but continued to ask questions of the informant as to the meanings, etc., of what he said; and then, later, asking himself questions about the relationship of what he heard to other things. Lowie noted (1937: 233–4), this was the chief significance of the *Baloma* monograph: Malinowski discovered functionalism as a de facto explanation of certain ideational and institutional aspects of culture where the belief in spirits of the dead were implicated.

Malinowski informs us that the Trobrianders (in particular, the Kiriwinians), have two separate sets of beliefs about the spirits of dead people: the *baloma* and the *kosi*. The former, upon death, leave the living and go to Tuma, a small island, where they stay indefinitely. The *kosi*, on the other hand, haunt the village where the deceased lived for a short time after death, but can return under certain circumstances. Malinowski noted that these two sets of beliefs were contradictory, but that the inhabitants shared them without any particular sense of this, and could shift from one belief to the other depending on context. The two sets were intimately bound with various other beliefs and practices, and the locus of either the *baloma* or *kosi* in these various social contexts was sufficient to guarantee their persistence.

Malinowski's informants told him that encounters with the spirits of the dead were frequent—although a few did say that some of these tales were fiction, or invented to impress the ethnologist. However, informants did not agree on the exact appearance and behavior of either the *baloma* or *kosi*: for instance, "the answers were vacillating and contradictory . . . has not crystallized into any orthodox and definite doctrine" (ibid.: 145).

Malinowski provides a series of demonstrations of how the beliefs are functionally related to other features of culture which require some certitude or guarantee; in particular, garden magic and pregnancy. The former is clearly a foretaste of the great two-volume treatise on garden magic (Malinowski 1935) to be published two decades later; and the latter had elements which are repeated in greater detail in *The Sexual Life of Savages* (1929). Malinowski was concerned with the fact that the Trobrianders, like the Australian Aborigines, seemed to lack knowledge of the physiological role of the male in conception—although they also believed that sexual intercourse was useful in "opening" the female to impregnation by spirits: the *baloma*. The *baloma* were also agents of reincarnation. Thus, the *baloma*, however "vacillating and contradictory" the accounts of some might be from person to person, nevertheless played a crucial role—"function"—in explaining the birth of children. Malinowski's own text provides a good illustration of the flavor of his commonsense functionalist approach, in which the context of field work is part of the descriptive results:

> I shall give a simple version of these events and discuss the details subsequently. When the *baloma* has grown old, his teeth fall out, his skin gets loose and wrinkled; he goes to the beach and bathes in the salt water; then he throws off his skin just as a snake would do, and becomes a young child again; really an embryo, a *waiwaia*—a term applied to children *in utero* and immediately after birth. A *baloma* woman sees this *waiwaia*; she takes it up, and puts it in a basket or a plaited and folded coconut leaf (*puatai*). She carries the small being to Kiriwina, and places it in the womb of some woman, inserting it *per vaginam*. Then that woman becomes pregnant (*nasusuma*).

> This is the story as I obtained it from the first informant who mentioned the subject to me. It implies two important psychological facts: the belief in reincarnation, and the ignorance of the physiological causes of pregnancy. I shall now discuss both these subjects in the light of the details obtained on further inquiry.
>
> First of all, everybody in Kiriwina knows, and has not the slightest doubt about, the following propositions. The real cause of pregnancy is always a *baloma*, who is inserted into or enters the body of a woman, and without whose existence a woman could not become pregnant; all babies are made or come into existence (*ibubulisi*) in Tuma. These tenets form the main stratum of what can be termed popular or universal belief. If you question any man, woman, or even an intelligent child, you will obtain from him or her this information. But any further details are much less universally known; one obtains a fact here and a detail there, and some of them contradict the others, and none of them seems to loom particularly clear in the native mind, though here and there it is obvious that some of these beliefs influence behavior, and are connected with some customs. ([1916] 1948: 190–1)

The important fact is that the *baloma* origin of pregnancy "functioned" (my term, but Malinowski's interpretation) to eliminate illegitimacy. Without a clear concept of sperm impregnation, the Trobrianders did not attribute conception to any form of sexual liaison. Even if a husband was absent for a year or more, and his wife had a child in the interval, the husband accepted it as his own since he "knew" that it was the result of spirit impregnation, not cohabitation with a rival. There has always been a certain skepticism about Malinowski's interpretation—a more subtle explanation would be that the *baloma*-impregnation belief is a way for a woman to ward off accusation of infidelity, and is one of those things that "everybody believes but nobody believes." Whispering could be rife behind the woman's back, based on an unspoken understanding that sexual intercourse is the real cause of pregnancy.

There follows a mini-treatise on field method, centering around the ambiguity of the details and the inconsistency of informant accounts. This begins:

> Two beliefs, quite contradictory to each other, may co-exist, while a perfectly obvious inference from a very firm tenet may be simply ignored. Thus the only safe way for an ethnological inquirer is to investigate every detail of native belief and to mistrust any conclusion obtained through inference only. (ibid.: 194).

This statement appears to be aimed at the speculative tradition of the late nineteenth and early twentieth century, when theoretical propositions were more important than facts, and particular ethnographic details were selected out of context in order to prove something—the same defective methodology that Boas had been criticizing. At any rate, in terms of standard histories of "ethnological theory," Malinowskian empirical functionalism performed the same task as Boasian historicism: a methodological reform movement; that is, to pursue ethnographic facts for their own sake and become certain of accuracy.

Malinowski's intensive field work led him to explore the full context of every concept, habit, and complex: ". . . the ordering, the classifying, and interpreting should be done in the field with reference to the organic whole of native social life" (ibid.: 212). That is, parts have meaning from their relationship to each other, and to the "whole." "In other words, there is a social dimension to a belief . . ." (ibid.: 213). However, he also allows for individual variation—individuals can have beliefs which are not "embodied in institutions" (ibid.: 218), in which case, the belief lacks a social dimension. But at the same time, idiosyncratic beliefs can contribute to the "whole" by introducing novelty and change. It is clear that Malinowski verged on a behavioral conception of culture, but like the functionalists in general, he did not pursue its implications. To diagnose the "social dimension" of a belief, and to show its role in "institutions" and its causal implications for behavior, was sufficient. All this was pure, basic functional analysis. Malinowski's theoretical "needs" functionalism was years in the future.

Kluckhohn's *Navaho Witchcraft*

Like Malinowski's *Baloma*, Kluckhohn's *Navaho Witchcraft* (1944) is a somewhat neglected work and often criticized for its innovative boldness. Functional explanations usually made book reviewers nervous—the explanations seemed too simple for the complex and arcane cultural behavior in the descriptive sections. In the early Classic era, the monographs that garnered the most kudos were the monster descriptive ethnographies that emanated from the great museums and departments, or as was the case in the United Kingdom, published in massive hardbound tomes by elite private publishers. Like *Baloma*, *Navaho Witchcraft* has detailed, specialized descriptive material, but it is much longer on methodological and explanatory commentary. It provides a concise, segmental explanation of why witchcraft exists, why it persists, and above all, how it serves useful needs in Navaho society.

Talcott Parsons and Evon Vogt (1962) wrote a biographical obituary of Kluckhohn which is reprinted in the book version of the 1944 monograph. In it they note that Kluckhohn's "catholicity of knowledge . . . made him, though so eminent an anthropologist never content with anthropology alone" (1962: xv, in the book). And this led to his "creative eclecticism" (1962: xx, *sic.*) which characterized his research and his entire career. His "catholicity of knowledge" and "creative eclecticism" were precisely what led more traditional members of the anthropological profession to reject much of his work and influence. These characteristics made Kluckhohn into the most distinguished multi- or interdisciplinary anthropologist of his time, accepting of ideas, concepts and theories from all sources, and sometimes questioning anthropological shibboleths in the process. While Kluckhohn was always closer to the inner circles of the profession than Gregory Bateson, his avant garde intellectual posture was not all that different. The difference was simply that Kluckhohn always managed to return to the fold: for instance, to publish an article on "The Concept of Culture" (Kluckhohn and Kelly 1945) when in fact much of his work demonstrated the inadequacies of the concept; to join with the demigod of the Classic discipline, Alfred L. Kroeber, to write a manifesto on the nature of culture and the nature of anthropology (Kroeber and Kluckhohn 1952).

The Monograph

On the first page of his Introduction Kluckhohn declares—as did Malinowski for his material in his early pages—that the practice of witchcraft does not necessarily conform to beliefs as told by informants to the ethnographer. What the Navaho called "the bad side" of human behavior (Kluckhohn 1944: 6) was particularly difficult to find out about because of the disjunction of belief and practice. And therefore the ethnological report must feature methodological as well as substantive analysis. And moreover, Kluckhohn makes it clear that he is not concerned with the problem of acculturation—that is, not concerned with an "aboriginal" as opposed to "acculturated form" (ibid.: 6)—thus dissociating himself from what, in the period, was viewed by many as a modern or contemporary avant garde theme in anthropology. *Navaho Witchcraft* is thus an account of witchcraft *as it was manifest during the ethnographer's visits*—not as it might have been in some precontact past. This was possibly the first time an ethnologist used the "historical present" as a vehicle for reporting cultural behavior.

The book is divided into two main parts, and each of these into sections. Section 1 is concerned with "Data," and this takes off with a discussion of methodology:

> Whether Navahos actually carried out rites of witchcraft—or at least whether such rites were carried out by many individuals at all frequently, is open to question as in the case of the Pueblo Indians. But there is no doubt that in both cultures belief in the existence of witches is manifested in expressions of fear of individuals and places and objects held to be associated with witchcraft. (ibid.: 5)

In other words, information the ethnographer obtains about cultural phenomena is strictly relative to the informants' ability or willingness to communicate. So Kluckhohn regarded the ambiguity of information as part of the context of witchcraft, not necessarily as an impedance to obtaining knowledge about it.

He continues with his sketch of a plan for future analysis and publication of the sociopsychological situation for each of his interviews on witchcraft, analyzing the circumstances of the fabrications, prevarications, emotional release, and so on. (The problem of prevarication became the topic of a study of Tarahumara witchcraft by Herbert Passin in 1942, two years before *Navaho Witchcraft*, which suggests that the idea of denial as a source of data rather than as an obstacle was in the air. Still, the data secured was sufficient to permit a listing of the chief categories of witching, about which he notes, "It must be insisted that it is the natives who have created these distinct categories—not the ethnologist" (ibid.: 23). Kluckhohn acknowledged, before the majority of ethnologists did, the problem of conceptual bias and imposition.

Section 9 is concerned with "Observed Behavior in Relation to Witchcraft." Kluckhohn poses the crucial question: "What warrant have we, therefore, for assuming that the Navaho (or many Navaho at any rate) actually believe these stories?" (ibid.: 53). The evidence, he tells us, is indirect—behaviors which "make sense" only if a strong belief in witchcraft exists—quite aside from the actual practice of witchcraft. The observed behaviors are as follows: the existence of medicines to ward off witching; the fact that there is good evidence that people have been killed as witches; that others are accused of being witches; and that a number of people actually believe themselves to have been bewitched. Kluckhohn acknowledges that while the data strongly indicate that a behavioral configuration of witchcraft exists, as evidenced by the materials noted above, he himself never observed any actual witching. This is an interesting admission; one is inclined to think that his emphasis on negative data might contain a hint of doubts about the validity of data appearing in many ethnological monographs of the period; or, what is more probable, his conviction that reports of witching is more a matter of beliefs and response to belief than it is of some literal description of behavior. Strong belief is as good as the real thing, in other words. (And here lies the frontier which—especially—short-term ethnographic investigation has always pressed against.)

Section 10 is "Participation." Kluckhohn tells us that in interview data from 500 individuals, he has 19 living persons who have been accused in local gossip of practicing witchcraft, and ten additional individuals who have since died. In the last thirty years prior to publication of the original monograph (1944), there were six public accusations or "trials" of supposed witches, and two so-called witches were clandestinely executed.

So we come to the crucial second main part of the monograph: "Interpretation," which is a major contribution to functional analysis. It is also—disregarding the particular theory used—one of the monuments of cultural anthropological interpretation, and while it continues to enrage postmodernists more interested in the anthropologist as a primitive thinker than in the thinking of primitives, it remains an illuminating portrait of how a particular pattern of behavior is built into the fabric of life in a tribal community.

Kluckhohn defines his approach as a "structural analysis," designed to show that "one fact bears a determinate relationship to another fact or set of facts. Are there any uniform modes of relationship between the data bearing on Navaho witchcraft and the data on Navaho history; between witchcraft beliefs and practices and Navaho social organization, Navaho economy, Navaho value systems?" (ibid.: 65). This is the basic way to phrase the functionalist approach: queries about the relationships of parts.

Kluckhohn goes on to examine explanations of the presence and meaning of witchcraft in the ethnological literature. He dwells briefly on the idea that witchcraft is essentially evil and destructive (in anthropology, the idea was reinforced by the popularity of Reo Fortune's *Sorcerers of Dobu* [1932]) and argues that this is bad science since any cultural complex must be handled within the context of its own culture—a basic relativistic proposition and one of the standby concepts of functional analysis as it was used by American anthropologists. He believes that witchcraft among the Navaho has a "euphoric effect," "perhaps even outweighing the dysphoric effects" (Kluckhohn 1944: 68). He expresses the hope that "this may influence anthropologists to examine without prejudice the contribution of any pattern assemblage to the total social system . . ." (ibid.: 68). (The language is representative of Kluckhohn's view on cultural patterning in functional and/or structural analysis.)

The first section is followed by "Distributional and Historical Comments," which is an attempt to account for Navaho witchcraft as a historical amalgam including Pueblo, Spanish, and perhaps other elements. He locates much of the Navaho belief system in described practices in Pueblo sources, but this, he decides, does not account for the observed and theorized linkages between witchcraft and various social phenomena—an obvious lead-in for functional analysis. History tells us something, but cannot answer questions about relationships between various cultural and behavioral elements.

So we come to section 3: "Navaho Witchcraft as Providing Culturally Defined and Adaptive and Adjustive Responses." This is the longest section in the monograph and was the most influential and controversial. It constitutes a full-dress social-cum-psychiatric-functional theory of Navaho witchcraft, and was controversial because it was based on what Kluckhohn freely admitted was incomplete data—data based on hearsay in part, and data lacking personal observations of actual witching practices. He calls it an "investigation of functional dependencies," or a "study in the interrelation of parts" (ibid.: 77). Here we begin to slide into technical terms: the "parts" and "dependencies" he speaks of are defined by his earlier summary of the descriptive materials, and also by the theoretical and conceptual language of functional analysis.

He announces his concepts, which derive from two main sources: the then current structural-functional social theory of Robert Merton (1949) and the psychiatric theory of Henry Murray (1938): *manifest* and *latent* functions from the first, and *adaptive* and *adjustive* responses from the second. Kluckhohn proposes that what he calls "cultural forms" survive only if they possess adaptive and/or adjustive responses: the first pertaining to the social system as a whole; the latter to the individual. The adaptive-adjustive distinction is clearly normative: it pertains to the fact that the individual can adjust to a maladaptive social situation, or that the adjustive behavior of the individual can influence the adaptive patterns in the society. If it is behavior of individuals we are speaking of, than how does one distinguish between the two types? (Or, is the whole argument tautological—survival *is* adaptation—adjustment *is* survival?)

However, such criticisms have a certain irrelevance. The fact is that the adaptive mode deals with systems, institutions, and culture-complexes like witchcraft, and it is actually possible to discover how the particular system or complex is significant for the ongoing operation of the larger whole. As for the individual, when he behaves in the context of the particular system or complex, his behavior implements the "adaptive" process for the society, *but* this does not mean that it will have the same significance—meaning or function—for him personally. It may run in the opposite direction. These two sets of distinctions have considerable analytical power, but there is no doubt that the closer you try to define their fit to a specific cultural context, the greater the ambiguity or tautology. And it was precisely this kind of now-you-see-it-now-you-don't quality of functionalist concepts that drove the critics wild.

Actually, Kluckhohn was well aware of the fact that functional analysis frequently lost sight of the "human individuals" in its effort to clarify and explain the operations of the social, noting that standard (sociological) structural-functionalism dealt with "abstracted parts of the social structure" (Kluckhohn 1944: 80). And this is why he theorized about the "adaptive-adjustive" nexus, and had to go to psychiatry for the concepts. And he was also aware of the criticism that functionalism could not deal with behavioral dynamics; for instance, witchcraft as a system of interacting behaviors and communications. He felt that the two sets of paired concepts went far to avoid the "ambiguities" inherent in standard functional analysis. They seemed to save functionalism from its critics, but at the same time used functional analysis to shed light on a particular "cultural form."

So the second set of paired concepts appears: Robert Merton's *latent* and *manifest* functions. Here we take a leap: the first set pertains, on the whole, to actual behavior, but the second seems to relate more to observer constructs rather than observed behavior. Moreover, the distinction, if it has any empirical reality, includes the empirical status of communication. If the subjects of the research tell you that such-and-such exists and does this or that, it is "manifest." But if they do not care to discuss it, and you find out about it via some indirect route, you call it "latent." This oversimplifies the situation because the topic could still be secret, suppressed, or simply lied about, but the point is basic: what is manifest and what is latent often is simply relative to such behaviors as secrecy, openness of dialogue, vocabulary, and so on.

What did Kluckhohn find when he applied these concepts or constructs to the witchcraft data? Since the monograph is a familiar one and its conclusions are part (or should be part) of the vocabulary of most cultural anthropologists, we may merely summarize them:

The manifest functions of witchcraft for the individuals are exemplified by obtaining wealth, disposing of enemies, and "being mean" (ibid.: 81). Witchcraft also helps people learn and have confidence in the folktales, chants, and curing ceremonials. And witchcraft also provides the Navaho with explanations for puzzling events—changes of mood, diseases, and so forth.

The latent functions of witchcraft for the individual consist of, e.g., the ability of an individual to gain power, given the "credence" of other people in witchcraft. Witchcraft can be a device, in other words, for gaining attention, exemplified by low-status people who throw fits or trance states at ceremonials, and who thereby may be spoken of as having witching power. Other latent functions concern the use of witchcraft as a means for indulging in socially forbidden behavior; e.g., to indulge in fantasies about incest by linking it to witching. Still another latent function of witchcraft (not clearly distinguishable from the previous one) is to provide an outlet for anxieties and insecurities. Finally there is the question of aggression and how the society permits its release—witchcraft is one of these mechanisms. These psychological functions—or adjustive functions for the individual—are given the longest space in the monograph; clearly Kluckhohn was inclined to dwell, in his personal version of functionalism, more on socio-psychological or behavioral phenomena than on purely cultural or structural—although the basic theoretical schema are couched in abstract social-science—not psychological—language.

His own summary of the anxiety and aggression domain of witchcraft functionality: "witchcraft is a major instrument for dealing with aggression and anxiety. It permits some anxiety and some malicious destructiveness to be expressed directly with a minimum of punishment to the aggressor. Still more anxiety and aggression is displaced through the witchcraft pattern assemblage into channels where they are relatively harmless or where, at least, there are available patterns for adjusting the individuals to the new problems created. Individual adjustment merges with group adaptation" (ibid.: 110). The final sentence is crucial: it displays Kluckhohn's awareness that the analytical concepts are not mutually exclusive, but are labels for behavioral tendencies—"patterns"—which take on varying semantic positions depending on context and level of social generality.

The monograph deals next with the ways witchcraft serves needs of the "local group" for solidarity and order. Accusations of witchcraft discourage the individual accumulation of wealth. (This has been found in many societies—individual wealth accumulation in small, weakly stratified communities is always a threat and is frequently dealt with through witchcraft accusation—for instance, Passin 1942, on the Tarahumara, where "witches" were rich men). Kluckhohn also uses the term "social control" in these final sections, and provides some historical data which he feels demonstrate the thesis: for example, in 1884, the leader Manuelito arranged the execution of "more than forty witches" (ibid.: 112), who were really noisy advocates of another armed uprising against the whites. If he had arrested these "troublemakers" and handed them over to the U. S. authorities, his prestige would diminish, so he used the witchcraft theme in order to have the Navaho deal with them. Similar strategies were apparently used by the Navaho to impede the spread of Ghost Dance manifestations. In general, Kluckhohn found that Navaho witchcraft flared up in periods of general stress and danger, and diminished in periods of peace and tranquility. Kluckhohn used classic, developed structural-functional theory here: "I am inclined to regard both the witchcraft and the ceremonial phenomena as alternative responses directed toward the preservation of a badly disturbed equilibrium" (ibid.: 117).

At the same time, Kluckhohn was aware that witchcraft, despite its favorable supportive functions in Navaho society, did entail what he calls "costs." Kluckhohn featured the positive side throughout the monograph but at the end of the monograph, he does acknowledge that all is not rosy:

> At the same time, witchcraft has its *costs* for the individual and the group . . . its *costs* is projected aggression and some social disruption. Probably, as a natural consequence of the insistence that witchcraft *does* have important adjustive and adaptive effects, the *cost* has been too little stressed. (ibid.: 120–1)

He goes on to note that possibly the most serious effect is that leadership is discouraged. The price of harmony and equanimity, achieved through the projection of fear and guilt to individuals who would be likely to act vigorously in leadership positions, is a general dampening of individualistic behavior, and this, in a reservation situation in which leadership is needed in order to ward off external threats to resources, has its negative consequences. This discussion of "costs" comes at the very end, and it has the appearance of something a critical reader of the original manuscript might have urged on its writer. I do not know; but what we say is that the general emphasis on homeostatic equilibrium in structural-functional theory appears in Kluckhohn's general theory of witchcraft among the Navaho, but that at the very end he attempted to modify this bias.[2]

Conclusions

The Malinowski piece represents what I called "early," and the Kluckhohn piece, "late" functionalism, and this is certainly appropriate given the dates of publication. More descriptive characterizations would be "empirical" or "commonsense" functionalism for the Malinowski monograph, and "theoretical" or "analytic" functionalism for Kluckhohn's. And of course this "theoretical" version was equivalent to what was known in its heyday as "structural-functionalism."

Malinowski's was a commonsense inquiry into relationships of parts, arising out of his observations in the field and his asking of questions about linkages of observed phenomena. The conclusions are presented as descriptive passages without resorting to second-order abstract concepts. Kluckhohn presented the empirical data and then drew upon preexisting, second-order theoretical ideas to interpret them. Empirical data was used, of course, but it tended to be subordinated to the classifications created by the concepts. And this procedure formed the target of the major critical effort directed at functionalism in the 1950s and 1960s.

However, there is no question that we learn more about the phenomena under investigation with Kluckhohn's approach than with

Malinowski's. Malinowski simply informs us how a particular set of beliefs and practices are connected to each other and to features of the social organization, and what purposes they seem to serve. But Kluckhohn also tells us something crucial about the nature of the phenomenon itself (witchcraft), and this is the gain from using second-order generalizing concepts which require behavioral and psychological data. The down side of this approach is simply our uneasiness about the applicability of these concepts to the particular phenomenon. They are, after all, applicable to any and all cultural behavior; therefore we question their relevance to the particular behavior under study.

Carrying this a bit further—it is possible to say that late functionalism, due to its use of second-order abstract concepts, involved a reality displacement: the phenomenon in question becomes something else: e.g., *witchcraft* becomes an *adaptive strategy*—and this displacement effect became another focus of criticism of the structural-functional approach. Cultural integrity was violated—considered an intellectual sin by late Classic era anthropologists. This violation was true for the patternist approach as well, which, as we noted earlier, was another version of primeval functionalism since it contained an implicit explanation of linkages. It would seem that you cannot eat your cake and have it too; if you want to theorize—generalize—about cultural behavior, you are going to have to sacrifice some verisimilitude, and this, in sum, was the critical attitude developing in the 1970s and 1980s and which evolved into a series of approaches which can be grouped as postmodern anthropology. These approaches try, usually unsuccessfully, to avoid theoretical constructs, etc., to present the raw material in such a way as to represent its essential meaning to the people concerned, without distortion. Kurt Wolff (see Bennett 1992) attempted this as far back as the 1940s and dedicated his career to the effort, but was never completely successful in overcoming the displacement effect.

Putting each of the two monographs into its time period, can we find any differences in the degree of confidence placed in them? The Malinowski piece represented new data, and new interpretations of the data. After its publication, exotic belief systems would never again be represented as oddities, divorced from other aspects of social behavior. The Kluckhohn situation differs: actually none of his conclusions about the adjustive and adaptive functions of witchcraft were particularly surprising, because they fitted into preexisting sociopsychological theories and findings. The idea of frustrated or displaced aggression, for example, had been used repeatedly in social psychological and psychiatric literature for a generation prior to publication of *Navaho Witchcraft* (e.g., John Dollard et al. 1939), and the conclusions made perfect sense to people who were familiar with this literature. Kluckhohn may have tried to show he was moving in new anthropological directions by giving witchcraft, in some contexts, a useful or even benign role, but this, as he himself acknowledges, might have been at the expense of alternative explanations or even a discussion of human evil. However this may be, my personal feeling is that the portrait of witchcraft functionality given by Kluckhohn is on the whole sound and meaningful. If the frame of reference—"late theoretical functionalism"—was defective, Kluckhohn's own conscientious data-collecting and judicious analyses and explanations saved the day.

As many others have noted, the chief villain in late structural-functional theory was the imposed theory of equilibrium and homeostatic fluctuation and feedback. This led Kluckhohn into dangerous waters when he theorized about the changing incidence of witchcraft in Navaho recent history, concluding that witching was associated with periods of social stress. That might be, but witchcraft in other societies is not necessarily so closely associated with the equilibrium quotient of the general society. It can exist or be diminished on the basis of other forces, some external to the social system, some internal.

Functionalism remains a vital tool in social and cultural analysis, since at root it is simply a series of basic questions about relationships among observed phenomena. The studious avoidance of functionalist language by many contemporary anthropologists while making perfectly reasonable functional analyses of their data, is a manifestation of intellectual faddism in the discipline.

Supplement:

Some Subsequent Studies of Witchcraft with Special Reference to Attempts to Distinguish between Social, Cultural, and Psychological Phenomena

Two monographic studies stand out in the Classic era anthropological literature on witchcraft: the 1944 Kluckhohn piece already examined, and the 1937 book by E.E. Evans-Pritchard: *Witchcraft, Oracles and Magic Among the Azande*. As with other cultural specialties, these were soon followed by comparative studies in order to obtain generalizations about the genesis and functions of witchcraft. On the whole the comparative research confirmed what so many other studies of other topics found: that beyond certain basic commonalities—in the case of witchcraft, the projection of one's misfortunes on others, revenge motives, and so on—the manifestations and linkages of witchcraft varied greatly from culture to culture.

Evans-Pritchard's volume is in many ways a precursor of Kluckhohn's book. Kluckhohn does not refer to the Azande monograph, and the omission is curious since there are theoretical links between the two: specific conceptions of the social functions of witchcraft; and the idea that witchcraft is not necessarily evil: it has integrative functions and also helps people to account for events which defy routine explanation. Moreover, both studies emerged out of an "applied" context: Evans-Pritchard dedicated his book to the local District Commissioner, and he also stated that he "hope(s) the present volume will be of service to political officers, doctors, and missionaries in Zandeland, and later to the Azande themselves" (Evans-Pritchard 1937: 3). Kluckhohn acknowledged the help of various personnel at the Navaho agency, and of course Kluckhohn had been in contact with the Indian Service on applied matters affecting the Navaho for some time. If one had to choose an American analogue to the kind of relevant ethnology represented by the Azande book and others of the British African ethnologists of the Classic era, it would be the series of coordinated investigations of the Navaho by Kluckhohn and his associates.

The Azande monograph was one of the seminal works we read in various graduate classes at the University of Chicago in the late 1930s and early 1940s. My course notes tell me we were deeply impressed by two things: one of them was the positive functions of witchcraft; but the other was Evans-Pritchard's demonstration that the Azande didn't really practice witchcraft, but used it as a convenient explanation of misfortune and disorder—that their "witchcraft" was really a myth, a useful fiction, and that the Azande knew full well that an unfortunate experience or incident was caused by real-world forces. However, they used witchcraft to explain how, for example, it happened that the individual experiencing the misfortune happened to be in the place that it happened. Evans-Pritchard also demonstrated that witchcraft helped to explain events that could not be easily explained, so that the witchcraft element was not really a supernatural force, but simply part of everyday reality—an annoying, irritating reality, but one that the individual had to cope with. Evans-Pritchard called it a "natural philosophy by which the relation of men to unfortunate events are explained . . ." (ibid.: 63). Findings like this impressed graduate students far more than the detailed descriptions of how witches were linguistically defined by the Azande, or how they were related to gender and social organization, or how spells and magical routines were organized.

The Evans-Pritchard book started its own trend toward witchcraft studies in British social anthropology, and Kluckhohn's Navaho monograph stimulated some studies by New World anthropologists. I do not intend to review all of this material, but some comments on key items are in order. The procession can begin with Monica Wilson's piece in the *American Journal of Sociology* in 1951 on the "witch beliefs" of the African tribal groups Nyakyusa and Pondo, with reference to social structure. She makes an attempt to combine cultural and social facets of the problem in honor, I suspect, of ongoing debates at the University of Chicago anthropology department where she was a visiting lecturer: "Many anthropologists are concerned just now with the relation between values and social structure. My subject is a facet of that problem. I shall try to show that witch beliefs are one expression of the values of a society and that these vary with the social structure" (Wilson 1951: 307). Her definition of witchcraft is Evans-Pritchard's: the use of special powers by individuals to harm others. The findings are logical: the Nyakyusa do not live with relatives, but their cattle are owned by kin groups: hence, persons accused of witching are non-related neighbors, not kinsmen. The Pondo, on the other hand, live with their kin, and correspondingly suspect kin of witchcraft, especially kin who have reasons: for instance, daughters-in-law often suspect their mothers-in-law and the relationship between the two is institutionally tense since the patrilineal residence pattern requires the bride to leave her home and reside with her husband and his kin. Thus, the patterns of witchcraft in these two societies which were similar in the sense of subsistence pursuits and general level of social development differed in accordance with variations in social organization and associated values. (Wilson did not cite Kluckhohn's monograph.)

Next in line is the article by S. F. Nadel, "Witchcraft in Four African Societies," published in the *American Anthropologist* in 1952. He selected two tribal groups in Nigeria and two in the Sudan. He considered his study to be one of "concomitant variations," and emphasized cultural factors—"cultural" in this case referring to mythology and other belief elements. For example, one of the tribes—the Korongo—had an elaborate explanatory cosmology and lacked witchcraft as either belief or practice. Another—the Mesakin—had no cosmological mythos and was "witchcraft ridden" (Nadel 1952: 27). It is tempting to attribute casual significance to these relationships but Nadel is cautious, since there were "too many instances of cultures combining explicit mythology with belief in witchcraft" (ibid.: 27). Another example concerned the Sudanese Nupe attribution of witchcraft to women, with men having ambiguous power; the Nupe, according to Nadel, have "a marked bias for dichotomous conceptions" (ibid.: 27). But among the Gwari, where witchcraft beliefs ignored sexual dichotomy, he also found much less in the way of dichotomous thinking and categorization. Other examples of the same order: logical consistency between general cultural attitudes and values and witchcraft beliefs and practices.

The Nadel piece seems dominantly cultural in orientation, and perhaps significantly was published in the *American Anthropologist.* Nadel's specialty was social structure and organization, but this piece was clearly in the cultural—"American"?—direction. (He cited neither Evans-Pritchard nor Kluckhohn.)

In 1960 Manning Nash published "Witchcraft as Social Process in a Tzeltal Community" in *American Indigena,* the international anthropological periodical issued by the Mexican *Instituto Nacional Indigenista.* Like the two previous papers, this one was brief, descriptive and almost undocumented, and simply adds a few exotic details to the corpus of knowledge about witches. It seems that the Tzeltal had "a fairly coherent body of conventional understandings" concerning witches (Nash 1960: 122): certain men had *nawal* or animal "familiars"—in the medieval European term. The owner of such an animal familiar can roam at night, transformed into the beast, and, on occasion, use the power the *nawal* confers to injure others. This was considered a form of *brujeria,* or witchcraft. The "social process" involves the means of identifying such witches, which is an involved procedure eventuating in curing ceremonies and conferences. If a diagnosis and an identification is made, the witch could be ritually murdered. Subsequently, the suspected murderers were subjected to a trial, which apparently could commonly result in acquittal, after considerable testimony from both sides. Nash sees the affair as a means by which a community can restore the balance and harmony lost when witchcraft accusations disturb them.

The only one of these early 1950s publications on witches that directly responded to both the Evans-Pritchard and the Kluckhohn arguments, is M. G. Marwick's paper, "The Social Context of Cewa Witch Beliefs," published in *Africa*, in 1952—and followed a decade later by Marwick's book on the Cewa, *Sorcery in its Social Setting* (1965). The 1952 paper contained a pointed review of the literature in witchcraft in an effort to establish what Marwick considered is the most appropriate context for analysis of the phenomenon. He begins:

> Witch beliefs, like many other social phenomena, may profitably be analyzed by the methods of several social scientists . . . the fundamental difference between the approaches of the social psychologist and the sociologist to witch beliefs is that, whereas the former focuses his attention on the individual as he participates in, and reacts to, these beliefs, the latter disregards individual attributes and concentrates on abstracted status-personalities, thus looking upon the beliefs as signs of tension in the network of inter-human relations that constitutes the social structure. (Marwick 1952: 120)

He then analyzes Kluckhohn's approach in *Navaho Witchcraft* and compares it to the Wilson paper dealing with the Nyakyusa and Pondo data. Marwick announces that he is in favor of the "sociological approach" to witchcraft studies. He notes that the Kluckhohn piece is "sociological in approach where it deals with the function of witch beliefs in conserving established social relations by underlining the group's value premises" (ibid.: 120). However, he continues: the "bulk of the analytical section, which bears the title, 'An Essay in Structural Dynamics' is, in my opinion, sociopsychological rather than sociological." He defines "sociopsychological" as "expressions of an individual's motives rather than as signs of tension in a system of interacting status-personalities" (ibid.: 121). He then observed that "Kluckhohn obviously does not have the same conception of the term *structural* as the British social anthropologists, e.g., Radcliffe-Brown" (ibid.: 121). Turning to the Wilson paper, he notes that it is "sociological in two respects. Firstly, it shows how the incidence of certain types of accusation can be directly connected with the nature of the social relations in which they occur" (ibid.: 121). (E.g., the mother-in-law–daughter-in-law relationship noted earlier.) The second "sociological" approach concerns an "indirect relation" between witch beliefs and social structure, namely, the way the beliefs can reinforce the "system of values" (ibid.: 121), and he exemplified this by the way the Nyakyusa attributed a "lust for food" among witches, which in turn reinforced the positive social value placed on keeping one's neighbors supplied with food. However, Marwick also says that Wilson did approach sociopsychological explanations in one or two instances. Seemingly, the criterion of what is sociological versus sociopsychological is the difference between viewing beliefs and actions in a purely individual motivational or emotional context on the one hand, and as a reflection of status positions, on the other. But Marwick also acknowledged mixed cases (in general, it would seem to me that the mixed cases are the most profitable, since they show the relationship between psychological factors like motivation, to social or group phenomena).

Marwick opened his essay with affirmation of the way witchcraft beliefs tend to support particular values and thereby "sustain the social structures"—a functionalist theme running through all the literature reviewed thus far, regardless of the particular approach used. He continued with what he viewed as the crucial precondition for a witchcraft episode: "strained social relations" (ibid.: 125). This condition he calls "social tension." And he uses Leopold von Weise's three types of "dissociative concepts" as his basic scheme.[3] These three types were: (1) *opposition or contravention*—which Marwick says is identical to his own "social tension"; (2) *competition*; and (3) *conflict*. That is, as tension or opposition arises in a group, it can result in either competition to see who prevails, or outright conflict. The scheme seems essentially commonsensical. He applied it to the Cewa and other cases by adding one important ingredient: Ralph Linton's paired concepts of *ascribed* and *achieved* status (Linton 1936; chapter 8). Elaborating, Marwick hypothesized that:

> (1) competition will tend to occur between persons in a social relation if their relative statuses are not ascribed by social structure, and that this competition will develop into tension and conflict if (a) the desire for the object or status compete for is intense and/or (b) social structure does not eliminate or regulate competition; and (2) that this tension will be projected into witch beliefs and subsequent conflict if there are no other adequate institutionalized outlets for it (Marwick 1952: 130–1).

He used the diagram and analogy of a ricocheting bullet: the tension will pop out at an angle, so to speak, if there is no other "adequate institutionalized outlet." As noted elsewhere, in the United States this was called the "frustration-aggression hypothesis," which is of course "psychological" in Marwick's terms. (This raises questions about the nature of the difference between psychological phenomena—or sociopsychological, to be exact—and sociological: substantive or terminological?)

Most of the text of the paper consists of descriptions of sources of "tension" in Cewa social structure, including twenty case studies where witchcraft might be expected to exist in accordance with the hypothesis in the previous paragraph. Seventeen of the cases did in fact have witching episodes. The three cases that did not fit the hypothesis involved psychological data, or as Marwick put it, ". . . if more details of the personalities of the 'witches' were available," the cases would be "susceptible to sociopsychological analysis" (ibid.: 232). He concludes that Cewa witch beliefs (and, presumably, the actual practice of witchcraft, although Marwick is unclear on this point) have "two main social functions": the first is "maintenance of the indigenous social structure, especially when its stability is threatened by modern social changes" (ibid.: 232)—the latter provision deriving from material in some of the case studies which related interpersonal tension and conflict to modernization processes and experiences. The first function is general and vague, and Marwick acknowledges this, noting that beliefs have stabilizing functions in all societies. (This is, of course, an example of the tautological "functions" which attracted criticism of the functionalist approach. That is, if beliefs exist in an ongoing social system, they have to be related to existing social and behavioral phenomena, and therefore, are "functional"—in disregard of the costs of maintaining them.)

The second function is more specific and has overtones of the useful generalizations presented by Kluckhohn:
". . . Cewa witch beliefs afford a means of rupturing social relations when these become too cramping or too pervasive" (ibid.: 232). This process is especially apparent in Marwick's analysis of lineage segmentation—conflicts commonly developed between branches of lineages, with departure and alienation resulting—the affairs often accompanied by witchcraft accusations. Marwick holds that social relationship systems in African societies frequently have to be "blasted away rather than quietly dismantled"—a generalization which surely transcends the African environment and is, in fact, abundantly exem-

plified on a worldwide basis in the 1990s by widespread ethnic, religious and national tensions.

There is another, and related contribution in the Evans-Pritchard and Kluckhohn style: the 1963 book edited by John Middleton and Edward H. Winter, *Witchcraft and Sorcery in East Africa*, containing ten case studies of various African tribal groups. In their introduction, the editors state that ". . . these beliefs are social, not psychological phenomena and must be analyzed as such" (Middleton and Winter 1963: 1). And this dictum characterizes the entire book, which is an institutionalized offering from "British social anthropology," but which like the other pieces we have reviewed, contains plenty of material on attitudes and values. And the editors acknowledge Evans-Pritchard and Kluckhohn, pointing out that the "modern study" of witchcraft and associated phenomena "rests on the work of these two men and their influence . . ." (ibid.: 2). And this means, as it did for Marwick—though in an equivocal manner—that Kluckhohn's psychiatric approach is as seminal as the more structural emphasis. As a matter of fact, Marwick, in his closing paragraphs, avows that his research "shows that a full understanding of witch beliefs and associated phenomena can be attained only by using—but not confusing—the methods of several social sciences, especially ethnography, sociology and psychology" (Marwick 1952: 232). He remarks that Kluckhohn attempted "an unsuccessful psychological analysis" (Marwick 1965: 306), but does not specify what he considered was "unsuccessful." Elsewhere, Marwick approvingly cites Kluckhohn's "socio-psychological" explanations.

Middleton and Winter seem to be more interested in the cultural versus sociological terminological dichotomy than the psychological-sociological. To illustrate, the authors give examples from the Azande and the Tallensi. The former concerns the gender-related practices regarding the transmission of witchery status we mentioned earlier: male witches can transmit witchery to sons but not to daughters but women witches can transmit to both sexes—and how these beliefs are consistent with Azande beliefs regarding procreation, and so forth. Middleton-Winter represent this as "cultural" explanation, since these ideas about witch origins are related to other cultural ideas and values. On the other hand, the material on the Tallensi provided by Fortes represents the "sociological" approach: witchcraft among these people is considered to descend in the female line, since their kinship system is patrilineal, and they believe that witchcraft threatens the solidarity of the male lineage group. This is defined by the authors as a "sociological" explanation. However, it would seem to me that both explanations are both cultural and sociological, since both involve ideas, values, and social groupings.

What did we learn about witchcraft in this twenty-five years or so of research? Well, we certainly found that witchcraft and witching are related both to general cultural values and also to groupings and practices considered to be social organization. How could it be otherwise? Witchcraft cannot exist in a vacuum; it must be part of the social process. Secondly, we have learned that witchcraft has both benign and destructive social functions: it promotes and reinforces interpersonal hostility, but it also provides a means for avoiding conflict, channelling off hostilities into smaller corners of the society; and also, upon occasion, assists in reestablishing harmony and promoting solidarity. Again, why not? If a society functions, so will its parts. The literature on witchcraft I have looked at contains no instance of a society falling apart because of rampant witchcraft—all the cases studied were those in which witchcraft was an anticipated and recurrent pattern of behavior and/or belief. However, there is no doubt that interpersonal hostility can take hold in a society and reach a point of destructive force, and witchcraft can become the vehicle of this force.

That is, from Evans-Pritchard on, the dominant theme in witchcraft studies partook of the functional, or "structural-functional" persuasion, and that tradition, while providing a vehicle for uncovering fascinating details and specific loci of witchcraft in odd corners of the world system, also produced some basic—even obvious—truths. The background issue is simply that in the European tradition, witches were evil, bad, and something you don't talk about. To study them is a somewhat daring venture. And to discover that witching is an expected and even useful part of social life was equally daring. So the importance of the findings was defined in part by the cultural biases of Western civilization.

And what of the conceptual issues? We have seen that the study of witchcraft in Classic anthropology included some confusion over a series of substantive concepts: culture, society, psychological phenomena, social phenomena, and so on—the terms eluding precise definition and overlapping in meaning. This background conceptual controversy owes little to witchcraft itself—it is an epiphenomenal product of the attempt of anthropologists to be social scientists, and to find the inherent and necessary ideas and methods.

Paradoxically, however, this "confusion" was productive of knowledge about witchcraft for the reason that Marwick implied: full knowledge of any social phenomenon requires a multidisciplinary or more accurately, a *multidimensional* approach. Thus, it was necessary to focus on "sociological phenomena," "psychological," or "cultural," in order to see the phenomenon whole. Kluckhohn came closer than any of the other researchers in seeing all sides of the situation, and in the opinion of this writer, his work, granted some defects, represents the most insightful contribution to the topic. To be sure, the Navaho handle witchcraft differently from African groups, but then each African group also has its own context for witching.

In 1942, the physiologist Walter Cannon published a paper entitled "Voodoo Death" in the *American Anthropologist* (Cannon 1942). Cannon had investigated a number of actual deaths attributed to witching in Haiti and described the physio-psychological symptoms. They turned out to be those of extreme alarm and anxiety: dehydration, adrenalin discharge, etc.—leading, in extreme cases, to shock and death. The study underlines the ultimate context of witchcraft: the fact that if one really believes in it, and if one is told that so-and-so is bewitching him, he will suffer from its effect, and possibly die. This tells me, among other things, that to be successful, witchcraft cannot be entirely secret: it must be a publicly acknowledged, though culturally "covert" part of social life.

Notes

1. I was particularly interested in Henry Maine's *Ancient Law* (1861) as a result of Robert Redfield's lectures in his history of anthropological thought course given at the University of Chicago in the late 1930s and early 1940s. Maine presented his history of legal institutions in the Orient and the Western world as a developmental sequence beginning with sacred and moral myths as sanctioning specific publishments and legal arrangements in tribal and village societies, and evolving into universalistic codes promulgated by emerging large-scale government authorities. I was intrigued by Maine's writings because while it could be viewed as an "evolutionary" presentation, it was based on actual known histories rather than speculative theories of social progress or development. Maine insisted on the need for accurate, country-based histories of growth and change, and concluded (in an anticipation of Marx) that legal codes appeared in various societies when people—the "plebeian" population, successfully challenged the "oligarchy" and its monopoly on legal procedures. And Maine was especially interesting because he was

the author of the first influential sociological polar typology: from *status* to *contract*. Maine's "functionalism" was even "earlier" than the "early" variety exemplified in this essay by the Malinowski piece. Maine realized, without making a special case for it, that all social institutions are interrelated, and that legal instrumentalities always had some close relationship with social organization, political power, and religious belief systems. He knew that social institutions and practices as well as religion had definite implications for customs, everyday and vice versa. Maine's descriptions of the growth and change of Hindu and Roman systems illustrates such functional interrelationships in great detail.

2. Eventually Kluckhohn went further in his critical stance on functionalist concepts, particularly "adaptation" and "adjustment". In a paper written for a volume of essays on the concept of adaptation, he spoke of the "limitations" of these concepts, particularly their failure to examine the:

> long- or short-term costs of "functioning" institutions. They are certainly incomplete, and I believe there are important elements of distortion in them. They do not enable us to deal with some outstanding problems, and they take no account of large masses of evidence that do not square with them . . . They emphasize out of all proportion the push of the total situation, neglecting the pull of ideas and of ideals. They constitute in fact a valuation in terms of survival and of adjustment, despite the common judgement of humanity that the "best adjusted" individuals often tend to be empty automations. (Kluckhohn 1949: 260–1)

   This was responding to the criticism of functionalism common to the period, and while the criticisms had validity, I still feel that although such concepts neglect some things, nevertheless they also tell us a lot about behavior in social situations.

3. Von Weise was a German systematic social theorist of the 1920s and 1930s who influenced a number of American sociologists, especially Howard Becker, who wrote a systematic sociology treatise based on the ideas (Becker 1932). Von Weise was a contemporary, more or less, of Max Weber, but on the whole lacked the historical content and grounding of concepts so useful in Weber, and which influenced Talcott Parsons. Becker and Parsons were, for a time, rival American social theorists, but the latter won the competition hands down.

Literature Cited

Becker, Howard. 1932. *Systematic Sociology, on the Basis of the Beziehungslehre and Begildelehre of Leopold von Wiese*. New York: J. Wiley & Sons.

Bennett, John W. 1992. "Surrendering to Loma and to Sociology and Trying to Catch Them: Some Recent Writings of Kurt H. Wolff." *Reviews in Anthropology* 21: 1–16.

Cannon, Walter B. [1942] 1965. "'Vodoo' death." *American Anthropologist* 44: 169–81. Reprinted in *Reader in Comparative Religion: An Anthropological Approach*, 2d ed., edited by William A. Lessa and Evon Z. Vogt. New York: Harper and Row.

Dollard, John, Neal E. Miller, Leonard W. Doob, O. H. Mowrer and Robert R. Sears. 1939. *Frustration and Aggression*, in collaboration with Clellan S. Ford, Carl Iver Hovland, and Richard T. Sollenberger,Institute of Human Relations, Yale University. New Haven, CT: Yale University Press.

Evans-Pritchard, E. E. [1937] 1968. *Witchcraft, Oracles and Magic among the Azande*. Reprint. Oxford: Clarendon.

Fortes, M. and E. E. Evans-Pritchard, eds. 1940. *African Political Systems*. London: Oxford University Press.

Fortune, Reo F. [1932] 1963. *Sorcerers of Dobu: Social Anthropology of the Dobu Islanders*. Rev. ed. London: Routledge.

Gregg, D. and E. Williams. 1948. "The Dismal Science of Functionalism." *American Anthropologist* 50: 594–611.

Harris, Marvin. 1968. *The Rise of Anthropological Theory*. New York: Thomas Y. Crowell.

Kluckhohn, Clyde. [1944] 1962. *Navaho Witchcraft*. Papers of the Peabody Museum of American Archaeology and Ethnology, vol. 22, no. 2, Harvard University. Reprinted with an introduction by T. Parsons and E.Z. Vogt. Boston: Beacon Press.

———. 1949. "The Limitations of Adaptation and Adjustment As Concepts for Understanding Cultural Behavior," in *Adaptation*, edited by J. Romano. Ithaca: Cornell University Press.

Kluckhohn, Clyde and William H. Kelly. 1945. "The Concept of Culture," in *The Science of Man in the World Crisis*, edited by R. Linton, pp. 78–107. New York: Columbia University Press.

Kroeber, A. L. and Clyde Kluckhohn. 1952. *Culture: A Critical Review of Concepts and Definitions*. Papers of the Peabody Museum of American Archaeology and Ethnology, vol. 47, no. 1. Cambridge, MA: Harvard University.

Linger, Daniel Touro. 1993. *Dangerous Encounters: Meanings of Violence in a Brazilian City*. Stanford, CA: Stanford University Press.

Linton, Ralph. 1936. *The Study of Man: An Introduction*. New York: D. Appleton-Century.

Lowie, Robert H. 1937. *The History of Ethnological Theory*. New York: Farrar & Rinehart.

Maine, Henry S. 1861. *Ancient Law, Its Connection with the Early History of Society and Its Relation to Modern Ideas*. (Latest reprint by Dorset Press.) London: John Murray.

Malinowski, Bronislaw. 1929. *The Sexual Life of Savages in Northwestern Melanesia*. London: George Routledge.

———. 1935. *Coral Gardens and Their Magic* (2 vols.). London: Allen & Unwin.

———. 1944. *A Scientific Theory of Culture and Other Essays*. Chapel Hill, NC: University of North Carolina Press.

———. 1948. *Magic, Science and Religion and Other Essays*. Selected and with an introduction by Robert Redfield. Glencoe, IL: The Free Press.

———. [1916] 1948. "Baloma: The Spirits of the Dead in the Trobirand Islands." In *Magic, Science and Religion and Other Essays*, pp. 125–227. Selected and with an introduction by Robert Redfield. Glencoe, IL: The Free Press.

Marwick, M. G. 1952. "The Social Context of Cewa Witch Beliefs." *Africa* 22: 120–35; 215–33.

———. 1965. *Sorcery in Its Social Setting: A Study of the Northern Rhodesia Cewa*. Manchester: Manchester University Press.

Merton, Robert K. 1949. "The Bearing of Sociological Theory on Empirical Research," in *Social Theory and Social Structure: Toward the Codification of Theory and Research*, pp. 21–82. Glencoe, IL: The Free Press.

Middleton, John and E. H. Winter, eds. 1963. *Witchcraft and Sorcery in East Africa*. New York: F.A. Praeger.

Murray, Henry. 1938. *Explorations in Personality: A Clinical and Experimental Study of Fifty Men of College Age*. New York: Oxford University Press.

Nadel, S. F. 1952. "Witchcraft in Four African Societies: An Essay in Comparison." *American Anthropologist* 54: 18–29.

Nash, Manning. 1960. "Witchcraft As Social Process in a Tzelbal Community." *America Indigena* 20: 121–6.

Parsons, Talcott and Evon Z. Vogt. 1962. "A Biographical Introduction to Clyde Kluckhohn's *Navaho Witchcraft*," in *Navaho Witchcraft* by Clyde Kluckhohn. Reprint. Boston: Beacon Press.

Passin, Herbert. 1942. "Tarahumara Prevarication: A Problem in Field Method." *American Anthropologist* 44: 235–47.

Spier, Leslie. 1921. *The Sun Dance of the Plains Indians: Its Development and Diffusion.* Anthropological Papers of the American Museum of Natural History, vol. 16, part 7. New York.

Wilson, Monica H. 1951. "Witch Beliefs in Social Structure." *American Journal of Sociology* 56: 307–13.

8

A Problem in Social Organization: The Use of Kinship as an Organizing Principle for Instrumental Activities

Co-authored with Leo A. Despres

With an Epilogue, 1996

The importance of kinship, consanguineal and simulated, in the instrumental activities of simpler peoples has long been recognized by ethnologists. In monographic studies like those of Malinowski (1935), Firth (1929, 1946), and Tax (1953), the role of kinship in technological performance, power relationships, and economic transactions has been described in detail. In recent research on non-Western societies which are undergoing industrialization, it has become evident that kinship and other forms of "pre-industrial" social organization are extremely important for organizing all types of economic and political activity. Comhaire (1956), Salz (1955), Nash (1956), and others have pointed out that kinship in the non-Western world is a tenacious sys-

Originally published in 1960 as "Kinship and Instrumental Activities: A Theoretical Inquiry," in the *American Anthropologist*, vol. 62, pp. 254-67. The inspiration for this paper came from my field research experiences in Japan, and Despres's in a New England factory (see bibliography). We wrote the paper in 1958-59 when we both were employed by different branches of Ohio State University. The paper was based on the results of a graduate seminar conducted by Bennett in 1958. We are indebted for much of the material and many features of the interpretation to the other members of the seminar: Donald Crim, Carl Lande, Arthur Neal, and C.H. Huang. Harold Gould was a member by correspondence. The paper has been slightly revised.

tem which is not only crucial in determining the course of change, but which also may become an instrument by which economic and political change might be introduced.

Ethnographic information on the instrumental functions of kinship systems has sometimes been used as evidence that while kinship has such functions in tribal society, they are weak or absent in industrial society. The proposition that extended kinship systems are incompatible with the needs of an industrial society has figured importantly in such approaches to acculturation and modernization as folk-urban theory and Weberian historical sociology. With research, cases which provide contrary evidence have been increasing in number (e.g., Despres 1958; Miner 1939; Levine 1955; Rubin 1951; Francis 1955). [And subsequently, Bennett and Ishino 1963.] While specific explanations have been given for these "exceptions," the increase in their number seems to call for a more systematic conceptualization than has heretofore been provided. This theoretical inadequacy motivated the authors to undertake an examination of kinship and instrumental activity based on a review of a number of typical cases from different societies. In the examination of the instrumental functions of kinship organizational models, the immediate problem confronting the authors was the complexity and variability of the phenomena. In Japan, for example, one finds work groups (*oyabun-kobun* systems) which have "boss-henchman" patterns of relationship characterized by simulated blood-kinship ties and serving specific economic and political objectives (Ishino and Bennett 1952; Ishino 1953). [And as a final version: Bennett and Ishino 1963.] Another Japanese system (with analogues all over the world) is called by Bennett the *nakama* [Bennett and Ishino 1963, chapter 6]. This is a system of hiring small groups of workers usually consisting of immediate neighbors and blood or affinal relatives. Such *nakama* display few ritual observances and no clear-cut simulated kinship ties, but nevertheless use watered-down role patterns reminiscent of the family. A different pattern is found in the Hindu *jajmani* system which consists of hereditary economic relationships of a lineage or kinship type existing between individuals or families of different castes (Gould 1958; Wiser 1936; [and Beidelman 1959; Harper 1959]). In the Philippines, kinship systems with instrumental functions take the form of bilateral kindreds which utilize both blood and simulated kinship ties for the purpose of organizing political factions and selecting candidates for high political office (Lande 1958; Sibley personal correspondence; Pal 1956). Still another variation in the use of kinship as the basis for instrumental activities is reported by Fallers (1956) in his book on "Bantu bureaucracy." In the villages of the southern Busoga, Fallers encountered instances of simulated clans which were formed without regard for actual kinship ties for the purpose of legitimizing property ownership and political authority.

Only two characteristics appeared to be generalizable across the entire range of cases we found for analysis in the anthropological literature:[1] (1) in each instance these systems were found to be associated with particular old, pre-industrial cultural traditions; and (2) the cases were predominantly associated with societies undergoing modernization. Aside from these two characteristics each case had its own unique dimensions and called for an explanation which had to take into account the specific historical and sociocultural context. At the same time, it seemed to the authors that cross-cultural comparison ought to yield more significant generalizations.

Assuming, therefore, that some kind of order must underlie the variability, the authors proceeded to experiment with a number of concepts which might yield the nature of that order. Considered first were standard techniques and models utilized in ethnological kinship analysis. These genealogical specifications were found to be inadequate for two reasons. First, they failed to provide an explanation as to why both bilateral and unilineal systems (as well as combinations of the two in some cases) were equally useful for organizing instrumental activity. (One would have expected that the flexibility of bilateral systems would make them more useful than unilineal systems in adjusting to changing economic and political conditions.) Second, orthodox kinship models failed to explain how such systems work; that is, how rational and instrumental decision could dominate the more traditional constellation of blood relationships while, at the same time, preserving that traditional constellation intact.

Next, the Parsonsian "pattern variables" were applied systematically to the data in search of a more generalized explanation.[2] It was found that if and when we were willing to infer the individual's values about other individuals and objects of social action (inferences for which we had very little data), the pattern variables could be systematically applied. This yielded a tentative classification approximating a "nominal scale" upon which each of the cases could be placed.[3] After considerable study, approximately twenty cases of kinship systems with instrumental functions were classified in this manner. However, two difficulties emerged which led us to conclude that the pattern variables were inadequate for a cross-cultural comparison. First, each case manifested a unique pattern which prevented us from developing a general typology in terms of which commonalities could be expressed. The difficulty here seems to be that the pattern variables force the social analyst to focus attention on the normative aspect of culture to the exclusion of other dimensions (e.g., the functions of tradition, the stability or instability of specific traditions, and so forth). In other words, the pattern variables appear to be adequate for deriving an interpretative explanation which renders the phenomena understandable to the observer when the cultural dimension can be assumed to be constant (e.g., for comparing different systems within the same culture). However, they are inadequate when the cultural dimension varies (e.g., when systems from different cultures or differing parts of one culture are compared).

The second difficulty with the pattern variables is related to the first. We found that the classification of a given case in terms of the variables depended upon which aspect of the case one took as the point of departure. For example, if the traditional cultural values of the Japanese *oyabun-kobun* systems were stressed, then the pattern variable, "collectivity orientation," seemed most appropriate for classifying the system (i.e., the members valued their group associations, rituals, and so on). On the other hand, if the system was studied with reference to the organization of instrumental activities performed, then "self-orientation" turned out to be the most appropriate classifier (i.e., the members worked for profit, wages, and so on). This need not be construed as a criticism of the pattern variables, since it would be permissible to use them heuristically or segmentally. However, our objective included not only analysis, but synthesis; that is, some way of handling the systems as wholes, within their social and cultural context. Here the pattern variables could give us little help.

Thus, at this stage the problem which confronted the authors was the familiar one [i.e., familiar to late Classic anthropology] of *bridging the gap between a cultural analysis on the one hand and a behavioral analysis on the other.* Kinship *structure*, insofar as it represents an historical and traditional system of symbols and meanings, is a *cultural* variable. The performance of specific tasks, whether it involves the production of specific products or services or the pursuit of political goals, is a *behavioral* phenomenon; that is, the patterns of behavior in the performance of tasks, unlike those guided by a system of symbols and meanings, are intimately related to conditions of time and place.

The difficulties which accompany any attempt to integrate the analysis of cultural systems (which, for analytical purposes, can be considered without regard to spatial-temporal dimensions) with the analysis of behavioral systems (which must be considered with reference to action in a temporal-spatial context) also prevented us from utilizing one or more of the various social typologies like folk-urban theory. Such theoretical constructs as folk-urban appear to be quite adequate for the analysis of long-range historical phenomena where temporal exceptions give way to the homotaxic assumptions made by the type. On the level of behavioral systems (e.g., a particular instance of a particular kinship system having specific instrumental functions) homotaxic assumptions cannot be made: the exceptions become the rule, so to speak. The difficulties in applying social or historical typologies to the analysis of action or of living societies can be appreciated when one compares Redfield's *The Primitive World and Its Transformations* with his *Little Community* (Redfield 1953, 1955).

From these exercises we found certain theoretically significant variables. On the one hand, there were specific rules or norms which governed the pattern of kinship relations, somewhat independent of the instrumental activities associated with them. In the Philippines, for example, there were rules which controlled the relationship of individuals in bilateral kindreds. These rules were supplemented by another set which governed the relationships between individuals who were related through the performance of traditional rituals such as Christian baptism. We also noted that there were other rules which governed the performance of instrumental activities. In the case of the *oyabun-kobun* system these rules related to job performance, job security, the organization of work activities, criteria of efficiency, or standards of quality of product. Finally, over and above these sets of rules, there existed historical and cultural patterns which not only provided the structural and ideological setting within which kinship rules and activity rules were related in given circumstances, but which also, in part, defined the role of kinship and its models in various situations.

For example, the role of kinship within a culture characterized by a caste hierarchy (as in the case of India) is different from the role of kinship within a culture characterized by the absence of caste. In India, one can certainly say that caste is the fabric of which the society is made and kinship is one means of preserving that fabric. Kinship principles come into play when members of families within castes inherit the economic functions or occupations associated with caste membership. In Japan, kinship is one means of preserving general hierarchal values. The ritual kinship within the *oyabun-kobun* system, however, is a means by which hierarchal values can be consciously and rationally exploited for economic and political purposes. In the Philippines, bilateral kindreds are one source of power in a more or less democratic culture. The consolidation of bilateral kindreds for political purposes is a means of increasing the power and wealth of kindred groups. In each case, the general culture, explicitly or implicitly, prescribes a somewhat different role for kinship. At the same time, it serves to define a particular relationship between kinship rules and the rules which govern instrumental activities.

By this time it should be evident that we found it necessary to distinguish between two basic components of the social organization of groups under analysis. First, we defined the *culture or ideology* of a group, a category consisting of certain rules and values associated with social relations, ceremonial life, economic activities, and any other aspect of social life. These cultural patterns define the "oughts" and "shoulds" of the relationships and activities of people. However, in the course of everyday social life, such norms may or may not be adhered to. Ideological systems tend to be equilibrious, relatively conservative, and available to individuals as general cultural knowledge. Now, while ideology logically can accompany any and all aspects of human affairs, we shall, for our special purposes, use the term chiefly to refer to the rules and norms—the model—of kinship relations.

We have chosen to refer to the second major component as *activity*. Logically this includes all activities: economic, religious, social, and so on. However, in our analysis we shall use activity primarily to refer to the "instrumental" aspect of our groups; that is, purposive economic and political activities. The nature of activity is such that there is likely to be constant change—to a greater degree, at least, than for cultural ideology. Instrumental activities constantly require adaptation to the material conditions which prevail at a given time and place. In addition, they constantly adapt to the changing technological scene, and to alterations in social life due to diffusion and social contact.

While activities can, in part at least, be oriented toward the sanctioning and maintenance of ideology (e.g., in a theoretical irrigation or "hydraulic society"), this orientation is usually continually qualified by conditions of subsistence and affluence. Consequently, groups and individuals come to possess rules or principles[4] of activity which are expressly developed for the purposes of making practical adjustments to a changing reality.[5]

From this viewpoint, then, activities are *not* conceived as being in equilibrium. The utility of the distinction between ideology and activity lies in the fact that the relationship of ideology to activity becomes problematic. The two may vary (from time to time and place to place) from complete independence to cases where the activity is almost an exact replica of the ideology. Thus, we can construct hypotheses about change and modernization which may be tested with available data. For example, when the ideological pattern differs appreciably from the form of the activity, we may ask how extensive changes in activities have to be to bring about significant changes in ideological patterns. When activity changes are extensive and rapid, and cultural or ideological patterns remain stable, what mechanisms exist or come into existence to circumvent potential conflict and provide for consistency? To what extent is the incompatibility of extended kinship structures and rational instrumental functions (as is the case in most Western societies) a matter of genuine structural incompatibility or a result of conflicting ideologies (e.g., kinship values versus bureaucratic values, or folk values versus urban values)?[6]

The data available to the authors on most of the cases were not sufficiently complete to answer these questions. However, systematic application of this theoretical approach to the available data suggested the possibility of generalizations that had not been forthcoming in our previous analyses. The case studies to follow represent typical variations in the comparative literature.

The *Oyabun-Kobun* and Related Systems in Japanese Society

Oyabun-kobun is a system of "boss-henchmen" relationships featuring simulated blood-kinship ties and serving various ideological, economic, and political objectives of Japanese society, including criminal groups. The system is culturally derived from a pattern of relationships in which the roles can be described in terms of Japanese familial-feudal institutions. Simulated or ritual kinship customs are known from early times in Japan (Asakawa 1903; Odaka 1950), but the specific oyabun-kobun pattern seems to have developed in the late feudal period (ca. early 1800s). [And in the early postwar Occupation period, economic conditions sparked a revival: 1995.] Thus, in addition to the emphasis on familism, or the traditional segmented patrilineal system characteristic of Japanese society, there is an emphasis on patterns of feudal hierarchy and *noblesse oblige*. In essence, the *oyabun-kobun* system utilized the "particularistic" principle of a blood kinship system in conjunction with hierarchal feudal patterns interwoven with the former by the existence of elaborate rituals (Ishino 1953; Ishino and Bennett 1952). [And Bennett and Ishino 1963, chapters 3, 4, and 5.]

The ideal roles of the participants may be outlined as follows: the oyabun typically is visualized as a simulated or "ritual" parent, to whom is owed the respect and loyalty expected of the father in traditional Japanese family organization. The kobun are considered as ritual children of the *oyabun*, and are expected to obey his orders and accept his decisions as to their needs. Ritual elaboration of the relationships includes a variety of ceremonies. One of these is the *jingi* ceremony in which a new worker formally applies for admission into a *kobun* group. Initiation ceremonies for new members include pledges of ritual brotherhood; the symbolic drinking of "blood" (wine, salt, fish) which is an element in the Japanese marriage ritual; and the bestowal of a new "family name" on the initiate. The blue *happi* coat, widely used throughout Japanese industry, may bear the crest and name of the "boss."

While on the level of traditional cultural ideology *oyabun-kobun* is a relatively stable system of symbols and meanings, on the level of activity it is sufficiently variable to give rise to cases representing a wide range of relationships of ideology to activity. That is, cases can be found where the ideological pattern is so rigidly adhered to that ideology and activity cannot be distinguished. At the same time, cases can be found where ideology and activity exist independently of one another. In the latter cases *oyabun-kobun*, as a system, often has little significance beyond that of a pattern of joking relationships.

The cases of *oyabun-kobun* systems which best illustrate the identity of ideological and activity patterns existed among certain provincial and special craft industries in the recent past, where the "master" had complete paternalistic authority over his apprentices, workers, and their families, and where the entire system of production is worked out in terms of these familial-feudal relationships patterns. Examples are the old craft-iron foundries (Odaka 1950); traditional fishing industries, where the boats were owned by one paternalistic entrepreneur who even furnished housing for his "sons" (his crewmen); and the traditional *kabuki* theater guilds, where even the name of the major actors descended to ritual sons (apprentices).

Another set of cases illustrates the use of *oyabun-kobun* patterns as cultural ideology upheld by ritual but in conjunction with an organization of activities which departs from these patterns. These cases can be found today in a number of industries, many urban, which involve seasonal or erratic labor recruitment, territorial monopolies, and sometimes a low level of skill. In these cases, the industrial tasks and direction of labor may be carried out with modern techniques and efficiency, but the *oyabun-kobun* ideology is used mainly at the managerial level in a ritualistic way to enforce monopoly, cement profitable economic combinations, and preserve a level of wages. Such examples can be found in the forestry and wood-products industries (Bennett 1958, [Bennett and Ishino 1963, chapters 6, 7, and 8]), urban construction industries, dockyard workers, street stall operator guilds, and criminal and racketeering groups. In many cases the term "boss-henchman system" can be used to describe the general structure of these groups.

A final group of cases includes those in which the ideological patterns of the *oyabun-kobun* system are utilized as techniques to organize labor but do not become part of the activities of labor. In many instances, due to various labor and ecological conditions (the underdevelopment of certain resources and techniques; situations of low wages but high demand), employers may adopt some of the patterns of the oyabun-kobun system in order to keep workers, outbid a competitor, or locate suitable deals, even though they do no take these patterns seriously as ideology, that is, as the one and only way. In the case of crews of lumbermen who work fairly regularly for single timber dealers [Bennett and Ishino 1963: chapter 8], it was found that the members of the group, the dealer and the lumbermen alike, used *oyabun-kobun* terminology in jest, and of course demanded none of the elaborate ritual that accompanies manifestations of the system in cases where it operates with traditional ideology as a norm for organization. In such cases, practical circumstances may cause the economic agents to resort to practices resembling the true *oyabun-kobun* system, but without its ritual or its compulsions. For example, in some of the earlier cases it is often as difficult for the worker with simulated kin rank to leave the group as it is hard for him to obtain membership. However, in this third type of situation, workers can leave when they wish, albeit with a certain amount of persuasion to stay, and are usually hired by normal business and methods. However, ritualized symbols are always available to call forth sentiments of loyalty, and so forth.

The Hindu *Jajmani* System

In the case of the Hindu *jajmani* system we find a hereditary system of economic relationships existing between individuals or families of different castes, whereby each provides the other with goods and services which the other needs, but which they are not permitted to provide for themselves due to caste rules of occupational specialization. However, kinship terms are not used, and the bonding principle is economic service, not family or kinship. The caste system provides the cultural ideology by which various groups within the community are related to one another. The economic needs of the Hindu community crosscut the caste hierarchy, but the ideological principles of caste prevent the higher-caste person (*jajman*) or family from performing menial tasks associated with food production and certain handicrafts. Thus, the *jajman* inherits a *purjan*, or worker, who has the right to serve the sons of men who were served by his father, and to obtain from them the traditional benefits in recompense. In terms of our theory, the *jajmani* system consists of a set of ritual principles or usages which provide for economic activities incompatible with caste in such a manner as to maintain the traditional cultural component of caste structure. In other words, cultural ideology is caste: activity principles are genealogical or "familial," in the sense of the "hereditary" feature. While caste prevents a man from associating with another of lower caste, particularly if the lower caste man is considered "unclean," an exception is made where the relationship is one existing between a *jajman* and *purjan*, even if the latter is a member of an unclean caste. This case represents an example where the principles of instrumental activity are entirely different and a variance with the cultural ideology in terms of which relationships are defined (Gould 1958; Wiser 1936).

Philippine Bilateral Kindreds

Philippine society, both Christian and pagan, is characterized by the presence of widely extended bilateral kindreds. Furthermore, kindreds among the Christian lowlanders are heavily augmented by the creation of essentially dyadic *compadre* (simulated kin) relationships among nonkinsmen. In one Christian village in the province of Cebu, Pal found that the average family head considers himself to be related to one-third of the 286 households in the village (Pal 1956: 9).

That cultural ideology in Philippine society merges extensively with economic and political activity is illustrated by the role bilateral kindreds play in such activities. Among lowland Christian groups Lande (1958) reports that the utilization of kinship ties is particularly striking in the sphere of political organization. One provincial political faction studied was traced back for a half century to the time when the first national elections were held in 1907. This faction has chosen its candidates for high provincial and national offices almost exclusively from among persons related to the faction's successive leaders by consanguineal, affinal, or simulated kinship ties. The bulk of its leaders in various municipalities of the province have also been connected to the faction's provincial leadership by such ties. Lande reports that such factions as a whole, when favored by skillful and popular leadership and by a strong likelihood of electoral victory, have been capable of a rapid and wide expansion along kinship lines—for each individual who becomes connected with such factions usually brings with him numerous kinsmen, compadres, friends, and followers. Furthermore, the introduction of American institutions has also served to augment a closer relationship between ideology and activity in the political realm. The necessity of organizing large combinations of politicians and voters in constituencies embracing entire provinces has led Filipino politicians, in the course of the past half-century, to recognize kinsmen far distant from themselves geographically and genealogically, and to enter into a far larger number of ritual kinship relationships than does the ordinary Filipino, Christian or pagan.

An African Political System

Kinship systems have dominated tribal African political and economic organization since before the beginning of the colonial era.

While in some areas of Africa modernization has effected a breakdown of traditional kinship systems (Little 1957), changes in other areas has resulted in a reorganization of kinship systems, sometimes along fictive lines, and the addition of new instrumental functions. Such seems to be the case among the East African Soga (Fallers 1955, 1956).

The culture of traditional Soga society consists of several interlocking authority systems characterized by a highly stratified hierarchy ranging from the royal family at the apex down to local village headmen. Patrilineality and a system of ascribed rank provides the central basis for political authority in the traditional pattern. The royal group's authority, property, and religion extended beyond its own members to the entire state, with the ruler's rank taking precedence over any other. The actual governing of the state involved an administrative staff of commoners who are involved in "patron-client"[7] relationships with the ruler. Since the traditional tribal principle of family seniority was acknowledged by the British colonial administration, evidence of family genealogies became crucial in establishing legitimate political order. Since genealogical claims could seldom be validated and court decisions were often based on the traditional power structure, strong personal followings became of major importance.

In the villages of southern Busoga, Fallers encountered instances of simulated or fictional clans which were formed by the association of men in the community without regard for actual kinship ties. Given legal recognition, these fictional clans represent a re-establishment of traditional Soga ideology for the sole instrumental purpose of handling problems of property and political succession where traditional lineages have been disrupted especially by sleeping sickness. Fallers states, "These simulated kin relationships have emerged under colonialism as devices for re-enforcing authority in a system that has come to operate through pressure politics" (1956: 122–31).

In terms of the theory utilized in this paper, Soga society is an illustration of a relationship between ideology and activity in terms of which the former is rationally constructed and instrumentally used to achieve organization in the latter. The situation thus resembles some *oyabun-kobun* groups, although the cultural base is very different.[8]

Conclusions

The analysis of cases of kinship with instrumental functions suggests consideration of a more general character. It would seem that two general functional types emerge from the analysis. Consistent with the theoretical framework suggested in this paper, these types may be defined in terms of a means-end schema.

1. The first type is characterized by what we shall call a reciprocal means-end relationship between the ideological patterns on the one hand and the activity patterns on the other. It is illustrated by the cases of Philippine bilateral kindreds, some *oyabun-kobun* groups, and the Hindu *jajmani* system. This type is characterized by the use of the cultural ideology (kinship rules, values) as a means for organizing instrumental activities. At the same time, the pursuit of these instrumental activities is a means of reinforcing the continuity of the traditional culture. In the Philippines, for example, the cultural ideology or rules of bilateral kinship are employed instrumentally as a means of organizing political factions. In turn, political factions serve as a means for consolidating and increasing the political and/or economic power of bilateral kindreds. In the *jajmani* system the cultural rules of hereditary descent are employed to organize economic activities in such a manner as to maintain the traditional caste patterns of Hindu society. A similar pattern seems to characterize those traditional cases of *oyabun-kobun* in which there is a fusion of the ideological and activity system (e.g., the old craft-iron foundries, kabuki theater guilds).
2. The second type is characterized by what we shall call a nonreciprocal means-end relationship between the cultural system and the activity system. This type is characterized by the fact that the culture is exploited in order to organize instrumental activities. In turn, the pursuit of instrumental activities is not directed toward maintaining the continuity of the traditional culture but toward the consolidation of economic and political power within specific groups. This functional type is illustrated by the *oyabun-kobun* "boss-henchman" groups—especially in criminal organizations—and by the institution of fictive clans in the villages of southern Busoga in East Africa. In the former instance, *oyabun-kobun* principles are used mainly at the managerial level in a ritualistic way to enforce monopoly, cement profitable economic combinations, or preserve a level of economic return. In the latter instance, fictive clans emerge primarily to legitimize economic and political power in accord with rules set up by the colonial administration which have not adjusted to the fact that traditional clans based on blood relationships no longer exist.

The primary advantage of recognizing the possibility of two functional types emerging in the relationship of kinship systems to instrumental activities is that it avoids a static conception of structural properties as well as the assumption of unidirectionality of change. The analysis of the above cases suggests that *any* type of kinship structure can be rationally employed in the organization of instrumental activities. Under changing conditions the relationship to such changes may result in the reinforcement of the traditional culture. In other instances it may produce a situation in which the traditional culture is not seriously considered other than for the possibilities of exploiting it. In still other instances the culture may be maintained on the level of ideology but ignored completely for purposes of organizing economic and political activities (a third functional type?). The specific direction the relationship may take remains problematic, and, at this point at least, directs our attention to the specific historical sociocultural circumstances surrounding a given case.

The above analysis also would seem to have theoretical implications of a more general character. First, it seems to raise issues pertaining to the boundary-maintaining mechanisms of social and cultural change which anthropologists to a large extent seem to have ignored [at least, at the time of writing]. Second, it contains implications as to the kind of theory that might prove to be adequate for the analysis of modernization phenomena.

As to the first problem, the analysis suggests that there are sets of conditions which serve as definite boundaries within which social and cultural change occurs. These conditions include the characteristics of systems of symbols and meanings on the one hand and the specific temporal-spatial circumstances within which activities occur on the other.

With respect to modernization, our analysis suggests that an adequate theory would take into account the functional relationships existing between the boundary-maintaining mechanisms mentioned above. This would seem to direct attention to such questions as the following: (1) Under what circumstances do changes in systems of meaning and symbols occur? (2) Under what circumstances do changes reflect merely a new use made of existing traditional cultural patterns? (3) What is the tolerance of a culture for changes in activity patterns; in other words, how extensive can economic and political changes be without effecting changes in traditional patterns of value orientation?

(4) What can the history of a particular society tell us about the relationship of that society's culture to the kinds of activities which have characterized it? Such questions imply that an adequate theory of modernization must bridge the traditional gap existing between a cultural analysis on the one hand, and a behavioral analysis on the other, if generalizations are to be more meaningful than the summary statements characteristic of many acculturation studies.

Epilogue, 1996

The "theoretical inquiry" phrase in the original title ("Kinship and Instrumental Activities: A Theoretical Inquiry") referred to our attempt to use Parsonsian variables to analyze the case material: an attempt which we report was only partially successful. Therefore, part of the paper can be viewed as an operative critique of some aspects of structural-functional theory. However, the distinction between culture—"ideology"—and behavior—"activity"—which we derived in part from Raymond Firth's distinction between "structure" and "organization" or adaptive social behavior can be considered a late structural-functional product. The argument prefigures the critiques of the culture concept in my later papers and in the chapters of this book, as well as my later work on social and economic adaptation. After the paper was published, I received a number of letters, about half of them from kinship-devotees who seemed to feel that Despres and I were ignoring the more important functions of kinship in the spheres of tracing descent, family organization, and ritual. Certainly we had no such intention. While we were not trying to undermine Classic kinship studies, we did feel that the—at the time—almost exclusive concern for kinship as genealogical phenomena had resulted in serious neglect of kinship as a model for organizational structure and behavior in social contexts other than familial. We felt that the ethnological bias tended to assume that the only true and valid concept of kinship was the genealogical, and that the use of kin ties as models for economic and political interaction was, somehow, inauthentic. A possibly more important criticism is the ambiguity of our two types: the one designed to protect and enhance tradition; the other simply to use cultural tradition to get the instrumental tasks performed. I feel that probably these are not to be viewed as types, but shifting objectives and emphases which can change as the nature of the tasks change.

Despres agrees with this criticism of the two types, but he also points out in a letter (1996) that the ambiguity might be resolved. "Why not use the distinction between 'adaptation' and 'adjustment,' introduced, I believe by Henry Murray, and used by Clyde Kluckhohn in his *Navaho Witchcraft* monograph?" (see chapter 7). Despres points out that adaptations more or less reflect institutionalized adjustments—that is, people find ways to cope with changing problems and these coping devices may or may not become standard. When another change occurs, people "adjust" to the new conditions, and eventually these adjustments, when and if generally accepted, become "cultural"—that is, traditionalized adaptative behavior. There always exists a gap between accepted or culturally standardized adaptations and individual coping adjustments—but at the same time, they are always in some sort of process of change and synthesis.

Notes

1. About twice as many cases were found than appear as examples in this article. References to most of these can be found under Literature Cited.
2. The "pattern variables" were developed by Parsons in his theory of social action to describe the normative orientation of action. They consist of very general terms defining a set of universal dimensions or properties of norms of social behavior and interaction. Thus, they are inherently patterns of cultural values (Parsons 1951: 79). Parsons maintained that there were only five basic pattern variables and these could be used to describe any system of social action (ibid.: 59). The first three of these pattern variables are derived from the individual's orientation to social objects or to other individuals. These three pattern variables are: (a) affectivity versus affective neutrality, (b) self-orientation versus collectivity orientation, and (c) universalism versus particularism. The last two pattern variables derive from the properties of social objects in a given social situation. These two pattern variables are (a) ascription versus achievement, and (b) specificity versus diffuseness. A complete analysis and definition of these pattern variables can be found in "Values, Motives and Systems of Action" (Parsons and Shils 1951: 47–275).
3. Sidney Siegel defines a nominal scale as one which simply uses symbols to classify an object, person, or characteristic. It represents measurement as its weakest level because of the limitations imposed by the formal properties of such scales. For an analysis of these properties see Siegel (1956: 22–3). The authors believed that if a nominal scale could be devised it would permit us to take a systematic sample of kinship systems with instrumental functions, note the frequency of appearance of specific types, and infer the statistical significance of appearance of specific types relative to other types.
4. As noted previously, these "principles" might also be considered as "values" or even "ideology," since, logically, cultural ideas can be attached to any human activity. However, we feel it necessary to discriminate between the relatively

static overall principles or "ideology," and the changing, adjustive rules of activity procedure. In doing so, we are in disagreement with the tendency in structural-functional social science to unite all "values" in a single analytical category and make them uniformly functional in social life.

5. The sources of our distinction between ideology and activity are as follows: Raymond Firth makes a similar distinction between "social structure" (ideology) and "social organization" (activity) (Firth 1951: 22ff, 1955: 1–18, see also 1954). Our distinction also closely resembles certain definitions used by Talcott Parsons. He defines culture as an ordered system of symbols and meanings which have the property of being learned, shared, and communicated. He defines an "action system" as something existing at a particular time and place, and which can exist independently of a given cultural system—or in agreement with it, in conflict with it, and so forth. (Parsons 1951). Other paired distinctions emerging from the Harvard school are related to ours; for example, Kluckhohn's original definitions of "normative" and "behavioral" patterns; and more recently, Clifford Geertz's "logico-meaningful" and "causal-functional" types of "integration" in social life (Kluckhohn 1941; Geertz 1957).
6. In a study of the use of a bilateral kindred to organize work activities in a New England brickyard, Despres observed that such kindreds could also be found in certain departments in a local woolen mill. In those departments where supervisors did not particularly adhere to bureaucratic values, kinship principles seemed to be utilized quite efficiently in organizing work activities. In those departments where supervisors were recruited from outside the community and did not share in a commitment to kinship values, the extension of kinship in work activities seemed to be in constant conflict with the bureaucratic values held by supervisors. In such departments, kinship was certainly an obstacle to the efficient organization of work activities (Despres 1958).
7. We have found it useful to distinguish wherever possible between "patron-client" and "boss-henchman" systems. The latter term connotes a system characterized by stern authority on the part of the boss, and relative servility on the part of the henchmen. The former is characterized by a more benevolent or paternal role on the part of the patron, and a somewhat more objective attitude on the part of the client; that is, he remains in the system so long as it serves his needs. It is not always possible to make this distinction, due to lack of data given in publications, and of course many systems combine features of both. And both are "hierarchal" social groups.
8. Another system which seems to be similar to these is reported for San Carlos, a Guatemalan community (Gillin 1951; Tumin 1952). In San Carlos two relatively autonomous ideologies coexist: that of the indigenous Indian population and that of the Ladinos. While the Indians, in general, desire little more than to work their own land, this desire has been largely frustrated by the Ladinos who own most of the land. The loss of land ownership by the Indians has tended to produce marked disruptions in traditional Indian life. In response to these tensions, the Indians have added to the religious pattern of godparental ties that of extracting from one's Ladino compadres a sense of obligation to provide certain privileges such as the rental of *milpa* land, economic security for Indian widows and orphans, and preferential treatment from Ladino legal authorities when one gets into trouble. Hence, a ritual kinship ideology is employed primarily to pursue instrumental activities.

Literature Cited

Asakawa, Kanichi. 1903. *The Early Institutional Life of Japan*. Tokyo: Tokyo Shueisha.

Beidelman, Thomas O. 1959. *A Comparative Analysis of the Jajmani System*. Monographs of the Association for Asian Studies, 8. New York: J.J. Augustin.

Bennett, John W. 1958. "Economic Aspects of a Boss-Henchman System in the Japanese Forestry Industry." *Economic Development and Cultural Change* 7: 13–30. Also appears as chapter 6 in Bennett and Ishino 1963.

Bennett, John W. and Iwao Ishino. 1963. *Paternalism in the Japanese Economy: Anthropological Studies of Oyabun-Kobun Patterns*. Minneapolis: University of Minnesota Press.

Comhaire, J. L. 1956. "Economic Change and the Extended Family." *Annals of the American Academy of Political and Social Science* 305: 45–52.

Despres, Leo A. 1958. "A Function of Bilateral Kinship Patterns in a New England Industry." *Human Organization* 17: 15–22.

Fallers, L. A. 1955. "The Predicament of a Modern African Chief: An Instance from Uganda." *American Anthropologist* 57: 290–305.

———. 1956. *Bantu Bureaucracy*. Cambridge: East African Institute of Social Research.

Firth, Raymond. 1929. *Primitive Economics of the New Zealand Maoris*. New York: E. P. Dutton.

———. 1946. *Malay Fishermen: Their Peasant Economy*. London: K. Paul, Trench, Trubner and Co.

———. 1951. *Elements of Social Organization*. London: Watts.

———. 1954. "Social Organization and Social Change." *Journal of the Royal Anthropological Institute* 84: 1–20.

———. 1955. "Some Principles of Social Organization." *Journal of the Royal Anthropological Institute* 85: 1–17.

Francis, E. K. 1955. *In Search of Utopia: The Mennonites in Manitoba*. Glencoe, IL: The Free Press.

Geertz, Clifford. 1957. "Ritual and Social Change: A Javanese Example." *American Anthropologist* 59: 20–54.

Gillin, John. 1951. *The Culture of Security in San Carlos*. Middle American Research Institute, no. 16, Tulane University.

Gould, H. A. 1958. "The Hindu Jajmani System: A Case of Economic Particularism." *Southwestern Journal of Anthropology* 14: 428–37.

Harper, Edward B. 1959. "Two Systems of Economic Exchange in Village India." *American Anthropologist* 61: 760–78.

Ishino, Iwao. 1953. "The *Oyabun-Kobun*: A Japanese Ritual Kinship Institution." *American Anthropologist* 55: 695–707.

Ishino, Iwao and John W. Bennett. 1952. *The Japanese Labor Boss System*. Interim Technical Report no. 3, Research in Japanese Social Relations, Ohio State University.

Kluckhohn, Clyde. 1941. "Patterning As Exemplified in Navaho Culture," in *Language, Culture and Personality: Essays in Memory of Edward Sapir*, edited by L. Spier. Menasha: Sapir Memorial Fund.

Lande, C. H. 1958. *Politics in the Philippines*. Unpublished Ph.D. diss., Harvard University.

Levine, S. B. 1955. "Management and Industrial Relations in Postwar Japan." *Far Eastern Quarterly* 15: 57–75.

Little, Kenneth. 1957. "The Role of Voluntary Associations in West African Urbanization." *American Anthropologist* 59: 579–96.

Malinowski, Bronislaw. 1935. *Coral Gardens and Their Magic* (2 vols.). London: Allen & Unwin.

Miner, H. M. 1939. *St. Denis: A French Canadian Parish.* Chicago: University of Chicago Press.

Nash, Manning. 1956. "The Recruitment of Wage Labor and Development of New Skills." *The Annals of the American Academy of Political and Social Science* 305: 23–31.

Odaka, Kunio. 1950. "An Iron Workers' Community in Japan: A Study in the Sociology of Industrial Groups." *American Sociological Review* 15: 186–95.

Pal, A. P. 1956. *A Philippine Barrio: A Study of Social Organization in Relation to Planned Cultural Change.* Unpublished Ph.D. diss., Cornell University.

Parsons, Talcott. 1951. *The Social System.* Glencoe, IL: The Free Press.

Parsons, Talcott and E. A. Shils. 1951. "Values, Motives and Systems of Actions," in *Toward a General Theory of Action*, edited by Talcott Parsons and E. A. Shils. Cambridge, MA: Harvard University Press.

Redfield, Robert. 1953. *The Primitive World and Its Transformations.* Ithaca, NY: Cornell University Press.

———. 1955. *The Little Community: Viewpoints for the Study of a Human Whole.* Chicago: University of Chicago Press.

Rubin, Morton. 1951. *Plantation Country.* Chapel Hill, NC: University of North Carolina Press.

Salz, B. R. 1955. *The Human Element in Industrialization.* American Anthropological Association Memoir no. 85.

Sibley, W. E. n.d. Personal correspondence on research pertaining to Philippine work groups.

Siegel, Sidney. 1956. *Nonparametric Statistics for the Behavioral Sciences.* New York: McGraw Hill.

Tax, Sol. 1953. *Penny Capitalism: A Guatemalan Indian Economy.* Institute of Social Anthropology Publication no. 16, Smithsonian Institution.

Tumin, M. M. 1952. *Caste in a Peasant Society: A Case Study in the Dynamics of Caste.* Princeton, NJ: Princeton University Press.

Wiser, W. H. 1936. *The Hindu Jajmani System, India, A Socioeconomic System Interrelating Members of a Hindu Village Community in Services.* Lucknow: Lucknow Publishing.

9

Psychology and Anthropology: Modes of Interface as Represented in the Work of F. C. Bartlett, Abram Kardiner, Ralph Linton, and Gregory Bateson

Introductory Note

This essay differs from others insofar as the two works analyzed in the chapter were produced by psychologists rather than anthropologists. However, both authors were deeply influenced by anthropology and participated in seminars and research ventures with the anthropological discipline. F. C. Bartlett was the founder and dean of British social psychology; Abram Kardiner was a practicing and teaching psychiatrist at Columbia University (where he came into association with Ralph Linton and his students). The chapter therefore has two dimensions: the first is an examination of the interface between psychology and anthropology; the second is historical: the Bartlett book pertains to the early Classic; the Kardiner, the middle and late Classic. The central issue, of course, is the problem of disciplinary interaction: the difficulties experienced by two separate disciplines, with their own interests and terminology—not to mention views of human nature—in getting together and creating a synthesis. It is assumed that by patching social-behavioral disciplines together, one enlarges knowledge. So far as I am concerned, the jury is still out on this issue. There is no doubt that disciplinary cooperation can help solve certain problems,

---

Written in 1995 for this volume.

since disciplines have a way of ignoring data: what is my independent variable is your dependent, and vice versa. But whether the cooperative solution of specific problems feeds a larger knowledge or image of human nature is undetermined. Some believe the more information we have about human behavior, the more complex the picture becomes. Perhaps the more we know, the more pessimistic the image becomes and the less willing we are to face up to it.

I. The Interface

Overview

Psychology was one—perhaps *the* one—discipline in the human sciences with which Classic cultural anthropologists repeatedly found it desirable—or dutiful—with which to interact. Papers advocating collaboration, or trying to determine why there was so little of it, began in the late nineteenth and early twentieth centuries and continued on down into the 1940s, when considerable interaction developed between the fields of personality psychology and cultural anthropology. In 1927 Alexander Goldenweiser opened an essay on "Anthropology and Psychology" with the sentence, "Anthropology, the science of man, and psychology, the science of mind, must obviously be related in more than one way" (1927: 69).[1] Yes. But the problem was that these relationships were being required of separate whole disciplines, and therefore the quite different methods and outlook on the nature of human behavior tended to discourage the more able practitioners. As Goldenweiser put it, most scholars probably preferred to restrict "their interpretations to unit concepts belonging to the same theoretical level as the data to be interpreted" (1927: 69); for instance, anthropologists with descriptive cultural data to generalize about culture; psychologists with psychological data on behavior to focus on psychological generalization.

Thus, both disciplines had a tendency to define their problems and methods idiosyncratically. The basic problem, at least for anthropology, concerned the definition of "psychology." Did it refer to some aspect of behavior, or did it simply define a particular discipline? What about the separate branches or subdisciplines of psychology—were some of them more congenial to the solution of anthropological problems than others? In the most informal sense, an ethnological treatise which describes the behavior and attitudes of people in any life context is offering the reader "psychological" material. In the strictest case, a culture or a tribal society could be analyzed by a psychiatrist and interpreted with special concepts which explained and predicted behavior. Occasionally critical syntheses appeared as the work of single individuals: for example, in 1927 Malinowski published *Sex and Repression in Savage Society*, which was broader in scope than it sounds since it contained a critical examination of certain theories of Sigmund Freud in relation to their European origins and their inapplicability to the Trobriand islanders.

The first serious attempt to use psychological testing techniques by an anthropologist—and still one of the few in all the literature—was made by W. H. R. Rivers in the 1890s when he gave Melanesians color perception tests during the Torres Straits expedition (Rivers 1902); and then a few years later, in India, where he tested various sense perceptions of the Toda (1905).[2] (Another early example is Seligman 1924; see also Rivers 1926). Seligman noted that because of the limitations of the tests themselves, and linguistic problems of color nomenclature, it was hard to tell whether "natives" saw the same colors as Europeans.

Beginning in 1860 and continuing until 1890, the psychologists Lazarus and Steinthal (1860–90) began the publication of a serial entitled *Zeitschrift für Völkerpsychologie und Sprachwissenschaft*, which included separate sections on "Social psychology," "The psychology of Culture," and "The concrete psychology of peoples," under the generic heading of *Völkerpsychologie*. Wilhelm Wundt (1916) was the most eloquent spokesman for the approach, which implied that the psychology of *das volk* contained peculiar and distinctive features not found in the mentality of civilized peoples. Aspects of nonliterate culture thus were seen as based on inherited psychological characteristics. The issue was eventually run to ground by Boas in his book, *Mind of Primitive Man* ([1911] 1938), and we shall have more to say about it later. Difficulties behind the controversy were caused by the fact that behavioral similarities and differences observed in differing settings could be interpreted in different ways, including the ideological. Those who wished to establish political and ideological positions might stress doctrines of superiority and inferiority; or the "outside" group could be designated as the source of evil or distorted judgements.

Classic era anthropologists relied heavily on the verbal statements of informants, supplemented by their own observations of behavior. But psychologists of the same period relied on impersonal or indirect methods where possible, since their approach was ideally based on empirical—experimental—methodology. Moreover, the unit of analysis was fundamentally different: anthropologists used the "culture"—the group tradition—as the base for data collection and interpretation; while psychologists traditionally used individuals. While anthropologists were led to make critical discriminations between group patterns of thought and behavior, psychologists largely ignored the group dimension, and in the view of anthropologists, attributed phenomena to the individual which the anthropologists insisted were really the result of cultural conditioning (not to mention the unexpressed or unadmitted cultural conditioning of the psychologist himself).

Another feature of the results of occasional cross-disciplinary collaboration was the multiplication of subdisciplinary fields and topics. A random check on titles of the books in my library furnishes the following: psychological anthropology; ethnopsychology; cross-cultural psychology; social psychology; folk psychology; biosocial psychology; culture and personality; cognitive anthropology. This reduplication and mirror-imagery of combined or overlapped fields does not provide much assurance that the two disciplines could produce synthetic and multidimensional answers to crucial questions about human behavior and its group context.

If we examine two historical analyses of the interface, one from the viewpoint of a psychologist (Jahoda 1982), the other from that of an anthropologist (Bock 1988), we discover that in both Classic and post-Classic anthropology there existed no formal, generally accepted protocol of "psychological anthropology" or "anthropological psychology"—only occasional and distinct researches, or the random use of insights and concepts from one or the other's field. Bock states that "all psychology is cultural" (1988: 211), and Jahoda that the proper topic is "cross-cultural psychology" (1982: 1), but neither author provides a coherent, well-developed scheme—only examples of typical researches, with their often ambiguous conclusions. The two books cited above have markedly divergent tables of chapters (Table 9.1 summarizing and reducing chapter titles to their essentials.)

Both writers classify the topics of interface in terms of what they believe their disciplines want to learn from the other. Naturally, some

Table 9.1: Topical Contents of Two Texts on Psychology and Anthropology

Jahoda (1982)	Bock (1988)
Personality	Perception
Socialization	Motivation
Social Behavior (i.e., social psychology)	Cognition
Magical Thinking	Psychoanalysis, etc.
Collective Representations	Configurations of Culture and Personality
Classifications—Natural and Symbolic	Basic and Modal Personality
Personality and Symbolism	National Character
	Psychohistory
	Social Structure and Personality
	Ethology
	Ethnosemantics
	Cognitive Development
	Alternative States of Consciousness
	Selfhood

of the same material occurs in both books, often under differing rubrics, and there are also complementary omissions. Jahoda's "Social Behavior" is a chapter which cites a number of classic anthropological studies of social structure and interpersonal behavior which he felt illuminated some basic tenets of social psychology; for instance, the way research like Victor Turner's analysis of factional conflict in kin groups illustrated sociopsychological propositions about the way groups channel individual behavior. But Bock did not even mention this material since it would not be "psychological" in his view: rather, the ethnological study of social networks. On the other hand, Bock believed Erving Goffman's (1967, 1969) interactionist approach to social behavior was a clear example of psychological anthropology, but Jahoda did not mention any of this material and on the basis of his conception of psychology, would not have considered it as belonging to the discipline. It probably would have been, in his view, "sociological."

The point is that the disciplines are heterogeneous: as we noted in the beginning, all data deriving from observing human behavior or hearing people talk, is "psychological" *or* "cultural," depending on whose professional axe is being ground. There are no precise analytical distinctions here, and probably never will be—so what is one man's meat is the other's bones.

In a paper entitled "An Anthropologist Looks at Psychology," published in the *American Psychologist* in 1948, Clyde Kluckhohn noted that "anthropology has more deeply influenced psychology than academic psychology has influenced anthropology" (1948: 439). The reasons, Kluckhohn felt, were based on the differing methodological styles mentioned previously, and what Kluckhohn called "temperament." Anthropology was, especially in the 1940s, very much a fieldwork science, and was repelled by the hard-science approach of psychologists—above all, by their view of human behavior as some kind of mechanical process. Their avoidance of difficult or ambiguous phenomena—feelings, aesthetics, ritual, and the like—gave them, in the anthropological view, a bland and picayunish profile. Kluckhohn felt that the reason for the strong mutual attraction of psychoanalysis and anthropology (in the 1940s) was because both fields not only avoided "hard science," but were also curious and excited about the emotional and irrational elements of human nature.

In Kluckhohn's view, the most "extraordinary" failure of rapprochement concerned the anthropological neglect of *social* psychology. Since the two fields were apparently studying the same basic problem—the influence of group atmospheres on human thought and behavior—there should be more contact. However, the expansion of social psychology took place during an era when anthropologists were busy collecting descriptive tribal data, so they had no time for minute clinical investigations and theories of perceptual behavior. Moreover, in the 1940s, when social psychology began to really investigate things that anthropologists *were* concerned with—cultural values, for example—anthropologists were so preoccupied with Freudian-based personality theory that they ignored social psychology. But in any case, they probably would not have shown much interest since professional sociopsychological research was all theory-oriented. For example, the results of a particular vital experiment like Jerome Bruner's (1973) work on perception of the value of various coins as related to physical properties like their size and weight, said little of importance to a student of an exotic culture—although it did have vital significance for a behavioral theory of culture.

Kluckhohn felt that what anthropologists really wanted (needed?) from psychology was "a formulation of the . . . raw stuff [universal human characteristics] that all cultures act upon" (1948: 442). And this is still a problem for both psychology and anthropology: precisely what is this "raw stuff," and does it really exist? Is the general socialized nature of the human species—a point on which all the human sciences basically agree—such that there really is no "raw stuff" except in very early infancy? Anthropologists in general take over after the neonatal stage, and examine the socialized behavioral products. The psychologist starts with the infancy stage and goes on from there, studying the process of mentation in individuals.

Ralph Linton joined the Classic chorus on the interdisciplinary issue in 1939–40 with a paper in the *Journal of Social Psychology* entitled "Psychology and Anthropology." Linton did not even mention the earlier phase of cooperation of the two disciplines on racial differences, especially intelligence. He was concerned entirely with culture and personality: "Where the two disciplines meet and indeed overlap is upon the fronts of ethnology and personality studies and here there appears to be a series of problems that neither can solve unaided" (Linton 1939–40: 115). What were these problems? His answer is very general: individuals "cannot be understood" except in relation to [their] social and cultural environment" (ibid.: 117), and studies of "social response and cultural change" require knowledge of the personalities of the people involved in these processes (ibid.: 118). This paper was written just after Linton had begun collaboration with the psychiatrist Abram Kardiner, which produced the material we shall discuss later, and therefore may be testament to the difficulties of the collaboration.

So basically the paper was about "cross-disciplinary work," as Linton called it, and the message had a pessimistic note:

> When a worker in one developing science tries to borrow from another developing science, what he usually gets are the findings and conclusions of several years before. The ghosts of defunct theories have a way of haunting the halls of other disciplines for at least a generation after they have been given decent burial in their original homes . . .. To cover two fields simultaneously and carry on original research is an almost impossible task . . .. The only valid basis for cross disciplinary studies is team work between specialists each of whom knows a great deal about one discipline and enough about the other to understand what his team mate is trying to say. (ibid.: 118)

There is also a paragraph about the first Kardiner book that resulted from a seminar Linton helped arrange and attended, and the tone is at best neutral:

> The investigator [i.e., Kardiner, who was attempting to diagnose the basic personalities of tribals] had to deal with information collected by persons whose interests and training were cultural rather than psychological, and as one of the contributors I can testify that the information which I was able to supply on actual motivations of behavior, not to mention native personalities, was scanty and subject to the disadvantages of all unchecked subjective judgement. (ibid.: 119)

In other words, psychologists wanted precise descriptions of *individual* behavior, but the ethnologist collected data from individuals in order to describe group actions and beliefs, and typically did not reformulate these data into categories like motivation or personality type: "However for the present most anthropologists deal in terms of either total culture or discrete culture elements and neither of these concepts is what the psychologist needs" (ibid.: 121).

Trying to be helpful, Linton then listed what he felt were the essential frames of reference which the psychologist needs in order to make better sense out of his reconstructions of personality. Basically these were social, not cultural: "The concept of culture thus becomes of real value to the personality psychologist only when it is linked with the concept of social structure" (ibid.: 124). And social structure, for Linton, mainly concerned *status*—the status of the individual in a social system determines much of his outlook and behavior. That is, he acquires "culture" from the vantage point of particular social positions. Here Linton simply reasserts the essence of chapter 8 of *The Study of Man* (1936).

Race and Culture

In 1925 the social psychologist J. R. Kantor wrote an impressive paper for the *American Anthropologist* entitled "Anthropology, Race, Psychology and Culture." The argument of the paper began with an indictment of the psychology discipline for its preoccupation with biologically derived problems, and for interpreting human behavior in biological and physiological terms. (This was on the whole true for the period—later, of course, with the increasing development of clinical, personality, and psychiatric psychologies the picture changed.) Kantor also faulted the anthropological profession for not concerning themselves "with important intellectual circumstances prevailing in their own culture" (Kantor 1925: 267), meaning by this two things: first, the way anthropology was unconsciously biased by Western "animistic cosmology" in its persistent attempt to find racial psychological endowments; and second, the tendency for anthropologists to adhere to the authority of spokesmen for a particular "cultural ideology." The latter referred to the older generation of social scientists who believed in race differences and possibilities of inferior-superior endowments (a habit Boas attacked vigorously).

Moreover, Kantor was remarkably contemporary in his views on the question of biological and cultural sources of behavior: he held that "mentality" was not a single trait or endowment, but rather an adaptive response to environment; indeed, all "psychological phenomena are in no sense qualities or faculties of an organism but really concrete activities" (ibid.: 270). Thus mentality—and all aspects of it, including intelligence and temperament—is "nothing but a name for a kind of action" . . . "interactions of psychological organisms (human and infra-human animals or being) with the stimuli objects and circumstances around them" [sic]. And of course this conceptual approach led Kantor to invalidate most psychological and intelligence tests, since, as he put it, they "are obviously nothing more than stimuli to performances which are without the trace of a doubt products of culture development" (ibid.: 269). One wonders what both psychology and anthropology might have been like if scholars had taken Kantor's ideas seriously.

Beginning in the 1890s, Franz Boas and others developed a powerful critique of speculative evolutionary anthropology primarily on methodological grounds (e.g., Stocking 1968). Boas, in particular, having been trained in nineteenth-century physical science, had an empirical outlook quite different from the "armchair scholars" in England and the Continent who used data freely in order to prove their theories of cultural change and progress. The basic theme in much of this nineteenth-century material was the idea that "primitive man" or "primitive races" were fundamentally different and on a "lower plane of development" from the civilized. It was assumed on the whole that the differences were probably biologically determined. The theory was controversial in its day, and no two writers agreed completely on all the details. Gradually the issue crystallized around two propositions: that races differed in basic biological endowment; and that primitive people thought and behaved differently from civilized—also probably based on biological inheritance.

Boas led the opposition, at least in anthropology. In his *Mind of Primitive Man* he concluded:

> There is no fundamental difference in the ways of thinking of primitive and civilized man. A close connection between race and personality has never been established. The concept of racial type is misleading and requires a logical as well as a biological definition (Boas 1938: v, introduction to the revised edition).

Boas's argument was based on scientific typology. He held that "race" or any human group with reasonably distinctive physical traits—and, although the issue was moot, distinctive behavior patterns—had to be established by statistical evidence accumulated by scientists. The impressionistic approach that dominated racial description in the nineteenth and early twentieth centuries was prone to guesswork. Ideal types can be a valid tool, but it is also vital to discuss the incidence of empirical variation within these types. Boas felt that the evidence was beginning to show that the variation within types was often greater than the differences between types.

In pre-Classic anthropology, the concept of culture was barely distinguished from the idea of race, and behavior based on custom and precedent was more or less assumed to be wedded to biological type. Secondly, races were customarily portrayed as fixed types, unvarying through time. Boas in his own research (the famous study of descendants of immigrants; 1912, and Boas and Boas 1913) had tried to show the plasticity of physical types, and wrote in *Mind* (chapter 5) that any attempt to compare types across time and space cannot—or does not—take into account variation due to factors that are not biological or psychological (e.g., the physical environment, diet, exercise, and so forth).

However, the lasting influence of Boas's book, so far as Classic anthropology was concerned, lay in his analysis of the concept of culture (actually only one chapter dealt with race differences and "racial" psychology). He rejected the nineteenth-century ideas about culture as a vague reality outside of direct human control, or as an artifact of various forces: the physical environment, economic levels, or geographic regions. His naturalistic demonstration of cultures as a projection of human group behavior was the dominant theme in ethnology for the next thirty or forty years (although Kroeber's abstract superorganicist views had considerable influence on academic theory).

As time passed, the issue of race intensified, under the influence of European doctrines of racial superiority and inferiority. By 1938, the year of the revised edition of Boas's *Mind*, Hitlerian doctrines had become a target for liberal thinkers on the race issue, and it was time for a pulling-together of the research on the themes developed by Boas and others in the 1920s. Otto Klineberg, a social psychologist, took up the challenge, and his book, *Race Differences* (1935) went into two editions and many printings. Along with Boas's *Mind*, it became an essential document in the scientific refutation of racist doctrines of superiority-inferiority at least in the United States, and the two books were frequently paired as texts in courses on race differences taught in the 1930s and 1940s. (I used them both in a course on "human variation" as late as 1962.)

Klineberg's book supplied the detailed research materials that Boas's did not. Boas used what was available at the time, but his main goal was to clarify the rhetoric of culture, race, and human variation generally, and not to foster detailed experimental work. This was Klineberg's job: the social psychologist did what no anthropologist was trained to do: analyze the dimensions of difference and similarity from the viewpoint of quantitative methodology of the controlled experiment. He also made a repeated plea for better ethnological data on comparative tribal behavior.

It occurs to me that if scientists had had any serious influence on political ideology and social thought in the first half of the twentieth century, the whole notion of racial differences as expressive of superiority and inferiority in coping with the world should have been laid to rest once and for all. But the notions persisted: as late as the mid-1920s there still were American sociologists and other professionals with noticeably racist ideas. And some anthropologists—at least prior to Boas—had dallied in racist doctrines and concepts of pure types, superior psychological tendencies, and so on. Such ideas persist, although they tend to be disguised as "ethnic" differences. *The Bell Curve* (Herrnstein and Murray 1994) represents on the whole a reversion to the defective scientific typologizing of the early twentieth century, and critiques like Fraser's *The Bell Curve Wars* (ed. 1995) as well as Gould's, *The Mismeasure of Man* (1981) are still necessary to keep the monster down—just as similar works required refutation in Boas's day. The trouble with race—seen physiologically or psychologically—is that it has become imbedded in political ideology; in the classifying and categorizing obsession of science; and the "sharpening" tendency in human perception: the tendency to perceive differences in people and to relate these perceptions to doctrines of biological differences, and the resulting use of the typology created to justify discrimination.

The Porteus Experiment

The most intensive Classic era attempt to use Western behavior and intelligence psychological tests on tribal peoples was that of Stanley D. Porteus, a clinical psychologist at the University of Hawaii, in the 1920s (Porteus 1931). By the 1920s, psychological testing of all kinds was in its ascendancy, and many of the tests still used today, albeit in revised versions, were also available then. Porteus worked with the Australian Aborigines for a year in 1928, on invitation from the Australian National Research Council to visit Australia and carry out a series of investigations on the mental status of the aborigines of that continent. With the exception of one or two minor studies involving small groups of half-castes as well as full bloods, nothing whatever had been attempted. . . . here in Australia are the remnants of a Stone Age people, cut off, in all probability from other racial contacts for thousands of years. . . . in short we could measure the influence of nature, with nurture held as an irreducible minimum. (Porteus 1931: v)

> That is, Porteus believed that the Aborigines, presumably cut off from intermarriage with other populations, had evolved their own psychological and cultural dispositions, and so the results of the tests would test nature-nurture propositions. Vague doctrines of racial purity underlay the approach, but there was no blatant racist stereotyping.

The results were published in a 403–page book, half of which was a general history and descriptive ethnography, organized with the help of A. R. Radcliffe-Brown, "with whose general program of research this study was linked" (ibid.: vi). That is, the entire project was conceived and carried out with anthropological sponsorship. Porteus tested groups near Alice Springs and on the northwest coast, and the fact that all the groups had been in contact with missionaries and other Australians for many years was acknowledged but not considered to be a problem for the design. Tests used included a battery of "psychophysical tests," measuring musculature, quickness of response, etc., since at the time other investigators had claimed correlations between certain performance factors and intelligence. The battery of tests for pure intelligence was chosen to avoid linguistic contamination or incomprehension, with tests like the Goodenough Draw-a-Man and the Goddard Form Board being used—the best available at the time. However, Porteus began suspecting that these tests were likewise contaminated with what he called "civilized" or the "white man's" concepts.

The general results of the entire study are probably best characterized as confused and equivocal. In the first place, Porteus, although not a believer in doctrines of inferiority and superiority, nevertheless had certain expectations of the performance of the Aborigines based on implicit conceptions of the "primitive mind;" e.g., "The childish delight in the highly coloured object, the naive joy of possession, the eagerness and cupidity displayed for the white man's gifts, were conspicuously absent" (ibid.: 16). (I recall reading this and similar passages for a term paper I wrote in an anthropology course in 1935, and being pleased to learn that the Australian Aborigines were not as childlike or "primitive" as they were supposed to be!) When the subjects began showing variant responses which did not clearly place them vis-à-vis subjects from other tribal populations in the world, Porteus seems to have been at a loss for interpretation. He fairly consistently found that Aborigines scored high on tests reflecting their experience—for instance, visual acuity—and low on tests involving language or skills associated with formal schooling. Aborigine children in school, for example, often scored higher than adults. The meaning of the results seemed clear enough, but Porteus had considerable difficulty reaching conclusions. He persisted in thinking that there must be some kind of inheritance factor associated with tribal status. For example, with respect to the Rote Memory Span Test,

> On the whole the Caucasian group have the best rote memories for digits, being ahead of the Oriental groups at each age except at eleven years. Similarly the Chinese except the Japanese slightly at each age level. . . . When the Australian digit span is compared it is seen that they lag hopelessly behind even the nine-year-old children of the other racial groups. Judging from my twenty years experience of clinical examinations, I would say this indicates a fundamental disability in aboriginal learning capacity. (ibid.: 387)

Porteus exhibited a willingness to accept any test group, however defined—racial, national, local, random, and so on—as equivalent to every other such group for comparative purposes. This repeatedly led him to ambiguous conclusions like the above, in spite of his relative sophistication on the problems of testing people with culturally bound instruments.

II. A Social Psychology Alternative: Bartlett's Psychology and Primitive Culture (with a foreword on G. H. Mead)

Social psychology is anybody's meat—there are versions of it in all the social disciplines: there is psychological social psychology (at least three versions); sociological social psychology; philosophical social psychology; and combinations of these. But there is no real "anthropological social psychology" because, as suggested previously, anthropologists felt that Culture did the trick: people were socialized in their culture, and that was a sufficient theory of "social psychology."

The philosophical basis of most versions of social psychology is found in the writings of George Herbert Mead, a scholar who spent most of his career at the University of Chicago, telling philosophers, sociologists, and psychologists what was transpiring between the individual and society. Widely unappreciated, but powerfully influential in certain circles, no one since has been able to conceptualize the process in such simple language (G. H. Mead 1934, 1938).

Mead's approach to the concept of self (see Mead 1934, part 3, especially sec. 21 and 22) resembled Sigmund Freud's: humans have a "self," or self-consciousness, a psychological process apparently not found in other animals. This self is forged in social relations with other people. Mead called his approach, "social behaviorism," and apparently viewed it as an expansion and correction of pure Watsonian behaviorist psychology. The component of the self which was directly derived from social interaction was called the "Me"—the attitudes and behaviors constituting the Me are shared, in varying ways and degrees, with those of the others with whom the person had been interacting. However, the second component of the self consists of the "I" (Freud's *ego*)—that is, a person's awareness of his needs, interests, and feelings, as over against the Me.

Now, the Meadian theory of the "social self" had no clear relationship to the humanistic theories of the nineteenth and early twentieth centuries which led to the idea of culture. In this context, anthropology emerged from a different intellectual tradition—one in which the self was either taken for granted or simply ignored as epiphenomental. If the individual was mentioned, it was assumed he was simply a bearer of the group culture. Moreover, anthropology took a long time to learn the rather elementary lesson posed by Mead: that a human is not all Me, but also has an I; that is, he is capable of reflecting upon and criticizing the content of his behavior derived from his interactions with society—in other words, that it was impossible to understand or explain human behavior by knowledge of culture alone. It was not really until the late Classic and early post-Classic eras that this reflexivity was fully grasped by anthropologists.

The following quotation from *Mind, Self and Society* summarizes the Meadian theory of self and also relates it to the larger social milieu:

> I have been presenting the self and the mind in terms of a social process, as the importation of the conversation of gestures into the conduct of the individual organism, so that the individual organism takes these organized attitudes of the others called out by its own attitude, in the form of its gestures, and in the others in the community to which the individual belongs. This process can be characterized in a certain sense in terms of the "I" and the "me" being that group of organized attitudes to which the individual responds as an "I."
>
> What I want particularly to emphasize is the temporal and logical preexistence of the social process to the self-conscious individual that arises in it. The conversation of gestures is a part of the social process which is going on. It is not something that the individual alone makes possible. What the development of language, especially the significant symbol, has rendered possible is just the taking over of this external social situation into the conduct of the individual himself. There follows from this the enormous development which belongs to human society, the possibility of the prevision of what is going to take place in the response of other individuals, and a preliminary adjustment to this by the individual. These, in turn, produce a different social situation which is again reflected in what I have termed the "me," so that the individual himself takes a different attitude. (G.H. Mead 1934: 186–7)

Mead also contributed a major philosophical sociopsychology of perception as part 2 of his *Philosophy of the Act* (1938) (based in part on Alfred North Whitehead's writings, especially *The Concept of Nature*, 1920). The burden of the argument was simply that perception cannot possibly be understood without taking into account the temporal social and environmental contexts: a purely empirical psycho-physical approach can yield nothing but abstract material parameters. Mead held that perception of something presupposes a process which began *prior* to the act of perceiving; that perception always involves a *selec-*

tion of phenomena; and that perception frequently involves error and distortion.[3] Here, as in the case of his analysis of self, Mead created still another ingredient of a sociopsychological theory of Culture (although he never used the term culture), and we graduate students at the University of Chicago in the 1940s considered it so. The reason it did not enter formally into the theoretical corpus of anthropology was, I believe, because the Meadian argument was simply taken for granted, a kind of given, or as simple confirmation of what anthropologists had been saying all along.

Now to proceed with Bartlett: The fundamental problem for pre-Classic and many of the early Classic anthropologists was the *origin* of customs, beliefs, taboos, or concepts of the universe. These cultural elements had to come from somewhere, and theories of slow osmosis—the gradual emergence of a particular cultural element as a general group process—were too vague and inconclusive. There had to be more specific origins, and finding an explanation or rationale was one of the main purposes of Bartlett's 1923 book:

> Suppose we find, for instance, that the members of some particular primitive group are in the habit of meeting together to practise certain ceremonial rites. Here is a fact which we must try to explain. We study . . . the ceremonial, and it seems . . . that the practice must spring from, or a least be accompanied by, certain beliefs. Now we picture some individual, setting him, for the time being, entirely outside his special group. Some striking occurrence in his life leads him to associate an animal, let us say, with the birth of a child, or with the securing of food. By the inevitable laws of association, acting upon him just as they might conceivably act on any other individual in any other natural environment, he connects the animal with the child, or the food, and may come to regard the first as the cause of the second. More than this he persuades others of the connexion. The spreading belief, also by a common psychological process, finds dramatic expression in a form of ritual. (Bartlett 1923: 8–9)

This is an early-twentieth-century British social psychologist, describing the familiar mode of explanation used by E. B. Tylor and Sir James Frazer (Bartlett cites both) to account for the origins of cultural elements—the detailed example analyzed by Bartlett was the famous Frazer explanation of the origin of totemism. Bartlett rejected this type of explanation: ". . . the attempt to find the beginning of social customs and institutions in purely individual experience may be essentially a mistaken one" (ibid.: 11). And here, of course, he agreed with the American critics of nineteenth-century speculative ethnology, especially when the speculative origins were used as fact, and made into crucial steps in cultural evolution. But Bartlett rejected the method on unique grounds: "The individual who is considered in psychological theory, in fact, is never an individual pure and simple. The statements made about him always have reference to a particular set of conditions" (ibid.: 11). That is, human individuals are members of social groups, but the individual-experience theory of origins assumed that the individual thinks up the custom on his own, whereas in most cases influences from the group provide the stimulus, model, or direct source of the idea or behavior (a position in essential agreement with the Meadian "Me").

Bartlett argued that the only valid case where individual experience can be used as an origins explanation is when we "interpret individual to mean pre-social" (ibid.: 12). That is, if it is known that the individual taken as the point of origin was not affiliated with a group, at least a group of any size or significance. So in the study of primitive groups, the psychological investigator must recognize that he is dealing with individuals who are—in contemporary terms—already socialized and the possessors of a body of ideas and customs. It is therefore risky and largely meaningless to assume that some particular individual was the inventor or originator of a custom or ritual—although psychological processes, properly handled, can explain the meaning and changes of culture.

Bartlett then presented the problem by analogy: the psychological experiment—one which, say, involves a test of perceptual discrimination, like that of particular sounds. Bartlett asked why such experiments often show a sudden improvement in the behavior of the subject? Can the subject of the experiment be taken as an individual who is innovating, originating some kind of behavior? Bartlett stated that "The analogy between the position of the experimentalist and the student of primitive culture is, in this respect a perfect one" (ibid.: 15). The pattern of change on the part of the subject suggests, Bartlett seemed to say, that individuals can originate forms of behavior which can be transmitted to others. Although, as noted previously, one cannot assume that the change in behavior (in this case, the improvement in test performance) is entirely individual in origin, since the subject is not "pre-social". Bartlett was aware that behavior changes in a learning or perception experimental context was not exactly the same as the question of an attitude, a belief, or a ritual. But that is not the point: from the standpoint of the psychologist, it makes little theoretical difference whether one is speaking of a tribal custom or a percept, since the psychologist deals mainly with individual behavior. In both or all cases of innovation or behavior change one must perform a certain amount of speculation as to the exact circumstances and history of the incident and the situation which might have called it forth. And these circumstances, of course, can include learned precedents.

So:

> We can now see clearly the principle which ought to guide us in our search for psychological explanations of behavior in the primitive group. Our attempt . . . is to understand the antecedent conditions of response, and we want to know how far back we must go in our inquiry. (ibid.: 16)

At this point the reader of Bartlett's book will ask: Was Bartlett interested in explaining primitive behavior, or was he interested in illuminating some crucial problems in psychological analysis by studying primitive behavior? He does not really answer these questions, although it seems reasonably clear that Bartlett was more interested in doing psychology than anthropology. So the book was not so much an attempt at collaboration between the disciplines as it was a matter of a psychologist using anthropological data. This involves some other matters which we shall return to later.

To continue with Bartlett's argument: how did he solve the problem of "antecedent conditions" and the distance one must go into the past to find data? It is important to note that while Bartlett began his disquisition by citing a pre-Classic ethnological methodology which he acknowledged had been largely discredited, he nevertheless determined that residing in the heart of this methodology is a genuine problem: how does novel or changed behavior originate? And this problem should be—could have been—of equal interest to the anthropologist. Bartlett wrote his book in the transition zone between the nineteenth-century speculative "origins" anthropology and the descriptive-historical anthropology of the twentieth century. As he put it, there were two extreme positions: one in which questions of origins were viewed as the only question worth asking, and the other which considered that "*no* questions of origin are worth study" (ibid.: 17). He tries to carve out a position between these extremes, specifying the actual period of time during which the individual behavior and the changes in "social response" emerge. That is, to think of the ethnological investigation as a kind of sociopsychological experiment.

Bartlett insisted that the mental processes of "primitive man" were no different than those of civilized humans: he rejected all attempts at psychologizing primitive mentality in which the *content* of thought and behavior is confused with the nature of the mental processes involved. The argument is identical to that proposed by Boas, although Bartlett does not say so. Bartlett attempted to denature the whole myth of primitiveness by noting that the idea assumes that anything not up to the standards of modern culture is viewed as "something strange and far off" (ibid.: 23), and therefore is somehow qualitatively different from the mentation of modern humanity. He felt that the difficulties of studying the mental life and behavior of primitives was exaggerated, due largely to this notion of strangeness—that is, the concept of "exotic," as I have called it.

As a social psychologist he had to take one additional step: to determine that nature of the "conventions and institutions" (ibid.: 25) which formed the setting and the sources of influences on primitive behavior. And this would call for superlative fieldwork and analysis of data. Short of knowledge of this material, one would need to dissect individual behavior into separate individual components, which he regarded as a "hopeless task."

A second main ingredient of Bartlett's theory required him to determine the nature of the "fundamental tendencies" toward behavior, emotions, and cognition characteristic of the human species. This was an alternative phrasing of the "instinct" concept, which, as codified by William MacDougall, had been used by psychologists in the first twenty years of the twentieth century (MacDougall 1908). Bartlett avoids the term "instinct" because by the early 1920s the concept was receiving criticism by behaviorists and learning theorists. Still, the species must have *something* in the way of inborn "tendencies," however these might be masked by learned cultural habits. And this reworking of the "tendencies" in the experience of individuals was Bartlett's problem.

He began his demonstration with a chapter on the "fundamental forms of man's social relations," and these were of two major types: those, like MacDougall's "instincts," which are part of biological inheritance; and then the "directly social" instincts: "sympathetic induction of the emotions," suggestibility, imitation, "and probably play," gregariousness, self-assertion, self-abasement, possibly the "parental instinct," "perhaps pugnacity," and a "social form of constructiveness" (Bartlett 1923: 28). In other words, he viewed a majority of the classic "instincts" as forms of social behavior that to a greater or lesser degree, and with varying relationships to each other, are to be found in all humans. To these, Bartlett would add the following: the "tendency toward primitive comradeship, the tendency of assertiveness," and the "tendency of submissiveness" (ibid.: 28) (and some more vaguely defined others which we can omit). Bartlett acknowledged that these combine and interrelate, but together they make up a list of basic behaviors which all members of the species manifest in appropriate (or, perhaps, inappropriate, also) circumstances. They constitute a definition of the inherent social nature of *Homo sapiens*.

Next, Bartlett added additional "fundamental forms" which he, as a social psychologist, was particularly concerned with. These were, simply, the "group differences tendencies" (ibid.: 29). These behaviors "cluster about a group's established institutions and act directly as determining factors of individual social behavior." He stated that it is impossible to list these, since they are of endless variety—although they always function within the various parameters (not Bartlett's term!) established by the various social "tendencies" or instincts. In other words, Bartlett proposed that human behavior exhibits a domain of determined responses which constitute the social nature of the species, but that this array of responses must always be set in a context of responses which derive from particular historical social situations (i.e., "culture"). These latter responses are much more numerous in *Homo sapiens* than in any other animal species. And the total sum of behaviors of humans at any given moment is a synthesis of the determined or instinctive responses and the learned responses particular to groups. This was, on the face of it, a sociopsychological restatement of a theory of human behavior which included both the biological givens and the learned external responses. Thus, instead of saying or implying that man's behavior is an artifact of his culture, Bartlett opted for a statement of what would today be called human plasticity.

Bartlett attempted to document his approach with a variety of analyses of particular and common forms of tribal behavior. He found that most of these were social in nature; that is, they involved individuals doing things together, with a varying amount of ritual or symbolic content; and above all, with varying levels and type of participation, for instance:

> From the point of view of the community we may assert that a specialised ten-

> dency toward, say, a particular form of ceremonialism is displayed. Yet when we turn to the individuals concerned, we find wide differences of attitude adopted towards, and even during, the practice of the ceremonial, and this in spite of the fact that the group as it engages in the ritual shows all the marks of common action. (ibid.: 47)

The significance of this problem was that as a psychologist, Bartlett was supposed to handle individuals—yet, while all the individuals in this situation are manifesting varied or even unique attitudes and perhaps other behaviors, as well, they were also agreed on the basic form of participation and the fact that the ceremonial is valid and significant in the social life of the community (*vide* Malinowski's concern over individual variation in the *baloma* beliefs). Bartlett observed that this type of empirical situation illustrates the fact that "sociology" cannot dispense with the knowledge of individual behavior, nor can "psychology" dispense with information on group behavior. He implied that the two approaches need something like social psychology as a way of linking them. The same, of course, would apply to anthropology: the Classic era largely dispensed with the level of individual behavioral analysis (although Boas, the great formulator of the Classic, gradually drew closer to a position like this). Even "culture and personality" was less involved with individuals and more with standardized personalities made up of cultural ingredients, and as a result, kept gravitating toward cultural determinism of behavior.

Now, what does this all mean with reference to "psychology and primitive culture?" Here Bartlett makes clear that if "primitive culture" means anything, it is that the corpus of "group differences responses" is very large for the various communities and groups constituting the social universe. But even more important is the fact that the "group difference tendencies" (i.e., the "culture") originate historically in particular communities, and this historical emergence then becomes "problematic" (ibid.: 52). That is, one cannot ignore the question of empirical origins. Bartlett acknowledged that the origins of strictly individual behaviors is not knowable—and here he is implicitly disavowing the doctrine of cultural determination of individual ideas and behavior. That is, the psychologist studies individual behavior simply at face value, but he must know the "origins" or at least the historical provenience of the "group differences" behaviors in order to distinguish this component from individual behavior. Moreover, the "origins" of the group difference patterns might well be particular individual behaviors, and this must be determined; it is, more or less, the goal of the psychological (i.e., sociopsychological) study of primitive culture (note that Bartlett does not even mention diffusion or borrowing here—although he does handle it later in the book).

Bartlett accomplished this in a series of chapters dealing with particular issues. His setpiece analysis appears in chapter 3, and deals with the folktale, which he considered to be a "social product" insofar as it is recited in groups, exemplified various "group difference tendencies," and usually involved descriptions and interpretations of social and individual behavior in social contexts. He used folklore material from various sources but in particular, Franz Boas's "Comparative Study of Tsmishian Mythology" (1909–10; see also Maud 1989), which Bartlett regarded as the most complete and detailed study of comparative folklore in the literature. Boas not only recorded the tales, but also details of social organization and cultural behavior to which the folktales relate—thus providing Bartlett with one statement of the "origin" of the particular "group differences tendencies" he is concerned with here (i.e., folklore). Bartlett analyzed the tales and discovered that the various behavioral tendencies described earlier all appear in the material. Among other observations, he notes that the storyteller is always influenced by the group listening to his rendition, and this constantly introduces a note of change into the material, and imposes different endings and other details on the corpus of material. The material describes forms of comradeship, of assertiveness, submission, and so forth. This type of analysis has become more or less standard in the scholarly folklore discipline, but its theoretical significance as a demonstration of the interplay of group and individual behaviors and ideas was never fully developed either by folklorists or ethnologists.

The book continues with five more chapters, each dealing with empirical or theoretical issues connected with the general approach, the "contact of peoples"; the "transmission of culture by borrowing"; the "diffusion of culture"; the "elaboration and simplification of culture"; and the "intensive study of the special group" (which concerns the proliferation of subgroups in modern society). Each of these chapters applies the basic ideas about the interplay of the individual and the cultural levels of analysis.

Of course, by the 1980s analyses of this type were fairly routine, and even formed the basis of the postmodern anthropology. Working with older ethnological materials, Bartlett's conclusions often sound trite or naive. But this is not really the point: the approach, the theoretical position, for the early 1920s, represented a clear-cut program for anthropology that would have included the individual and the culture in a single synthetic approach, and one can regret that anthropologists of the period did not grasp its significance.[4]

Culture and Personality: The Linton and Kardiner Episode

We have seen that from the turn of the century through the 1920s the "psychology" that anthropologists attended to was, in the main, an inquiry into learning and perceptual capacities, and on the whole individuals were taken as representative of the "culture"—or even entire species. There of course were a few exceptions, like Daniel Brinton's (1902) involvement with Kraepelian psychiatry. But in the 1930s a very different approach began to develop, one informed by new therapeutic disciplines of personality psychology associated with Sigmund Freud and other European "mind doctors." By the 1920s, Freudian ideas had become de rigueur in educated circles and were beginning to appear in American anthropology, especially in the works of Margaret Mead and Ruth Benedict.[5] Freud and his compatriots were in one sense part of a larger intellectual tradition: German humanistic philosophy, and this element also was important in Benedict's *Patterns of Culture*, where she acknowledged her intellectual debt to Wilhelm Dilthey (Benedict 1934: 52).

Now, the emergence of a concept of individual personality as some kind of private organization of behaviors unique to that individual was influenced by the development of a strong consciousness of self and the idea of human rights in the Western democracies—ideas that had been developing since the Enlightenment. Gardner Murphy's 1947 book, *Personality: A Biosocial Approach to Origins and Structure*, was an apotheosis of this trend: the idea of personality as a unique system of individual organized behaviors and ideas, with the materials coming from anthropology, sociology, and social psychology to create what he called a "field theory" of personality. This meant that "personality is considered here as a flowing continuum of organism-environment events" (Murphy 1947: 21).

This was a mouthful, but Murphy meant that personality should not be conceived of as *types*, but as a behavioral *process*. For him, the individual personality existed in a field of influences and stimuli, constraints and opportunities, possibilities and inhibitions, all provided by a milieu which could be learned and made part of a personality. No two personalities were exactly alike, but Murphy acknowledged, particularly in his "Part Six, Individual and Group," that in societies with particularly tight social systems, characteristic forms or tendencies could appear. But even in such cases, personality type could be seen as variable, not constant—behavioral possibilities which might appear in certain situations but not in others. The idea was not grasped immediately either in psychology or in the social sciences, and to some extent the whole Linton and Kardiner episode displayed confusion over types versus processes.

The Classic era contained a number of intense intellectual episodes each of which proclaimed a new field of theory, but many of these would peter out when the promises could not be kept or the interest simply faded. The attempt by a New York psychoanalytic psychiatrist, Abram Kardiner, and a Columbia anthropologist, Ralph Linton, to create a new approach in the emerging field of culture and personality via a series of clinical seminars, was an instance of this tendency. The concept of "basic personality," announced by both participants with gravity and a certain amount of fanfare, turned out to be a version of the old typological approach to culture and, especially, a reworking of Ruth Benedict's "configurations." In essence, typological theory assumed that it was possible to locate a central behavioral and ideational tendency in the life of a people—a culture, or a society—even if one grants a certain amount of variation around the central theme. And, lo and behold, this psychological type—personality generalized—turned out to be a virtual restatement of "a culture." So the central epistemological problem was whether there was any meaningful way to distinguish between the two concepts—personality and culture.

Ralph Linton, in his foreword to the first of the two books produced by Kardiner in his seminar with a group of collaborating anthropologists, tried to distinguish the culture/personality approach from Benedict's theories:

> the concept of a group basic personality structure will prove valuable to anthropologists in several connections. It suggests a type of integration, within a culture, based on the common experiences of a society's members and the personality characteristics which these experiences might be expected to engender. This sort of integration differs sharply from that which the functional anthropologists have made a focal point in their researches and from that posited by Benedict in her well known *Patterns of Culture* . . .. The integration whose existence has been demon-

> strated by Dr. Benedict is of a totally different sort. It consists in the domination of a particular culture configuration by a particular attitude or affect around which the bulk of the culture's content is organized. (Kardiner 1939: viii–ix)

At the time this passage was written, Linton and Benedict were reported to have been at odds over intellectual and professional issues, and there is a hint—"totally different sort than . . ."—of an attempt to disavow Benedict's thesis. However, the Kardiner notion of "basic personality" was really very similar to Benedict's "configuration" since the "culture" being analyzed was treated as isolated and integral. That is, the concept of "basic personality," like Benedict's configurations, applies only where the circumstances provide the kind of integrity and consistency of behavior represented. As both Linton and Kardiner eventually realized, the existence of multiple status and subcultural social environments in complex, changing, or large-scale societies make the use of the concept of "basic personality" subject to many qualifications. Throughout the history of the psychological-anthropological interface in the Classic era, there were attempts to translate these ideas into precise "scientific" concepts, but in fact the ideas graded into one another and really involved a search for how one might express the commonalities—or, more dynamically, the social and mental bonds between members of any group. Certainly this search was nothing new: it may well be the central issue in the history of Western and Oriental philosophy.

Kardiner himself attempted to distinguish his "basic personality" from Benedict's "configurations" by noting that her concepts pertained to cultures that were "dominated by an *idée fixe*"—that is, isolated societies which had an opportunity to develop their central philosophy more or less without influence from other peoples (Bartlett's "group differences tendencies"). This kind of social existence presumably induced a strong sense of self—but self as defined in terms of an attachment to tradition, which in turn produces a fear of corruption and loss. Linton stated that societies more open to external influence cannot develop this kind of configurated culture, and instead, one must search for a "basic personality type" (BPT) in the behavior of the population: that is, what they all share in the way of values, response patterns, etc., becomes the BPT. Therefore a society can have a BPT in spite of a considerable amount of internal variation and deviance from several sets of norms.

Well and good. However, as noted earlier, this made the BPT, and Benedict's and others' "configurations" to be all matters of demographic or statistical degree, and not holistic or integral phenomena.

The entire Linton/Kardiner affair was really a continuing seminar report. Kardiner was responding to the growing literature on culture and personality coming out of anthropology departments, but he was not inclined to do original fieldwork (unlike Alexander and Dorothea Leighton, who worked on the Navaho with Clyde Kluckhohn, or Eric Homburger Erikson, who worked with anthropological sponsorship on various Plains reservation groups (Erikson 1950). Kardiner published in 1939 the first in the series of three books in the collaboration: *The Individual and His Society*, which consisted of chapters based on the seminars. The procedure involved presentations of ethnological data by seminar members. The seminar presentations were then written up by Kardiner who used his theoretical framework to diagnose the personality materials. Thus the book consists of a series of psychocultural portraits of various societies done secondhand. Linton wrote the Foreword to the book.

In 1945, the other two books in the series appeared: Kardiner and Associates, *The Psychological Frontiers of Society*; and Linton's own small offering, *The Cultural Background of Personality* (1945b). The "Frontiers" book followed the organization of the earlier one, and included chapters on the Comanche, and another on the Alorese, who appeared in the first book—and this time giving Cora du Bois coauthor credit. The third society analyzed was Carl Withers's *Plainville, U.S.A.* (West 1945). And there were several theoretical and methodological chapters. On the whole, the book made no intellectual advance beyond the earlier one, but the data analysis and techniques of presentation were more carefully done.

I have already discussed the concept of "basic personality type" and commented on its ambiguities. Kardiner was a Freudian, but with eclectic interests, who noted his debts to Wundt, Freud, Breuer, Kohler, Watson, and so on, in an effort to portray his own approach as a kind of mainline branch of psychology. Kardiner was an early critic of Freud's methods of data collecting and interpretation, but he acknowledged the fundamental significance of Freud's ideas about repression, defense mechanisms, and the concepts of id, ego, and superego. And these concepts provided a bridge into the social sciences, since they dealt with the social substance or sources of personality. In Kardiner's view, the study of society or culture was equivalent to a Freudian analysis of an individual personality, and the chapters dealing with the various cultures or societies have the feeling of being diagnoses rather than ethnographic descriptions.

The specific concepts, in addition to "basic personality," included the crucial set: "Key Integral Systems," e.g., Maternal Care, Induction of Affectivity, Early Disciplines, Institutionalized Sibling Attitudes, Induction into Work, Character of Participation in Society, Marriage, Reality Systems, Projective Systems, Techniques of Production, and so on—the total list has fourteen of these "integral systems," each expanded into detailed subtypes, and they included both intimate emotional experiences of the individual, as well as institutionalized social and cultural phenomena. That is, emotion and attitude are on the same level, presumably, as techniques of production, status, religion, and so on. This is where many scholars got off the bandwagon, because it looked like a setup. Causal responsibilities could be switched around from one "integral system" to another, simply because they were all "systems" affecting the individual. This was a form of psychological reductionism: culture, in such a view, was reduced to what an individual perceived and experienced. Yet, both Linton and Kardiner (much as did Kluckhohn—see chapter 14) kept insisting on the separateness and autonomy of "culture" and "personality" as concepts and phenomena.

Now, the "basic personality structure" is formed out of the sum total of experiences in these "integral systems" by a process of—what: maturation, learning, imitating, growing up? Then came a step that caused endless controversy: Kardiner believed (e.g., 1945: 29ff.) that "institutions" were "derivatives" of the "basic personality structure." This was puzzling since the list of "integral systems" also included some of the "institutions." A chicken-and-egg affair, and while it is possible to defend this line of reasoning, since culture can be conceived as a continually evolving adaptive feedback system, Kardiner did not make this defense, but left the systems argument up in the air (systems theory applied to social data was really twenty years in the future). And Kardiner did not state—so far as I can determine—that *all* "institutions" were derivatives of the basic personality, only that *some* were—"the greater the number of institutions that we can place as derivatives" (ibid.: 29) is a function of the amount of data "the ethnographer" supplies "us"—the psychological analyst—with. But again, that data also defines the "integral systems." How do you break into the process in order to be sure what is chicken and what is egg? What is antecedent or consequent? What is past and present? Are these questions relevant?—they may be for a psychologist, like Bartlett, but really not for the Classic anthropologist.

Kardiner then placed special emphasis on what he called "projective systems" (one of the integral systems concepts), and this idea also attracted criticism. Kardiner here was tackling what Freud had dared to discuss in various papers—the behaviors and ideas associated with religion, magic, taboo, totemism, art, literature, and so on—behavior and cultural content that defied analysis with the techniques and theory of the earlier experimental psychological tradition. Kardiner simply had to deal with this material if he wished to make a real contribution to the anthropology-psychology interface. He contrasted "projective systems" with "rational systems" (the latter what Talcott Parsons would call "instrumental patterns" or systems—goal-accomplishment systems involving means and ends, with varying degrees of rational choice of means to accomplish the ends).

Kardiner asserted that in the typical primitive society, the training which led to participation in the shared basic personality structure or type would begin in infancy and continue throughout life, and thus the basic personality—or the individual's share in it—is produced, as he said, "in actual experience"—although in another passage he discusses "learning," and it is not clear what the difference between learning and experience really might be in the process of formation of the basic personality—or the extent to which the individual shares in it—points that Kardiner never really discussed or cleared up.

And then there was the concept of "security system," to which an entire chapter was devoted in the earlier 1939 book, but which is simply omitted in the 1945 book (although there is a single one-word index reference to the word "security"). Even in the 1939 book the concept was nothing special: it simply was concerned with how people convince themselves that they feel secure or that the system around them offers a secure existence, and so on. He related security systems to basic personality in a series of thumbnail-sketched tribal societies, and much of the data had more to do with available resources and technology than with psychodynamics.

Now aside from the ambiguity and uncertainty of the conceptual apparatus, which might have passed with a B-minus in a graduate term paper, how do the portraits of the basic personality, etc., of the various societies stand up? The answer simply is that where the data was rich, as in Cora du Bois's Alorese material, the portrait sounds like a solid ethnography, with plausible psychological trimmings. Where the data was thin, or where Kardiner "and Associates" were using a fragment or two from a particular society in order to make a point, the reaction of the reader is negative or doubtful. Certainly none of the ethnology-based accounts are as convincing as the accounts of adult Navaho culture or Plains tribes childhood experiences in the Leighton and Erikson books mentioned earlier (or for that matter in a dozen or so full-dress culture-and-personality monographs that appeared in the 1950s and early 1960s—subsequent to the Kardiner episode).

Kardiner dwelt exclusively on concepts relating to personality, while Linton tried to formulate the culture concept side of the collaboration (if that is what it was, although there are those who think that Linton was really drawn into the affair somewhat against his will). However, Linton seemingly played a role not dissimilar to that of Clyde Kluckhohn vis-à-vis Talcott Parsons in the Harvard Social Relations episode (though of course Parsons was a sociologist not a psychologist). Linton's little book, *The Cultural Background of Personality*, was really the text of a series of lectures he was invited to present at Swarthmore College in 1943. He used some of Kluckhohn's pet notions, especially culture patterning and overt and covert culture. However, the longest passages were devoted to Linton's own chief concept: *status*, and the way a person's position in society has much to do with his behavior. The chapter or lecture on Personality, although the longest in the book, has little or nothing of Kardiner in it, and instead could have been written by a social psychologist insofar as it dwells on the way behavior, attitudes, values, etc., are shaped by social situations and the general culture. This has sometimes been read as a demonstration of Linton's basic unwillingness to accept Kardiner's psychiatric interpretations. Linton also accepted the idea that a "new science devoted to the dynamics of social behavior (1945b: xiv) was emerging from the collaborative work of "Psychologists, Anthropologists, and Sociologists," and here he again shows the influence of the "social relations" and other "interdisciplinary" approaches popular at the end of the war (and which Linton made some effort to document in his *Science of Man in the World Crisis* (1945a).

The Bateson Alternative: Toward a Behavioral Anthropology

Gregory Bateson's masterpiece, *Naven* (1936), an account of a recurrent ceremony practiced by the Iatmul people of New Guinea, provided an alternative to the Kardiner-Linton culture-and-personality approach insofar as Bateson did not use tests or dogmas derived from psychology or psychiatry, but behavioral data derived from careful, persistent ethnographic investigation. The interpretations were based on a version of both structural-functional and culture-pattern theory. Bateson's book of 286 pages on a single ceremony was a tour de force.

In essence the *naven* ceremonial dancers reversed the gender roles (a case of "ritual gender" rather than "ritual kinship" as in Chapter 8): men dressed and behaved like women, and women like men. Bateson wanted to know why these role reversals took place, in the contexts of Iatmul social organization and culture. (In some respects his problem was Bartlett's: how do such customs and ceremonials really come about?) Now, the *naven* was a ceremonial performed for a variety of reasons—but all were associated with one feature of the kinship system: the mother's brother (lau) would arrange the ceremony for his sister's children (laua). That is, the Iatmul had a matrilineal descent system like the Trobrianders, in which parental relationships were skewed toward the maternal line. A *naven* could be held for any significant event associated with the *laua*—an accomplishment, a killing, change of status, etc. In short, *naven* was an important part of the Iatmul socialization system. But what puzzled Bateson was the fact that gender roles and behavior were switched.

Since the biological father was not recognized, the mother's brother had to replace him. And the Iatmul went a couple of steps further than other societies with a similar problem: they tried to convey the ethos—the emotional context—of feminine motherhood roles by having the men dress as women—but they also had to scorn or satirize the relationship with comic clothes and behavior, since men are not *really* women. Bateson took a whole book to get the interpretations to make sense, and when they did, the thing turned out to be quite understandable. It was simply that the symbols were exotic from the Western point of view.

There were two chief contributions: the first was Bateson's concepts of *ethos* and *eidos*, specific configurationist ideas which represented an improvement over the vaguer concepts proposed by Benedict and others. *Ethos* in general referred to satisfaction, dissatisfaction, sadness and joy, as related to activities and valued states of being. While ethos was depictive, Bateson accompanied it with a dynamic concept, "affective function," defined as "relations between details of culture and the emotional needs of individuals" (Bateson 1936: 32). The *eidos* was defined as the "cognitive aspects of details of cultural behavior" (ibid.: 30), and this was accompanied by "pragmatic functions." This way of grouping concrete culture patterns implied that a dialog or dialectic should arise between the ethos and eidos: for example, between the emotional needs of people and their behavior designed to promote social and physical survival. Ceremonials like the *Naven* might well be the ritual means of relieving the anxieties or conflicts these situations would generate or reinforce.

Except for the Malinowski piece mentioned, no one had been able to achieve a coherent, logical analysis of this kind of dialectical system, and in any case, the picture of social behavior emerging from the analysis transcends the kinds of generalizations that the early Benedict and Mead approaches were capable of. John Dollard (1937) called *Naven* a "brilliant and difficult book." (See also reviews by Radcliffe-Brown 1937; Powdermaker 1940; Spiro 1958; and Wolff 1944).

Another contribution of Bateson's book was what he referred to as a "fundamental circularity of phenomena" (1936: 117) in the cultural process. This concept was particularly worrisome to S. F. Nadel, who commented on it at length in his 1938 review of the book. The process was exemplified by the building of large ceremonial houses, which gratify the emotional sense of pride;—but the building of such houses also validated the "normality" of pride in the culture. That is, an ethos sentiment or emotion interacts with an eidos component—or an "emotional function" with a "pragmatic function." Bateson believed that the functional "system of society" was composed of such "circular phenomena." Twenty years later it would be called a feedback process. In any event, it bothered Nadel who felt that the circularity was the result of focussing on a limited number of components, and if one should "extend the relations to other contents of culture, there is no circularity at all" (Nadel 1938: 46). That is, inevitably starting points and causal factors would be discovered.

This seems to me a restatement of the Bartlett problem: while you cannot find the initial causes of *individual* behaviors, you should attempt to find the beginnings of *cultural* phenomena, so I suppose one could say that Bateson was confusing individual and social levels of analysis. This criticism was frequently levelled at the proponents of cultural configurationism.

However, I do not believe that this is very important. Bateson had got hold of a basic process: the way the behavior of people in a society with standardized expectations, values, etc., begins to perform systematically, i.e., with feedback mechanisms: A produces B, and then B influences A, and so on. I know of no other empirical analysis of this "circularity" prior to Bateson's which attained his clarity and provided as much empirical data. The principal accomplishment of *Naven* was to provide an analysis of social behavior which I believe exceeded anything the Freudians and neo-Freudians were able to offer at the time.

Childhood and Society

Reviewing the culture-and-personality materials produced in the middle and late Classic era, one central problem was the way childhood and even infancy experiences could influence the behavior of adults. This was a question derived mainly from Freudian theory, and even psychiatrists who had long given up on the accuracy of Freudian predictions, tended to accept the importance of "childhood and society." The results of these inquiries tended to confirm what was known all along: that childhood experiences are relevant to the study of adult behavior, but their role varies. The individual learns and changes throughout life, and the more varied his experiences, the more likely that childhood experiences will be overlain and can be extinguished. The tighter and more homogeneous the experiences of the individuals in a social group, the more likely childhood will play an important role in their adult life. That is, childhood socialization is most relevant to adult behavior in "folk societies" like some of the tribal communities studied in culture and personality research. But even these are subject to qualification, since many of them were in states of transition. The early culture-and-personality theorists underplayed the significance of human teachability and learnability, and this was directly traceable to the dominance of Freudian-derived psychiatric theory.

One basic difficulty of the culture-and-personality research of the

1940s was that culture on the whole was taken as a static given rather than as a variable. In Kardiner's seminar studies, for example, the "culture" of the various groups was described first, then followed by an analysis of childhood experiences—and of course concordances were found. This seemingly demonstrated the accuracy of the childhood thesis, but what it really did was simply reaffirm or recapitulate the ethnography. The problems of consistency, adaptation, and interaction between instincts or "universals" and learned behavior that social psychologists like Bartlett were concerned with were largely lost in the effort. Theoretical material with more dynamic dimensions, like Irving Hallowell's (1945) seminal paper on learning and acculturation, or Bateson's clinical examination of the interplay of sexual roles and ceremonial values just discussed, were in the minority. And Margaret Mead's and Bateson's observational work in Bali (Bateson and Mead 1942) where they watched the interplay between adult and child and the translation of some of the themes of this interaction into ceremonials and everyday problem situations, while illuminating, was difficult and expensive to perform (for further discussion of the Bali study, see chapter 13).

The best of the culture-and-personality monographic studies were similar to Gordon MacGregor's *Warriors Without Weapons* (1946): a straightforward account of the way Plains Indian values underlay the outlook of young men and women, and required them to attempt to perpetuate the aboriginal existence in an environment utterly inappropriate to such behavior. This approach brought attitudes, values, everyday existence, resources, and even some aspects of childhood training, into a synthesis that made considerable sense. In my opinion, it was in these depictive monographs—produced in the late 1950s and into the 1960s, that psychiatry and anthropology began to achieve a useful descriptive synthesis.

The 1990s: A Postscript

The "culture-and-personality" movement, as so named and defined in the 1940s, has not really survived. The issues it tackled were so indigenously Freudian, and the data so variable from study to study, that its practitioners became fewer and fewer. To do it well, one required intensive fieldwork, and when this was done, it was difficult to distinguish the results from a good depth ethnography. However, interest in some of the methods persisted, and books on Freud's ideas occasionally appear (e.g., Heald and Deluz 1994). An interest in personality and "self"—as it tends to be called—also continues, but in a broader, eclectic approach, using a variety of philosophical, cultural, and psychiatric ideas (e.g., Jordan and Swartz 1990; McCall 1990; Morris 1994). By far the largest subfield is *ethnopsychology*, a field deeply rooted in psychology, and representing an invasion of the discipline by anthropological ideas (much as something called by educationists "ethnology" represents the specialized use of ethnographic field techniques to study classroom behavior). However, the ethnopsychology field also has attracted anthropologists, often as members of cross-disciplinary teams. Ethnopsychology (there is also a small field called ethnopsychiatry, pertaining to indigenous techniques of therapy developed in tribal and other relatively independent societies) is in a sense the survivor of the work on race testing and attitude surveying done by psychologists in the Classic era, plus the work on social psychology using subjects from different cultural settings. (For instance, D'Andrade and Straus 1992; Price-Williams 1975; Matsumoto 1994; Gaines 1992; Segall et al. 1990.)

And then there is "cognitive anthropology" (e.g., Cole et al. 1971; Crapanzano 1992; Dougherty 1985; d'Andrade 1995), a kind of synthesis of several minor subfields from the Classic: depth linguistic analysis; the study of values and meaning; research on ritual; elements of ethnomusicology; and folklore studies. Perhaps the latter are the primary source: the study of folklore in the Classic era was a separate discipline, although occasionally ethnologists would join forces. By the end of the Classic, folklore studies were moving in the direction of studies of meaning with linguistic and philosophical trimmings. "Cognitive anthropology" has by no means absorbed folklore studies, but folklore's theoretical interests have certainly been appropriated by anthropology.

Notes

1. In addition to the Goldenweiser piece, see the following early papers: Boas 1910; Hocart 1915; Kantor 1925; Kroeber 1918; Linton 1939–40; Lowie 1915.
2. W. H. R. Rivers was an M.D. and a practicing psychiatrist who started as an anthropologist in India. His experiences with World War I veterans, whose psyches were fragmented by the horrors of trench warfare, gave him a kind of training and insight into the depths of human experience that would have equipped

him to handle the "culture and personality" theme far more sensitive and realistically than Abram Kardiner, whose therapeutic experience was largely confined to New York intellectuals. An account of Rivers's talents appears in the trilogy of novels by the British writer Pat Barker. (1991; 1994, 1996). The third novel, *The Ghost Road*, is in part constructed arounds Rivers' memories of his experiences in Melanesia during the Torres Straits Expedition. He recalls episodes of Melanesian behavior, particularly ritual, and finds analogs in the behavior of his soldier patients.

3. The relevant passage from G. H. Mead:

> There are two characteristics of perceptual experience which I have already indicated, but which I wish to again emphasize. The first of these is that perception of physical things presupposes an act that is already going on in advance of perception and is a process within which perception lies; . . . The second characteristic of the perceptual situation to which I am referring is its essentially social character. By the social character of the act I mean that the act calls out an activity in objects which is of a like character with its own. . . . this social character of the perceptual process is an abstraction from a much more concrete social attitude . . . attitudes of irritation or affection toward inanimate things . . . (G.H. Mead 1938: 149–50).

4. The approach represented by Bartlett's book eventually emerged in a subfield called "cross-cultural psychology" (Triandis and Lambert 1980, especially Otto Klineberg's (1980) chapter), distinguished from "social psychology" on the basis of the concern for cultural comparison. Traditional experimental social psychology was concerned primarily with the problem of how social attitudes influenced judgement and perception. Cross-cultural psychology is more concerned with the way perception and behavior, in similar or comparable circumstances, will vary from culture context to context. By the 1970s, the name of Donald T. Campbell was prominently associated with the field (Campbell 1963, 1964, 1975). Campbell also collaborated with Melville Herskovits on problems of comparative behavior and attitude. Some of Bartlett's themes were retained in the later cross-cultural field; for instance, the problem of psychological universals (see Lonner 1980), who handles the problem as a matter of how anthropology, biology, and linguistics defines "universals."
5. References to Freud and his theories, particularly those dealing with culture history and social phenomena, began to appear in the anthropological literature in the early years of the century (e.g., W. H. R. Rivers's paper, "Freud's Concept of 'Censorship'" (1920); and his earlier paper, "Dreams and Primitive Culture" (1918). It is worth noting that Alfred L. Kroeber spent two years actually practicing psychoanalysis after a year of training at Stanford (for an account, see Theodora Kroeber 1970: 104–18). His experience surfaced in five papers, republished under the generic title, "Psychologically Slanted," in his lifetime collection of essays (Kroeber 1952). Only two of these really dealt with Freud, and both concerned Totem and Taboo (Kroeber 1920, 1939). On the whole Kroeber kept his psychology-psychoanalysis separate from his anthropology, and anyone not aware of his psychoanalytic experience would be puzzled by this inveterate culturologist-historian's repeated sympathetic reviews of works like Benedict's *Patterns of Culture*. (Further discussion of Kroeber's attitude toward psychology may be found in chapter 10, and of the ideas of Benedict and Mead in chapter 13.)

Literature Cited

Barker, Pat. 1991. *Regeneration*. London: Viking.

———. 1994. *The Eye in the Door*. New York: Dutton.

———. 1996. *The Ghost Road*. New York: Dutton.

Bartlett, F. C. 1923. *Psychology and Primitive Culture*. New York: MacMillan.

Bateson, Gregory. 1936. *Naven: A Survey of the Problems Suggested by a Composite Picture of the Culture of a New Guinea Tribe Drawn from Three Points of View*. London: Cambridge University Press.

Bateson, Gregory and Margaret Mead. 1942. *Balinese Character: A Photographic Analysis*. New York Academy Science, vol. 2.

Benedict, Ruth. 1934. *Patterns of Culture*. Boston, MA: Houghton Mifflin.

Boas, Franz. 1909–10. "Comparative Study of Tsimshian Mythology." *Thirty-first Annual Report of the Bureau of American Ethnology*. Washington, DC: Smithsonian Institution.

———. 1910. "Psychological Problems in Anthropology." *American Journal of Psychology* 21: 371–84.

———. [1911] 1938. *The Mind of Primitive Man*. Rev. ed. New York: Macmillan.

———. 1912. *Changes in Bodily Form of Descendants of Immigrants*. New York: Columbia University Press.

Boas, Franz and Helene M. Boas. 1913. "The Head-Forms of Italians As Influenced by Heredity and Environment." *American Anthropologist* 15: 163–88.

Bock, Philip K. 1988. *Rethinking Psychological Anthropology: Continuity and Change in the Study of Human Action*. New York: W. H. Freeman.

Brinton, Daniel G. 1902. *The Basis of Social Relations: A Study in Ethnic Psychology*. New York: G.P. Putnam's Sons.

Bruner, Jerome S. 1973. *Beyond the Information Given: Studies in the Psychology of Knowing*. Selected, edited, and introduced by Jeremy M. Anglin. New York: Norton.

Campbell, Donald T. 1963. "Social Attitudes and Other Acquired Behavioral Dispositions," in *Psychology: A Study of Science*, vol. 6., edited by S. Koch, pp. 94–172. New York: McGraw-Hill.

———. 1964. "Distinguishing differences of perception from failures of Communication in Cross-Cultural Studies," in *Cross-Cultural Understanding: Epistemology in Anthropology*, edited by F.S.C. Northrop and H. Livingston, pp. 308–36. New York: Harper and Row.

———. 1975. "On the Conflicts between Biological and Social Evolution and between Psychology and Moral Tradition." *American Psychologist* 30: 1103–26.

Cole, Michael, et al. 1971. *The Cultural Context of Learning and Thinking: An Exploration in Experimental Anthropology*. New York: Basic Books.

Crapanzano, Vincent. 1992. *Hermes' Dilemma and Hamlet's Desire: On the Epistemology of Interpretation*. Cambridge, MA: Harvard University Press.

D'Andrade, Roy G. 1995. *The Development of Cognitive Anthropology*. Cambridge: Cambridge University Press.

D'Andrade, Roy G. and Claudia Strauss, eds. 1992. *Human Motives and Cultural Models*. Cambridge: Cambridge University Press.

Dollard, John. 1937. "Review of 'Naven' by Gregory Bateson." *American Sociological Review* 2: 567.

Dougherty, Janet W. D., ed. 1985. *Directions in Cognitive Anthropology*. Urbana: University of Illinois Press.

Erikson, Eric H. 1950. *Childhood and Society*. New York: Norton.

Fraser, Steven, ed. 1995. *The Bell Curve Wars: Race, Intelligence, and the Future of America*. New York: Basic Books.

Gaines, Atwood D., ed. 1992. *Ethnopsychiatry: The Cultural Construction of Professional and Folk Psychiatries*. Albany, NY: State University of New York Press.

Goffman, Erving. 1967. *Interaction Ritual*. Garden City, NJ: Anchor.

———. 1969. *Strategic Interaction*. Philadelphia, PA: University of Pennsylvania Press.

Goldenweiser, Alexander. 1927. "Anthropology and Psychology," in *The Social Sciences and Their Interrelations*, edited by W. F. Ogburn and A. Goldenweiser, pp. 69–88. Boston, MA: Houghton Mifflin.

Gould, Stephen J. 1981. *The Mismeasure of Man*. New York: Norton.

Hallowell, A. Irving. 1945. "Sociopsychological Aspects of Acculturation," in *The Science of Man in the World Crisis*, edited by R. Linton, pp. 171–200. New York: Columbia University Press.

Heald, Suzette and Ariane Deluz, eds. 1994. *Anthropology and Psychoanalysis: An Encounter through Culture*. London: Routledge.

Herrnstein, Richard J. and Charles Murray. 1994. *The Bell Curve: Intelligence and Class Structure in American Life*. New York: Free Press.

Hocart, A. M. 1915. "Psychology and Ethnology." *Folklore* 26: 115–137.

Jahoda, Gustav. 1982. *Psychology and Anthropology: A Psychological Perspective*. London: Academic Press.

Jordan, David K. and Marc J. Swartz, eds. 1990. *Personality and the Cultural Construction of Society: Papers in Honor of Melford E. Spiro*. Tuscaloosa: University of Alabama Press.

Kantor, J. R. 1925. "Anthropology, Race, Psychology, and Culture." *American Anthropologist* 27: 267–83.

Kardiner, Abram. 1939. *The Individual and His Society: The Psychodynamics of Primitive Social Organization*. New York: Columbia University Press.

———. 1945. *The Psychological Frontiers of Society*. With the collaboration of R. Linton, C. Du Bois, and J. West. New York: Columbia University Press.

Klineberg, Otto. 1935. *Race Differences*. New York: Harper & Brothers.

———. 1980. "Historical Perspectives: Cross-cultural Psychology before 1960," in *Handbook of Cross-cultural Psychology: Perspectives*, vol. 1, edited by H.C. Triandis and W.W. Lambert, pp. 31–68. Boston: Allyn and Bacon.

Kluckhohn, Clyde. 1948. "An Anthropologist Looks at Psychology." *The American Psychologist* 3: 439–42.

Kroeber, A. L. [1918] 1952. "The Possibility of a Social Psychology." *The American Journal of Sociology* 23: 633–50. Reprinted in Kroeber, pp. 52–6.

———. 1920. "Totem and Taboo: An Ethnologic Psychoanalysis." *American Anthropologist* 22: 48–55.

———. 1939. "Totem and Taboo in Retrospect." *The American Journal of Sociology* 45: 446–51.

———. 1952. *The Nature of Culture* (anthology selected by the author). Chicago: University of Chicago Press.

Kroeber, Theodora. 1970. *Alfred Kroeber, A Personal Configuration*. Berkeley: University of California Press.

Lazarus, M. and H. Steinthal. 1860–90. *Zeitschrift für Völkerpsychologie und Sprachwissenschaft*. Berlin: Ferd. Dummler.

Linton, Ralph. 1936. *The Study of Man: An Introduction*. New York: Appleton Century.

———. 1939–40. "Psychology and Anthropology." *Journal of Social Psychology* 5: 115–26.

———. 1945a. *The Science of Man in the World Crisis*. New York: Columbia University Press.

———. 1945b. *The Cultural Background of Personality*. New York: Appleton-Century-Crofts.

Lonner, Walter J. 1980. "The Search for Psychological Universals," in *Handbook of Cross-cultural Psychology: Perspectives*, vol. 1, edited by H. C. Triandis and W. W. Lambert, pp. 143–204. Boston: Allyn and Bacon.

Lowie, Robert H. 1915. "Psychology and Sociology." *American Journal of Sociology* 21: 217–29.
MacDougall, W. 1908. *Introduction to Social Psychology*. London: Methuen.
MacGregor, Gordon. 1946. *Warriors without Weapons: A Study of the Society and Personality Development of the Pine Ridge Sioux*. Chicago: University of Chicago Press.
Malinowski, Bronislaw. 1927. *Sex and Repression in Savage Society*. New York: Harcourt, Brace.
Matsumoto, David R. 1994. *People: Psychology from a Cultural Perspective*. Pacific Grove, CA: Brooks/Cole.
Maud, Ralph. 1989. "The Henry Tate—Franz Boas Collaboration on Tsimshian Mythology." *American Ethnologist* 16: 158–62.
McCall, Catherine. 1990. *Concepts of Person: An Analysis of Concepts of Person, Self, and Human Being*. Brookfield, VT: Gower.
Mead, George H. 1934. *Mind, Self and Society*, edited by C. W. Morris. Chicago: University of Chicago Press.
———. 1938. *The Philosophy of the Act*, edited by C. W. Morris. Chicago: University of Chicago Press.
Morris, Brian. 1994. *Anthropology of the Self: The Individual in Cultural Perspective*. Boulder, CO: Pluto Press.
Murphy, Gardner. 1947. *Personality: A Biosocial Approach to Origins and Structure*. New York: Harper & Brothers.
Nadel, S. F. 1938. "Review of 'Naven' by Gregory Bateson." *Man* 38: 44–6.
Porteus, Stanley D. 1931. *The Psychology of a Primitive People*. New York: Longmans Green.
Powdermaker, Hortense. 1940. "Review of 'Naven' by Gregory Bateson." *American Anthropologist* 42: 162–4.
Price-Williams, Douglass R. 1975. *Explorations in Cross-cultural Psychology*. San Francisco: Chandler & Sharp.
Radcliffe-Brown, A. R. 1937. "Review of 'Naven' by Gregory Bateson." *The American Journal of Sociology* 43: 172–4.
Rivers, W. H. R. 1902. *Reports of the Cambridge Anthropological Expedition to Torres Straits*. Cambridge: Cambridge University Press.
———. 1905. *The Todas*. Oosterhout: Anthropological Publications.
———. 1918. Dreams and Primitive Culture. *Bulletin of the John Rylands Library* 4: 387.
———. 1920. "Freud's Concept of the 'censorship.'" *The Psychoanalytic Review* 7.
———. 1926. *Psychology and Ethnology*. London: Kegan Paul, Trench, Trubner.
Segall, Marshall H. et al. 1990. *Human Behavior in Global Perspective: An Introduction to Cross-cultural Psychology*. Boston: Allyn and Bacon.
Seligman, C. G. 1924. "Anthropology and Psychology: A Study of Some Points of Contact." *Journal of the Royal Anthropological Institute of Great Britain and Ireland* 54: 13–46.
Spiro, Melford E. 1958. "Review of 'Naven' (2d ed.) by Gregory Bateson." *American Anthropologist* 60: 970–1.
Stocking, George W. 1968. *Race, Culture, and Evolution: Essays in the History of Anthropology*. New York: Free Press.
Triandis, Harry C. and William Wilson Lambert, eds. 1980. *Handbook of Cross-cultural Psychology: Perspective*, vol. 1. Boston: Allyn and Bacon.
West, James (pseud. of Carl Withers). 1945. *Plainville, U.S.A.* New York: Columbia University Press.
Whitehead, Alfred North. 1920. *The Concept of Nature*. Tarrner lectures delivered in Trinity College, November 1919. Cambridge: University Press.
Wolff, Kurt H. 1944. "A Critique of Bateson's 'Naven.'" *Journal of the Royal Anthropological Institute* 74: 59–74.
Wundt, Wilhelm. 1916. *The Elements of Folk Psychology*. London: Allen & Unwin.

Introductory Note to Chapters 10 and 11

The overall objective of Classic anthropology was to find a concept of culture which could serve whatever purpose of analysis and explanation was at hand. In the case of A. L. Kroeber, some of whose work is reviewed in chapter 10, this search occupied a lifetime, but he was no closer to an all-purpose definition at the end than at the beginning. In the case of Walter Taylor, whose single book is the focus of chapter 11, the search was devoted to a conception of culture which could serve Americanist archaeology. Kroeber was never really sure what culture was; but Taylor underlined the importance of the distinction between *C*ulture and culture*s*, and felt that archaeology needed to do more with Culture and perhaps less with the separate, site-specific little artifact collections that occupied so much of the Classic archaeologists' attention. Although Taylor recognized the existence and importance of universal Culture, he, no more than Kroeber, was able to specify its dimensions or to provide a convincing portrait of its regularities. Kroeber selected simple things—like dress fashions—to analyze and thereby to illustrate the cultural regularities that presumably characterized the behavior of the species, but in the long run Kroeber found little of a convincing theoretical nature to say about Culture—other than to assert its existence.

Part of the problem was the inherent difficulty of selecting, from the vast treasure trove of human activities and objects (Edward B. Tylor's "That complex whole") those phenomena that particularly revealed Culture. Kroeber never did decide, and while he denied it, he really settled for a *ding an sich* conception—Culture is Culture. Taylor, on the other hand, had a more workable conception: "culture consists of ideas"—the models and concepts in people's heads. But the trouble with Taylor's definition was simply that it was hard to find the evidence of ideas in material artifacts. But Taylor thought, I think correctly, that archaeologists could do more if they tried. That, in essence, was his message.

10

A. L. Kroeber and the Concept of Culture as Superorganic

But the greater human intelligence in itself does not cause the differences that exist. This psychic superiority is only the indispensable condition of what is peculiarly human: civilization. Directly, it is the civilization in which every Eskimo, every Alaskan miner or arctic discoverer is reared, and not any greater inborn faculty, that leads him to build houses, ignite fire, and wear clothing. The distinction between animal and man which counts is not that of the physical and mental, which is one of relative degree, but of the organic and the social, which is one of kind. The beast has mentality, and we have bodies; but in civilization man has something that no animal has.

—*Kroeber ([1917] 1952: 26–7)*

Kroeber's 1917 Paper Entitled "The Superorganic"

Distinctions of degree—distinctions of kind, and the dualisms arising from these logical forms are among the foundation stones of Classic anthropology. So much has been written on the origins, history, semantics, and textbook definitions of the culture concept that I shall refrain from following that trail to its end. In this essay, I shall look at Kroeber's classic papers on the "superorganic," dress fashions, and civilizational configurations as examples of the consequences of his

Written in 1995 for this volume.

way of conceptualizing culture. Except for a late denial (discussed later) of the idea that culture was a matter of "kind," Kroeber on the whole stuck to his approach throughout his career, although he was always willing to examine and approve other ways of handling "cultural" data. On the other hand, once one accepts Culture as a distinct universal entity—something unique and integral for man—then any kind of contents can be shoe-horned into the frame. The superorganic concept inevitably creates its own multidimensional or multilevel discourse.

The Superorganic paper[1] was a procedural pronouncement: it supplied still another Americanist criticism of nineteenth- century European anthropology, along with Boas's writings, and it set a particular intellectual tone which characterized Classic anthropology for much of the twentieth century. Kroeber was shooting at what he called the "confusion" in anthropological circles over the social and biological components of the human species, and how this confusion established the groundwork for doctrines of racial superiority and inferiority.[2] He felt that the confusion was due to faulty "analogic reasoning:" the belief that since physique could be inherited biologically, so could social phenomena. Thus, the doctrine of the inheritance of acquired characters was the ultimate target of his critique. His establishment of culture as some kind of separate or distinct entity was, at least in part, an artifact of this demonstration—or perhaps a means to an end. He threw out hints in his writings that he might have consciously exaggerated the breadth of the gap between animal and man, in order to establish the fact that humans had something no animal had, and that this "something" was not biologically inheritable. In any case, he phrased his critiques carefully, allowing for possible evidence from the other side:

> . . . little really satisfactory evidence has been produced to support the assumption that the differences which one nation shows from another—let alone the superiority of one people to another—are racially inherent, that is organically founded. It does not matter how distinguished the minds that have held such differences to be hereditary—they have in the main only taken their conviction for granted. The sociologist or anthropologist can, and occasionally does, turn the case inside out. . . . Real proof, to be sure, is as wanting on one side as on the other. ([1917] 1952: 33–4)

Behind Kroeber's arguments there lay the classic dualisms—all of them slippery and dependent on definition. The question of whether animals have "culture" is still alive: if you take purely quantitative measures, then certainly the anthropologist can say that for all practical purposes, animals lack it. But if you take a technical or behavioral measure, then the still-accumulating evidence that primates, birds, and other species do use and even make tools, suggests some sort of cognitive mapping—and cognitive maps, from a strict neurological standpoint, are the psychological basis of culture. Kroeber acknowledged the borderline cases (which continue to appear, like the 1996 information that New Caledonian crows can make tools out of twigs). However, Kroeber would have asked whether these crows could establish a universal religion?

Kroeber proceeded through a series of setpiece discussions of current issues and writings which permitted him to make his main point: that civilization—Culture, The Social—is a thing in itself, and not reducible to biological—"organic" phenomena. He discusses the work of le Bon, Spencer, Galton, Pearson, and Marett—all of whom, in varying ways and degrees implied an organicity of human behavior and civilization. Does this mean that civilization is mental? Yes, Kroeber argues, civilization is in the minds of men, but not in their biological heritage: "Of course civilization is not mental action itself; it is carried by men, without being in them" (ibid. 1952: 38). He makes the point over and over: a kind of metaphysics, really: culture or civilization is made possible by biology and psychology: humans have to do the work, the "mental exercise"—but once in existence, culture is a creation, a thing "carried by men." Separate, autonomous, but also imbedded in the human domain. Thus the "mental" is really part of the "organic:" it helps create civilization, but civilization is nonetheless separate from it—and if so, then is "civilization" not a real entity, with its own laws?

Much of the Superorganic paper is devoted to a discussion of invention, particularly the apparent inevitability of invention as a response to need. The fact that several key inventions were probably discovered more or less simultaneously in different areas where comparable needs emerged, was grist for Kroeber's mill. And certainly the accumulating evidence in later years on domestication of plants and animals independently or simultaneously in various parts of the world tends to validate this particular point. Edward Sapir, in his critique "Do We Need a Superorganic?" (1917) hit hard on such materialistic emphases, implying that Kroeber was stacking the deck, since material phenomena by their very nature—what later could be called instrumental necessity—would exemplify the kind of automatism that Kroeber saw in the civilization process. Sapir and others called it "determinism," thinking particularly of Kroeber's metaphysical insistence that the human *individual* really had nothing much to do with culture. Kroeber was right in a way—there *are* aspects of culture which have strong physical imperatives, but this does not mean that all of civilizational phenomena are so, or that individuals do not have much to do with the process.

"There can be only one kind of organicness: the organic on another plane would no longer be organic." And of course this holds for the Social too: the Social by any other name would not be social: "the thing we call civilization, transcends them (the organic) for all its being rooted in life" (Kroeber 1952: 51). (Curiously, Kroeber never used the term "superorganic" in the text of the paper.) While civilization is thus a thing unto itself, it does not determine the nature of the individual human in any simple manner. "Because culture rests on the specific human faculty, it does not follow that this faculty, the thing in man that is supra-animal, is of social determination" (ibid.: 48).

Take the case of language. Kroeber used two full pages to discuss the question of whether language—really *speech*—is "organic" or "social." He acknowledged that animals use sounds to communicate, and cites the "experiments" of several ancient kings to test whether children have any natural, biologically determined speech which could manifest itself independently of social contact. The experiments, like the one tried by the mogul Akbar, who shut the kids up all alone for presumably a long period, only to have them come out unable to speak, tended to prove the opposite. Kroeber has a disquisition on "ouch" as an utterance expressing pain, and therefore a candidate for an organic, species-specific-inheritable element of speech. The results were negative. Even at this primitive level, he decided, different "nations" have different sounds to express pain. Kroeber's whole argument, of course, is now subject to a certain amount of criticism on the basis of "deep structure" theories; knowledge of the process of language acquirement by children; and the increasingly better-understood complexity of animal communications. However, while none of these new writings really refute Kroeber, they do suggest that the flat dualisms—humans have language and animals do not, and speech is social and animal utterances organic—require very careful qualification.

Actually, Kroeber did acknowledge that animal behavior is not all instinct—"the mental activity of the animals is partly instinctive, partly based on experience" (ibid.: 31–2)—but again, since 1917 much more is understood about the importance of learning in animals—and even "teaching" in mother-offspring relations, plus the way learned behaviors involve adaptive changes in behavior that may appear to be "instinctive." In general, in order to make the broadly valid point that humans are way ahead of animals in that they can reason and learn at a much higher level, and thereby create "civilization," Kroeber underestimated the mental powers and behavioral capacities of animals. He widened the gap between the species and man, and in the past eighty or ninety years the gap has been narrowed. But obviously a gap remains.

A year later, in 1918, Kroeber published "The Possibility of a Social Psychology," and it is here that Kroeber introduces his first formal analysis of the term "superorganic," in the form of a graphic portrayal of "levels:"

The table shows that "social psychology" meant for Kroeber a kind of master science of culture. The "social" is the final or emerging product which comes to stand alone; the "psychology" refers to the mental acts that bring it about. He notes in the introduction to the edited version of the paper appearing in his 1952 anthology that in 1917 and 1918 modern social psychology did not really exist (Kroeber had obviously not read Bartlett—see preceding chapter), and he simply used or invented the term to describe his conception of the ideal way to study culture. The point echoes the Superorganic paper: he suggests that the absence of a true "social psychology" is the consequence of the basic confusion among "sociologists" about the separateness of the organic and the social. That is, if it is assumed that human behavior is merely a reflection of, or simply caused by organic

Table 10.1: Kroeber's Classification of "Levels"

	Formulation of Processes	Depiction of Phenomena
Superorganic phenomena	Social psychology	Culture history
Mental organic phenomena	Psychology	Biographic history
Vital organic phenomena	Physiology	Natural history
Inorganic phenomena	Physics, chemistry	Astronomy, geology

***Source*: Kroeber [1918] 1952: 54**

processes, then there would be no need for a separate cultural science. This paper is, in reality, a justification for the existence of cultural anthropology—and cultural anthropology is defined as a kind of history. The basic point of both papers is simply that "civilization" is a human thing—but still a thing apart, with its own dynamics and history. And human things cannot be handled with the methods of "science"—as Kroeber conceived science:

> It is true that what is ordinarily called "science" as distinguished from history, that is, the kind of science which resolves into quantitatively describable factors or operates with them, has practically no achievements to its credit on the plane of the superorganic. It might therefore be doubted whether such a science is possible in the superorganic plane of culture. ([1918] 1952: 55)

Years later, Leslie White, operating with his Marxist-inspired version of a superorganic theory of culture, did indeed seem to accept "scientific" analyses of civilization with regard to energy utilization. And Kroeber himself, in his dress-fashions research, used quantitative measurements of bodily proportion to establish regularities or configurations. However, presumably such simple quantification was a legitimate exception to the rule—perhaps he was really thinking of the mathematics of chemistry or physics and the use of such data to prove complex hypotheses and theories about essence or lawful processes with universal relevance. Kroeber rejected this kind of science with respect to the study of civilization or culture simply because he perceived the latter as purely historical phenomena, continually evolving and changing. But the problem is simply that once one postulates a phenomenon in kind, it is extremely likely that there will be a search for laws—generalizations of a universal character—and certainly Kroeber was not immune to that temptation in his later work. So he denied the existence of laws of history, but later went ahead to discover some.

The graphic outline in the social psychology paper is based on the distinction between what Kroeber calls the "explanational and the depictive sciences"—a distinction which he continued to play with, and which Kluckhohn eventually borrowed as a tool to classify the various methodological modes and substantive phenomena in anthropology (Kluckhohn 1947).[3] In other words, "superorganic phenomena" may operate as processes of "social psychology"—that is, thinking and cogitating in social situations, which produces behavioral change (if that is what is meant here); but when the superorganic is described, written down, it takes the form of "culture history." The lower levels of reality in the diagram are not strictly comparable to the superorganic, or as Kroeber writes, ". . . the more basal the dimension in which a class of science operates, the more readily is the transition from the depictive treatment to the determination of mechanisms accomplished" (Kroeber 1952: 54). I suppose this means, for example, that the history of the universe provided by astronomy can be directly described and understood with physico-chemical processes;—the latter *are* the history, so to speak. But when you get into higher levels, like the superorganic, it becomes more difficult to translate sociopsychological processes into some form of unfolding narrative. The causal connections are confused or vague, and so on.

Such differences in the properties of the various levels of the diagram should have tipped Kroeber off to a defect in this mode of classifying scholarly fields. The point is that, for example, the superorganic has material phenomena in it which can inform the scholar about important historical facts. For example, chemical composition of potsherds can trace movement of people and culture contacts.

The "social psychology" paper also establishes the etymology of the term "superorganic." Kroeber said he borrowed it from Herbert Spencer: "It was he who first employed the word "superorganic."[4] Spencer certainly held a concept of "culture" (Kroeber 1952: 56). However, Kroeber also notes that Spencer was unclear about the implications of superorganicism, and constantly went over the line into organic analogies without clearly distinguishing their causal irrelevance for the superorganic. True. And yet Kroeber tells us in the very next paper reprinted in his 1952 anthology—"Historical Reconstruction of Culture Growths and Organic Evolution" (a paper originally published in 1931), that he had a lifelong interest in classification of "shapes, structures and functioning qualities" of animals—and also of cultures and languages. This comment is immediately followed by "It is clear I am not by temperament a social scientist" ([1931] 1952: 57). That is, Kroeber seems to be saying that social scientists are not interested in formal classifications—he calls this "natural history," and therefore presumably social science is something else.

Actually a full and final exposition of the concept of "superorganic" did not appear until 1948, in Kroeber's critical essay on Leslie White's "View of Culture" ([1948] 1952: 110–17). Kroeber delineates no less than ten major propositions which he feels characterize White's work, and then comments on each. The first of these concerns the "series of levels" on which phenomena can be studied, and Kroeber implies agreement with White—and well he might, since the whole superorganic business was based on the idea of levels each of which had its own properties and possibilities of analysis. The second of the ten propositions concerns "reductionism," or the fact that usually the phenomena of one level can be explained by the properties and processes of the levels below it, and here again Kroeber seems to be in agreement with White. And the third proposition—which states that some aspects of each level *cannot* be explained by reductionism—is also generally approved. However: Kroeber begins to have doubts with Proposition No. 5, which concerns the question of separate and distinct phenomenological identities for the "levels;" especially culture. This section contains the famous passage where Kroeber explicitly disavows his tendency to conceive of the superorganic—culture—as an independent entity, but admits that he had been "ambiguous."

> As of 1948, it seems to me both unnecessary and unproductive of new difficulties, if, in order to account for the phenomena of culture, one assumes any kind of entity, substance, kind of being, or set of separate, autonomous, and wholly self-sufficient forces. I do not find that I have ever explicitly declared my belief in such. But I do find that I have been ambiguous . . . .(ibid.: 112)

It was precisely this persistent "ambiguity" that led Classic era anthropologists to accuse him of excessive super-superorganicism. And of course Kroeber criticizes White for more than ambiguity on the issue of culture-as-kind, and disavows White's tendency to look for laws, forces and other self-contained cultural phenomena. All this decades-long furor and fuss concerned a class-concept, "culture," that was proposed as a distinct phenomenon requiring cataloguing or definition. Once one attempts to define an "analytical abstraction," and one full of heterogeneous phenomena, there is no limit to the possibilities of controversy.

In his paper on White, Kroeber wrote, in reference to Bidney's arguments about causation,

> The efficient causes of cultural phenomena questionably are men: individual personalities who are interpersonal and social relations. It seems to me this cannot be denied and that there is neither use nor honesty in trying to whittle any of it away. But the manifestations of culture come characteristically in certain forms, patterns,

> or configurations . . . while persons undoubtedly make and produce these cultural forms . . . our knowledge of persons and societies of persons, has failed conspicuously to explain the cultural *forms*. (ibid. 1952: 114)

This passage gets at the crux of the whole matter. *Kroeber simply could not conceive of a scholarship which reduced cultural patterns to individual or even group psychological or behavioral data. There simply had to be some additional reality to these "forms," and so forth.* And it was the anthropologist's duty to discover them. In no significant sense did this differ from White's views.

Curiously enough, Kroeber did not refer anywhere in his paper to White's occasional use of a definition of culture as the human means of adapting to the environment. White himself pushed this in only a few pieces, and its implications seem to have escaped White, just as it did so for Kroeber. (We shall note in the next chapter that Taylor *did* pay attention to this view, and rejected it.) To have seriously entertained an adaptational concept of culture would have actually bridged the Kroeberian gap between the idea of culture as originating in human mentalities but at the same time existing separately from individuals; it also would have allowed Kroeber to introduce a culture-level concept of human behavior into the argument. That is, humans invent culture as a way of establishing ways and means of survival, and once established, they persist in memory, and hence take on what rhetorically appears to be an independent existence.

As Marvin Harris pointed out (1968: 333–40, with the help of the historian Philip Bagby) the real issue in the superorganic controversy was not whether culture was autonomous in kind, but rather the semantics of concept and construct formation; that is, a problem of scientific logic and language. Classic anthropologists tended to confuse words with things: if you create a word-concept, Culture, then you tend to believe in its existence, and therefore you have to define it—give it definitional reality. For Kroeber, this basic confusion over language and phenomena was based, I believe, on his desire to be known as a historian rather than as a scientist. In his view, historians create the phenomena of history by writing about it, and therefore the anthropologist or ethnologist (although as with other matters, Kroeber was ambiguous here), when he describes a culture, he in a sense creates it. (See chapter 1, where I suggest that ethnology was, in a sense, a matter of writing "stories" which then seem to endure as myths.) Again there is potential here for semantic confusion: stories or depicted cultures *are* "real" in the sense of stories, accounts, literary or scientific creations, and that is the end of it. *But they lack the "reality" of the phenomena on which the accounts are based.*

Where does this leave us? the dogmatisms, ambiguities, and inconsistencies of Kroeber's writings- –as well as its truths—have tantalized historians of anthropology, and I shall not add anything further to that discussion. The problem for this book is the consequences of Kroeber's vague or general idea that culture is a matter of kind; that it cannot be reduced to mental or organic phenomena, even though—paradoxically—these phenomena necessarily underlie it or provide the basis for its existence. The whole affair came about as a result of insisting on a *name*: culture or civilization, and *that* insistence, of course, was based on the desire to distinguish man from the animals. However, this is really a matter of shades or degrees of various behaviors, and the problem could have been elucidated empirically, without resorting to a general term or concept.

Kroeber's Research on Dress Fashions (1899–1940)

Dress fashions? I recall my own wonderment at this choice of topic for major research on culture by the famous Alfred Louis Kroeber when I first encountered it in Robert Redfield's course on ethnological theory in 1940. I was still laboring under the naive belief that you choose topics for research on the basis of their intrinsic importance, or because they had major economic, political, or aesthetic significance in history. It took me a while to get the idea that in Kroeber's view, any aspect of culture was as good as any other if your mission was to determine regularities and processes. Or, put the other way around, that if you believed—even ambiguously—in the phenomenological independence of something, then any aspect of that thing could be used to determine its nature and dynamics.

Kroeber started thinking about dress fashions in 1899, wrote his first piece on it in 1919, and the final version in 1940 had Jane Richardson as a coauthor (Richardson and Kroeber 1940). Richardson was a distinguished British anthropologist who more or less specialized in "material culture." The fact that Kroeber played with these data for half a century suggests either monomania or some inner conviction about the subject matter. He never really told us, flat out, why he tackled women's fashion, but the implications are fairly clear: in the first place, it was part of culture, and in Kroeber's view, any part is as good as any other if you are searching for regularities. Second, Western fashions for women had a continuous, meticulously detailed history over two or more centuries. Third, it was possible, by using simple conversion formulae, to obtain quantitative measurements of the phenomena involved (as noted previously, this seemed to contradict his argument in the Superorganic discussions of the uselessness of quantification in the study of culture, but no matter). But Kroeber could have found equivalent time-series quantitative data in basic machinery, houses, or weaponry, so the choice of dress fashions is still somewhat mysterious. Possibly it meant to him a more human or aesthetic component of culture, and Kroeber was generally on the side of humanistic phenomena.

Kroeber and Richardson did not announce their objectives, what they expected to find, or problems to solve—the discussion is entirely dominated by the data on dress proportions and their changes, and how these fluctuate in possible relationship to one another. The authors, in other words, were satisfied to get what they got with the statistical program used—a program which uses nothing more sophisticated than standard deviation and coefficients of variability. The 1940 monograph is remarkable for its pedestrian descriptive statements, of which the following is an example:

> First of all, it is clear that the proportionate amount of deviation varies among the six dimensions dealt with. Thus, skirt length, the absolutely largest dimensions, has 5.9 as its highest five-year mean percentage deviation (Table 2), while 19 out of 30 values are under 1.0. Waist length rises to a maximum of 10.8, and only thrice falls below 1.0 . . . .([Richardson and Kroeber 1940] Kroeber 1952: 360–1)

After pages of this they do come to a finding—"possible causes of changes in variability" (ibid.: 368). This would seem to have been either the problem they wanted to handle, following the preliminary findings in Kroeber's older papers on the subject, or it is an empirical finding of the 1940 joint study—the authors do not tell us which. This entire section on "Causes of Variability" is worth quoting in full:

> Causality of Change
>
> We are now in position better to weigh the several possible causes of changes in variability.
>
> The primary factor would seem to be adherence to or departure from an ideal though unconscious pattern for formal clothing of women. The consistent confor-

mity of variability to certain magnitudes of proportion—mostly a conformity of low variabilities to high magnitudes—leaves little room for any other conclusion.

A second possible explanation, that high variability is a function of extremes of proportion, falls as such. It is true for a full waist and a narrow or short skirt, untrue for slender waist or full or long skirt. The explanation holds only so far as it is subsumed in that of the basic pattern.

A third possible explanation, that generic or nonstylistic factors unsettle fashion at certain times, is not eliminated, but is pushed into the background of further investigation. After all, such a cause would be an ultimate, not an immediate one. It may well be that unsettled times make for unsettled styles. Revolution, Napoleonic and world wars, struggles over the rights of man, communism and fascism, the motor and jazz, may contribute to fashion's trying to stretch and disrupt its fundamental stylistic pattern. But while such an influence is easily conjectured, it is difficult to prove. In any event, there seems no clear reason for the specific fashion extremes which such a set of causes might be thought to produce. Social and political unsettlement as such might produce stylistic unsettlement and variability as such; but there is nothing to show that it would per se produce thick waists, ultra-high or low ones, short and tight skirts. If there is a connection here, it seems that it must be through alteration of the basic semiunconscious pattern, through an urge to unsettle or disrupt this; and that when increased fashion variability occurs, it is a direct function of pattern stress, and only indirectly, and less certainly, of sociopolitical instability. In short, generic historic causes tending toward social and cultural instability may produce instability in dress styles also; but their effect on style is expressed in stress upon the existent long-range basic pattern of dress, and the changes effected have meaning only in terms of the pattern.

Concretely, it would be absurd to say that the Napoleonic wars, or the complex set of historic forces underlying them, specifically produced high-waisted dresses, and World War [I] low-waisted ones. They both probably did produce an unsettlement of style, which, however, resulted in extremity of high- and low-waistedness respectively.

Herewith arises another question: whether the crests and troughs of waves of fashion, its periodicities discussed in section 1, are perhaps also to be sought not in anything inherent in fashion, but rather in more general historic causes. In favor of such a view is the heavier clustering of trait extremes in Revolutionary-Napoleonic and in World War [I] and immediately subsequent decades. But again there are crests also in the intervening period. What is specifically characteristic of the agitated periods is not so much extremes of dimension or proportion, as extremes of high variability; and these in turn correlate with certain minima and maxima of proportion, but not with their opposites. The significant fact remains that high variability is not associated with any dimensional crest, but always with only one of a pair of opposing extremes. This throws us back on the basic pattern as something that must be recognized.

Now one can indeed accept this basic pattern, but accept it as something intrinsically tending to remain more or less static over a long period, or the whole of a civilization; and then attribute the more marked variations from it to broader historic disturbing causes, rather than to anything stylistically inherent and tending from within toward swings away from and back toward the pattern. On this view the century-long cycle which we have found to hold for most of our fashion traits would not be a property of style per se, but a by-product of the fact that Europe happened to be generically disturbed in the decades around 1800 and 1920. (ibid.: 368–9)

Now, the above may be taken to represent the level of generalization or explanation that Kroeber deemed appropriate for cultural analysis. "Causality" to him meant the existence of a "pattern," either "ideal" or "unconscious," and it is the adherence to or departure from such a "pattern" that explains the existence of various forms of variability in the measurements, and their relationship of these forms to each other. The only citation of a possible causal force other than the statistically-defined "pattern" is "unsettled conditions," but Kroeber was skeptical since such vaguely defined social forces cannot explain the changes in specific dress proportions, like, say, tight versus loose skirts. Kroeber and Richardson make no explanations for such changes, and obviously do not believe it is profitable to attempt to find them: ". . . is easily conjectured but difficult to prove" (ibid.: 369).

Now, what they *did* find, and which has a certain significance, is that over the span of years (varying from 300 to 150) the maximum and minimum dimensions of various proportions of dresses alternate "with fair regularity" about every fifty years. Annual changes occur, but they are of lesser magnitude and the proportions eventually tend to go back to the starting point. But over the years the accumulation of small changes tend to produce a secular pattern and this pattern is a kind of mean around which the variability for shorter intervals revolves. However, the authors also found two periods of especially marked variability, and these were associated with the Revolutionary-Napoleonic wars, and the period around and between the two twentieth-century World Wars.

The authors concluded that the nature of variability and the long-term patterns, plus the high variability associated with disturbed eras, tells them that "the role of particular individuals in molding dress style is slight" (ibid.: 370). In other words, if you can find trends, patterns, etc., then individuals do not count—there is something in the cultural phenomenon itself that induces the rhythms. So goes the metaphysics.

The amazing thing about all this is the total absence of any inquiry into the institutional and behavioral factors which actually create and influence dress fashions: the snob elite; gifted designers and their ateliers; shifting tastes, body symbolism, economic marketing, the price of raw materials, and so on. In other words, this fashions research, from Kroeber's early work to the final product, at no point asked the obvious question, "what, exactly, *are* dress fashions? Who creates them, wants them, and why?" In several passages, as noted, Kroeber rejected such cultural-reality issues, implying that they were essentially unknowable or matters of speculation, since he believed individuals have nothing to do with the movements and regularities of civilization. Or, in his own terms, you cannot know the superorganic by an inquiry into "psychological" attitudinal and behavioral phenomena. This is beyond what he later called "ambiguity" on the superorganic issue: Kroeber—at least in this context—really *did* have confidence in the superorganic.

Kroeber was a dogmatist and a kind of materialistic mystic, believing, at times, in forces and movements outside the immediate ken, but possibly discoverable if one used the right methods. It was no good asking people to describe the meaning of their experience if you were trying to find out something about the social and cultural settings in which this experience occurred. He distrusted the individual because he had theorized that "psychology" had nothing to do with civilization once created, and he stuck with this doctrine through most of his career, making an effort to modify it in 1948, as his contribution to a rather confused and febrile debate with David Bidney and Leslie White (for a useful résumé, see Harris 1968: 332–33; and my discussion in the next section).

Kroeber's Studies of Civilizational Configurations

As his career wound down, Kroeber became more and more preoccupied with—interested in—a set of questions that historians had been puzzling and fighting over for a century or more. Kroeber deals with some of these in the introduction to part 5 of his 1952 anthology. For example:

> *How are civilizations to be delimited* from one another? . . . [there is the problem of] the *"footnote cultures" of little backward peoples*, especially when situated among large advanced nations . . . they may have some of the taxonomic interest of isolated survivals in organic evolution . . . *the qualitative separateness of cultures. . . . overall pattern limitation, reconstitution, or atrophy and disintegration* [of civilizations]. How far is it legitimate to infer from particular style patterns to an overall whole culture pattern? The problem of relating the statistic concept of a regionally-limited type of culture, the "culture area" of anthropologists, to the flow of culture in history. . . . (all quotes from 1952: 330–1, italics added)

Now what in the world was a California anthropologist doing with such problems?—problems of *Weltgeschichte* that the best of the universal historians since the Renaissance had tried to solve? Certainly the questions suggest "civilization" is something more than the superorganic, which was Kroeber's chief claim to theoretical status. His implied answer can be guessed: culture was culture, and even if you had spent much of your life investigating the life of California Indians as it was in the past, you nevertheless knew something about civilization, since every little bit is part of the whole. Microcosms. And the "footnote cultures" (marvelous phrase) might even suggest organic analogies: would Kroeber have used the term in 1917?

The work actually started with the "cultural intensity and climax" final section in the useful monograph *Cultural and Natural Areas of Native North America* (Kroeber 1939). The book was an attempt to rescue the topic—first explored by Clark Wissler—of tribal culture areas and their concordance with physical environmental features. This approach was based on the museum mentality: classification—but neglected human adaptive skills which override and reshape the environment, even at tribal cultural levels—something Kroeber should have been more aware of. So concordances might be close at low-energy levels of technology, but far apart at more skillful or resource-abundant levels. Kroeber knew this, but apparently he felt that it was necessary to drop the other shoe and pull together the evidence, vague or equivocal as it was in many cases, once and for all.

In some respects Kroeber's notion of culture-as-kind was most clearly represented in this section of his 1939 book. He defines "intensity" as follows:

> What we call intensity of culture therefore means both special content and special system. A more intensive as compared with a less intensive culture normally contains not only more material—more elements or traits—but also more material peculiar to itself, as well as more precisely and articulately established interrelation between the material. ([1939] 1952: 337)

That is, *a culture* (not just culture-in-general) can be analyzed by a technique of nominal quantification—"more" of this or "less" of that, and thereby ranked as more or less intense. Each of the six major cultural-natural areas of native North and Central America Kroeber selected to discuss in this section, he said, had "at least one climax or focus of cultural intensity" (ibid.: 337). By this he meant that most cultures or culture areas (he seems to equate them, but this could be purely terminological) display a temporal process of increasing complexity or specialization (not clear from his text whether these are the same or different), so that every culture has its day, so to speak. But some have longer days than others. He also proceeds to count the "culture elements that have index value for systematization" (ibid.: 337). The judgements as to which cultures in a comparative pair or group have more intense climax development than others is mainly subjective, with simple common sense indicators, like centralized religious practices, written language, sophisticated pottery design, agriculture, and so forth. So it is no surprise, for example, that the Pueblo rank above the Shoshone, or the Aztec above the northern barbarian Mexican tribes from whence they came to the south where intense climaxes were already under way. And Kroeber was concerned about the questions of whether intensity can develop purely internally, in isolation, or as a result of diffusion—and, the expectable answer was, of course, both: ". . . high intensity cultures are the most absorptive as well as the most productive" (ibid.: 339). And Kroeber was confident that high-intensity cultures and high-climax areas within them have considerable time-depth; that is, if the data displayed these characteristics in the historic period, it was with "a reasonable degree of assurance" (ibid.: 339) that these conditions prevailed in the archaeological past as well. But how far back? If cultural intensity-climax is a growth or developmental phenomenon, then it obviously has a history, so at some point in the archaeological past there must have been low intensity with vague climaxes.

The argument seems elementary: nothing really new has been introduced. The prehistorians and ethnohistorians of the late 1930s and 1940s were doing routine empirical research of the same type: judgements of "intensity" or "complexity," were made as commonsensical propositions. Kroeber was simply crystallizing these everyday understandings.

The search for high-level generalizations about "culture or civilization" came to a final focus in the massive 1944 tome, *Configurations of Culture Growth.* Theodora Kroeber (1970: 170–2) provides a detailed publication history of the book which informs us that he had considerable difficulty persuading publishers to accept it—all 846 pages of it. Harcourt Brace tried to get Kroeber to cut the manuscript, but he refused, and eventually the University of California Press printed the whole text—no doubt as a loss-leader monument to this distinguished anthropologist who had made major contributions to scholarship and to the renown of the institution. Kroeber spent seven years writing the book, and in 1957 attempted to capsulize its essence in a slim volume, *Style and Civilization*. It is clear from this version that he thought of the work more or less in the same category as the writings of universal historians like Spengler, Toynbee, or Sorokin: "My ultimate aim in these chapters is an inquiry into civilization: what are its characteristics, its essential nature, its features in the past, its future prospects" (Kroeber 1957: 1). He uses the fashions-research as a model, and distinguishes his work from these three universal historians by his use of *style* as a central concept. Style, he says, is "highly definite," "distinctive," "readily recognized," and styles have "predictive value" (ibid.: 2). The rhetoric is similar to papers written by others during the period on ceramic typology as an indicator of archaeological cultures and their diffusion and blendings, and so one might say that Kroeber made an inquiry into civilization from the point of view of a historical-archaeological anthropologist. While the whole enterprise was subjective or judgemental he did avoid *highly* subjective judgements, and concentrated on simple formal analysis (his lifelong habit: an avoidance of sophisticated intellectual analysis).

The ethnographic context keeps turning up: in a general discussion of the meaning of "style" he lists the various central features of diets and cooking as they vary across the great civilizational blocks: "thus East Asiatic bowls replace our plates, chopsticks our knives and forks; and these in turn entail distinctive postures, manipulations, and etiquettes . . ." (ibid.: 5). This kind of descriptive list-making is common in early Classic anthropology: it is the essential style of Robert Lowie's *Are We Civilized?* (1929), a book I examine in chapter 14. The rest of Kroeber's first chapter is a résumé of the findings of the dress-fashion research, with particular emphasis on the variability within the long-term cyclical trends or waves. This particular finding captivated Kroeber: it apparently was a revelation of cultural movement and rhythms, and a precursor of the *Configurations* work.

But this first chapter was his prologue, his declaration that an anthropologist could play ball with the historians of civilization. In chapter 3 he tries to come to grips with the main issue: the way stylistic analysis can shed light on the nature of civilization. This is a meandering argument that begins with an attempt to assess the role of the individual genius in the development of civilization, and ends with a somewhat puzzled attempt to explain why analysis of "whole cultures," like Benedict's *Patterns*, seems to turn into psychological analyses. As usual, Kroeber moves between culture as a creative mental phenomenon and culture as something which humans bear, but which somehow exists independently of them. He moves back and forth in this chapter, as in his entire career, between these alternatives, never really deciding why he should so move—seemingly not realizing that the issue is largely a semantic one. If you are convinced that culture is Culture, a *ding an sich*, but at the same time have to admit that humans create it, you are going to see it either as an isolate or separate entity, as human psychology, or as whatever—depending on the context of the discussion or frame of reference. (Clyde Kluckhohn got out of the tangle by calling culture an "analytical abstraction.")

But the chapter also contains an attempt to deal with the problem of "style" in the organic world, and in general, the analogic relationship of biological patterning to culture. The essence of the argument is as follows:

> In man, who has culture, the same species-individual relation and hereditary mechanisms are of course present, but they have become much less relevant, because of a new factor, consisting of the products, tangible and intangible, of individuals living in groups. They maintain an existence of their own, which is associated with the groups of individuals, in fact is dependent on them, and yet the products also have a certain independence, in that they largely affect and modify one another . . .. The cultural products, not bound by heredity, are far more plastic than the individuals . . .. This in turn enables them to influence other cultures in the direction of increased change . . . while culture as well as life has continuity, it shows, within the limits set by life, far greater and more rapid variability. (Kroeber 1957: 75–6)

So culture is, Kroeber feels, the ideal medium for style, whereas the organic world is not, since it changes slowly and its forms have been "painfully acquired by aeons of selection" (ibid.: 76).

This passage contains all of the ingredients in Kroeber's dogma of culture: dependence on humans, and then contradictorily, its apparent life of its own. The "products of culture," Kroeber wrote, "influence one another." However, one must ask, since culture is the creation of humans, how can it influence itself? Culture is not its own cause—causation resides in humans, and if one "product" is said to influence another one, it means that a relationship is established in somebody's mind (e.g., Bennett 1976). Kroeber acknowledges formal similarities between the organic and the cultural worlds, and recognizes they are analogies, but he always seemed to be seeking something of greater moment or significance in these analogies. While he acknowledged the substantive and processual differences between the two worlds, he seems to feel that this does not exhaust the matter. It did not occur to him that human actions can influence the organic world empirically, via technology, the extinguishing of species, the transformation of environments. Of course there are relationships between the two worlds, but they are not to be analyzed with analogic reasoning. It is true that much of our knowledge of the human impact on Nature is recent, but enough of it was available when Kroeber wrote his book to have permitted him to include it in his frame of reference (after all, he wrote a book on culture-environment relations in North America).

His avoidance of hard data and complex relationships between phenomena are probably echoes of his rejection of the role of scientist. Arguments by analogy, by the use of reason and philosophical argument, are all consistent with his choice of history as the proper role for the student of culture. Kroeber wrote review essays on the works of both Oswald Spengler and Arnold Toynbee, finding much to admire and also a certain amount to criticize. Spengler, he felt, was closest to anthropological thinking in that he was a thorough relativist and searched for relativity in all branches of human culture. Toynbee's work was "marked by illuminating insight" ([1943] 1952: 378), but he wrote too much (*this*, from the author of an 800–plus page book full of details on ancient civilizations derived from available publications).

Was eight years of hard work really worth the results? Well, yes, so far as Kroeber was concerned, because in the concluding chapter he states that he found two things he did not expect. First, he found "no evidence of true law" (Kroeber 1944: 761); that is, the rhythmic or repetitive occurrence of "florescence." The periods of flowering of great accomplishments and ideas rise and fall, come and go; some cultures have them more than once, some never—that is, assuming that subjective contentual value judgements of "florescence" can be accurate—and more of that problem in a moment. Second, and this is implicit in the whole undertaking: pure cultural relativity prevents the exercise of judgement, of intellectual presence in the writing of culture history. Kroeber made no bones about his departure from strict relativity in this book: it is loaded with personal assessments of good and bad, high and low. And with this, Kroeber parted company with the science-minded, analytic cultural relativists of the late Classic era.

But Kroeber continues to dodge the issue, or avoid the obvious.

Consider the following passage:

> What it is that binds high-value culture patterns to such transience—lower-grade ones can apparently go on with much less change and much longer—is far from clear. It may be something in the constitution of the human mind. But direct psychological explanations have never got anyone very far in reducing the phenomena of history to order, and I shall not fall back on them. This much is clear: the patterns which we adjudge as of higher quality are selective from among a number of potentialities. They cannot remain undifferentiated and attain quality. As they begin to select, early in their formation, they commit themselves to certain specializations, and exclude others. If this arouses conflict with other parts of the culture in which the pattern is forming, the selection and exclusion may be abandoned, the pattern as something well differentiated be renounced, and nothing of much cultural value eventuate. If, however, this does not happen, but the other patterns of the culture reinforce the growing one, or at least do not conflict with it, the pattern in question tends to develop cumulatively, in the direction in which it first differentiated, by a sort of momentum. Finally, either a conflict with the rest of its culture arises and puts an end to the pattern, or it explores and traverses the new opportunities lying in its selective path, until less and less of these remain, and at last none. The pattern can be said to have fulfilled itself when its opportunities or possibilities have been exhausted. Or more exactly, the value culmination comes at the moment when the full range of possibilities within the pattern is sensed; the decline, when there remain only minor areas of terrain to be occupied. After this, development may quietly subside, the results achieved being retained as institutions, but with repetitive instead of growth activity; and quality atrophies. (Kroeber 1944: 763)

Why is it "far from clear" that "high-value culture patterns" are transient? Why do the patterns select from a number of potentialities? Why do high-grade patterns require supplementation? Why do they get committed to particular phenomena and then specialize in them? Why do culture patterns reinforce one another? Conflict with one another? Why do patterns seem to lose steam and wind up as "institutions?" Why does the quality then seem to atrophy? Substitute a major-league baseball team for "patterns" and Kroeber's passage becomes an excellent description of a team progressing through the season by improving its pitching staff and eventually winning the league pennant, entering the World Series, winning it, and then declining to last-in-the-league for the next three seasons, while the fans ask "why?" (If Kroeber could use dress fashions, I can certainly use baseball.)

Kroeber suggests that it "may be something in the constitution of the human mind" (and this suggests another substitution: the term "human mind," or "people" instead of culture patterns in the quotation. To me, it is obvious that this is the way people behave: they develop an interest in something, learn what must be learned, are reinforced by rewards—for instance, renown, a prize, a payoff—and then work even harder and see the project through to the end, after which there is a letdown: success has been achieved, let's take it easy for a while and save money and energy. This is primate compulsive behavior, or the achievement-strategic behavior of any intelligent mammal. So *of course* what Kroeber found in the movements of growth and change in culture was the way the mind—or mind-and-body works in strategic behavior. There are sociobiological elements here, although I do not intend to push that too hard. But if you ever watched a cat attempt to catch a bird, you will see the same curve of accomplishment and falloff; with a possible later renewal of the energetic attack; but often, with repeated failure, a tendency to abandon the behavior. Cats can learn. They experience boredom.

The mystery of A. L. Kroeber is simply that he *must* have known that the rhythms he found in cultural florescence match patterns of human and mammalian behavior. However, he had declared himself years before on the "psychology" issue: once culture is in hand, then psychology cannot help explain it. Wel', maybe not "psychology," but certainly *behavior* can. But like most of the Classic anthropologists—with the exception, of course, of the patternists, especially Margaret Mead and Gregory Bateson, psychological explanations were taboo. And Classic concepts of behavior or behavioral dynamics were immature (again, with the exception of at least Gregory Bateson—see chapter 9). Culture for Kroeber, despite his disavowals, was still a matter of kind, a *ding an sich*. Human behavior was vague, epiphenomenal, and there was no adequate theory of it at hand. The absence of the behavioral—and, of course, the cognitive—element in Kroeber's writing is tragic: with it, he could have found out so much more about "culture."[5]

As noted, Kroeber opened the discussion in the final windup chapter with a denial of "laws" or regularities . . . "nothing cyclical, regularly repetitive" (Kroeber 1944: 761). However, in the long quoted passage, he did in fact discover a number of regularities, and also repeated phenomena—"patterns" is the term he uses. Are patterns "regular," even repetitive? Granted that "laws" may be too strong a term, "patterns" would appear to possess something along those lines. And what about the years of research on dress fashions, and the interesting findings of cyclical patterns of proportions and their changes? We are once again confronted with rhetorical inconsistencies. What did Kroeber mean by the "laws" he says he did not find? In the language of the nineteenth and early twentieth century, the word meant invariable, predictable, always recurrent phenomena, as one finds in chemistry or physics. Kroeber, as *historian*, knew that nothing this definite happened in history. But he also used the terms "regularity" and "cycles" and most certainly he *did* find some of both. Kroeber seemed to eat his cake and have it too: he wanted to find regularities, but also to distinguish himself from the glib perpetrators of cultural evolutionary generalizations.

Dipping into the content chapters of *Configurations* is hazardous and frustrating, because of Kroeber's recitations of comings and goings, rises and falls, all presented in verbal arithmetic: more or less, first phase or later phase, increasing specialization, impulses from above or below, exhaustion setting in, and so on. No really hard data, no attempt at explaining the possible, and in so many instances, the actual historically *known reasons* for these "patterns." Why did he so scrupulously avoid presenting the evidence?

Perhaps he had something else in mind. Take, for example, the section on the rise of the Japanese state, in chapter 10: he noted that the florescences of art and literature occurred in her peaceful eras, and their decline in the periods of recurrent feudal warfare. However, most aesthetic interests were continuous throughout Japan's history, and therefore often do not show patterns of growth and decline—only fluctuation that depends as much on interests and "fashion" as on social conditions. And there are some startling exceptions as I shall note in a moment. The problem, as other critics have pointed out, is with the concepts of "florescence," growth, decline, etc., as these are based on subjective judgement. Even so I do not feel that these are probably not the main point: Kroeber was ultimately dependent on incomplete available literature, and for ancient periods, on the vagaries of preservation.

But suppose we gave him the benefit of the doubt, and agree that to some degree intense civil warfare in medieval Japan *did* inhibit artistic expression. This is a "pattern," so—now—is the pattern repeated in some other civilization? Apparently he did not think so, or did not research the matter, concluding that it is distinctive for Japan. Therefore it cannot be a generalization about "configurations of culture growth." But another cavil: suppose this proposition is not an either-or proposition? Suppose some forms of artistic expression actually increase in periods of war, and others diminish? War, in other words, can stimulate artistic expression as well as stifle it—it depends on other aspects of the general culture and the attitudes of the military leaders. In most of Japan's feudal history, many of the leaders were, in fact, patrons of the arts: *The Chrysanthemum and the Sword*, Benedict's tour de force masterwork, published only two years after *Configurations*, celebrated this patronage by the intellectual samurai.

Résumé

In the last analysis, A. L. Kroeber worked very hard to establish a distinctive intellectual base of operations for anthropology—a base which differed from psychological science, from natural science, and from academic history, although he admitted anthropology shared certain things with all three—perhaps most with the last. His breadth of knowledge of human culture surpassed most of his contemporaries, but he seemed more interested in philosophizing about the method and approach of anthropology than in empirical research. His fieldwork and published ethnological material concerned humble peoples with limited expressions of culture, but his long-term interests focused on high civilizations. His subject-matter interests and techniques or logic of investigation seem appropriate to archaeological research, but he never dug a site or analyzed a batch of artifact material. His conception of anthropology was Olympian: anthropologists were supposed to be able to handle any culture, any civilization—since, perhaps, he tended to equate the two, culture *and* civilization (although not always—another of his inconsistencies). Any aspect of human culture, however, grandiose or trivial, was equal to every other—at least from the standpoint of its capacity, with the right treatment, to reveal the secrets of the phenomenon. Culture was, after all, granted some confusing double-imagery, the *Superorganic*.

This is not a very promising career review for a major figure in a scholarly discipline. What, precisely, was A. L. Kroeber up to? And why is his stature still one of gray eminence in a discipline which on the whole showed little real interest in his central theses and interests? I believe, first, that the contradictions and confusion in his scholarly record mirror the complexity and perversity of the subject matter: human behavior and endeavor. The persistent attempt to define culture, and then to validate the definition by passive scholarly research, was the consequence of insisting on giving a name, an identity, to the distinctive features of human behavior—features which do not stand alone in the animal kingdom, but alone enough so as to encourage a separate rhetoric. The rhetoric inevitably will turn out to be contradictory and full of reification, no matter who speaks it. Kroeber is revered because he was the first anthropologist to get himself caught in these inevitable semantic contradictions of humanistic scholarship. Kroeber sensed this problem, and perhaps his insistence on history rather than science as his academic home was one result.

But this still does not explain his persisting eminence. In the last analysis, Kroeber gave a kind of Olympian dignity to anthropology—something no other scholar of the period managed to do as well. Franz Boas was a researcher primarily, and he contributed a series of fine-grained, exotic works which meant a great deal to the inner core of the profession but did not really command major attention elsewhere. Eminence he had, but it was as patron and teacher. Kroeber sought universalism in his work, and at its best, his work had it. He was Anthropology's Scholar, a man who hoped to rank with the greats—people like Herodotus or Toynbee. And he certainly sought such identification in his frequent comments and reviews on the works of people like them. He was also a great organizer of symposia, a man who spoke *for* and from *within* anthropology, to the intelligentsia. His presence was proof that anthropology was something more than potsherds and phonemes and basketry.

Kroeber's Olympian dignity conferred authority on the search for a concept of culture. This, more than any one theoretical issue, characterizes the Classic era. And neither Kroeber nor any other Classic anthropologist with the possible exception of Clyde Kluckhohn knew that once you asserted the reality of culture in any sense whatsoever, you were hooked, although Kluckhohn couldn't really admit it. You had to account for it; you had to find its meaning and substance. The search is not yet over, but the sensible anthropologist tends to ignore it and does what he can to make sense of his chosen subject matter.

Notes

1. All page citations to the paper are to Kroeber's own edited anthology (1952).
2. And that is exactly how Kroeber himself saw the paper in retrospect: "Looking

back thirty years on my essay called "The Superorganic" I am struck by the sense that pervades it of a great need for freeing cultural phenomena from the oppression of biological thinking" ([1948] 1952: 116).

3. I reproduce Kluckhohn's diagram since it represents the classic "five fields", as intersected by the history vs. science dichotomy. Kluckhohn wrote the piece at my invitation for the Central States Anthropological Bulletin (1947), in a years when I was program chairman, and he acknowledged that it was based on a chart prepared by Robert Redfield, and used in Redfield's course on theory at Chicago. Kluckhohn also acknowledged a "critical reading" of the diagram and its explanation by A.L. Kroeber.

Figure 10.1
Interrelations of the Various Fields of Anthropology in Terms of Subject Matter and the Logical Character of the Problems, with an Indication of the Related Disciplines

ANTHROPOLOGY

Zoology Paleontology Anatomy Osteology Geology	Physical Anthropology Primatology Human & Primate Evolution Racial History of Man Somatology	(Anatomy) (Osteology)	Physical Anthropology Constitutional; Anthropology Race Mixture Growth Studies	General Biology Genetics Statistics Physiology General Medicine
	HISTORICAL	BIOLOGICAL Applied Anthropology CULTURAL	ANALYTIC	Psychosomatic Medicine Psychiatry
Paleontology History Classical Archaeology Egyptology & Oriental Studies Geography Philology	Archaeology Folklore Culture History Topical Ethnology Historical Linguistics	(Ethnography) (Speech)	Culture & Personality Social Anthropology Ethnological Theory Dynamic Linguistics	Sociology Psychology Human Geography Statistics Philosophy Economics Political Science Jurisprudence

Kluckhohn's explanation of the diagram:

"Leaving applied anthropology to one side, it may be said then that three types of interest guide anthropological workers in their activities. The first is concerned primarily with simple description and classification. The second is essentially historical. The interest is in the what? where? and when? of unique events, in establishing the sequence of these events, in discovering the patterns as well as the events of history, and in depictive integration. Historical anthropologists, on the other hand are as least abstract as possible. A vivid concreteness is the hallmark of the best historical anthropology, as of history in general. The third type of anthropology . . . is abstract and analytic. It is interested in the particular only to understand the general. It studies processes in order to find out the recurrent regularies in those processes."

4. However, Jan Christian Smuts used the concept in his 1926 book, *Holism and Evolution* (Smuts 1973), and C. Lloyd Morgan (1923) provided the definitive formulation of "levels."
5. Perhaps the ultimate paradox in the Kroeber saga was his attitude toward psychological matters. As we have noted, he rejected psychological explanations of culture—but at the same time seemed to applaud attempts like Ruth Benedict's. And even more surprising is that with the exception of a couple of short reviews or essays, he ignored Freud and therapeutic psychology, even though he had formal psychoanalytic training and was, for a year or so, a practicing analyst. I am not implying that Kroeber got the idea of the superorganic from these writers; only that the idea of emergent "levels" of phenomena was very much in the air in the period, 1915–1925, and in this sense Kroeber's paper represents the anthropological version of the idea.

Literature Cited

Bennett, John W. 1976. *The Ecological Transition: Cultural Anthropology and Human Adaptation*. London: Pergamon.

Harris, Marvin. 1968. "Kroeber," chapter 12 in *The Rise of Anthropological Theory*, pp. 319–42. New York: Thomas Y. Crowell.

Kluckhohn, Clyde. 1947. "Some Remarks on the Branches of Anthropology and on Anthropology's Relation to Other Disciplines." *Central States Bulletin* 2(1): 2–9.

Kroeber, A. L. [1917] 1952. "The Superorganic." *American Anthropologist* 19: 163–213. Reprinted in Kroeber, pp. 22–51.

———. [1918] 1952. "The Possibility of a Social Psychology." *The American Journal of Sociology* 23: 633–50. Reprinted in Kroeber, pp. 52–6.

———. [1919] 1952. "On the Principal of Order in Civilization As Exemplified by Changes of Fashion." *American Anthropologist* 21: 235–63. Reprinted in Kroeber, pp. 332–6.

———. [1931] 1952. "Historical Reconstruction of Culture Growths and Organic Evolution." *American Anthropologist* 32: 149–56. Reprinted in Kroeber, pp. 57–62.

———. [1939] 1952. "Cultural Intensity and Climax," in *Cultural and Natural Areas of Native North America*, by A. L. Kroeber, pp. 222–8. University of California Publications in American Archaeology and Ethnology, vol. 38. Reprinted in Kroeber, pp. 337–43.

———. [1943] 1952. "Toynbee's *A Study of History*." *American Anthropologist* 45: 294–9. Reprinted in Kroeber, pp. 373–8.

———. 1944. *Configurations of Culture Growth*. Berkeley: University of California Press.

———. [1948] 1952. "White's View of Culture." *American Anthropologist* 50: 405–14. Reprinted in Kroeber, pp. 110–7.

———. 1952. *The Nature of Culture* (anthology selected by the author). Chicago: University of Chicago Press.

———. 1957. *Style and Civilizations*. Ithaca, NY: Cornell University Press.

Kroeber, Theodora. 1970. *Alfred Kroeber, a Personal Configuration*. Berkeley: University of California Press.

Lowie, Robert H. 1929. *Are We Civilized?* New York: Harcourt, Brace & Co.

Morgan, C. Lloyd. 1923. *Emergent Evolution: The Gifford Lectures, Delivered in the University of St. Andrews in the Year 1922*. London: Williams and Norgate.

Richardson, Jane and A. L. Kroeber. [1940] 1952. *Three Centuries of Women's Dress Fashions: A Quantitative Analysis.* University of California Anthropological Records, vol. 5, no. 2, pp. 111–54. Partially reprinted in Kroeber, pp. 358–72.

Sapir, Edward. 1917. "Do We Need a Superorganic?" *American Anthropologist* 19: 441–7.

Smuts, Jan Christian. 1973. *Holism and Evolution* (reprint). Originally published 1926 by Macmillan, London. Westport, CT: Greenwood Press.

11

Walter W. Taylor and Americanist Archaeology's Search for a Concept of Culture

Introduction

This essay deals with aspects of the intellectual development of North American archaeology, especially work in the eastern half of the continent, which I came to know as a graduate student and young professional. While I was active in archaeological research and writing in undergraduate college and graduate school, events in the World War II period plus the multidisciplinary intellectual atmosphere of the University of Chicago led me into the never-never land of cross-disciplinary social science. But I never lost my curiosity about the prehistoric past, or the tantalizing semantic and methodological problems surrounding the analysis of ambiguous objects and inverted stratigraphy.

Americanist archaeologists in the Classic era increasingly conceived of their activities as constituting a discipline, but whether it was merely affiliated with, or perhaps wholly contained within, the academic field of anthropology was a matter of indecision. While Americanist archaeologists assimilated many ideas from sociocultural anthropology—an inevitable consequence of the comprehensive effort by all fields to reconstruct the history and culture of American Indians—it also created problems based on the fact that the inherent limitations of archaeological data prevented full participation in the intellectual appa-

Written in 1996 for this volume. (I received the news of Walter Taylor's death as I was reading the first proofs of the chapter.)

ratus of the larger discipline. Walter Taylor's book, *A Study of Archeology* (1948), exemplified the ambivalence: while he endeavored to define archaeology as a distinct discipline related to many fields, at the same time he advocated closer intellectual involvement in anthropological concepts in general. However, because archaeology's data are mostly material, specialized and fragmentary, it was difficult to use conceptions of culture that relied on behavioral and ideational data (see Dunnell 1971: 121–7).

Historical Overview

Before anthropology became a formally recognized scholarly field, the remains of long-gone human occupations were up for grabs. That is, anyone with a shovel, curiosity about the past, and a yen for exotic objects (or objects one could sell at a profit) could strain his back to bring them to the surface. A few of the early North America diggers—for example, Thomas Jefferson (1944)—had serious intentions of reconstructing the past—although since the ancient inhabitants of North America were manifestly not relatives of the European immigrants who settled the continent, most excavators were inclined to be more preoccupied with exotic artifacts or mysterious origins and identities of the "vanished races"—as they were often called, than with actual ways of life or historical relationships. This early digging gave rise to a steady output of summary volumes, beginning in the early years of the nineteenth century, most of them hybrid tracts, designed for sale to the curious public and also as guides for the other diggers and speculators. (For detailed accounts of nineteenth-century archaeology see Willey and Sabloff 1973 and subsequent editions.)

One early-nineteenth-century synthesis volume is Josiah Priest's *American Antiquities and Discoveries in the West, Being an Exhibition of the Evidence that an Ancient Population of Partially Civilized Nations Differing Entirely from those of the Present Indians Who Peopled America Many Centuries Before its Discovery by Columbus, and Inquiries into their Origins, with a Copious Description of Many of their Stupendous Works, Now in Ruins, with Conjectures Concerning What may have Come of Them, Compiled from Travels, Authentic Sources, and the Researches of Antiquarian Societies* (1834, 4th ed). Yes, this is the complete title of the book, and it tells the reader exactly what to expect. Notice that the "discoveries" pertain to peoples allegedly not related to the Indians. Priest, like the diggers whose labors he was synthesizing, simply could not believe that the Indians they knew in the late eighteenth and early nineteenth centuries could possibly have been responsible for the giant earthworks in the eastern United States. This idea gave rise to the term, "Mound Builders," which persisted well into the twentieth century, even after it had become obvious that the builders must have been the Indians. Henry C. Shetrone of Ohio, a prominent pre-anthropological excavator, entitled his 1930 book, *The Mound Builders*, and as late as 1966, Gordon Willey used the term "Mound Builders I and II" for burial and temple mounds in the eastern United States (Willey 1966—who used the term purely descriptively). However, by the mid-1930s the important doctrine around most anthropology graduate schools was the need to get rid of this term or concept referring to a separate race of "mound builders."

The notion that Native Americans were not responsible for the more imposing sites and artifacts was certainly one of the factors that led to the free excavation of burial places and the storage of the remains in museum basements and research areas. The idea that these remains might represent ancestors or relatives of living tribal groups simply didn't occur to most archaeologists, and it was only in the late 1980s and 1990s that representatives of the reservation groups near the sites demanded return of skeletal material and artifacts. By 1995 some Indian spokesmen even began denying the archaeologically established facts of cultural development and even biological evolution—in effect cutting the ground out from anthropological archaeology. The affair was exasperating because in very few cases could any proof be found of the kinship of living Indians and the stored skeletal material. All archaeologists could do was simmer with repressed outrage. Some tribal groups, of course, took an intelligent approach, and even established professional excavation programs and museums.

Anyway, according to Priest's fascinating accounts there might be a Roman fort in Marietta County, Ohio; remains of the lost tribes of Israel (in various places); evidence of "Mexican natives" having migrated up the Mississippi; Egyptian mummies in Kentucky; remains of "White nations" prior to the European invasions and settlements; and other possible identifications. Withal, though, Priest was cautious, and most of his cultural attributions were "supposed" (the habit persists: e.g., Barry Fell 1976). And some of the simple descriptive passages were accurate in detail, and capable of contemporary identification in terms of now-known cultural provenience (for other early accounts of American prehistory, see Atwater 1820; Bradford 1843; Lapham 1853; Squier and Davis 1848; Foster 1874; Haven 1855—the Haven piece is especially interesting: for a description see Meltzer 1996).

Semi-professional archaeological work began in the early nineteenth century in local historical and antiquarian societies (the American Antiquarian Society was publishing monographs as early as 1820, including Caleb Atwater's pioneer accounts of the Ohio mounds). This work was carried on mainly by accomplished hobbyists, usually professionals like doctors, lawyers, and naturalists. But Americanist archaeology's association with the anthropological fraternity began in the Smithsonian Institution in the late 1840s, under Joseph Henry, and from the 1880s continued in the U.S. National Museum, across the Mall (see Hinsley 1981 for details). John Wesley Powell, a geologist and explorer, established the Bureau of American Ethnology in the Smithsonian in 1879, and thereafter both Washington institutions were fully committed to anthropology. As noted previously, the objective was to learn as much as possible about the American Indians, so all the specialty fields were represented: physical anthropology, linguistics, ethnology, archaeology. In the 1890s, when the university departments of anthropology began to form a critical mass, the center of gravity of the profession began to shift away from the Washington institutions.

The archaeologists of the Smithsonian and the National Museum in the nineteenth century usually lacked formal training in archaeology or in anthropology generally, but were willing to learn by doing. However, beginning in the last decade of the nineteenth century and continuing into the twentieth century, young people were being trained in anthropology and archaeology in the universities, and they formed the first cadre of professional archaeologists. They viewed archaeology as part of anthropology, but also to some extent as a separate but coordinate discipline.

The next step was taken when the anthropological profession began turning out highly trained persons with a full panoply of anthropology courses as well as from one to three seasons of inaugural field work experience. This began in different institutions at different times. Representative early ones were California, Pennsylvania, Harvard; middle-period examples were the midwestern state institutions plus the University of Chicago, which got under way with formal field-training digs in the early 1920s. Among the pioneer anthropologists and ethnologists who trained these people, names like Clark Wissler, Fay-Cooper Cole, Roland B. Dixon, A. L. Kroeber, Alexander Goldenweiser, A. V. Kidder, were prominent. These were people who considered anthropology to be a historical science and who saw no particular difference between the general methods of anthropology and archaeology. And these men trained what became the first "scientific" generation of archaeologists—people like W. C. McKern, James Griffin, William Ritchie, Philip Phillips, Emil Haury.

The transitions differed—in some cases where some work had been done in old university departments, the transition was simply a matter of a graduate student, after a little extra training elsewhere, coming back home and replacing his senior professor—the senior professor having had only limited exposure in the 1910s, let us say, to "scientific" archaeological methods. In other cases it was an outright replacement of an older, essentially self-trained digger who had occupied a position at a state historical society for years, by a young anthropology-archaeology Ph.D. hired from the nearby state university. In a few cases the incumbent, an unusually sophisticated older generation person simply continued in service, becoming a trainer of anthropological-archaeologists until his retirement. And so on. But in most cases, the transition involved the replacement of a person of semi-professional background by a university-trained anthropological archaeologist.

The result of the process was to imbue archaeology with the anthropological ethos, and that meant, by and large, a strong need to subscribe to a formal definition of culture. Patty Jo Watson (1995), in a 1993 Distinguished Lecture to the American Anthropological Association, devoted her text to an account of contemporary concepts of culture as held by archaeologists covering the period from the 1940s to the 1990s. These definitions or conceptions cover the waterfront, from purely ideational and even ideological, to materialistic; from humanistic to operationally scientific (Watson 1995: 690).

The Emergence of Scientific Method

With the preemption of archaeology by anthropology—or did the archaeologists themselves insist on being included in the fold?—the practitioners rapidly developed a strong feeling of guilt over the sloppy methods of the pot-hunting past. Distinguished older-generation figures—like H. C. Shetrone—who worked in the 1920s, were by the late 1930s viewed as unskilled and out-of-date. Anthropology departments began appearing in elite universities in the latter quarter of the nineteenth century, but it was not until the expansion of higher education and the acceptance of social science as a legitimate teaching subject in the mid-1910s that anthropology departments came to be seen as a necessary part of the university curriculum. The number of such departments (or subdepartments as part of sociology) increased tenfold in the first three decades of the twentieth century.

Academization, then, meant scientization, and for anthropology, this meant a search for a *scientific* concept of culture and its handmaiden, ethnology. For archaeology, it meant three things: (1) improved methods of excavation and better stratigraphy; (2) superior techniques of artifact description, and above all; and (3) precise chronology. All of these in the pre-Classic era were approximate or slipshod. Many of the digs had focused on large, single sites like burial mounds or especially conspicuous architectural ruins. The detailed stone and potsherd artifact load was often small, or even when large, or consisting of fragments, it might be shovelled into boxes and ignored in favor of more spectacular finds. The finer and complete pieces were in the hands of private collectors, usually minus data on provenience. And of course the background information to link up cultural materials was largely lacking, so the artifact yields of excavations were often unconnectable to anything else. The major goal of this pre-Classic archaeology was to recover interesting remains of vanished civilizations, not to reconstruct history or to research human ecology, trade economics, or social organization. These were "academic" matters.

Field methods—techniques of excavation and preliminary analysis of the artifact material—was the first of the three necessities for a truly scientific archaeology to get attention by the anthropological archaeologists in the eastern United States, and more or less simultaneously, in the Southwest (although I am concentrating on the East). A significant step in the direction of improved techniques was initiated by Fay-Cooper Cole, the chairman of the Anthropology Department at Chicago, along with his chief archaeologist, Thorne Deuel, later Director of the Illinois State Museum. Cole and Deuel created something they called the "Chicago Method," and began, in the early 1920s, a series of excavations in Illinois counties.

The first field party, which included graduate students Robert Redfield, Fred Eggan, and Harry Hoijer—all professors of anthropology in the Department in later years—went to Jo Daviess County in the far northwest corner of the state in 1925, to survey a series of burial and effigy mounds—a southward extension along the Mississippi River of Wisconsin Woodland cultures. None of the excavation results (1926–32) were published until the 1940s, when I found the notes and artifacts in the Chicago Archaeology Laboratory. Dr. Cole suggested I work up the material, which I did. It was eventually published by the University of Chicago (Bennett 1947). The materials included the notes and artifacts produced by an indigenous excavator in the county, William B. Nickerson, between the years 1896–1907 (the artifacts actually had been presented by him to the Peabody Museum many years before, and the museum kindly presented them back to us at Chicago on my request). Nickerson was a trained surveyor who also worked as a telegrapher for the Illinois Central Railroad in Galena, and did archaeology as a hobby. Independently he developed all the same techniques Cole and Deuel called the "Chicago Method": located the loci for all finds with a transit, measured profiles and ground plans, and so on (for an account of the Nickerson episode, see Bennett 1942).

After the Jo Daviess digs, Cole and Deuel invaded Fulton County with the "Chicago Method," and the results were published in 1937 as *Rediscovering Illinois* (Cole and Deuel 1937). Methods of excavation and analysis were described in detail. The chapter, "Classification of Cultures" utilized the so-called "McKern System" in its first major professional application (discussed later in this chapter). The excavations were presented with ground plans and profiles and drawings of associated artifacts. The interpretations were presented as a series of several cultural horizons with associated skeletal material, in an effort to reconstruct the "cultural history of Fulton County." Some of the better-represented horizons were given names that had already appeared in the earlier literature—Woodland, Hopewellian—although the "black sand" and "red ocher" materials would later receive the label "Early Woodland" and "Archaic," respectively, by others. There were a number of errors of assignment and interpretation, but on the whole *Rediscovering*—not Illinois, but at least *Fulton County*—was a good piece of work, and the best or most "scientific" monograph on eastern U. S. archaeology to be produced in that period. There was a certain amount of resentment in some circles over the fact that Cole and Deuel claimed authorship of methods, concepts, and names that were really in the behind-the-scenes public domain of the emerging anthropological archaeology in the Midwest (not to mention the Nickerson case!). And in some respects *Rediscovering Illinois* was out-of-date at the moment of its publication. The ceramic typology was simplistic, and by the mid-1930s James Griffin and others were well advanced on more sophisticated methods of pottery and artifact analysis. The use of the "McKern System" of cultural classification was already—only four or five years after its initial presentation—receiving considerable criticism for its confusion of chronology and culture-type criteria.[1] The point is that once large bodies of material were available to scientifically and professionally trained and dedicated operators, progress was extremely rapid. The middle and late 1930s witnessed an explosion of effort and critical intelligence in archaeological methods.

Willey and Phillips: Theory and Method of the Historical and Comparative Approach

Now, let us jump ahead to 1958, and the publication of what became, for about a decade, the most influential book on the methods resulting from the efflorescence of scientific-anthropological archaeology. In 1958, Gordon Willey and Philip Phillips of Harvard published a definitive version of *Method and Theory in American Archaeology* as a kind of windup statement of the impressive accomplishments of the previous two decades of research (earlier versions appeared in sections in anthropological journals). These decades had been spent in an attempt to determine once and for all the basic chronology of cultural development in the Americas—this was the Classic era's great archaeological accomplishment. By the mid-1950s it was possible to say that no really new cultures were to be found; that from then on it was a matter of filling in details. The book therefore celebrated the triumph of Americanist archaeology under the aegis of the Classic era anthropological discipline.

The approach of the book can be grasped in its introductory chapter of just seven pages: the authors called it "processual interpretation." They rejected "functional" because it seemed to narrow the focus to just one kind of process, and they were implying the existence of several: presumably, ecological, demographic, economic, and so forth.

Despite this breadth of outlook, the book is conservative because it dwells primarily on historical reconstruction—"the historical-developmental approach"—of the broad culture sequence of North America. They proposed (or really articulated current doctrine) five "stages," starting with the oldest: lithic, archaic, formative, classic, post-classic. "Stages" is somewhat misleading because while the lithic and archaic are found nearly everywhere in North and even Middle America, as we move into the higher-level "stages" we are dealing not with the entire continent or region, but only with a few districts that achieved quasi-urban status. In this and other contexts the book demonstrates the difficulties of combining cultural and temporal-developmental criteria of classification.

Willey and Phillips openly stated that archaeology is "dependent" on anthropology—or to be precise, *American* archaeology is.

A significant statement in the first chapter concerns the concept of culture:

> Some Americanists have been drawn into the extreme position that sees in culture an independent order of phenomena, intelligible in terms of itself alone—the "cultural superorganic." Most of us, without subscribing to the superorganic view of culture, have nevertheless operated "as if" it were a fact. In our opinion, even this moderate position, though operationally expedient and to a certain extent inevitable, is ultimately detrimental to the main task of archaeology, which is to organize its data in terms of a real world, a world in which cultural and social phenomena (to name only these) are inextricably intermingled. (Willey and Phillips 1958: 3)

Some comments are in order. First of all, the "as if" statement has a familiar ring because it is similar to Kroeber's position (see chapter 10): his denial of culture as a *ding an sich*, but operating in his own research as if he really thought it was. Secondly, the authors wished to handle archaeological data in a "real world" context, which apparently included the "inextricable" fusion of social and cultural phenomena. So obviously they looked forward to reconstruction of social organization as well as cultural ideas. But in any case, by asserting that archaeology is part of or "dependent on" cultural anthropology, the philosopher or methodologist of archaeology was required to entertain a concept of culture.

The Willey-Phillips book represented, for the late Classic, the mainline doctrine on Americanist archaeology—the one that had produced the most stimulating and useful information up to that point. The main task of Classic era Americanist archaeology was defined as a portrait of the progression of cultural development in North America, as a corrective to pre-Classic concerns for spectacular ruins and intriguing artifacts. Willey and Phillips in essence were celebrating the success of that reform movement.

The authors recognized that this accomplishment generated some methodological and philosophical problems. The principal one concerned the difference between classifications based on *time* and those based on *form* (meaning any substantive or material phenomenon). The crucial issues had surfaced in the Midwestern Taxonomic Method (more familiarly called—as we noted a while back—the "McKern System"). This classification was constructed as a hierarchy of sets, with the lowest category—the *component*, as an assemblage of obviously related material in a particular site; the next category, the *focus*, a geographical entity composed of similar components; the *aspect*, a geographical grouping of foci; the *phase*, a grouping of Aspects; and finally, the overall, overarching *pattern*. In the eastern and midsection of the continent, there were just two *patterns*: Mississippian and woodland. As classifications based on form alone the McKern System was useful, but problems accumulated as soon as any particular body of materials was divided into the categories. Some sites had two or more components, often mixed together in what seemed to be the same time period. There were transitional cases, where, for example, components of both Mississippian and woodland-pattern material were fused, contemporaneously.

The hierarchical form of the diagram often seemed to *imply* that stuff at the bottom was younger than the materials and categories above—but while that was just a spatial illusion, in some cases it was real, by accident or other reason. Moreover, the arrangement of the various sets often did not coincide with formal properties. Suppose there are three foci, the similarities among which are sufficient to postulate the existence of an aspect. Now, the foci would represent, in most instances, say, three groups of sites. Now, it was often the case that the three foci, while placed on a horizontal plane in the diagram, actually represented a considerable span of time—with Focus 1 being many years older than Foci 2 and 3. Second, while the foci more often than not corresponded to actual geographically located sites, the aspects and phases, not to mention the pattern, were really constructs. The three above foci, gathered together analytically, would thus be *called* an aspect, but whether they actually had, say, political relations was not something the classification could tell you. And, what relation any of the scheme's categories had to actual ethnic and linguistic entities was, in most cases, either a mystery or a matter of guesswork. Griffin and others worked for years on the "Fort Ancient Aspect" material, eventually postulating that the material represented the prehistoric culture for one branch of the Siouan-speaking peoples. But without indigenous historical data there was no way to be absolutely sure, and this uncertainty eventually produced or refined the subdiscipline of ethnohistory and the "direct-historical approach" (Wedel 1938) in archaeology.

Now, the Willey-Phillips stages or eras were cultural-typologies with distinctive objects; but also, time periods. This simultaneity of object and time has always been a problem for archaeologists, but it is a consequence of the multidimensional nature of human behavior, and professional historians gave up worrying about it years ago. Their solution was to focus on events and sequences of events, the influence of these events, and the significance of the ideas of great movers and shakers, and so on. In other words, *writing history*—and defining history, more or less, as the unfolding of the confused and wayward manifestations of human behavior. Archaeologists would like to be able to do the same, but the paucity of the data makes it very difficult. So repeatedly, they fall back on these logically disturbing and often misleading form-*cum*-temporal classifications.

While archaeologists could handle the problem of classifying artifacts, it was necessary to call for help from natural scientists with respect to the establishment of firm chronologies. This work began in the Southwest, at Arizona, where astronomers had noticed that tree growth rings reflected the history of moisture maxima and minima through the centuries. By constructing master charts for particular regions and districts, and eventually for the Southwest as a whole, it became possible to date these sites by examining the rings in the wood or charcoal found in them. Fay-Cooper Cole inaugurated a tree ring lab at the University of Chicago in the late 1930s, under New Mexico anthropologist Florence Hawley, but the complexity of tree species and growth plus variability of moisture conditions made dendrochronology difficult in the Midwest and East, except in a few cases, like the bald cypress for the Southeast.

However, the search for better dates continued. Physicists and chemists continued to work on elapsed-time methods, and eventually the half-life of carbon-14 and related forms of dating using the decay rates of radioactive substances, became the most reliable. By the end of the Classic, various methods of dating were well established in Americanist archaeology, and had become a multidisciplinary undertaking in their own right. The physical sciences in a number of universities found it a source of additional research revenue, and often solicited the help of the archaeologists in the anthropology departments to obtain funds to establish a facility.

These methods of classification and dating were the handmaidens of what Willey and Phillips called the "historical-developmental approach" (and other labels, depending on what chapter you read). But the meaning was consistent: in their own words, "Culture-historical integration, as we have seen, is the descriptive process concerned with cultural forms, with plotting these forms in space and time, with defining their relationships and inferred functions" (Willey and Phillips 1958: 61). A broad program: it was not merely historical reconstruction, but included an attempt at establishing sociocultural relations, and above all, inferring their functions. They went on to say, "There is, we think, common agreement that these are archaeology's primary tasks, on the descriptive level of organization" (ibid.). The rest of the chapter consisted of an exposition of the descriptive-stage classification, and the rest of the book consisted of chapters on each of these stages as it was manifested in various parts of North America.[2]

The presentation of these stages exemplifies the peculiar rhetoric that developed in North American archaeology in the Classic era, for example:

> Middle Woodland period cultures in Georgia and contiguous portions of adjoining states are difficult to classify. These are unified by common participation in the southern Appalachian or Complicated Stamp pottery tradition, a ceramic development grounded in the simple and checked stamp styles of the early Woodland phases such as Mossy Oak and Deptford. . . . Cultural development in peninsular Florida tended to pursue a course of its own which renders terms like "early Woodland" and "middle Woodland" somewhat meaningless . . . .(Willey and Phillips 1958: 161)

The passage shows how cultural classification began to move away from the quasi-official "McKern System" and make use of whatever criteria seemed useful: pottery decoration; known time horizons; or unique facies that didn't fit any existing category. And "difficult to classify" horizons were becoming more numerous than those confidently placed. Finally, single traits, like the method of stamping pottery, could be used as the sole criterion for classifying a whole regional complex (note that the "aspect" and "phase" categories are missing in the passage quoted. So we have "cultures" tagged by pottery, or a type of mound, or the style of burials, ignoring everything else. Perfectly legitimate, but it really makes sense only to archaeologists—it was a shorthand lingo developed in conferences and taverns, and around the campfires and dining tables of the field camps. It certainly had little or nothing in common with ethnological description; these archaeological "cultures" were constrained creations of academia and they became the symbol of what Walter Taylor felt was wrong with archaeological theory.

Walter Taylor's Critique of the "Historical-Developmental" Approach[3]

The answer, of course, was to find a new way to think about archaeological data, and new definitions of the old concepts. This sort of exercise had been going on in sociocultural anthropology for several decades, as the field passed through a series of "schools:" evolutionism, historicism, culture patternist, functionalism, *Kulturkreis* theory, and various topical specialties. At the end of World War II functionalism had reached an apex, and was beginning its decline. But archaeology had begun dabbling in functionalist interpretation during and shortly after the war, with names like Frank Setzler and Paul Martin in the vanguard. I was enthusiastic over these developments, as any Chicago anthropology student who admired Fred Eggan and Clyde Kluckhohn would have been, and committed myself in a summary paper on them (Bennett 1943). So the time was ripe for something new.

How new? Archaeologists on both sides of the Atlantic had repeatedly mentioned the need for the extraction of more detailed and culturally oriented information from excavated material. Grahame Clark published his *Archaeology and Society* in 1939—its very title was a shocker in some graduate departments, because for many people, archaeology had nothing to say about society. Clark, however, adopted the essential Taylor position a decade before the publication of *A Study of Archeology*: he discussed the need for reconstruction of economic life and the desirability of providing information on "social, intellectual, and spiritual life." He concluded with remarks on the significance of archaeology's knowledge of the past for modern life. Clark does not describe how these reconstructions were to be made in detail, and the bulk of the book concerned standard approved methods of excavation, dating, and analysis. I eagerly read the book in the 1940s and we discussed it at length at Chicago, and the general consensus was simply that Clark's recommendations were mainly appropriate for a European context, where you generally had better links between the past and present.

Now, Taylor was recommending *full* contextual cultural analysis for Americanist archaeology, especially the *North* American situation—where the data were often especially scanty. In 1940 Clyde Kluckhohn published a much-cited paper on the need for more culturally and problem-oriented analysis of Mayan prehistory, and this seemed appropriate because the Middle America data were relatively lush. Kluckhohn spoke as an anthropologist, and the paper was understood at the time as a kind of manifesto to archaeologists from the cultural-anthropology side. Since Kluckhohn was Taylor's thesis advisor, Taylor's thesis-book might be viewed as the North American descendent of Kluckhohn's Maya paper.

Many in the profession felt the chickens were finally coming home to roost: for years the identification of Americanist archaeology with anthropology had been given lip service, but now it appeared that this was not enough. But paradoxically Taylor seemed to deny that archaeology was part of the discipline of anthropology: "As an autonomous discipline, it [archeology] consists of a method and a set of specialized techniques for the gathering or 'production' of cultural information" (Taylor [1948] 1983: 44). But then a few pages before the final sentence of Chapter 2, he defined cultural anthropology as ". . . the comparative study of the statics and dynamics of culture, its formal, functional and developmental aspects" (ibid.: 39). "Cultural information," presumably. The chapter also deals with history, and Taylor concluded that insofar as archaeology can produce data on the past in a correct chronological sequence it is linked to history—or actually what he called "historiography," since he was emphasizing the *writing* of history. An archaeological report is therefore a kind of written history (this usage is similar to Kroeber's identification of history as cultural description—Kroeber 1931, 1935). Taylor emphasized the impossibility of truly *re*constructing the past, because nobody—historian, archaeologist, anthropologist, or novelist can really do this. One can only *construct* a past as it seems to the analyst, using the best information and ideas he can command.

James Deetz pointed out in what is perhaps the only genuinely favorable disquisition by an Americanist archaeologist on Taylor (Deetz 1988), that the most insightful chapter in the book is this second one, on the relationship of history to anthropology. It is curious that none of the reviewers nor the critics and commentators took it seriously. However, the relationship of history to anthropology during the 1930s and 40s was regarded as a highly technical sideline, as in the case of historical reconstruction (see chapter 7); or a theoretical matter for Kroeber and Boas to argue about, but not a vital methodological issue. Ethnology was still by and large under the aura of the virtuoso complex, in which the ethnographer and writer was considered the ultimate authority on the "culture" he presented to the reader. As Deetz paraphrased Taylor's position, history, or what Taylor called *historiography*, is "value-influenced construction of past reality" (Deetz 1988: 16).

Taylor went on to note that ethnology is also a construction of the past, because the culture the ethnographer records and eventually writes up is now in the past (in spite of the early Classic habit of putting everything into the present tense, the so-called ethnographic present). Therefore, archaeology and ethnology or cultural anthropology join hands—they can be viewed as participants in the same general endeavor.

Taylor was really defining archaeology as a kind of *meta-discipline*—a field of study within but also between other disciplines, supplementing and sometimes transcending their goals and accomplishments. (The term had not been invented so Taylor could not have used it.) But there were other contradictions: Taylor remarked that "The archeologist, as archeologist, is really nothing but a technician" ([1948] 1983: 43), and by this I suppose he meant that stripped of his affiliations with history and anthropology, and ignoring his product, which is a form of historiography, the archaeologist, doing his thing in the field, is nothing more than a scientific digger, a soils engineer, an architectural analyst. So archaeology is not any one of these things all the time, but can be any of them depending on context.

Patty Jo Watson notes, "Walter Taylor made a strenuous effort to align Americanist archeology with Americanist sociocultural anthropology by taking the traditional, Tylorean culture concept as a central tenet in his argument" (Watson 1995: 689).[4] Taylor's chapter 4 is entirely devoted to "A Concept of Culture for Archeology." The title is interesting because up to that time, so far as I can tell, nobody had really required archaeology to subscribe to a highly formal definition of culture. In other words, Taylor was proposing (without, I suspect, being fully aware) that culture was something whose definition varied depending on your purposes. His exposition is tedious, and when examined closely, it turns out to contain not one but several definitions. The Kroeber and Kluckhohn 1952 monograph on culture concepts devotes two pages to Taylor's discussion, but even they missed some of the details. The first and most forthright Taylor definition is simply that *culture consists of ideas*: the ideas that lie behind the artifacts and other material remains found by the archaeologist.[5] Taylor was possibly influenced by Albert Blumenthal who in the 1940s was the foremost spokesman for the ideational definition of culture (Blumenthal 1937a, 1937b, 1940; all of his papers are in Taylor's bibliography).

A second Taylor definition, related to the first, concerns the "mental constructs" that people learn in life. Taylor felt that if enough of these constructs—behavior patterns, ideas, techniques, and so on—were held by enough people (no percentages provided!), then one has *a culture*. This seems equivalent to Robert Redfield's "common understandings" definition of a "folk society." And this concept, of course, implements Taylor's third set of definitions: the "holistic" and the "partitive." The holistic is Culture as a universal phenomenon; while the partitive refers to particular local expressions of this universal entity. The "shared mental constructs" then constitute the essence of a particular culture. Finally, and in the fourth place, Taylor rejected the idea of a superorganic, but at the same time, he kept referring to holistic culture as a kind of thing or entity, so he got caught in the Kroeberian contradiction: denying a separate reality for culture but at the same time talking about it as if it were.

Why did Taylor emphasize an ideational concept of culture? As noted, this was by no means foreign to anthropology: certainly "ideas" were always at least one component of culture in most textbook definitions. One reason is simply that Taylor had been trained as an anthropologist at the graduate level by Clyde Kluckhohn, a culture-concept theorist. Another reason was, of course, his own philosophical rationale: that for an archaeologist, culture is not the material objects alone, but the concepts or the "cognitive maps," as they would be called in the post-Classic, which configure the material remains. But the third and most important reason was simply that Taylor could not escape from the fact that archaeologists dig up *human* remains and the physical *artifacts of human life* and, therefore—*culture*. Taylor resisted calling archaeology anthropology, but he could not deny that archaeology, just like anthropology, deals in Man and Culture:

> It is an integral part of this major aim to make every effort to interpret the concrete, empirical findings of archeology in terms of culture itself, of cultural behavior, and of the non-material results of cultural behavior whereby the materialistic and "lifeless" data may be given depth and life. (Taylor [1948] 1983: 96)

Taylor's rhetoric here is typical of the Classic era: how in the world does one distinguish between "culture itself" (is not this superorganicism?), and "cultural behavior," and the "non-material results of cultural behavior?"[6] It is easy enough to guess and to use terms like "cognitive map" which appeared much later, but at the time, the available vocabulary was limited, and the urge to incorporate everything into "culture" was strong.

Taylor noted that Ralph Linton was hazy over the distinction that Taylor made between "holistic" and "partitive" because, according to Taylor, he ignored that while items of a *culture* are shared; items in holistic *Culture* can be either shared or not. The argument suggests that to know holistic Culture is to be a philosopher, or a pure anthropological theorist—whereas to know *a* culture is simply to *construct* it from the ethnographic or archaeological data. *Cultures* are empirical; *Culture* is a philosophical or what he called a "mental construct," or an "analytical abstraction"?). This suggests, of course, the superorganic, but then Taylor avoided the idea of a separate reality for culture by using the "mental construct" formulation.

So we come, finally, to the "conjunctive approach"; chapter 6—the longest in the book. To define this approach was, in fact, Taylor's main objective. Curiously, the best definitions of the approach are not to be found in this chapter, but in earlier ones. Chapter 6 is devoted to a rather pedestrian listing of methods and categories of data—nothing new, really, even in 1948. Taylor simply lists the data categories used in sophisticated archaeological circles of the time.

Taylor presented the conjunctive approach as a desirable alternative to the "comparative or taxonomic approach" (ibid.: 9), which, it would seem, is really the classificatory aspect of the historical-reconstruction approach. The latter, Taylor believed, was concerned entirely with relationships between the data from various sites at geographical and temporal removes. That is, the construction of aspects, phases, patterns, etc., was for Taylor a matter of constructing *external* relationships of the components and foci—and in the hands of Classic operators like Willey and Phillips, before and after Taylor, it was a matter of constructing culture history. The conjunctive approach was devoted to *internal* relationships among the site data: how, for example, the size of a pueblo ruin implied particular population magnitudes and economic status. Taylor felt that inquiries such as this would reveal culture, whereas the taxonomic approach revealed taxonomy and historical sequence, although he acknowledged that the approaches were for some purposes complementary.[7]

I always had difficulty understanding why Taylor drew such a hard distinction between the taxonomic-developmental approach and his own conjunctive approach. I felt they were simply two stages of the work necessary to reveal the full context of a vanished cultural situation. (And I argued this with Taylor over a two- and-a-half week period in Seattle, in December, 1948, while I was waiting for a flight to Japan and he was teaching temporarily at the University of Washington.) Anyway, "conjunctive" really meant connective, interrelated, and so it has continued to mean this into the 1990s, although few archaeologists use the term.[8] Later, we had other conversations when he was at Southern Illinois University and I was at Washington University, only a couple of hours apart, but we found it difficult to communicate because by that time I was thoroughly immersed in applied and economic-ecological anthropology, and if there was one thing Walter detested it was applied work.

A Study of Archeology is, in the last analysis, another Classic era anthropological document in search of the concept of culture. Taylor's bibliography lists no less than sixty-nine references which relate to the concept and definition of culture. It would be interesting to note the extent to which Taylor's ideas about the concept were picked up by others in the 1950s. However, it is difficult to find specific references to Taylor's ideas on culture in subsequent archaeological writings (at least in the 1950s and even into the 1960s). To some extent the book was shunned or deliberately ignored by the professionals. But Taylor may have had more impact than was generally acknowledged at the time. Definitions and discussion of the concept of culture began appearing in general archaeology texts and an increasing number of articles appeared on methodology and theory. For example, the 1956 Society for American Archaeology Memoir No. 11, *Seminars in Archaeology: 1955*, includes several papers exploring aspects of the culture concept in the context of specific case studies. In their piece, Willey and Phillips (1958) note similarities in their paper with respect to "levels of [analytical] organization" (observation, description, explanation) to Taylor's ideas. However, Willey and Phillips were primarily concerned with the second or "descriptive level" of analysis and they were fundamentally vague with respect to definitions of culture. In their words, culture (and civilization) are "the maximum units reflecting the major segmentations of culture-history" (Willey and Phillips 1958: 48). This differed from the Taylor anthropologically oriented concept.

In what was probably the preeminent introductory text to archaeology during the 1960s and early 1970s, Hole and Heizer, *An Introduction to Prehistoric Archaeology* (1965 and subsequent editions), devoted five pages to a discussion of "Culture," distinguishing between "culture" as used by anthropologists and "The Archaeological Culture," and an entire chapter titled, "Analysis of Culture Process" (in which culture is viewed as a "system"). Curiously, Taylor is not cited in these discussions and occurs only in a list of "General Works about Archeology" and in reference to the chapter, "Historical Reconstruction in Archeology."

Culture as system, or the "sociocultural system," begins to dominate the archaeological theory literature of the late 1960s and 1970s (cf. Hole and Heizer 1965; Watson et al. 1971; and the British text, David Clarke's *Analytical Archaeology* 1968). Robert Dunnell's *Systematics in Prehistory* (1971), also has a discussion of the culture concept and archaeology's relationship to sociocultural anthropology, history, and science (see pp. 121–7). Dunnell's objective, like Taylor's, was to distinguish archaeology (actually what Dunnell calls the study of "Prehistory") from anthropology and history; but unlike Taylor, prehistory is defined as a separate, *scientific* discipline and only related to sociocultural anthropology in that they share a common concept, that of culture. Dunnell's concept of culture "is to be understood as meaning *shared ideas*—and nothing more" (1971: 121).

Perhaps, with his "conjunctive approach," Taylor really thought like an anthropologist rather than an independent disciplinarian of archaeology—the role he advocated. In two later short pieces, Taylor understood that the field really operates on the basis of "probabilities" (Taylor 1972: 32; also Taylor 1969: 384) rather than certainties; or what might be a mathematical approach to the problem of inference. That is, the ambiguous data on artifact use, meaning, function, etc., which plagues archaeological interpretation, requires a good deal of educated guesswork, and Taylor tried to find a way of disciplining the method. This also led Taylor to cultivate a healthy skepticism over the rather overblown scientizing and philosophizing of the "new archaeologists" (as they were called in the 1960s and 1970s)—which required more certainty of identification and interpretation than archaeological methods could possibly provide. He elaborated on this point with reference to the culture concept, noting that archaeologists would find Leslie White's adaptational concept of culture awkward to apply because it was so difficult to pin down adaptive processes and behaviors when all you have are a collection of artifacts that happened to have been preserved.[9]

Taylor's position in the history of Americanist archaeology is not easy to pinpoint. His important writings are confined to *A Study of Archeology*, and his actual excavations to a single report on some of his Mexican work, edited by others, and not as yet available as this is being written (although reports on parts of the assemblage have appeared, e.g., Gilmore 1947, Bryant 1975). But the famous book went through seven printings, presumably all sold out, which speaks for itself. Lewis Binford, considered by some a kind of successor to Taylor with respect to both the specifics of his archaeological theory and also to his gadfly functions, has noted that Taylor's book was important in his own development (Binford 1972: 2ff.). Binford represents the generation immediately succeeding Taylor, and began his university career at the University of North Carolina, later transferring to the University of Michigan. He read Taylor's book while still at North Carolina, was enthusiastic, and consulted it repeatedly during his Michigan period. Binford noted that with respect to the *conjunctive approach*, "Taylor had the aims but not the tools" (Binford 1972: 8); that is, the ideas were good but Taylor's presentation lacked methodological precision: he failed to tell the profession *how* to do what he wanted them to do. Binford, in other words, seemed here and elsewhere in his book, to imply that he supplied the tools that Taylor did not.[10]

Postlude

Sociocultural anthropology was engaged in an intense search for sophisticated theory—a search which started in the 1920s, really, but hit a peak in the 1940s and early 1950s. The Parsonsian venture, with its antecedents in Max Weber and Bronislaw Malinowski, the early beginnings of social ecology, the controversial resurrection of evolutionary theory, the sociological systematics of the British, and so on—all of this existed while archaeologists were still counting potsherds—so to speak. William Longacre, in a 1996 unpublished paper, remarks that "American archeology was badly out-of-step with American anthropology." The statement is somewhat equivocal—"out of step" sounds like criticism, but the fact is that archaeology was still engaged in a vital task: the depiction of the basic historical progression of human endeavor in crucial parts of the world, and especially the United States east of the Mississippi. That is, while I believe that archaeologists may have felt "out of step," and also felt guilty about the fact they were not producing high-level theory, or reconstructing *whole* cultures and not just pottery types, they really were not prepared for intellectually sophisticated endeavors. And I think that one reason Taylor's 1948 book was resented was because of the guilt and frustration. Taylor, not a real digger himself, and a student of that fancy Harvard anthropologist, Clyde Kluckhohn, had some nerve! My own recollections of the period also tell me that Taylor's book was probably read more carefully by sociocultural anthropologists than by archaeologists.

In the light of the 1990s, criticism of the specifics of Taylor's proposal for an enlarged archaeology is not very meaningful. Archaeology was heading in those directions before he wrote and published, and it has continued to do so. The typological and developmental approaches which he criticized, have of course continued to flourish, because they represent a necessary function: one simply has to get a grip on the temporal unfolding of human activities and their mutual influence and interaction. And various segments of the "conjunctive approach" that Taylor advocated have all become parts of the discipline and most are represented by specialized subfields and position papers. The more the merrier. Taylor deserves the cordial gratitude of the whole archaeological community for shaking it up at a crucial time in its development. But he also deserves the applause of the anthropological profession for contributing a valuable document on the theory of culture.

Notes

1. First description of the "McKern System," officially termed the Midwestern Taxonomic Method, was in a pamphlet by the National Research Council (McKern, Deuel, and Guthe 1933). McKern was an early student of Kroeber's at the University of California and eventually director of the Milwaukee Public Museum. He was one of the first anthropologists trained by the first scientific archaeological generation to take a major job at a major American museum. The classification was given its first hearing and revision at the Indianapolis Archaeological Conference in 1937, which is also considered the founding ceremony for modern Midwestern archaeology.
2. One can compare the position taken by Willey and Sabloff, in the first edition (1973) of their book, *History of American Archaeology*: they define archaeology as "the study of the human cultural and social past whose goals are to *narrate* the sequential story of that past and to *explain* the events that composed it" (Willey and Sabloff 1973: 11, emphasis original). The "narrate" part is, of course, identical to their "historical reconstruction" theme; but the "explain" element is new: the authors seemingly had come around the Taylor-Binford et al. position which seeks more than simple sequential portrayal. And on the same page, we find that "Archaeology is also allied with anthropology." Not "dependent on," in the Taylor formula, but simply "allied to." By the mid and late 1970s, there was a sharp reaction to what many North Americanists saw as overreliance on cultural anthropology as a source of ideas, and a drift back into a more generic or multidisciplinary "scientific" approach.
3. I lack details concerning the writing and publication of *A Study of Archeology*, but Taylor's own introduction to the original 1948 edition—reprinted in the 1983 printing—provides an outline. The thesis was written in 1942–43 as a doctoral dissertation at Harvard, with Clyde Kluckhohn as thesis advisor. The thesis is organized differently from the book version and was given the title, "A Study of Archaeology: A Dialectic, Practical, and Critical Discussion with Special Reference to American Archaeology and the Conjunctive Approach." A typewritten message is taped onto the first binding page before the title page: "ACE ARCHAEOLOGIST SPIRITUAL REJUVENATION KIT; Placed here by the GIDEONS. This book is rated PG, parental guidance suggested."

   After Taylor received his Ph.D. he entered the armed forces and spent about three years in the European theater. Upon his return, a group at Harvard encouraged him to prepare the thesis for publication, and helped him get a Rockefeller Fellowship in the Humanities. Taylor lists the following people as instrumental in assisting him on this venture: Clyde Kluckhohn, W. H. Kelly, J. C. Kelley, Henry Collins, Frank Setzler. Apparently the people mentioned above arranged to have the American Anthropological Association publish the book in 1948 as Memoir no. 69. There were several later printings—the 1983 printing contains a history (Watson 1983). Most of the publications that Taylor approvingly notes as exemplifying his "conjunctive approach," including some by the present writer (e.g., Bennett 1943, 1944), were published between the writing of the thesis and its later publication. In other words, archaeology was already moving toward Taylor's own objectives and approach in the late 1940s.
4. I feel that Watson is in partial error when she says that Taylor used Tylor's definition of culture. Tylor did not really say it consisted of ideas, but rather, and simply, a "complex whole" that makes up "culture or civilization"—and then

follows it with an enumeration of items and institutions, *some* of which were more or less mentalistic.

5. The ideational conception of culture is not new, and became significant in literary and artistic circles in the latter half of the nineteenth century. The following is a passage from the manifesto for symbolist painting (echoing a similar manifesto for symbolism in literature written in 1886): ". . . objects can have no value *qua* objects. They can only appear to him [the artist] as *signs*. They are letters in an immense alphabet that only a man of genius knows how to spell out . . ." (Aurier 1891).
6. Some of Taylor's critics noted the verbosity of this chapter on the culture concept, and questioned whether it was really necessary that archaeology invest in cultural semantics. I can echo that feeling, but on the other hand acknowledge that the preoccupation with the concept was inevitable, given the decision to tie archaeology's banner to anthropology. Taylor's "conjunctive approach," if fully implemented, probably needed a culture concept no more urgently than it would have needed concepts of technological innovation, resource use and environmental adaptation, subsistence dependencies, and the like. This situation has by no means changed: it continues to generate separatism between archaeologists, who, on the one hand, feel that sociocultural anthropology really has little to offer; and those who, on the other hand, continue to celebrate the union, and strive to interpret artifact materials in cultural terms.
7. Taylor's 1954 paper on the "history and theory" of Southwestern archaeology (1954) is something of a surprise because he seems to approve of most of the methodologies developed in the Southwest, including ceramic typology and historical sequencing and classifications, aspects which—at least with respect to Eastern archaeology—he appeared to criticize as excessive or short-sighted. He also congratulates the Southwestern workers for always relating their excavated materials to culture complexes, especially the Anasazi-Pueblo indentification. That is, the Southwestern archaeologists were, at least in part, doing what the "conjunctive approach" advocated: always keeping living cultures in mind, and doing one's best to interpret archaeological materials with respect to the living survivors. And Taylor also chides Easterners for their long-term dominance of Southwestern archaeology, and their obsession with the "field expedition" concept: the packing of the station wagons and the long trip west, the suitable romantic clothing, and so on (all features which I became familiar with during the summers of 1933, 1935, and 1937, when I participated in Southwestern archaeological projects all sponsored by Eastern archaeologists). Paul Martin provides a favorable commentary on Taylor's paper. However, Martin *should* have been favorably disposed, since his "functional" attempts at interpretation of small Pueblo sites was a precursor of Taylor's "conjunctive approach."
8. They never got into the habit of using Taylorian rhetoric because the book was anathema—and incidently this bothered Walter Taylor. The reception of *A Study of Archeology* was decidedly mixed. Some of the comments and reviews exhibited a suppressed sense of outrage; few were favorable, but some acknowledged that Taylor made some good points. The European reception (e.g., Daniel 1951) was generally more cordial than the American, and usually managed to point out that the "conjunctive approach" was nothing new considering the work of prehistorians like V. Gordon Childe (1944) or Grahame Clark (1939). Among the American reviews and comments, Richard Woodbury's—five years after publication—was typical: a kind of thin-lipped rejection. Woodbury noted that "the few printed reviews and comments on *A Study of Archeology* express a striking range of

opinions, and are generally at variance with the widespread verbal criticisms evoked by this publication" (Woodbury 1953–54: 292). This comment refers to what I allude to in the chapter: the fury with which the then rather small archaeological fraternity reacted to Taylor's unstinting criticism of minor divinities like James Griffin, A. V. Kidder, and Emil Haury. Woodbury faults the book for its dogmatic and crusading objectives, and for its "patronizing attitude." Woodbury cites Robert Burgh's critical attack and Irving Rouse's dismissal of the conjunctive approach as too time-consuming and too expensive. The Burgh critique (1950), appearing as a "Comment" in the *American Anthropologist*, faulted Taylor for some of his contradictory statements and for errors of interpretation of artifact material Taylor used as examples of his recommended methods. He concludes, "Taylor develops his conceptual scheme for the conjunctive approach by the inadmissible device of altering his premises as often as is required by the dictates of his abstract plan, as is evidenced by the contradictions . . ." (Burgh 1950: 117). As I said, the fraternity was furious.

Bruce Trigger, in my opinion, contributes the best (and shortest!) modern critique of the book. He observes many of the contradictions and inconsistencies, but does not dwell on them, instead simply pointing out that:

> His [Taylor's] work was mainly important as a critique of current standards of archeological research and as a call for archaeologists to recover and analyze archeological data in far greater detail than they had done hitherto. The result was to reinforce the trend toward functional interpretation already under way in American archeology rather than to challenge the basic tenets of Boasian historical particularism. . . . (Trigger 1989: 270)

Taylor's sensitivity over the restrained reception of *A Study of Archeology* is apparent in his introductory essay to Mark Leone's *Contemporary Archaeology* (1972):

> Perhaps the popularly held view that my criticism of Americanist archeology was a polemic aroused such partisan and defensive animosity that the message of the rest of the volume was lost. . . . the older generation taking umbrage but maintaining a dignified silence and largely ignoring my insurgency . . . .(Taylor 1972: 29)

He goes on to say that later generations came to accept his ideas but by that time the real origins of the approach had begun to grow dim. Later comers had adopted the ideas; hence these later writers were often cited as the source of the approach (ibid.: 29–30). He faults critics like Gordon Willey and Paul Martin, who felt that *A Study of Archeology* had to be taken with a grain of salt, or words to that effect, since Taylor had not produced an archaeological site report or artifact analysis based on his conjunctive approach. Taylor remarks,

> . . . it has always seemed to me that both Binford [who was also named in Willey's critical remark] and I have provided our colleagues with enough pertinent material for them to chew on for quite a spell. The fact that they have not chosen to do so and have been waiting so patiently for us to provide them with . . . masses of material objects . . . appears to me to be more a commentary on their outlook and standards of value than a justifiable demand on us. (ibid.: 30)

It is interesting to note that in this passage, as in others in the 1972 essay, Taylor pairs himself with Binford (see, also, Taylor's (1969) review of Binford and Binford), but at the same time, criticizes the Binfords for producing "an explicit restatement of an old one"—that is, a position adequately expounded by Taylor himself (Taylor 1969: 383).

9. By the 1970–1980s archaeologists began to use sociologist Robert Merton's (1968) concept of "middle-range theory," a term which refers to the wide range of useful "empirical generalization" characteristic of much research on social phenomena. A careful consideration of Taylor's conjunctive approach suggests that it approximates (prefigures?) the statics/dynamics version of "middle-range theory" as popularized by Binford (1977, 1981; see also Raab and Goodyear 1984). However, Taylor should be credited with originality because he developed it entirely out of his knowledge of archaeological methods and thought.
10. To some extent, I have always felt that the relationship of archaeology—especially Americanist—to general anthropology resembles the relationship of rural sociology to general sociology. Like the rural sociologist who aspires to deal in general theory and patterns, but who must rely on the urban-and-world-based social theory of the general sociologist, largely inapplicable to the rural scheme, the Americanist archaeologist has tried to utilize the sociocultural concepts and theories rooted in the study of living communities. In both cases—sociology and archaeology—the level of theory used is often at best only partly applicable to the cultural data derived from research.

Literature Cited and Some Consulted Works

Atwater, Caleb. 1820. *Description of the Antiquities Discovered in the State of Ohio and Other Western States*. Transactions and Collections, vol. 1. American Antiquarian Society.

Aurier, Albert. 1891. *Le symbolisme en peinture*. Mercure de France, 9 Feb. 1891.

Bennett, John W. 1942. "W. B. Nickerson—Pioneer in Scientific Archaeology." *American Antiquity* 8: 122–4.

———. 1943. "Recent Developments in the Functional Interpretation of Archaeological Data." *American Antiquity* 9: 208–19.

———. 1944. "The Interaction of Culture and Environment in the Smaller Societies." *American Anthropologist* 46: 461–78.

———. 1947. *Archaeological Explorations in Jo Daviess County, Illinois: The Work of William Baker Nickerson (1895–1901) and the University of Chicago (1926–32)*. Chicago: University of Chicago Press.

Bidney, David. 1944. "On the Concept of Culture and Some Cultural Fallacies." *American Anthropologist* 46: 30–44.

Binford, Lewis R. 1962. "Archaeology As Anthropology." *American Antiquity* 28: 217–25.

———. 1972. *An Archaeological Perspective*. New York: Seminar.

———. 1977. "Introduction," in *For Theory Building in Archaeology*, edited by
L. R. Binford, pp. 1–10. New York: Academic Press.

———. 1981. *Bones: Ancient Men and Modern Myths*. New York: Academic Press.

Binford, Sally R. and Lewis R. Binford, ed. 1968. *New Perspectives in Archaeology*. Chicago: Aldine.

Blumenthal, Albert. 1937a. *The Best Definition of Culture*. Marietta, OH: Marietta College Press.
———. 1937b. *Culture Consists of Ideas*. Marietta, OH: Marietta College Press.
———. 1940. "A New Definition of Culture." *American Anthropologist* 42: 571–86.
Bradford, A. W. 1843. *American Antiquities, and Researches into the Origin and History of the Red Race*. New York.
Bryant, Vaughn M., Jr. 1975. "Pollen As an Indicator of Prehistoric Diets in Coahuila, Mexico." *Bulletin of the Texas Archeological Society* 46:.
Burgh, Robert F. 1950. "Comment on Taylor's 'A Study of Archaeology,'" with a rejoinder by Walter W. Taylor. *American Anthropologist* 52: 114–9.
Case, C. M. 1927. "Culture As a Distinctive Human Trait." *American Journal of Sociology* 32: 906–20.
Childe, V. Gordon. 1944. "The Future of Archaeology." *Man* 44: 18–9.
Clark, Grahame. [1939] 1957. *Archaeology and Society*. 3d ed. London: Methuen.
Clarke, David L. 1968. *Analytical Archaeology*. New York: Columbia University Press.
Cole, F. C. and T. Deuel. 1937. *Rediscovering Illinois*. Chicago: University of Chicago Press.
Colton, H. S. 1942. "Archaeology and the Reconstruction of History." *American Antiquity* 8: 33–40.
Daniel, Glyn E. 1951. "Review of 'A Study of Archaeology' by W. W. Taylor." *Man* 51: 82–3.
Deetz, James. 1988. "History and Archaeology Theory: Walter Taylor Revisited." *American Antiquity* 53: 13–22.
Dunnell, Robert C. 1971. *Systematics in Prehistory*. New York: Free Press.
Fell, Barry. 1976. *America B.C.: Ancient Settlers in the New World*. New York: Quadrangle.
Foster, J. W. 1874. *Pre-Historic Races of the United States of America*. 3d ed. Chicago: S.C. Griggs and Company.
Gilmore, Raymond M. 1947. "Report on the Collection of Mammal Bones from Archaeological Cave Sites in Coahuila, Mexico." *Journal of Mammalogy* 28: 147–65.
Griffin, James B. 1937. "A Classificatory System As a Working Base for the Study of North American Archaeology." *Indianapolis Archaeological Conference*, pp. 48–50. National Research Council, Division of Anthropology and Psychology, Committee on State Archaeological Surveys.
———. 1943. *The Fort Ancient Aspect, Its Cultural and Chronological Position in Mississippi Valley Archaeology*. Ann Arbor, MI: University of Michigan Press.
Haven, S. F. 1855. *Archaeology of the United States*. Contributions to Knowledge, vol. 8. Washington, DC: Smithsonian Institution.
Hinsley, Curtis M., Jr. 1981. *Savages and Scientists: The Smithsonian Institution and the Development of American Anthropology, 1846–1910*. Washington, DC: Smithsonian Institution Press
Hole, Frank and Robert F. Heizer. 1965. *An Introduction to Prehistoric Archeology*. New York: Holt, Rinehart and Winston.
Holmes, W. H. 1915. "Areas of American Culture Characterization Tentatively Outlined As an Aid in the Study of Antiquities," in *Anthropology in North America* by F. Boas et al., pp. 42–75. New York: G. E. Stechert.
Jefferson, Thomas. [1788] 1944. "Notes on the State of Virginia," in *Basic Writings of Thomas Jefferson*, edited by Philip S. Foner. Garden City: Halcyon House.
Kelley, Jane H. and Ronald F. Williamson. 1996. "The Positioning of Archaeology within Anthropology: A Canadian Historical Perspective." *American Antiquity* 61: 5–20.

Kluckhohn, Clyde. 1940. "The Conceptual Structure in Middle American Studies," in *The Maya and Their Neighbors*. New York.

Kreiger, Alex. 1944. "The Typological Concept." *American Antiquity* 9: 271–88.

Kroeber, A. L. 1931. "Historical Reconstruction of Culture Growths and Organic Evolution." *American Anthropologist* 32: 149–56.

———. 1935. "History and Science in Anthropology." *American Anthropologist* 37: 539–69.

Kroeber, A. L. and Clyde Kluckhohn. 1952. *Culture: A Critical Review of Concepts and Definitions*. Papers of the Peabody Museum of American Archaeology and Ethnology, vol. 47, no. 1. Cambridge, MA: Harvard University.

Lapham, J. C. 1853. *The Antiquities of Wisconsin*. Contributions to Knowledge, vol. 7. Washington, DC: Smithsonian Institution.

Leone, Mark P. 1972. *Contemporary Archaeology: A Guide to Theory and Contributions*. Carbondale, IL: Southern Illinois Press.

Longacre, William A. 1996. "1966 and All of That: Gordon R. Willey Synthesizes North American Archaeology." Paper presented at the Sixty-first Annual Meeting of the Society for American Archaeology, New Orleans, LA.

MacNeish, Richard S. 1978. *The Science of Archaeology?* North Scituate, MA: Duxbury.

Malinowski, Bronislaw. 1939. "Review of Six Essays on Culture by Albert Blumenthal." *American Sociological Review* 4: 588–92.

McKern, W. C. 1937. "Certain Culture Classification Problems in Middle Western Archaeology." *The Indianapolis Archaeological Conference*, pp. 70–82 National Research Council, Division of Anthropology and Psychology, Committee on State Archaeological Surveys, Washington, DC.

———. 1939. "The Midwestern Taxonomic Method As an Aid to Archaeological Culture Study." *American Antiquity* 4: 301–13.

McKern, W. C., T. Deuel and C. E. Guthe. 1933. On Midwestern Taxonomic Method. Unpublished ms., National Research Council.

Meltzer, David J. 1996. "Separating Learning from Folly, Fancy from Fact: Samuel Haven and the First Synthesis of American archaeology (1856)." Paper presented at the Sixty-first Annual Meeting of the Society for American Archaeology, New Orleans, LA.

Merton, Robert K. [1949] 1968. *Social Theory and Social Structure*. 3d ed. New York: Free Press.

Preucel, Robert W., ed. 1991. *Processual and Postprocessual Archaeologies: Multiple Ways of Knowing the Past*. Occasional Paper no. 10, Center for Archaeological Investigations, Southern Illinois University, Carbondale, IL.

Priest, Josiah. 1834. *American Antiquities and Discoveries in the West*. 4th ed. Albany: Hoffman & White.

Raab, L. Mark and Albert C. Goodyear. 1984. "Middle-Range Theory in Archaeology: A Critical Review of Origins and Applications. *American Antiquity* 49: 255–68.

Rouse, B. I. 1939. *Prehistory in Haiti, a Study in Method*. Publications in Anthropology, no. 21, Yale University, New Haven, CT.

Schwartz, Douglas W. 1968. "North American Archaeology in Historical Perspective." *Actes du 11ème Congrès International d'Histoire des Sciences*, vol. 2, pp. 311–5.

Setzler, F. M. 1942. "Archeological Accomplishments during the Past Decade in the United States." *Washington Academy of Sciences Journal* 32: 253–59.

Shetrone, Henry C. 1930. *The Mound-Builders*. New York.

Society for American Archaeology. 1956. *Seminars in Archaeology: 1955*. Society for American Archaeology memoir no. 11.

Squier, E. G. and E. H. Davis. 1848. *Ancient Monuments of the Mississippi Valley*. Contributions to Knowledge, vol. 2, Smithsonian Institution.

Steward, Julian H. 1941. "Review of 'Prehistoric Culture Units and Their Relationships in Northern Arizona,' by H. S. Colton." *American Antiquity* 6: 366–7.

———. 1942. "The Direct Historical Approach to Archaeology." *American Antiquity* 7: 337–44.

Taylor, Walter W. 1948. *A Study of Archeology*. Originally published as Memoir 69, American Anthropological Association. Reprinted privately in 1964 by W.W. Taylor. Reprinted by Southern Illinois University Press, Carbondale, in 1967 and 1983.

———. 1954. "Southwestern Archaeology: Its History and Theory," with comments by Paul S. Martin and Irving Rouse. *American Anthropologist* 56: 561–75.

———. 1969. "Review of 'New Perspectives in Archeology' by Sally R. Binford and Lewis R. Binford, eds." *Science* 165: 382–4.

———. 1972. "Old Wine and New Skins: A Contemporary Parable," in *Contemporary Archaeology: A Guide to Theory and Contributions*, edited by Mark P. Leone, pp. 28–33. Carbondale, IL: Southern Illinois University Press.

Trigger, Bruce G. 1989. *A History of Archaeological Thought*. Cambridge: Cambridge University Press.

Watson, Patty Jo. 1983. "Foreword (to the 1983 edition)," in *A Study of Archeology* by Walter W. Taylor, pp. ix-xvi. Carbondale, IL: Southern Illinois University, Center for Archaeological Investigations.

———. 1995. "Archaeology, Anthropology, and the Culture Concept." *American Anthropologist* 97: 683–94.

Watson, Patty Jo, Steven A. Leblanc and Charles L. Redman. 1971. *Explanation in Archeology: An Explicitly Scientific Approach*. New York: Columbia University Press.

———. 1971. "The Normative View of Culture and the Systems Theory Approach," chapter 3 in *Explanation in Archaeology: An Explicitly Scientific Approach* by P.J. Watson, S.A. LeBlanc and C.L. Redman, pp. 61–87. New York: Columbia University Press.

Webb, William S. 1938. *An Archaeological Survey of the Norris Basin in Eastern Tennessee*. Bulletin 118, Bureau of American Ethnology.

Wedel, Waldo R. 1938. *The Direct-Historical Approach in Pawnee Archaeology*. Smithsonian miscellaneous collections, vol. 97, no. 7.

Willey, Gordon R. 1966. *An Introduction to American Archaeology*. Englewood Cliffs, NJ: Prentice-Hall.

Willey, Gordon R. and Philip Phillips. 1958. *Method and Theory in American Archaeology*. Chicago: University of Chicago Press.

Willey, Gordon R. and Jeremy A. Sabloff. 1973. *A History of American Archaeology*. San Francisco, CA: W.H. Freeman.

Woodbury, Richard B. 1953–54. "Review of 'A Study of Archaeology' by W. W. Taylor." *American Antiquity* 19: 292–6.

12

Applied and Action Anthropology: Problems of Ideology and Intervention

With a Supplement: The Career of Sol Tax and the Genesis of Action Anthropology

> *It is characteristic of the anthropologist that if he does continue his work of education into what is close to the political realm, he acts as an independent agent, taking upon himself the ultimate responsibility for satisfying his conscience in terms of the obligations he feels toward his colleagues and toward his fellow men.*
> *—Sol Tax, "The Uses of Anthropology"*

> *Moreover, the recipe for action that must be drawn from applied anthropology thus far is that of caution, of modest expectations as to what can be accomplished by planning, of hu-*

This is a shortened and reorganized version of a paper originally published with the title "Applied and Action Anthropology: Ideological and Conceptual Aspects," *Current Anthropology*, vol. 36, Supplement, pp. S23-53 (1996). Republished with permission from the Wenner-Gren Foundation and the University of Chicago. The paper was originally conceived as a kind of tribute to Sol Tax, who died in 1995. Confining the paper to just two varieties of practical anthropology means that I ignore other types—Stephen Polgar, for example, distinguished four: "applied, action, radical, and committed" (Polgar 1979). I also neglect "advocacy"—an increasingly popular mode among anthropologists who wish to influence public policy but avoid the complications of both applied and action forms of practice (for discussion of advocacy, see Fetterman 1993; Peattie 1968; and Jacobs 1974).

> *mility as to what may be predicted with present instruments for observing and conceptualizing, of preference for* vis medicaturix naturae *in many social situations.*
> —*Clyde Kluckhohn,* Mirror for Man

> *We only do applied anthropology if someone is going to apply it. We have to have a consumer.*
> —*Margaret Mead, "Discussion" in* Anthropology and Society

Applied Anthropology: History and Concepts

The term "applied anthropology" is used in both Britain and the United States to refer mainly to the employment of anthropologists by organizations involved in inducing change or enhancing human welfare. In recent years the term has become a generic designation, with labels from the "hyphenated" or institutional anthropologies used to describe specific topical interests.[1] Applied has sometimes been represented as a distinct professional field, but it has not been possible to establish standards of performance and rules of certification.[2] The topical coverage is too diverse, and the roles played by the applied anthropologist are equally varied (see Peterson 1987; and van Willigen 1993: 3–5, who lists no fewer than fourteen roles!). For this and other reasons the history of applied anthropology is not easily written.[3]

HIstorically, applied anthropology is rooted in the contact of Western civilization with tribal and peasant cultures. The earliest formal activity consisted of compiling descriptions of such peoples for European consumption; the work of Peter Martyr d'Anghera (MacNutt 1912), an Italian scholar who created ethnographic reports and compilations for the Vatican and the King of Spain in the sixteenth century, is perhaps the first serious modern attempt. The practice continued well into the nineteenth century, and the materials formed the basis of theoretical "armchair" anthropology.

Perhaps the first appearance of a contemporary social conscience in connection with anthropology was the English organization in the 1840s designed to foster "protection" to the "native races" movement protesting the treatment of indigenous populations in British colonial enclaves (Reining 1962). The organization also represented an ancestor of the Royal Anthropological Institute. However, a true "applied" or interventionist initiative did not appear until the 1920s as an adjunct of colonial administration in Africa, and an American analogue, concerning Native American reservation administration and problems, began in the late 1930s. However, American applied anthropology really has a triple origin: the early work in Native American reservations (with the combined scholarly and practical work of Clyde Kluckhohn and associates, with the Navaho being the most distinguished example),[4] the Harvard Business School studies of the sociocultural basis of industrial organization,[5] and the studies of American rural communities sponsored or stimulated by the Bureau of Agricultural Economics and Rural Welfare in the Roosevelt Administration's Department of Agriculture.[6] These activities underscored the topical diversity of Applied, although they shared a conceptual kinship in the idea of interdisciplinary (or *multi*disciplinary) research and theory. At the same time, the majority of the participants were trained as anthropologists, and most of them had done classical ethnographic field work. Lloyd Warner, a participant in the Harvard Business School projects, did his doctoral research on the Australian aborigines (Warner 1937), and Conrad Arensberg did community cultural studies in rural Ireland. Kluckhohn married a sociologist and had broad social-science training at Harvard, but he conducted extensive ethnographic work with the Navaho. Fred Richardson and Elliot Chapple also did fieldwork, and Margaret Mead, who became one of the founders with these two men of the Society for Applied Anthropology in the 1940s, had cut her teeth on the cultural psychology of Oceanic societies.

The orientation toward multidisciplinary approaches and concepts has its roots in the difficulties of using single-factor or reified concepts of social phenomena in Applied work. A rejection of single-factor causation is what underlay the Harvard interdisciplinary movement, which in the 1950s surfaced in the form of the academic Department of Social Relations. This department was based on the structural-functionalist theory of Talcott Parsons, who claimed that social reality is divided into three parts: culture (anthropology), society (sociology), and personality (psychology). But Applied practice went further: it had to investigate and manipulate many phenomena other than those described in these three realms (economics, for example).

This multidisciplinary approach implied a threat to the panculturalism or whole-culturalism of the Classic era. The transition away from the culture-dominated Classic era began in the 1940s and was interrupted in one sense, and reinforced in another, by World War II (see below). This transition was characterized by confusing statements from people like Mead and Kluckhohn who defended and promoted the culture concept but who, in their own work, branched out into other disciplines—for instance, Mead to psychiatry, Kluckhohn into sociological functionalism—although both endeavored to translate these approaches into anthropological culturalism wherever possible. I believe it was the implied threat to the core idea—Culture—that led to the unease and hostility with which much Applied work was greeted by many academic anthropologists.

However, there is this question: if the founders of the Society for Applied Anthropology really saw the world in multidisciplinary terms, why did they insist on calling it applied *anthropology*? The answer has already been implied: they perceived anthropology as the one single-but-multidiscipline; and Ralph Linton's famous *Study of Man*, published in 1936, marks the beginning of broader, eclectic theoretical approaches. And just after the war, in 1945, Linton edited *The Science of Man in the World Crisis*, a book that staked out a claim for anthropology as the organizing practical discipline for the social sciences. Of course, a simpler answer to the question is that the founders were all trained, more or less, in the anthropological discipline, and one does not readily deny one's natal home.

The applied work done by anthropologists and their social science colleagues during World War II was extremely broad: studies of military occupations and their reforms, research on military and civilian morale, information-gathering "intelligence" work, updating Peter Martyr (!) on the life of peoples largely unknown to Western scholarship, work on democratic reforms in government and education, public opinion surveys on the domestic front, and so on. As the war ended and the postwar occupations began to liquidate their control over Japan, Germany, and former colonies and islands, many of these anthropologists came home, ready to exercise their multidisciplinary conscience. On the other hand, others of these wartime refugees returned to anthropology with an aggressive pro-cultural, pro-anthropological viewpoint which seemed to say, "now it's time to make good on all those promises of theory made in the Classic era." Whatever the source, and with elite leadership from Kroeber and other survivors, they went to work on this task, and in the 1950s the discipline began to reject the multidisciplinary view of the prewar period.[7]

But applied anthropology, which couldn't afford to reject this view for reasons already stated, continued the multidisciplinary tradition both in its membership and its practice. The (American) Society for Applied Anthropology remains officially hospitable to all disciplines and topics, and its meetings are attended by social scientists of all kinds. Its periodical, in a statement printed on its back cover, invites participation from all disciplines: "*Human Organization* publishes articles dealing with all areas of applied social science."[8] Still, the word *anthropology* persists in the name of the organization, and in the generic title given practitioners, regardless of their actual disciplinary affiliations.[9] A quick check on the affiliations of authors in *Human Organization* articles over the 1980–1990s period shows that a little less than 60 percent have fairly definite anthropological orientations or degrees (though over half were not working for anthropological departments), so there remains a bias in the field toward the discipline of anthropology. However, judging by the language in many of the articles, and occasional self-identifications, at least half of all anthropologically affiliated writers would probably identify themselves as institutional anthropologists: "ecological", "economic", "development", "medical", and "educational" being the principal subfields for this period.[10]

As a result of this disciplinary fragmentalization, the topics and geographical coverage of the journal changed through the years. In 1966, Jozetta Srb, a professional writer, was commissioned to make an analysis of the authorship and topical coverage of *Human Organization* from its founding in 1941 (Srb 1966). She showed that from the first issue in 1941 to the mid-1960s the topics had not only increased in number, but had changed according to world conditions and problems. "Community studies" dominated for a decade; by 1966 "developmental change," as it was called then, constituted a single general focus, with many subdivisions. In the years after 1966, however, civil rights, race issues, and human rights problems in general would increase in number.

American applied anthropology became intensely preoccupied with fieldwork methods in the 1950s and 1960s (e.g., Dean and Whyte 1958; Leighton, Adair and Parker 1951; Richardson 1950; Rodman and Kolodny 1964). Field methods, with some exceptions, had been generally taken for granted by the "virtuoso" [see chapter 6] academic ethnologists through the 1920–1950 period, with the topic of "primitive languages" and their translation being perhaps the main issue to receive some attention [e.g., the interchange by Margaret Mead and Robert Lowie (Mead 1939; Lowie 1940)]. Field methods became important for Applied because of the responsibilities of application: you have to be *sure* of what you consider to be knowledge of human behavioral proclivities when the fate or fortunes of real people—not merely ethnological subjects—depend on it. Moreover, the practitioner had to prove to his employer that his stuff was accurate, which required statistical samples, surveys, scientifically constructed questionnaires, and coefficients of association.

The sources of the explanatory concepts used in Applied studies have always been eclectic and have become more so as the institutional anthropologies have gathered steam in recent years. However, from the beginnings of the American Applied field in the 1940s there was a consistent emphasis on cultural attitudes and values as the explanations of last resort and the use of anthropological versions of standard social-science ideas: for example, "acculturation" in lieu of "social change." But there is no doubt that despite the rhetorical emphasis on anthropology the majority of Applied work could not have been done without the help of concepts from other social disciplines. The goal is not to produce general theory but to solve problems, and whatever works, works. More important is post hoc assessment of consequences, and this is done rarely, because organizations sponsoring Applied work seldom care what happens after the assigned budgeted task is completed.[11]

Finally: when you apply anthropology, just what is it you apply? (cf. Angrosino 1976). The question is rarely asked because there is no really satisfactory answer. We have already noted that the field has to be essentially multidisciplinary in its theoretical and methodological resources. And while the conventional answer to the question was 'the culture concept,' this really meant relativism: an attitude of tolerance and acceptance of any form of social reality, an attitude that frequently contradicted the demands for change embedded in the assigned tasks. However, if to "apply anthropology" means to translate cultural relativism into conservation of local ways and adaptations—that is, make sure that change is not overly punishing, or that any induced change has a beneficial effect—then Applied Anthropology is at root a value-oriented endeavor. However, "values" were taboo during the Classic era with its professed adherence to objective scientific methods! Still, the humanist-liberal ideology of the field kept coming through in the choice of topics and the critical appraisals of change projects appearing at the end of, for example, the case studies published in *Human Organization*.

Applied Anthropology: Ideology

To engage in practice requires purpose, and purpose requires guidance from values. Values function at two levels in Applied: they sanction particular interventions and purposes, and they can defend and justify the activity of practice itself. This latter function is distinctive for the practicing social sciences, since they also believe in the value-freedom of scientific activity. Hence special defenses or rationales had to be supplied. (And I shall discuss some of these in a later section on "Intervention.")

In many cases it is not possible to distinguish between these two levels of ideology, and we shall not do so in great detail in the rest of this section. In general, applied anthropology has had two dominant ideological positions: the earlier, paternalistic orientation of British colonial-applied anthropology and the egalitarian outlook of the American anthropologists. The difference between the two positions was not great, and perhaps mainly one of rhetoric: the British were inclined to use the jargon of the colonial era with its implied condescension toward "natives," while the Americans were prone to use the language of American liberalism, for instance, "people have equal rights to benefits," or "people should be treated with dignity."

A. C. Haddon's little 1921 book (actually the text of a lecture), *The Practical Value of Ethnology*, is a good statement of the original British position: Haddon stated that "colonialism ran roughshod over backward people" (1921: 30), and then went on to point out that anthropology can show administrators how to deal with these people: "Obviously, the only satisfactory method of dealing with savage, barbarian or more civilized peoples is to behave in a considerate way to them, and according to my experience, they will respond because they are gentlemen" (ibid.: 31). However, there was always need for what he called "control," created by "the application of anthropology to current statecraft," and in winding up, he cites an address to the American Folklore Society by Frank Russell, "Know, Then, Thyself" (published in *Science*, 1902) which advocated the study of the "new science"

(Russell 1902: 562) of anthropology in order to understand the "savage and the barbarian" (ibid.: 567). Thus, the British colonial-anthropology position was essentially paternalistic: tribal people were to be protected, their cultures understood, their lives bettered. Since it was believed colonial administration was often wrong- headed, anthropologists as members of the dominant race had a *special* obligation to help: "we shall then have appreciation without adulation, toleration not marred by irresponsible indifference nor by an undue sense of superiority" (ibid.: 567).

A step beyond this classic paternalism appeared in the 1935 book, *Anthropology in Action*, by Gordon Brown and Bruce Hutt—the former a British social anthropologist, the latter a colonial administrator for one district of the Iringa tribe in Tanganyika. This collaboration between anthropologist and administrator was subtitled "An Experiment," and came at the end of a decade or so of sporadic interaction between ethnologists in the field and the administrators who were their official hosts. It was a period of doubt and skepticism as to the value of anthropology, since the anthropologist was assumed to have few skills in policy-making and administration—doubts which came through nicely in an "Introduction" by one P. E. Mitchell, the colonial secretary for Tanganyika, who had to approve the experiment (see also Mitchell 1930). Mitchell laid it on the line: ". . . it would be for the administrator to ask questions, and for the anthropologists to answer them . . ." (Mitchell in Brown and Hutt 1935: xviii). And in the concluding chapter the authors assured Mr. Mitchell of their compliance, when they wrote that anthropologists "would refrain from criticism of the action taken by the administrator" (Brown and Hutt 1935: 231), since the latter must take into account a great many factors other than those the anthropologists were concerned with. And that remains, with some complicating factors, the situation today for socioeconomic development-oriented applied anthropology in the Third World. Certainly the volume of information supplied by anthropology for planning has increased, but the role of the anthropologist in day-to-day operations remains pretty much that of a wise but rather passive advisor or evaluator.[12]

Although Radcliffe-Brown produced some early writings on the topic (Radcliffe-Brown 1931), Bronislaw Malinowski was the intellectual father of British applied colonial anthropology: he defined the field and trained a whole generation of field workers (e.g., Raymond

Firth 1931) as ethnologists-with-a-conscience. His matter-of-fact approach is exemplified by the following comment:

> Thus the important issue of direct versus indirect rule needs careful study of the various processes by which European influences can reach a native tribe. My own opinion, as that of all competent anthropologists, is that indirect or dependent rule is infinitely preferable. . . . (Malinowski 1929: 23)

And this research, this study of processes and institutions, is the job of the anthropologist, while he suggests ". . . leaving to statesmen (and journalists) the final decision of how to apply the results" (Malinowski 1929: 23; also Malinowski 1930; and see Ian Hogbin 1957 for an interpretation of Malinowski's role). By 1935, as we have seen, this meant that the anthropologist is there to answer questions but not to pose them. But of course Malinowski believed that the anthropologist should be free to voice his opinions in the scholarly journals, like *Africa*. (For later discussions and versions of British applied anthropology, see Forde 1953 and Henshaw 1963.)

To turn to the American tradition, it is necessary to point out that the absence of an *acknowledged* colonial system obscured the overt paternalism so evident in the British case. At the same time, the *role* of the anthropologist was basically similar: he was a member of the dominant majority, secure in his social and ethnic identity, and with the same benevolent attitudes toward the "natives." No matter how earnest he might be in his gesture at solidarity with the "target population" he was still not subject to the constraints of their position. He has been free to go and to participate in whatever sector of the larger society he may choose.

However, the rhetoric of American Applied ideology was different from the British; it derived from basic turn-of-the-century American egalitarian populism—that anything that deprives people of their needs or desires should be changed or reformed. Of course, this ideology was updated in the rhetoric of the New Deal and its egalitarian-oriented paternalism. Laura Thompson, "the Great Articulator of Applied ideology" in the 1950–1960s period, put it this way, first giving her basic behavioral credo:

> In essence it symbolizes both the desire and desirability of human beings to fulfil themselves individually and collectively to the maximum of their physical-emotional-intellectual powers, and to do so both as single personalities and in relation to other personalities . . . .(Thompson 1965b: 290–1)

The job of the applied anthropologist is to help make this possible. In a slightly earlier paper she called it a "responsibility" of the anthropologist: "probably never in the history of the discipline have anthropologists operated effectively in positions of such responsibility in human terms" (Thompson 1965a: 283).

A paper published in *Human Organization* in 1965 by Theodore Brameld, an education historian and pioneer education ethnologist, echoed the "self-realization" theme enunciated by Thompson, but also pointed out that anthropologists have to respect the individual—and some individuals prefer to live in minimal interaction with society. Brameld extended this to the small group and community: its distinctive and integral local culture has to be respected by the anthropologist.

On the other hand, if we go back to the 1940s, the ideology expressed in the early literature has little overt relation to liberal-humanist values. The viewpoint combined professionalism with social engineering: applied work must be done scientifically, and if done so it will also enhance the scholarly position of the discipline. Margaret Lantis (1945) felt that the practitioner must guard against inserting his prejudices into practice, in order to render the local culture accurately, so as to: "Know their prides and prejudices"; "Their Culture is their Truth"; "The Innate Strength and Intelligence of the Common People" (she was approvingly citing remarks she heard at a conference in Washington on local agricultural assistance participated in by anthropologists and sociologists). In other words, the way to render a true vision of the culture and needs of local people, and thereby help them accept the shocks of culture change, is to be a *scientific anthropologist*. The professional credo of anthropology thus became coterminous with the appropriate ideology for successful applied work. This, in Lantis' terms, was the "public service" of anthropology, and it was an essentially uncritical attitude: anthropology, if done "scientifically," could do no wrong. The credo implicitly assumed that anthropology was omniscient (ignoring, for the moment, its ignorance of worldly matters). Margaret Mead's views were similar, though generally more realistic than Lantis's.

These positions of the American school were chewed over through the 1960s, 1970s, and 1980s, with little change. Sol Tax explains why, in the final chapter for the 1964 edition (omitted in a later edition) of his edited book, *Horizons of Anthropology*, that applied anthropologists, alone among the social scientists, never created a professionally defined and accredited practical training cadre. As self-identified professional anthropologists, they had to remain apart, to preserve cultural objectivity and a sympathetic identification with the population under study. Thus, the anthropologist "acts as an independent agent, taking upon himself the ultimate responsibility for satisfying his conscience in terms of the obligations he feels towards his colleagues and toward his fellow men" (Tax 1964: 255). But Tax believed that these "colleagues" were not only fellow professors or graduate students, but the subjects he is working with and for.

With the emergence of open cultural and political dissent in the late 1960s and 1970s, the mixed humanist-paternalist-scientism of applied anthropology came under attack, along with nearly every other ideological and ethical aspect of the discipline. The colonial past simply could no longer be ignored, and so New Left-inspired ideologies began to be heard. Roger Bastide's (1971) book, *Applied Anthropology*, took a neo-Marxist position. Although his arguments are none too clear, some thoughts come through: anthropology must accept the fact that it is a product of Western civilization and that the West is responsible for the oppression and exploitation of native peoples—peoples now engaged in revolutions of liberation. Applied anthropology should assist in these revolutions. Still, Bastide knew that this is complicated, because some of the indigenes strive to enter the bourgeoisie, who the Marxists regarded as the exploiters! So what is to be done? Anthropologists should fight against marginalization and new forms of exploitation, and help the people, farmers, or urban squatter groups, decide for themselves what they want to achieve. Applied anthropology in Bastide's terms should be both be an "experimental science," designed to create a new theory of change, and a "practical" science, to help the deprived classes achieve a better life. And this practical field must be as much art as science. Anthropology must acknowledge that true science can exist only if man is free to pursue liberty. And this means that the anthropologist must divest himself of the superstitions of class prejudice and unreason: that is, "cultural bias." Well.

Applied Anthropology: The Academic Critique

Through the years anthropologists have engaged in criticism of applied anthropology which falls into five main categories.

The first of these is that applied anthropology has *no theory of its own* and that it borrows only superficial ideas from academic or scholarly anthropology or other disciplines. Actually, Applied, especially in its early years, benefitted more from sociology or economics than from anthropology, given the fact that anthropologist knew very little about the modern world. And much academic anthropological theory was (is?) simply not relevant for practice.

To reverse the issue: it seems to me that details of the theory of change as developed by anthropologists over most of a century have been tested by the Applied people, but the results are largely ignored by the academic theorists (mainly, I suppose, because they are still preoccupied with cultural essences rather than social change). The point is that the "tests" were usually made in the context of specific, everyday situations and lacked rhetoric which cut ice with the intellectuals. To paraphrase a typical example: "We found that acceptance of wells dug by power equipment was much more easily come by than irrigation canals dug with locally made wooden shovels." Basic principles of the relationship of change processes to material culture and symbolism might be imbedded here, but, if so, they are not apparent as written. However, applied anthropologists have from time to time assembled such statements as collections of case studies of change or as thinkpiece essays,[13] but much of this material is considered thin or trite by scholars. From the scholarly point of view, theoretical statements of cultural behavior should be phrased in exotic terms, like symbolism or some other behavioral or mental process; thus, if theory is hidden in simple empirical generalizations, it is not identified as theory. But this also means that applied anthropologists test social-behavioral theory by *using* it and constantly rediscovering its basically mundane nature. Actually the paucity of general theory in Applied also can be viewed as a boon, since it excuses practitioners from becoming involved in the persistent transient intellectual controversies and faddism in anthropology.

The lack of power to really effect change or influence policy is the second criticism and is often voiced by the applied anthropologists themselves, especially when writing for academic periodicals. These tend not to be very convincing because they usually dodge the basic issue: that influence on planning and policy is based on actual power in all political systems, and that power is defined, in the administration of social affairs, by those who command the authority to order punitive sanctions or who are endowed, by some even higher authority, with the right and power to dictate change (recently, Nancy Scheper-Hughes (1995) has demanded a "militant anthropology!"). However, there is always informal persuasion, and certainly applied anthropologists have had numerous successes at this: talking to their superiors and co-workers and getting them to accept modified versions of the plan. This sort of activity became a fine art in the British colonial service and probably as well in American Indian affairs, especially, perhaps, during the administration of the Bureau by anthropologically trained Philleo Nash.

However, until the basic organization of bureaucracy changes, the role of anthropologists and friends will be largely advisory, and their power largely informal, a matter of individual ability and diplomacy. The question of roles is especially critical in development anthropology, because as often as not the anthropologist is ambivalent about the way the change programs may affect the target population (for discussions, see Bennett 1988; and also Bennett 1993–96). Aside from all the complaints, the practitioner frequently has really nothing much to offer; his best effort really boils down to nay-saying or qualification: he says, in effect, "do it my way and it will be easier" or "I wouldn't do it at all because it will cause pain—or resistance." This is not the rhetoric of directed power, but of consultation.

A third criticism concerns *The high failure rate of many applied anthropologically conceived or advised projects*. This has sometimes been represented as the proof of theoretical inadequacy or basic ignorance on the part of applied anthropologists. The criticism seems foolish to me, given the high rate of failure in *all* human affairs, whether advised by anthropologists or others. In actuality, many of the "failures" are really successes, if you take into account the fact that in social life we often learn best from mistakes. In addition, the expected rate of success in the administrations that plan such projects is usually low. In the 1970s and 1980s USAID was content with at best a 20 percent success rate in its pastoralism projects, as measured against the expected accomplishments listed in the "project papers." But an anthropologist implicated in some phase of a project with something in the 10–20 percent success rate would be tarred with the failure brush. (For details, see Bennett et al. 1986. See, also, Hirschman 1967 and Tendler 1975 for discussions of problems of failure and unanticipated consequences in development work.) Some of the "failure" critiques also stem from a few disasters or at least awkward projects where the applied anthropologists had difficulties with the indigenous population, sometimes being asked to leave the site. Cornell University's long-term team study of Vicos, an Andean community, experienced problems of this kind.[14]

Another area of criticism concerns the *paucity of training programs.* This is in part a function of the fact that applied anthropologists have tended to be part-time employees since so many applied jobs are temporary or strong on consultantship but without career opportunities. A second reason is the diversity and disparateness of the subject matter. Since any institutional aspect of contemporary society in any nation can become a focus of applied work, it becomes difficult to establish training for specific needs and subjects. What can be done is training in field methods and in the diplomacy needed to handle the "target populations" (as well as the bosses). Very few formal, degree-offering training programs exist: the University of South Florida's is the best known and best publicized, but other anthropology departments offer routine courses, seminar training sessions, and some fieldwork opportunities. (For descriptions of the South Florida training program, see Angrosino 1981, 1982. Van Willigen 1987 is a manual of practice issued by the National Association for the Practice of Anthropology, American Anthropological Association.)

A final area of criticism concerns the *ethics of intervention in the lives of "target populations" and the publication of information obtained from Applied research.* From its British beginnings in the colonial era, applied anthropology has exhibited uneasiness with its role as information-gatherer and interventionist, since three domains of motives and preferences are always involved in practical activity: those of the people who are the subjects of the experiment or project, those of the organization running the project (the employers); and those of the applied social scientists (the employees). This is a much more complicated situation than encountered in ordinary scholarly research and one that inevitably generates ethical conflicts. Moreover, because a measure of historical guilt is involved in much Applied work, the conflicts are easily heightened.

Probably most ethical issues are simply not resolvable; they tend to peter out or are set aside with a series of compromises. And these compromises vary by situation given the endlessly variable contexts of social action and change. Attempts at setting forth basic ethical principles in Applied—and in anthropology and ethnology generally—took the form of codes of ethics,[15] or sets of principles anthropologists are advised to follow in order to safeguard their own position with the employer, to ensure the well-being of the "target population," and to save their own conscience from being placed in ethically contradictory positions.

The early codes for Applied tended to emphasize the practitioner's role vis-à-vis his employer. However, as time passed, this emphasis on the ethical problems of the applied anthropologist himself changed toward the human subjects of the work: whether, for example, developmental change was in their interest or not; or whether publication of the results of the research, even when names and places were disguised, constituted a breach of confidence. These issues became important as economic development and political nationalization drew the indigenes into the world of legality and human rights.

The Ethics of Intervention

The intervention issue has some special aspects worthy of extended comment. In the background lie some absolutes common to democratic humanism in Western culture. One of these is the admonition against being one's "brother's keeper"; intervention for the sake of bettering the lot of "brother" is acceptable ethically, providing it is done freely, without expectation of some recompense or payback. "Payback" then becomes an ethical issue: it involves commercializing or corrupting the act of intervention. Imbedded are other values, such as the Christian idea of *love* as freely granted with no special motive of gain to the person offering the love.

Well and good, but people continually intervene in the lives of other people; this is, in fact, a prime requisite of organized society. Redfield's elaboration of the *Gemeinschaft* concept was a rendition of a world without the necessity of *formal* intervention, since society functioned harmoniously on the basis of local benign interactive correction based on "common understandings." This was in part a romantic fiction (significantly it was called an "ideal type" and was a product of nineteenth-century German romantic social thought), since in most small communal societies rigorous, purposive, sanctioned intervention takes place almost daily in order to maintain the "moral order." The intellectual prestige the "folk society" scheme acquired during the 1940s is testimony to the nostalgia built up around tribal culture by the Classic era ethnological program. After World War II the "folk society" idea was rapidly eclipsed, as anthropologists began taking a more realistic view of human behavior at all levels of social development.

Another concept associated with intervention is the fear of inverted gratitude, that is, the idea that those who help other people are never really forgiven for it. This is often elaborated into a fear of retaliation on the part of the presumed benefactor, and this in turn, can lead to alienation and separation.

In face of confusion over the ethics of intervention it is apparent that in order to intervene—that is, to execute a program of intentional benevolent intervention—a special rationale is required which offers a way through the contradictory pathways. We have seen that this rationale has varied through the years: for the British in the late nineteenth and early twentieth centuries it was a matter of the "white man's burden," which eventually became negatively identified as "paternalism" as the former colonials sought and acquired political freedom (and the possibility of retribution). Another important ethic is "responsibility," or, as Robert Rubenstein (1986: 273) put it, responsibility toward the target population and responsibility toward the employer (see also Berreman 1968). I shall focus here on the first rather than the second meaning. As noted previously, this involves confrontation between the self and the other: the practitioner on the one hand (i.e., his career interests and intellectual objectives), and on the other, what he "owes" to the people he is studying and presumably benefitting. Does he have the responsibility of helping them, of protecting them against exploitation, which means acting against his employer, or of simply seeing to it that nothing he does will injure them? And a third dimension is the responsibility to scholarship or "science," as it is called in much of the earlier literature on the subject. How can one judge this three-way list of responsibilities when one or two are always going to be in some kind of conflict?

Let us dwell on the question of *responsibility of benefaction*; that is, is the "success" of the intervention (or at least the anthropologist's role in the intervention process) a responsibility that must be shared by the anthropologist? At this point we join forces with the pluralistic moral order of our times: the answer, given by probably every practicing anthropologist in the development field, is that (paraphrasing) "it is my responsibility to *do my best* to ensure favorable outcomes, but I cannot guarantee it." That is, perhaps he or she is saying "that it is really not my responsibility—if anything, I pass it on to someone else, because I want to live to be a practicing anthropologist another day."

I do believe that the "responsibility to science" ethic quoted as a defense against ethical strictures is tricky and probably spurious in most cases where it is used. If Thomas Kuhn's idea about the social determination of basic scientific paradigms is mainly correct, then most scientific ideas have an important element based on projections from the culture of their time, and will change sooner or later. The Classic era is littered with ideas which commanded fervent attention and dimensions of "responsibility" for a while. And the economic development field, which has dominated Applied for several decades, is likewise strewn with passé predictive theories, many of them unrealistic or inappropriate to the circumstances of Third World socioeconomic structure (see Cochrane 1971 for a highly personal critique).

So—exactly what is intervention? Intervention for what? The term itself is vague because it is difficult to find a clear pattern in the welter of situationally specific cases. There can be major intervention in religious systems, as in the case of the Christianizing of "natives" all over the world; and there can be minor intervention in the methods of drawing water, substituting a drilled well for a seeping spring. And the ethical responsibility associated with such extremes of intervention also ranges from massive to trivial.

In the last analysis, as with so many ethical issues in a pluralistic cultural framework, it is "up to the individual." The disquisitions on the ethics of intervention in applied anthropology literature boil down to this: that the individual practitioner must decide whether he really ought to do the work, and how best to do it to minimize harm.

Therefore, *minimization of harm* is probably the most frequently adduced ethic for practical anthropology. It has two main forms: (1) the ethic and advisability of accepting a job or task if the possibility of harm is great, and (2) the ethical aspects of continuing in the job if it becomes apparent that harm is probable. The underlying issue is what sociologists call "unanticipated consequences," a strong pattern in human affairs, or what Albert Hirschman, the analyst of economic development projects, called the "hiding hand" (Hirschman 1967). In the face of such uncertainties ethical questions are difficult to answer, and "it depends on the situation or the individual" is once again the conventional way of settling accounts. Guilt once again enters the arena as a contingency, resulting from harm done as a result of unanticipated consequences. (For some practitioners, one way of minimizing these unpleasant possibilities is to accept relatively minor interventionist assignments.)

So far as the second aspect of responsibility is concerned—the responsibility one owes to one's employer—this clearly lies behind the insistence on the part of the applied anthropologist that he or she must be able to eat his cake and have it, too: accept employment but maintain a considerable degree of independence and freedom to criticize the boss or defend the human subjects against undesirable consequences. In colonial anthropology this was simply forbidden: the administrator was the decision-maker, and the anthropologist the information-gatherer. But this restrictive role has never been acceptable—at least in theory—to American applied anthropologists. The issue figured in the Tax Action Anthropology Rebellion which, as we shall see later, held that the only way to retain one's academic and moral conscience in practical work is to avoid employment by the powers that control the scene; that is, *altruistic* versus *assigned* intervention, the former with a larger quotient of personal responsibility. Let the subjects control the problems being researched, not the bureaus. Fine, but this usually doesn't work very well in practice, because the subjects would frequently just as soon stay the way they are, in which case the practitioner has to accept the further responsibility of telling them what he thinks is good for them (paternalism again!).

Finally, we come to the issue of exposure or publication. I consider that at the moment of writing, this issue has achieved a certain resolution. The guidelines on publication of results of Applied investigations are fairly clear, and, for the most part, the practitioners follow them. The classic trouble case, documented in *Human Organization* during the late 1950s and early 1960s, is the "Springdale" episode, involving the premature and unauthorized publication of a teamwork community study made by Cornell University in a small upstate New York town. Arthur Vidich, the senior author of the book, *Small Town in Mass Society* (Vidich and Bensman 1958), had been a member of the research team and had agreed not to publish any of the results without review and permission with his supervisor, Urie Bronfebrenner. After his departure from the project, and acceptance of an academic job, he prepared a book manuscript with Joseph Bensman, a professional writer but not a member of the original research group. The townspeople took major offense at the book and satirized it in a Fourth of July parade with the town's major citizens riding on a float wearing masks identifying them as the psuedonomic characters from the book, and an effigy of the book's main author afloat on a manure spreader. University deans and presidents were harangued, suits were threatened, and the general uproar made the pages of the *New York Times* and eventually, *Human Organization*. The last word was had, I feel, by William F. Whyte, the editor of *Human Organization*, who responded to one of Vidich's attempted defenses with the following: "We are convinced the Vidich-Bensman answer will not serve. [Vidich] seems to take the position that he has a responsibility only to science. Has the researcher no responsibility to the people whom he studies?" (Whyte 1958).[16]

And the collective answer is, of course, "yes." The Vidich-Bensman case changed the rules once and for all. After the episode nobody in Applied could entertain the possibility of publishing without some consultation with the project director and the subjects of the research. And that is where the matter stands at the time of writing.

Action Anthropology: Genesis

A moment ago I referred to Sol Tax's rebellion against the "employment" approach of applied anthropology. This 'rebellion' produced what came to be called Action Anthropology, whose principal difference from applied anthropology was its voluntaristic approach. This was designed to avoid the basic paternalism of Applied, with its overtones of guilt and co-optation. In the 1950s, Sol Tax, although a staunch anthropologist and an active participant in the Society for Applied Anthropology, became increasingly dissatisfied with the alternating paternalistic and technocratic slants of Applied.[17] Tax's participation in the Society for Applied Anthropology began to diminish, but as interest in his Action anthropology began to develop in the late 1950s and 1960s, Human Organization published several articles and communications concerning it—most of them favorable. By the 1970s Action was considered one approach in an enlarged Applied anthropology.

Action anthropologists were expected to help communities as volunteer scholars, using their own funds or with the help of research grants. The human subjects were to be treated as equal participants, and the goal was to help them articulate their grievances and then conduct discussions in which the various parties tried to find ways of meeting needs or solving problems. In essence, this was "community development," a field which led practical social science in the first Development Decade of the 1950s, when rural life and economy was considered a major target of postwar reform in the former colonies (and which also was very much in the air in Chicago, in the form of Saul Alinsky's "Back of the Yards" movement—discussed in a moment).

Action anthropology was born in, and largely confined to, a single research venture: the famous Fox Project, involving the study of a community on the Fox Indian reservation property in Iowa. The basic methodology of this project resembled Robert Redfield's approach in Latin American communities, in which, of course, Tax had collaborated (see Rubenstein 1991 for the correspondence of Redfield and Tax on fieldwork during the Latin American period). The method required a team of students supervised by a senior professor, with members of the team assigned particular topics or emphases, and with the work expected to continue over a period of years.

Tax's Exposition of Action Anthropology

Tax wrote several papers defining and justifying Action from the early 1950s into the 1960s, and the text became the basis of lectures in his travels as a representative of *Current Anthropology*. The version I use here was entitled "Action Anthropology" and appeared in *Current Anthropology* in 1975. (A footnote tells us that its original form was a lecture given at the University of Michigan in 1958 and published in the *Journal of Social Research* at the University of Ranchi, in the State of Bihar, India, in 1959.[18] And still another version appeared in 1952, in the journal *America Indigena*.[19])

In the 1975 paper Tax says that anthropology's central concept is Culture, and that this concept features the notion of lifeways diversity, which in turn "enriches" the materials available to anthropologists to define alternative solutions to social problems. We might paraphrase Tax's several long passages in the following way. Awareness of social problems is a "world-wide syndrome" (Tax 1975: 514), and it is the responsibility of the anthropologist to help people convert their awareness of social need into social action. This intervention must be *done in the field*: "I cannot imagine action anthropology except in the context of field work" (Tax 1975: 515). He defines fieldwork as a "clinical or experimental method of study" (Tax 1975: 515); that is, it is "study," or research, and at the same time it is aimed at real-life problems of the population under study. Here lies the essence of Action: while it is something the academic anthropologist does as research, it is simultaneously something he does for humanity. A neat trick, because the anthropologist must obtain his own support or funding yet avoid employment by any agency in charge of the basic resources the group under study requires in order to survive.

But Tax felt that Action goes even further. The worker must be "willing to make things happen." The Actionist must encourage change, foster it, encourage the informant-participants to experiment with changes in their habits and institutions and discover new values. And to do all this is to transcend the contemporary cognitive apparatus of the discipline—as Tax asserts, "current theory is never enough" (Tax 1975: 515). You cannot find, either in conventional academic theory or in the conventional culture, enough ammunition to provide the necessary guidance for the actuality of social behavior in change [the ideas here would seem to be related to Firth's (1954, 1955) concepts of "structure" and "organization"]. In other words, Tax, like any other practicing social scientist in any era or nation, discovered that current social behavior and existence does not necessarily conform to social theory or to cultural values.

And he went still further. He stated that the "basic problem" the action anthropologist deals with is "community organization" and that "his chief tool is education" (1975: 515). The Actionist must use "art and experience" as well as theory and method; that is, action anthropology emerges from the life and career and hopes and fears of the anthropologist as much as it does out of the lives of the people under study, and that he must convey these feelings to the people and encourage them to respond (see Scheper-Hughes and other deconstructionist anthropologists).[20]

Such ideas articulated in plain English were a challenge to the American Anthropological Association Old Guard and many Society for Applied Anthropology stalwarts as well. At the time Tax was saying these things the Chicago department was in the hands of inner-core specialists like David Schneider, and critical responses by the Peabody-Chicago-Berkeley axis to Tax's ideas were echoing through the profession. By 1975, when the paper was published in full format in *Current Anthropology*, the ideas were on the whole expected and accepted, but back in the 1950s and 1960s they were strange and shocking. (However, Margaret Mead made similar points, although with a different rhetoric, during the late 1950s and early 1960s at American Anthropological Association, Society for Applied Anthropology, or American Association for the Advancement of Science annual meetings.) Both Tax and Mead were in a sense the opening guns in the rebellions in the ranks of anthropology in the 1960s and 1970s, but curiously the two were at odds over the Applied versus Action issue all through this period.

Tax goes on to discuss the ethical and moral issues: "truth is important; anthropologists seek the full truth of social context; "freedom" is equally important: anthropologists must value freedom, because they cannot reveal the whole context of cultural diversity without it; "self-determination" is something we believe in, and help others to seek, although we should not necessarily impose this on others. But these and other values imbedded in Action are all, Tax seems to say, common human values; to advocate them should not cause anthropologists pangs of conscience since sooner or later all humans express or want them. (This sounds like Tocqueville: humans want and need freedom.) In a later paper Tax called it "the freedom to make mistakes" [Tax 1956]); they want to run their own affairs; but they can benefit from help from knowledgeable and concerned professionals. Whether they *want* such help was, of course, one of the issues not usually faced by the Actionists, and constituted one theme exploited by critics (e.g., Thompson 1976: 2).

Action Anthropology: The Academic Critique

Some academic criticisms of Action have been suggested, and others can be anticipated: that Action was a kind of "social work" was a frequent slur heard at meetings and occasionally in print; that Action was a violation of correct scientific method or logic; others claimed that Action was really a figment of Tax's peculiar methods of fieldwork and could not be done by anyone else. Some critics still felt that values had no place in "science," especially when you mixed them as casually and vigorously as Tax seemed to advocate.

I can add one. If Tax and his co-Actionists were really serious about discovering social problems and solutions in the context of everyday, ongoing behavior and attitudes, they needed something better than the American Classic era cultural anthropology of the time to do it. Tax did say that available theory was inadequate, but perhaps he failed to look far enough. Not only, as suggested earlier, did he not employ concepts from British social anthropology, but he also ignored the Harvard-based Behavior Science or Social Relations theory which, although waning in this period, still retained a considerable following in anthropology. Tax, by pushing classic four-field Anthropology as the sole or at least major source of ideas, was rejecting or neglecting the multidisciplinary approach, and I believe it was a fairly conscious rejection since Tax was at intellectual odds with the "Harvard gang" just as he was estranged and uneasy in the presence of Margaret Mead and the "applied gang." The former represented, in his view, a break with Anthropology; the latter the takeover of decent, liberal reformist anthropology by the technocratic Applied people. In one sense, Action anthropology was simply Tax's way of declaring his independence of both groups. However, this entailed, especially in the case of the Social Relations concepts, a certain cost: the neglect of more systematic approaches to social behavior. And in the annals of the Actionists one finds references to disordered note-taking, mind-changing, and other things which are an inevitable part of fieldwork, but given the goals of the Actionists, a frustrating impediment. What do these folks we are studying *really* want? And who are we to tell them? What new problems will emerge when we solve the old ones?

Some light would have been thrown on such questions if Action had used an adaptational approach to social behavior. Instead, Tax insisted on Culture as the master concept—because of his inveterate faith in Classic anthropology and its basic diversity and eclecticism. Even the conventional Parsonsian "pattern variables" would have helped: what values or ideas are universal in the community, and which ones specific to situations? Do the people seek diffuse understandings of social roles, or specific ones? And so on. Tax was not overtly hostile to this kind of conceptualizing, and much of it was done routinely in the field, as commonsense observation, but it is fairly clear in his writings that he did not feel comfortable with formal modes of social thought. Throughout his career Tax was a kind of contained rebel, distrusting the social science establishment, but at the same time working for it and trying to improve it. [For more details on Tax's career and ideas, see the Supplement.]

Finally the precepts of Action were not unique (nor would Tax have claimed they were), since they shared much with Applied. And Action began to influence Applied. In any case, Tax was crystallizing a concrete and particular field situation, the Fox Community Project, in terms that were familiar to him from high school onward (e.g., Tax 1988: 2, where he says he held the basic values of anthropology from the "third year of high school").

Lisa Redfield Peattie, certainly one of the Fox Project students most responsible for the coming together of the Action approach in the field, later developed doubts on rather abstruse grounds. Influenced by the writings of Paul Diesing (1991), a philosopher, she noted that action anthropology used a John Dewey-inspired "means-end schema" in which both the discovery of the problem and the search for its resolution proceeded simultaneously, in their own real time. Peattie felt this schema violated the classic scientific scheme in use by *applied* anthropology; namely, through research one discovers what the problem is, and then does more research in order to find a solution (a "rational" or linear-temporal approach). Peattie was worried about the fact that in the "Deweyan" approach one must continually seek some sort of evaluation of procedure and conclusion, whereas in the linear approach the mode of evaluation "is clear": the worker either has done what he set out to do or he hasn't. Using the elliptical approach, Action needed constant discussion and argument and thus could easily devolve into a kind of group dynamic among the field workers and participants. The trouble with the linear approach, of course, is that it has strong tendencies toward authoritarian dictation of both problem and solution by the outside expert. In addition, the need for more research to define solutions means that the problem inevitably will be redefined, so the linear-rational approach is likely to dissolve into the Deweyan, because reflexivity is a fundamental characteristic of human behavior. I have engaged in both types of activity at different times and do not see a choice on abstract or logical grounds: it is all situational, it depends upon you, the field worker; the people studied; and the others in the background who call the shots or hold the ultimate power. Action anthropology's elliptical-participative decision making is as likely to be successful as Applied (linear-causal decisions) in its appropriate setting. *Both* are likely to be time-consuming, frustrating, and prone to mistakes (see Held 1984 on the problem of rationales for social action).

In the 1970s and 1980s many articles in *Human Organization* expressed ideas reminiscent of Action, although rarely, if ever, was credit given to the source (if it was a source—and that is difficult to judge, since Tax was writing on the verge of a general rebellion against establishment-oriented theory which blossomed in the 1960s and 1970s). For instance, Wayne Warry, in a 1992 paper published in *Human Organization*, and entitled "The Eleventh Thesis: Applied Anthropology as Praxis," defines his field as follows: "Praxis offers an important focus for practitioners of social science, one in which theory is integrated with praxis at the point of intervention." He goes on to advocate the "structuring of means-end relations on the basis of grounded reason and communicative action" and claims that "a praxis approach would involve study participants as equal partners in open discussion of theoretical assumptions that underpin the search for pragmatic solutions to everyday problems" (Warry 1992: 156). Action anthropology cast into fashionable 1980s "praxis" jargon?

Laura Thompson by the mid-1970s had joined the postcolonial critics who were attacking applied and development anthropology as handmaids of the exploiters. Her 1976 paper in *Human Organization* was an attempt to reformulate the role of Applied in a postcolonial world, and she summed up her prescription as follows:

> . . . an applied anthropologist may help a client group as consultant by defining the group's practical options in local, regional, national, and global contexts. Using understanding of group behavior in the context of its ongoing life situation, a clinical anthropologist may predict, within certain limitations, the probable effect that the selection of each option would have on the client community were it to be selected and implemented by the membership. Choice of a preferred alternative and its enactment, however, should remain the prerogative and responsibility of the client. (Thompson 1976: 6)

Although this passage has some characteristic Thompson phraseology, residues of the 1950s behavior-science era, it could also serve as a statement of the methodological approach of action anthropology, although in the same paper she criticizes Action for its lurking paternalism: did the Fox really ask for help, or did Tax's group tell them they needed it? (See also Thompson 1950, in which she uses the phrase "Action Research.") In any case, in this and other critical assessments of practical anthropology in this period of the mid-1970s and early 1980s one sees effects of the discipline's 1960s Era of Anxiety and Guilt. Tax seems not to have been influenced by the guilt element; for him anthropology and culture were their own excuses for being, and the most important thing was to avoid co-optation by the Big Boys who run the show. In any case, Thompson, although imbued with some of the ideas of Action and possessed of a generic humanism, still accepted the "employment" frame of applied anthropology.

Still another example is a paper by Anthony Paredes (1976) in *Human Organization* that defined "ethnographic enterprise" as a "transaction between human beings" and claimed that anthropological research should become a "palpable element in the stream of their (the researched group's) recent history". In a comment on the paper, Nancy Lurie, echoing Action—she was a member of the original Fox team—proposed that the ethnologist or applied anthropologist should become a "partner" with the community. These ideas were part of a growing restlessness among anthropologists who felt that the discipline was saturated with detached, inhuman approaches.

The origins of much critical commentary was not in the discipline but in left-humanist political ideology. Paradoxically, applied anthropology was identified by these critics with "colonial" and "elitist" postures, probably due largely to the extensive participation of anthropologists in socioeconomic development projects. But from the standpoint of methodology and the concepts that supported it in practical anthropology, the ideas of people-oriented research and the treatment of subjects as human beings to whom one owes a degree of love and assistance certainly had roots in action anthropology.

Although the Left was critical of anthropology as an "imperialist" undertaking, anthropologists sympathetic to such ideas nevertheless saw their discipline as a way out of exploitation via the doctrines of cultural tolerance, humanist identity, and respect for the local community. Tax's Action was precisely this kind of approach in that it obliquely answered the anti-imperialist Left criticism in anthropology with a populist doctrine of egalitarian participation and respect for the indigenous population. Yet, as several critics pointed out, such respect for the indigenes could also be construed as paternalism. Was paternalism inherent in Action, or was it an attitude openly held by Tax and his students? In the documentary evidence (Gearing et al. 1960) there is nothing that would justify accusing Tax of being "paternalistic." There is evidence, on the contrary, that he was aware of its dangers and did his best to avoid them. Above all, Tax insisted on discovering and using the desires and needs of the people and avoiding the preferences or values of the intellectual fraternity. Thus, Action had inevitable paternalistic implications but lacked the value-rationalized paternalism of so many previous episodes in the history of relations between Native Americans and the majority society.

So far as I could determine from the information available, Tax's Action did not foment rebellion on the Fox reservation, but it might have if it had lasted longer and had been more effective in raising levels of aspiration or expectation. Something of the sort did happen in Vicos, where the anthropologists obviously were not capable of changing the basic power structure: the landlords remained in power, and the tenants eventually, under the stimulation supplied by the project, protested.

Are anthropologists supposed to be revolutionary cadres? Well, if you encourage—train—local people to articulate their grievances, there is no telling where it will end up. It is my feeling that fear of such ambiguous or unpredictable outcomes is another reason why Action did not become a more influential mode of practice in anthropology. But perhaps even more fundamental is what I have called the "ambiguous engagement" (Bennett 1988) of anthropology with all forms of social practice: the desire to participate reined in by the fear of undesirable transformation or destruction of existing and integral cultures.

Supplement: The Career of Sol Tax and the Genesis of Action Anthropology

David Blanchard's paper in the Tax *Festschrift* (Hinshaw 1979) established the origins of Tax's ideas about "action" in his intellectual biography—details which I confirmed and added to in a daylong interview with Tax in the spring of 1994. Tax was born elsewhere, but grew up in Milwaukee. His parents were German immigrants, with a proletarian or lower-middle-class background, and were adherents of the 1848–style radicalism shared by many Germans who came to Milwaukee in the latter half of the nineteenth century. Tax spent his childhood listening to his father and older brother Ervin discuss socialist ideas and the need for the "little man" to defend himself against the Interests—ideas that were also part of the Populist heritage of the Midwest. The Milwaukee version was called "socialism," and the city had "socialist" mayors for years. Their main contribution consisted of public ownership of some city facilities, plus an advanced welfare system and excellent public education.[21]

Tax's own populist career started at age twelve, when as a volunteer newsboy he was arrested by the police for selling papers without a permit. A kind of school board-sponsored company union—the Newsboys' Republic—existed, and one had to belong to this in order to obtain a permit. The purpose was benevolent: to prevent newspaper publishers from exploiting children. Tax joined the Republic promptly and received his permit, thus cancelling the court trial he was subject to. However, Tax was outraged at such adult domination and after many battles took over the Republic and built it into a genuine union, winning bargaining rights—all before he was fifteen.

Tax went on to the University of Wisconsin-Madison (after an aborted semester at the University of Chicago), but had problems keeping up with his courses because of his editorial work on an independent student liberal paper and his strenuous promotional activities on behalf of Hillel and the student Liberal Club. Tax had difficulties with the Communist student organization which infiltrated and virtually destroyed the Liberal Club. Tax told me that this experience convinced him once and for all that extreme left-wing organizations with revolutionary ideologies were inappropriate for reformist advocacy in American society. In general, Tax's biography from early days in Milwaukee through his peripatetic college period defines an activist personality determined to defend the underdog and to avoid collaboration with the organizations in power, one who understood that anything worthwhile in life takes organization, determination, and intensive action.

Tax's undergraduate honors thesis written at Wisconsin (seen by both Blanchard and myself) distinguished two kinds of "science": "pure" and "therapeutic"; or to quote: "It would seem that the effort [speaking of the "therapeutic"] might at least have the best knowledge of its subject that it possibly can: and the pure science anthropology must furnish that knowledge" (as quoted in Blanchard 1979: 422). Tax continued to refer to this distinction in his student papers and reports over the next few years, but sometimes there is concern that "pure" science rarely offers the kind of information one really needs in order to do "therapeutic" practice, since it is preoccupied with basic theory rather than the nitty-gritty of everyday life. Attempts to apply his dialectic were made in his first pre-graduate study fieldwork experience with

Ruth Benedict's Mescalero Apache study, but he was unable to follow through since he was accepted as a graduate student at Chicago, where he went to study anthropology at the source.

He started his fieldwork as a Chicago student with short visits to various Algonquian tribes, including the Fox. But this, too was a brief episode, because Redfield soon sent him to Latin America to open the Guatemalan branch of the Redfield program. The next decade was spent there and in Mexico. The period also saw the early precursor of action anthropology, with Tax recording Indian demands for reform, experimenting with democratic methods of teaching, and running participative, nondirective fieldwork with parties of Mexican anthropology students. Throughout his Latin American episode, Tax never relinquished his conviction that anthropology students need to get closer to their informants in the field and to treat them as fellow humans, coupled with an intense conviction that the poor and exploited need help and protection. Blanchard suggests that the upshot of his Latin American fieldwork experience was "to conclude that anthropology had failed because it had not produced the data needed to solve social problems" (Blanchard 1979: 426).

Sol Tax was repeatedly disappointed by anthropology's inadequacies in the "therapeutic" field, yet he never deserted the anthropological ship. Why not? Because he believed that of all the social sciences, anthropology offered the most hope of humanistic, socially-rational application, and while anthropologists did not fully appreciate the need to treat subjects as equals, they nevertheless did so to an extent greater than the elitist sociologists and economists. And after years of research-associate status, much of it spent at a table-desk in a dead-end side hall of the Chicago department, Sol was appointed an associate professor with tenure. He then emerged as a major proponent of the "core" program of graduate education established by the department in the early postwar period. This program was a manifestation of his conviction (e.g., Tax 1955) that anthropology consists of four or five fields and that these must stay together because topical diversity helps implement value relativism, the basis of a humanist world view: "unity in diversity," he called it in a hectographed classroom leaflet used in the early core program. And this urge showed up again in his organizing activity on behalf of *Current Anthropology* (which quite possibly, more than any other professional event, kept the entire discipline from fragmenting in the 1960s and early 1970s).

In 1948 the Department asked Tax to start a field training program for ethnology students on the Fox reservation, recalling his brief work there twelve or so years earlier. Tax accepted the challenge, and that was the beginning of the Fox Project. Tax conveyed to the students in preparatory seminars his vision of a participative ethnography, in which the informants were co-investigators and the investigators were students of the informants.

Tax asked his field workers to ask themselves key questions: where are the Fox going, and what do they want out of life? Such questions were not ordinarily associated with anthropological fieldwork because depiction or reconstruction of tribal cultures were the principal objectives of the Classic era. The question implied that the Fox were in fact—in addition to their Native American identity—Americans in a small town with fears, hopes, and needs. Lisa Redfield Peattie, a member of the team, made some positive suggestions as to how to sponsor meetings and social occasions among the factions on the reservation, in order to foster better communication and get them thinking along constructive social-change lines. Tax at first rejected the philosophy behind this, but then rejected his rejection and wrote a long letter (Gearing et al., eds. 1960: 32) in which he discussed his old ideas about "therapeutic science," noting the need for inserting values into anthropological research and extending the whole procedure to include the informants or subjects—the Fox—as active participants in the intellectual process of assessing needs and finding values to support those needs. He called it "action research," and eventually this became Action Anthropology. For information on the Fox Project and its possible aftermath, the "documentary history" produced by Fred Gearing (et al. 1960) and other members of the project is the single best source, although a few articles on methods and results were produced, including Tax's own paper in *Human Organization* (1958). However, as is the case with so many applied anthropology projects, little or nothing in the way of follow-up research on the community organizational reforms was accomplished.

After the Fox Project, Tax participated in a number of marginal action projects or episodes with Southwestern and Northern Plains tribal groups, but none of these matured into a full-dress undertaking. The Fox Project students and other students of Tax did likewise: attempts to use Action in their subsequent individual fieldwork. Few of these later efforts seem to have taken place over a sufficient period of time to accomplish any substantial change in the communities, but Karl Schlesier's work with the Southern Cheyenne apparently bore fruit: the tribe seems to have developed a successful community action program (Schlesier 1974: 283).

If accomplishment is measured by economic and demographic magnitudes, then Tax's most successful Action endeavor was his community housing and development program in the Fifty-fifth and Fifty-seventh Street neighborhood around the University of Chicago (Tax 1959, 1968). Using his persuasive interviewing and group discussion techniques, coupled with intensive, deal-striking interaction with politicians and real estate people, Tax managed to build a series of new single and multiple-family units on the lots created by clearance of substandard and aging buildings. He was also able to get the residents to take responsibility for various community ventures designed to upgrade housing and income standards, which had the effect, according to critics, of keeping out lower-income and minority residents from deteriorated areas to the north. This type of project—emphasizing neighborhood voluntarism—was in the Chicago air as a result of Saul Alinsky's "Back of the Yards": a rehabilitation community-organization program designed to alleviate substandard conditions in the stockyard district and also to assist the labor unions in getting a better deal for the stockyard workers (Slayton 1986; Alinsky 1971). Tax of course knew Alinsky, and Alinsky once told me that while he admired Tax's energy he felt that the objective (never stated as such by Tax) of creating a barrier to protect the University district from demographic deterioration was not exactly admirable. (Maybe so, but it most likely saved the University of Chicago from moving to the suburbs.) Community organization or activist social work (many social work schools in the 1960s and 1970s created programs like this as field training for their degree candidates) was also in the air from the late 1950s on through the whole 1960–1970s era of social unrest and reformism (Borman 1979), and in that context Tax's approach simply represents the appearance of this general approach within anthropology.[22]

Codicil, 1997

After editing this essay for inclusion in the book, I sensed an abruptness and a lack of point. On rereading it, it seems to me that the underlying but only partially realized theme is the moral ambiguity of anthropology. That is, not merely the ambiguity of ethical and moral issues in Applied anthropology, but in the discipline as a whole. It all goes back to the concentration on tribal peoples during an era when these peoples were under the thumb of colonial powers. To study these populations objectively meant to ignore their dependent and exploited status; to help them, but at the same time to ignore their political position, created a de facto paternalism. But anthropology was not able to face up to this situation openly, since it had another mission: the development and maintenance of a scholarly academic field. In this sense, there really is not much difference between the general and applied anthropologies—both share in the moral ambiguity—and the correlated ethical dilemmas. Sol Tax was aware of these, and his "Action anthropology" was an attempt to come clean on the moral issue: openly espouse a moral stance and proceed to put it into effect in the field: to use the knowledge of the discipline openly and honestly to help people; and to ignore conscience worries about paternalism.

Another facet of the moral-ambiguity issue concerns anthropology's occasional willingness to develop critiques of civilized life, representing them as derived from anthropological knowledge and insights, when in fact there was very little in the corpus of the discipline to justify or document the criticisms. Margaret Mead struggled with this issue—she tried to escape the ambiguity by making a very careful selection of research data to justify or defend here diagnoses and remedies. She was not always successful.

Notes

1. Is it possible to calculate the number of applied anthropologists? The problem is that Applied is not so much a profession but a set of opportunities. Moreover, membership in the Society for Applied Anthropology is a poor index because many of these people, from various countries, were trained in disciplines other than anthropology, or combined anthropology and some other field in their professional training and activity. However, for what it is worth, a few figures can be inspected. First of all, there were, in the early 1990s, 1,900 members of the Society for Applied Anthropology, who also received the house organ *Human Organization*. For comparison, the membership of the AAA in the same period was 12,300. I was not able to discover how many of the 1,900 Society for Applied Anthropology members also belong to the AAA (because I could not get the AAA to answer letters or respond to phone calls). Taking a different approach, I looked at the "Interests" list of the associates' panel for *Current Anthropology*. These come from questionnaires the journal sends out at intervals to associates. The associates are found in about eighty-nine countries worldwide. Their Interests are

strictly salient responses: there is no pre-coding or later combining of entries. In 1994, there were 2,063 associates whose questionnaires had been tabulated, and exactly 65 of these had entered "Applied Anthropology" as one of their interests. Two persons had selected "Action Anthropology". However, I slightly reclassified and regrouped the entries, and a somewhat different picture emerged. If entries pertaining to culture change, economic development, economic, medical, educational, ecological, and social (i.e., the "institutional anthropologies") are added to the 67 in Applied and Action, the total is 882. And this can be compared with a total of 841 who provided interest entries for the purely cultural, symbolic, ethnological, physical, and psychological anthropology fields. This suggests that the institutional fields, plus fields which are concerned with the changes and problems of contemporary societies, either equal the older, conventional, or exotic interest areas or may even exceed them. It also implies that applied anthropology per se has been losing its role as the exclusive home for anthropologists interested in contemporary society.

The 1975 (and last) edition of the Wenner-Gren *International Directory of Anthropologists* contained a list of "Interests" for a total of 4,300 associates, over twice the number in 1994. This seems to be due to the fact that the associates list changes from time to time, as it should, since people are mortal and professions are constantly diminishing and expanding. The list of interests in 1975 was also much longer than the 1994 selection, and full of apparent and unexplained duplication. At any rate, exactly 159 Associates listed "Applied Anthropology". And when one adds institutional and social change fields (though represented in 1975 with rather different language and terminology) the number increases to over 3,000, so the pattern of the two samples is similar: relatively few respondents were willing, in both years, to select Applied (or Action) Anthropology, but pluralities and even majorities professed interests in the subject matters and topics usually or often associated with Applied work: contemporary society and its institutions, change, development, ecology, and so forth. (Too much should not be made of these CA data, since the salient-response system has terminological ambiguities. To get an accurate count of research and practical interests one would need a more carefully constructed questionnaire, and a certain amount of explanation and even pre-coding.)

N.B.: The single largest number of interests for both the 1994 and the 1975 data bases was archaeology.

Aside from numbers, the question of professional identity makes counting difficult. Some of the most significant applied work has been done by people who do not identify themselves as "applied anthropologists"—Richard N. Adams is a case in point. In my own case, I have generally synthesized applied and theoretical-academic data and theory, in the belief that there should be no real distinction between the two.

2. Strictly speaking, an essay on Applied Anthropology should include both archaeology and bio-anthropology. The latter has a long and distinguished record of applied forensic service to medicine, law enforcement agencies, and the military, not to mention manufacturers of furniture and clothing. Archaeology's applied phase is more recent. Perhaps the most striking example is the work of William Rathje (Rathje and Murphy 1992) on trash and garbage landfills, an undertaking which strikes some anthropologists as comical, but which contributes interesting information on the problems of waste and consumption patterns in industrial civilization. A radically different approach to application in archaeology is represented by a "Special Report" of the Society of American Archaeology (Lynott and

Wylie 1995), where the authors argue for "relevant" and "responsible" archaeology, that is, with significance for the preservation of cultural heritage. Archaeologists, says Wylie, should be "stewards" of the past (Pyburn and Wilk 1995: 71). No information is provided on precisely how to do this, but it should be pointed out that archaeologists have been participating with federal, state, and local heritage and site-protection groups for many years, with considerable success in the way of protecting sites, saving artifacts, discouraging private collector sales, and so on.

3. Most texts and readers in Applied contain a brief account of past developments, but this is usually biased in some direction or other and ignores one or another key activity. No one has attempted to pull all the case study reports and attempts at theoretical summation together - the job would be a formidable one, and its product hard to conceive of. But it needs doing. So far as the history of the field is concerned, useful documents are the first chapter in Eddy and Partridge (Partridge 1987), a typical reader-text; and the second chapter of van Willigen (1993). So far as material which will provide a view of the changing topics and concepts over the years, the best bet is a chronologically ordered list of reader-texts: e.g., Spicer 1952; Anthropological Society of Washington 1956; Adams and Preiss 1960; Arensberg and Neihoff 1964; Eddy and Partridge 1987. Barnett (1942) and Temple (1914) provide notes on pre-modern applied anthropology, and Richards (1944) reviews the early years of British Applied.
4. The work of Clyde Kluckhohn and his students and associates is a landmark in the history of anthropology—let alone Applied. The point is that Clyde simply did not draw a clear distinction between Applied and Pure, mainly, perhaps, because he was not really "employed" by some agency to do a specific job although he served as a participative consultant. Kluckhohn on the whole was academically self-directed (like Sol Tax was later in the Fox Project). For examples, see Kluckhohn and Kluckhohn (1971) on Navaho material culture; Kluckhohn (1944) on Navaho Witchcraft, a scholarly monograph on the sociopsychology of culture; Leighton and Kluckhohn (1948), on personality development of the Navaho; and Boyce (1974), summarizing the work on sheep-raising and other economic matters.
5. For a sampling of this 1940s work (although some of the items were written later, as retrospection) see the following: Barnard (1950) and Roethlisberger and Dickson (1964) for classic statements of Harvard industrial sociology; Chapple (1943) for a position paper on "anthropological engineering" which defines the prewar, technocratic New Deal-oriented ideology of Applied; Richardson (1945) for a position paper on "rural rehabilitation"—the New Deal Agriculture community program; and Warner (1940–41) for a paper on anthropological studies of modern communities.
6. A convenient sample is the series of "Rural Life Studies" produced by the USDA and republished in a collected edition by Greenwood Press (Culture of Contemporary Rural Communities 1978).
7. Ralph Nader, who in the early 1950s took his first anthropology course as a freshman at Princeton, later caught the essence:

> The interesting distinction students made between anthropology and sociology in the early fifties was that sociology was utterly boring . . . and anthropology was exciting and creative. Why? I think largely for three reasons. First, anthropology had come out of the late thirties and World War II with an image of problem solving. Anthropologists were pressed into service by a mobilized

society to look from their unique vantage point into various attitudes that had to be understood . . . in order to solve some of the problems . . . in the war effort. Kluckhohn, in *Mirror for Man*, of course, made a strong point of the functional relevance of anthropological knowledge by giving examples from that period. We were also told what an insightful study Ruth Benedict's *Chrysanthemum and the Sword* . . . was. . . . The second reason anthropology somewhat stood apart from sociology and other social sciences was its description of describing human behavior . . . in an interesting way. Third, anthropology tended to project a process of merciless self examination, both for society and individuals. . . . In short, anthropology had not sought a high perch on the abstraction ladder. . . . But something has obviously happened in the last two decades and not to the good. . . . Anthropology has developed its own restrictive taboos, its own little culture, and has been surrounded, if not strangled, by it. It has developed status symbols which proliferate trivia and, even worse, the quest for trivia as a status symbol in the profession. . . . (Nader 1975: 31–2)

8. Pronouncements on the multidisciplinary hospitality of the Society for Applied Anthropology and *Human Organization* were frequent in the 1950–1960 period, but have fallen off in the past two decades. It still constituted a definite philosophy in the mid-1960s, although a bit pessimistic and defensive. An example is the "From the Editor" piece in *Human Organization*:

   From the beginning, for example, the Society and its journal have expressed interest in the application of principles and methods from *all* sciences (biological and physical as well as social and behavioral) to the analysis and solution of human organizational problems. . . . Man was to be viewed whole, as a biologically and psychologically complex organism and as a social being existing in a changing physical and cultural environment which could be controlled scientifically. . . . In practice, the goal (whether valid or not) is yet to be achieved. (*Human Organization* 1966: 85)

9. The original name of *Human Organization*, in the period 1941–48, was *Applied Anthropology*. There was a vigorous debate at a Society for Applied Anthropology meeting in 1948 where it was decided to change the name in order to "give the journal a greater appeal and to create a wider audience" (*Human Organization* 1949a: 3). There was opposition from members who felt the advocates were overly fond of the wartime interdisciplinary outlook. Then, as now, the two issues of greatest concern in Applied, as well as in the larger discipline of Anthropology, were the merits of anthropological study of contemporary life and society; and the question of whether anthropology can "go it alone" without help from other disciplines, although this latter issue is no longer so relevant, given the institutional anthropological specialties, which borrow freely from neighboring disciplines.
10. One advantage of the institutional anthropologies is that one can do scholarly work but at the same time have it possess practical significance. For example, the monographic books published by the Society for Economic Anthropology via the University Press of America, deal with such topics as economic development, entrepreneurship, local markets, household economy, bargaining, and others. About half of the work reported in these monographs was based on contracted applied anthropology; but an equal amount represented doctoral, grant-supported research. The institutional anthropologies are simply a way that the anthropological discipline has found to echo the effort of the institutional social sciences, or to get

around the constraints and frustrations of a focus on the fading tribal societies and perform interesting and scholarly social research on the contemporary world.

11. However, the technique of post-hoc assessment of results of planned change projects is a standard procedure in economic development, and development anthropologists have participated in these evaluations. Typically, the anthropological member of the team is assigned the task of studying the social changes resulting from the project, and/or the way social and attitudinal factors may have sabotaged the project's goals. In the early 1980s I did an assessment of some of these project evaluation reports dealing with African pastoralism (Bennett et al. 1986) and on the basis of that work, plus basic ethnological and economic-anthropological studies of pastoral peoples, concluded that anthropologists had performed a competent job in determining the basic cultural-economic-ecology of pastoralism and its variants in different African environments. Much of the best information came from the evaluative post-project studies, a clear demonstration of how Applied work can actually contribute to more general anthropological knowledge. Even more—it showed how pressing social issues—like the need to "develop," sedentarize, or improve production among a particular people—can form the basis of stimulating ethnological research. This possibility is still not fully understood among the conventional academic adherents of the discipline. Comparative, post-hoc ethnological studies have been made in a few cases (e.g., the famous Oscar Lewis (1951) restudy of Redfield's Tepoztlan) but without reference to particular institutional sectors, or to change. Lewis simply tested Redfield's static depictions of Tepoztlan culture, and acquired different results—naturally.
12. The role of the anthropologist vis-à-vis the administrator doesn't change. H. G. Barnett (1956) wrote a little book, *Anthropology in Administration*, based mainly on his experience as a Trust Territories Anthropologist in Micronesia after World War II. This, in some respects, is an American parallel to the Brown and Hutt volume. And like that volume, the book contains an introductory statement by an administrator, in this case one J. A. McConnell, the former deputy high commissioner of the Trust Territory, who noted:

    > The expert scientist in his staff role should be a source of unbiased information and a neutral judge of the effect of alternative decisions. Whether he fully achieves this position depends in part on the nature of his relationships with his administrator. (preface to Barnett 1956)

13. See, for example, these collections of case studies of change: Spicer 1952; Adams and Preiss 1960; Arensberg and Niehoff 1964; Anthropological Society of Washington 1956; Clifton 1970; Maday 1975; Eddy and Partridge 1987. For books see the following: Boas 1928; Evans-Pritchard 1946; Kluckhohn 1949; A. Leighton 1949; Mead 1955; Erasmus 1961; Foster 1969; Weaver 1973; Bodley 1976; Wulff and Fiske 1987; Van Willigen 1991; Smith 1993.
14. For accounts of the Vicos study, certainly one of the applied-development anthropology classics, see the following: Dobyns et al. 1962; Holmberg and Dobyns 1962; Laswell 1962; Holmberg 1955.
15. See the "Report on the Committee on Ethics" in *Human Organization* (1949b); and the "Proposed Statement on Professional and Ethical Responsibilities: Society for Applied Anthropology" (*Human Organization* 1983), printed in various issues of *HO*. This is a revision of two earlier codes (e.g., *Human Organization* 1951), and includes more material on the interaction and exposure issues than the previ-

ous versions. Both this and the AAA Code of Ethics are often criticized for inhibiting energetic and penetrative field inquiry. For a thoughtful general paper on ethics, see Jorgensen (1971). Additional items are the following: Adams 1981; Chapple 1951; Dillman 1977; Fluehr-Lobban 1991; Gjessing 1968.

16. In addition to the Vidich-Bensman book, and William Whyte's editorial cited in the text, see the following for the Springdale story: Evans 1960–61; *Human Organization* 1958–59, 1959a, 1959b, 1959–60; Vidich 1960.
17. I myself witnessed one instance of the disagreement. It occurred at a meeting of the Society for Applied Anthropology Board sometime in the late 1950s (I cannot recall the particular year) at which Chapple, Richardson, Mead, and Tax were present (and myself, at which time I was a program chairman for a forthcoming meeting) and possibly one or two others (I suspect I am the only living witness!). But a vigorous argument ensued over several key issues: one involved the Code of Ethics which was in a state of debate at that time, another was editorial policy for *Human Organization*, and another concerned relations between the Society for Applied Anthropology and the United States Government on some issue long forgotten. Tax seemed to feel that the old-guard members were overly deferential with respect to large organizations, overly dependent on government support and funds, and overly concerned with applied anthropology as a distinct discipline in its own right. The administration of the Society for Applied Anthropology began to go downhill about this same time and during the 1960s reached a nadir with revelations of scandals concerning subscriptions and other things.
18. Tax spent about two weeks in Ranchi, where D. P. Sinha, an Indian ecological and economic-applied anthropologist, was teaching in a Department of Anthropology. Tax was selling the *Current Anthropology* network, and did so by delivering a series of lectures on anthropology and its role in the Third World rehabilitation. I visited the Ranchi department and worked with Sinha a month or so following Tax's visit, and received an account of how he managed to charm the administration and promote his Action-oriented conceptions of applied anthropology.
19. The first formal presentation of action anthropology to the anthropological profession occurred in November 1951, at the annual meeting of the American Anthropological Association in Chicago (a meeting which was my first in several years, since I had just returned from the Japan Occupation). A session, entitled "Applied Anthropology," and chaired by John Useem included two papers on Action by Sol Tax and Robert Merrill. Other panelists were John Adair, Edward Kennard, George Foster, and Jean Comhaire. As I recall the session, the tension between the classic Applied stance, and the participative, value-oriented Action approach, was apparent. Incidently, the first publications on action anthropology to appear in *Human Organization* were papers by Tax and Lisa Peattie in a symposium entitled "Values in Action" in *Human Organization* (Tax 1958). "Action" here did not refer to action anthropology, but to activist research in general. The other panelists were H. G. Barnett and Allan Holmberg, but their papers referred to the need to take account of values in scientific anthropology, not create or advocate values.
20. Or, in academic jargon: "the theory of practice asserts the primacy of subjective experience in the formation of objective knowledge" (Partridge 1987: 223).
21. Our Milwaukee paths crossed just once. Tax was eight years older, and in adolescence that meant an eternity. However, one of Tax's allies in the Newsboys' Republic wars was Frank Zeidler, later to become a longtime "socialist" mayor of Milwaukee. Zeidler, Tax's age, was a senior at West Division High when I was a freshman and sophomore there. On one occasion Zeidler gave a talk at a West

Division assembly on the Newsboys affair, along with Tax, and at which I was present due to a compulsory attendance rule (reconstructed during Tax-Bennett conversations in Spring 1994). Zeidler and I later became rival feature writers for the West Division student literary magazine. (Tax, on the other hand, went to a high school on Milwaukee's East side.) (The reader might wonder at such sophisticated activity in high schools in the 1920s, but High school education in Milwaukee at that time was probably equivalent to contemporary junior college.)

22. For a convenient bibliography of early studies of community-based development projects participated in by anthropologists in the 1950s and 1960s, see Arensberg and Niehoff (1964: appendix A), "A Selected List of Case Histories of Socioeconomic Change Projects." See Goodenough (1963) for an account of "community development" research. For some assessments of the development-anthropology subtype of Applied, see the following: Gow 1991, 1993; Mead 1955; Mair 1969; Poggie and Lynch 1974; Hoben 1982; Scudder 1987. The monographs published by the Institute for Development Anthropology in Binghampton, NY, provide an example of contemporary development anthropology literature. The IDA is also the preeminent anthropologically oriented contract research agency in the development field. For a polemical defense of development anthropology - as over against conventional Applied, see Cochrane 1971.

Literature Cited

Adams, Richard N. 1981. "Ethical Principles in Anthropological Research: One or Many?" *Human Organization* 40: 155–159.

Adams, Richard N. and J. J. Preiss, eds. 1960. *Human Organization Research*. Homewood, IL: Dorsey Press.

Alinsky, Saul D. 1971. *Rules for Radicals: A Practical Primer for Realistic Radicals*. New York: Random House.

Angrosino, Michael V., ed. 1976. *Do Applied Anthropologists Apply Anthropology? Essays on an Evolving Discipline*. Athens: University of Georgia Press.

———. 1981. "Practicum Training in Applied Anthropology." *Human Organization* 40: 81–85.

———. 1982. *Case Studies in Applied Anthropology Internship Training*. Tampa, FL: Center for Applied Anthropology, University of South Florida.

Anthropological Society of Washington. 1956. *Some Uses of Anthropology: Pure and Applied.* Washington, DC.

Arensberg, Conrad M. and Arthur H. Niehoff. 1964. *Introducing Social Change: A Manual for Americans Overseas*. Chicago: Aldine Publishing.

Barnard, Chester I. 1950. *The Functions of the Executive*. Cambridge, MA: Harvard University Press.

Barnett, H. G. 1942. "Applied Anthropology in 1860." *Applied Anthropology* 1(3):19–31.

———. 1956. *Anthropology in Administration*. Evanston, IL: Row, Peterson and Company.

Bastide, Roger. 1971. *Applied Anthropology*. Translated from the French by A. L. Morton. New York: Harper & Row, Publishers.

Bennett, John W. 1988. "Anthropology and the Development Process: The Ambiguous Engagement," in *Production and Autonomy: Anthropological Studies and Critiques of Development*, edited by John W. Bennett and John Bowen, pp. 1–29. Monographs in Economic Anthropology, no. 5. Lanham, MD: University Press of America.

———. 1993–96. *Human Ecology As Human Behavior: Essays in Environmental and Development Anthropology.* Expanded edition published 1996. New Brunswick, NJ: Transaction Publishers.

Bennett, John W., Steven W. Lawry and James C. Riddell. 1986. *Land Tenure and Livestock Development in Sub-Saharan Africa.* AID EvaluationSpecial Study no. 19. Washington, DC: U.S. Agency for International Development.

Berreman, Gerald D. 1968. "Is Anthropology Alive? Social Responsibility in Social Anthropology." *Current Anthropology* 9: 391–396.

Blanchard, David. 1979. "Beyond Empathy: The Emergence of Action Anthropology in the Life and Career of Sol Tax," in *Currents in Anthropology*, edited by R. Hinshaw, pp. 419–445. The Hague: Mouton.

Boas, Franz. 1928. *Anthropology and Modern Life.* New York: W. W. Norton & Co.

Bodley, John H. 1976. *Anthropology and Contemporary Human Problems.* Menlo Park, CA: Cummings Publishing.

Borman, Leonard D. 1979. "Action Anthropology and The Self-Help/Mutual Aid Movement," in *Currents in Anthropology*, edited by R. Hinshaw, pp. 487–513. The Hague: Mouton.

Boyce, George A. 1974. *When Navajos Had Too Many Sheep: The 1940s.* San Francisco, CA: Indian Historian Press.

Brameld, Theodore. 1965. "Anthropotherapy: Toward Theory and Practice." With comments by George D. Spindler and Morris E. Opler and a rejoinder by Brameld. *Human Organization* 24: 288–297.

Brown, G. Gordon and A. McD. Bruce Hutt. 1935. *Anthropology in Action: An Experiment in the Iringa District of the Iringa Province, Tanganyika Territory.* London: Oxford University Press.

Chapple, Eliot D. 1943. "Anthropological Engineering: Its Use to Administrators." *Applied Anthropology* 2(2): 23.

———. 1951. "Ethics in Applied Anthropology." *Human Organization* 10(2): 4.

Clifton, James A., ed. 1970. *Applied Anthropology: Readings in the Uses of the Science of Man.* Boston: Houghton Mifflin.

Cochrane, Glynn. 1971. *Development Anthropology.* New York: Oxford University Press.

Culture of Contemporary Rural Communities. 1978. Originally published by U.S. Department of Agriculture as "Rural Life Studies" nos. 1–6. Westport, CT: Greenwood Press.

Dean, John P. and William Foote Whyte. 1958. "How Do You Know If the Informant is Telling the Truth?" *Human Organization* 17:(2): 34–38.

Diesing, Paul. 1991. *How Does Social Science Work? Reflections on Practice.* Pittsburgh, PA: University of Pittsburgh Press.

Dillman, Caroline M. 1977. "Ethical Problems in Social Science Research Peculiar to Participant Observation." *Human Organization* 36: 405–407.

Dobyns, Henry F., Carlos M. Monge, and Mario V. Vazquez. 1962. "Community and Regional Development: The Joint Cornell-Peru Experiment: Summary of Progress and Reactions." *Human Organization* 21: 109–115.

Eddy, Elizabeth M. and William L. Partridge, eds. 1987. *Applied Anthropology in America.* 2d ed. New York: Columbia University Press.

Erasmus, C. J. 1961. *Man Takes Control.* Minneapolis: University of Minnesota Press.

Evans, William M. 1960–61. "Conflict and the Emergence of Norms: The 'Springdale' case." *Human Organization* 19: 172–173.

Evans-Pritchard, E. E. 1946. "Applied Anthropology." *Africa* 16: 92–8.

Fetterman, David M. 1993. *Speaking the Language of Power: Communication, Col-*

laboration, and Advocacy (Translating Ethnography into Action). London: Falmer Press.

Firth, Raymond. 1931. "Anthropology and Native Administration." *Oceania* 2: 1–8.

———. 1954. "Social Organization and Social Change." *Journal of the Royal Anthropological Institute* 84: 1–20.

———. 1955. "Some Principles of Social Organization." *Journal of the Royal Anthropological Institute* 85: 1–17.

Fluehr-Lobban, Carolyn, ed. 1991. *Ethics and the Profession of Anthropology: Dialogue for a New Era*. Philadelphia, PA: University of Pennsylvania Press.

Forde, Daryll. 1953. "Applied Anthropology in Government: British Africa," in *Anthropology Today*, edited by A. L. Kroeber, pp. 843–844. Chicago: University of Chicago Press.

Foster, George M. 1969. *Applied Anthropology*. Boston: Little, Brown.

Gearing, Fred O., Robert Mc. Netting, and Lisa R. Peattie, eds. 1960. *Documentary History of the Fox Project, 1948–1959*. A program in action anthropology, directed by Sol Tax. Chicago: University of Chicago.

Gjessing, G. 1968. "The Social Responsibility of the Social Scientist." *Current Anthropology* 9: 397–402.

Goodenough, Ward Hunt. 1963. *Cooperation in Change: An Anthropological Approach to Community Development*. New York: Russell Sage Foundation.

Gow, David D. 1991. "Collaboration in Development Consulting: Stooges, Hired Guns, or Muskateers?" *Human Organization* 50: 1–15.

———. 1993. "Doubly Damned: Dealing with Power and Praxis in Development Anthropology." *Human Organization* 52: 380–397.

Haddon, A. C. 1921. *The Practical Value of Ethnology*. London: Watts & Co.

Held, Virginia. 1984. *Rights and Goods: Justifying Social Action*. Chicago: University of Chicago Press.

Henshaw, Stanley K. 1963. "Applied Anthropology and Sociology in Tropical Africa." *Human Organization* 22: 283–285.

Hinshaw, Robert, ed. 1979. *Currents in Anthropology: Essays in Honor of Sol Tax*. The Hague: Mouton Publishers.

Hirschman, Albert O. 1967. *Development Projects Observed*. Washington, DC: The Brookings Institution.

Hoben, Allan. 1982. "Anthropologists and Development," in *Annual Review of Anthropology*, vol. 11, edited by Bernard J. Siegel, pp. 158–66. Palo Alto, CA: Annual Reviews.

Hogbin, H. Ian. 1957. "Anthropology As Public Service and Malinowski's Contribution to It," in *Man and Culture: An Evaluation of the Work of Bronislaw Malinowski*, edited by Raymond Firth. London: Routledge & Kegan Paul.

Holmberg, Allan R. 1955. "Participant Intervention in the Field." *Human Organization* 14(1): 23–26.

Holmberg, Allan R. and Henry F. Dobyns. 1962. "Community and Regional Development: The Joint Cornell-Peru Experiment: The Process of Accelerating Community Change." *Human Organization* 21: 107–109.

Human Organization. 1949a. "Editorial: Our New Look." *Human Organization* 8(1): 3–4.

———. 1949b. "Report of the Committee on Ethics." *Human Organization* 8(2): 20–21.

———. 1951. "Code of Ethics of the Society for Applied Anthropology." *Human Organization* 10(2): 32.

———. 1958–59. "'Freedom and Responsibility in Research,' comments by Arthur

Vidich and Joseph Bensman, Robert Risley, Raymond Ries, and Howard S. Becker." *Human Organization* 17(4): 2–7.

———. 1959a. "'Freedom and Responsibility in Research,' comments by Earl H. Bell and Urie Bronfenbrenner." *Human Organization* 18: 49–50.

——. 1959b. Principles of professional ethics: Cornell studies in social growth. *Human Organization* 18: 50–52. Reprinted from *The American Psychologist* 7:452–455.

———. 1959–60. "On Freedom and Responsibility in Research: Memorandum of Understanding Concerning Basic Principles for Publication of Program Research." *Human Organization* 18: 147–148.

———. 1966. "From the Editor (on Multidisciplinary Studies)." *Human Organization* 25: 185–6.

———. 1983. "Proposed Statement on Professional and Ethical Responsibilities, Society for Applied Anthropology." *Human Organization* 41: 367.

Jacobs, S. 1974. "Action and Advocacy Anthropology." *Human Organization* 33: 318–321.

Jorgensen, Joseph G. 1971. "On Ethics and Anthropology." *Current Anthropology* 12: 321–334.

Kluckhohn, Clyde. 1944. *Navaho Witchcraft*. Boston: Beacon Press.

———. 1949. *Mirror for Man*. New York: McGraw-Hill.

Kluckhohn, Clyde, W. W. Hill, and Lucy Wales Kluckhohn. 1971. *Navaho Material Culture*. Cambridge, MA: Belknap Press.

Lantis, Margaret. 1945. "Applied Anthropology As a Public Service." *Applied Anthropology* 4(1): 20–32.

Laswell, Harold D. 1962. "Community and Regional Development: The Joint Cornell-Peru Experiment: Integrating Communities into More Inclusive Systems." *Human Organization* 21: 116–124.

Leighton, Alexander H. 1949. *Human Relations in a Changing World: Observations on the Use of Social Sciences*. New York: Dutton.

Leighton, Alexander H., John Adair and Seymour Parker. 1951. "A Field Method for Teaching Applied Anthropology." *Human Organization* 10(4): 5–11.

Leighton, Dorothea C. and Clyde Kluckhohn. 1948. *Children of the People: The Navaho Individual and His Development*. Cambridge, MA: Harvard University Press.

Lewis, Oscar. 1951. *Life in a Mexican Village: Tepoztlan Restudied*. Urbana, IL: University of Illinois Press.

Linton, Ralph. 1936. *The Study of Man*. New York: Appleton Century.

———. 1945. *The Science of Man in the World Crisis*. New York: Columbia University Press.

Lowie, Robert H. 1940. "Native Languages As Ethnographic Tools." *American Anthropologist* 42: 81–89.

Lynott, Mark J. and Alison Wylie, eds. 1995. *Ethics in American Archaeology: Challenges for the 1990s*. Washington, DC: Society for American Archaeology.

MacNutt, Francis Augustus. 1912. *De Orbe Novo: The Eight Decades of Peter Martyr D'Anghera*. Translated from the Latin with notes and introduction, 2 vols. New York: G.P. Putnam's Sons.

Maday, Bela C., ed. 1975. *Anthropology and Society*. Washington, DC: The Anthropological Society of Washington.

Mair, Lucy. 1969. *Anthropology and Social Change*. New York: Humanities Press.

Malinowski, Bronislaw. 1929. "Practical Anthropology." *Africa* 2: 22–38.

———. 1930. "The Rationalization of Anthropology and Administration." *Africa* 3: 406–407.

Mead, Margaret. 1939. "Native Languages As Field Work Tools." *American Anthropologist* 41: 189–205.

———, ed. 1955. *Cultural Patterns and Technical Change.* A manual prepared for the World Federation of Mental Health. Paris: UNESCO.

———. 1975. "Discussion," in *Anthropology and Society*, edited by Bela C. Maday, pp. 13–18. Washington, DC: The Anthropological Society of Washington.

Mitchell, P. E. 1930. "The Anthropologist and the Practical Man." *Africa* 3: 220.

Nader, Ralph. 1975. "Anthropology in Law and Civic Action," in *Anthropology and Society*, edited by Bela C. Maday, pp. 31–40. Washington, DC: Anthropological Society of Washington.

Paredes, J. Anthony. 1976. "New Uses for Old Ethnography: A Brief Social History of a Research Project with the Eastern Creek Indians, or How to Be an Applied Anthropologist without Really Trying." With *HO* comments. *Human Organization* 35: 315–329.

Partridge, William L. 1987. "Toward a Theory of Practice," in *Applied Anthropology in America*, edited by Elizabeth M. Eddy and William L. Partridge, pp. 211–36. New York: Columbia University Press.

Peattie, Lisa. 1968. "Reflections of an Advocate Planner." *Journal of the American Institute of Planners* 34: 80–88.

Peterson, John H., Jr. 1987. "The Changing Role of an Applied Anthropologist," in *Applied Anthropology in America*, edited by Elizabeth M. Eddy and William L. Partridge, pp. 263–81. New York: Columbia University Press.

Poggie, John J. and Robert N. Lynch, eds. 1974. *Rethinking Modernization: Anthropological Perspectives.* Westport, CT: Greenwood Press.

Polgar, Steven. 1979. "Applied, Action, Radical and Committed Anthropology," in *Currents in Anthropology*, edited by R. Hinshaw, pp. 409–419. The Hague: Mouton.

Pyburn, K. Anne and Richard R. Wilk. 1995. "Responsible Archaeology Is Applied Anthropology," in *Ethics in American Archaeology: Challenges for the 1990s*, edited by Mark J. Lynott and Alison Wylie, pp. 71–79. Washington, DC: Society for American Archaeology.

Radcliffe-Brown, A. R. 1931. *Applied Anthropology.* Proceedings of the Australian and New Zealand Society for the Advancement of Science, 20th meeting, Brisbane 1930: 267–280.

Rathje, William L. and Cullen Murphy. 1992. *Rubbish!: The Archaeology of Garbage.* New York: HarperCollins.

Reining, Conrad. 1962. "A Lost Period in Applied Anthropology." *American Anthropologist* 64: 593–600.

Richards, A. I. 1944. "Practical Anthropology in the Lifetime of the International Africa Institute." *Africa* 14: 293.

Richardson, F. L. W., Jr. 1945. "First Principles of Rural Rehabilitation." *Applied Anthropology* 4(3): 16–37.

———. 1950. "Field Methods and Techniques." *Human Organization* 9(2): 31–2.

Rodman, Hyman and Ralph Kolodny. 1964. "Strains in the Researcher-Practioner Relationship." *Human Organization* 23: 171–182.

Roethlisberger, F. J. and William J. Dickson. 1964. *Management and the Worker: An Account of a Research Program Conducted by the Western Electric Company, Hawthorne Works, Chicago.* New York: John Wiley & Sons.

Rubenstein, Robert A. 1986. "Reflections on Action Anthropology: Some Developmental Dynamics of an Anthropological Tradition." *Human Organization* 45: 270–279.

———, ed. 1991. *Fieldwork: The Correspondence of Robert Redfield and Sol Tax.* Boulder: Westview Press.
Russell, F. 1902. "Know, Then, Thyself." *Science* 15: 561–71.
Scheper-Hughes, Nancy. 1995. "The Primacy of the Ethical Propositions for Militant Anthropology." *Current Anthropology* 36: in press.
Schlesier, K. 1974. "Action Anthropology and the Southern Cheyenne." *Current Anthropology* 15: 277–283.
Scudder, Thayer. 1987. "Opportunities, Issues, and Achievements in Development Anthropology since the mid-1960s: A Personal View," in *Applied Anthropology in America*, edited by Elizabeth M. Eddy and William L. Partridge, pp. 184–210. New York: Columbia University Press.
Slayton, Robert A. 1986. *Back of the Yards: The Making of a Local Democracy.* Chicago: University of Chicago Press.
Smith, Sheldon. 1993. *World in Disorder: An Interdisciplinary Approach to Global Issues.* Lanham, MD: University Press of America.
Spicer, Edward H., ed. 1952. *Human Problems in Technological Change: A Casebook.* New York: Russell Sage Foundation.
Srb, Jozetta H. 1966. "Human Organization: The Growth and Development of a Professional Journal." *Human Organization* 25: 187–97.
Tax, Sol. 1952. "Action Anthropology." *America Indigena* 12: 103–9.
———. 1955. "The Integration of Anthropology," in *Yearbook of Anthropology 1955*, edited by W.L. Thomas, Jr., pp. 313–28. New York: Wenner-Gren Foundation.
———. 1956. "The Freedom to Make Mistakes." *America Indigena* 16: 171–7.
———. 1958. "The Fox Project." *Human Organization* 17: 17–9.
———. 1959. "Residential Integration: The Case of Hyde Park in Chicago." *Human Organization* 18: 22–7.
———. 1964. "The Uses of Anthropology," in *Horizons of Anthropology*, edited by Sol Tax, pp. 248–58. Chicago: Aldine Publishing.
———, ed. 1968. *The People vs. the System: A Dialogue in Urban Conflict.* Chicago: Acme Press.
———. 1975. Action Anthropology. *Current Anthropology* 16: 171–7.
———. 1988. "Pride and Puzzlement: A Retro-Introspective Record of Sixty Years of Anthropology." *Annual Review of Anthropology* 17: 1–21.
Temple, Sir Richard C., Bt. 1914. *Anthropology As a Practical Science.* London: G. Bell & Sons.
Tendler, Judith. 1975. *Inside Foreign Aid.* Baltimore: Johns Hopkins University Press.
Thompson, Laura. 1950. "Action Research among American Indians." *The Scientific Monthly* 70: 34–40.
———. 1965a. "Freedom and Culture." *Human Organization* 24: 105–110.
———. 1965b. "Is Applied Anthropology Helping to Develop a Science of Man?" *Human Organization* 24: 277–287.
———. 1976. "An Appropriate Role for Postcolonial Applied Anthropologists." *Human Organization* 35: 1–7.
Van Willigen, John. 1987. *Becoming a Practicing Anthropologist: A Guide to Careers and Training Programs in Applied Anthropology.* NAPA bulletin 3, American Anthropological Association.
———. 1991. *Anthropology in Use: A Source Book on Anthropological Practice.* Boulder, CO: Westview Press.
———. 1993. *Applied Anthropology: An Introduction.* Rev. ed. Westport, CT: Bergin and Garvey.
Vidich, Arthur J. 1960. "Freedom and Responsibility in Research: A Rejoinder." *Human Organization* 19: 3–4.

Vidich, Arthur J. and Joseph Bensman. 1958. *Small Town in Mass Society: Class, Power, and Religion in a Rural Community*. Princeton, NJ: Princeton University Press.

Warner, W. Lloyd. 1937. *A Black Civilization*. New York: Harper.

———. 1940–41. Social Anthropology and the Modern Community." *American Journal of Sociology* 46: 785–796.

Warry, Wayne. 1992. "The Eleventh Thesis: Applied Anthropology As Praxis. *Human Organization* 51: 155–163.

Weaver, Thomas, ed. 1973. *To See Ourselves: Anthropology and Modern Social Issues*. Glenview, IL: Scott, Foresman, and Company.

Wenner-Gren. 1975. *International Directory of Anthropologists*. New York: Wenner-Gren Foundation.

Whyte, William F. 1958. "Editorial: 'Freedom and Responsibility in Research: the 'Springdale' Case." *Human Organization* 17(2): 1–2.

Wulff, Robert M. and Shirley J. Fiske. 1987. *Anthropological Praxis: Translating Knowledge into Action*. Boulder, CO: Westview Press.

13

The "Famous Lady Anthropologists": Ruth Benedict and Margaret Mead

With a Supplement: A Note on the Critique of Benedict's *Chrysanthemum and the Sword* by Japanese Scholars

Introduction

"Lady Anthropologists" is what the public called women in the profession during the Classic era, and there was quite a crew: Ruth Benedict, Ruth Bunzel, Dorothy Eggan, Esther Goldfrank, Alice Fletcher, Frederica deLaguna, Dorothy Lee, Margaret Mead, Hortense Powdermaker, Gladys Reichard, and of course the odd case of Elsie Clews Parsons, a wealthy patron of anthropology, but who also did ethnology. Most of them were students of Franz Boas, who deserves a posthumous medal from feminist groups for his pioneering effort to induct women into the social sciences. In general, Classic anthropology was well known for its acceptance of women—it was far ahead of sociology. The label, "lady anthropologists" is of course no longer used, but the feminist movement has glorified some of these women, especially Mead and Benedict, and they have become role models for later generations. In their day, they were singled out as the "famous"

Written in 1996 for this volume; Supplement based on an article co-authored with Michio Nagai.

lady anthropologists. Most of the women followed the leads of Mead and Benedict on intellectual matters, so that psychological and humanist styles of scholarship have come to typify the interests of the feminine contingent in the discipline.

Of this group we have already considered the work of Thompson, Goldfrank, and Eggan in the chapter on Pueblo Indian culture. Benedict and Mead get special attention in the present chapter, with reference to their contribution to scholarship and the public culture. Therefore the chapter is a companion to the following one, on "populist" anthropology, where I examine three books explicitly written by male anthropologists for public consumption or general readership. Both Benedict and Mead wrote books read by the public, but from a rather different perspective than those by the men. Above all, they conceived of scholarly work as having public significance. *Patterns of Culture* could be taken either as a popular or professional piece—and the reviewers split along precisely this line, as noted later.

Patterns of Culture is probably the all-time most widely-read serious work in anthropology. For thousands of readers, it was—and is—the one book in the field that was worth reading, and for years it represented the basic message of anthropology: that the world is divided into groups of humans who are capable of producing widely divergent but more or less equally valid forms of existence. *Patterns of Culture* was the first Penguin paperbound book published in the United States after World War II, and I was one of a panel of young teaching anthropologists who were asked by the British Penguin people to nominate a book in the discipline they should publish, in order to score in scholarly dignity and in sales. I think the majority of the panel agreed on *Patterns*. I was using it in what we called those days an "auxiliary text." The main audience at that time, of course, were ex-GI's, going to college on the Bill.

Margaret Mead's role is harder to assess. It is true that her three chief works on Oceania—*Coming of Age in Samoa*, *Growing Up in New Guinea*, and *Sex and Temperament* were all best sellers, with *Coming of Age* for a time keeping pace with *Patterns* as a public best seller. But none of these books by Mead equalled the philosophical impact of Benedict's: Ruth had a view of humanity, not merely a reinterpretation of adolescence and sex. Mead's fieldwork was always greeted with a certain amount of skepticism, and Freeman's (1983) savage critique has not helped. Mead's approach was a direct one: she let the public, both scientific and general, know how anthropology might save modern culture—or at least solve some intimate problems or change faulty values. She became a spokesman for a socially liberal applied anthropology and her often acidulous lectures to fellow anthropologists and conventions and conferences had an effect on various emphases and preoccupations of the discipline.

Benedict's Patterns of Culture

The book is remembered chiefly for the three chapters dealing with the Pueblo Indians, the Dobuans of Melanesia, and the Indians of the northwest Coast of North America (principally the Kwakiutl). But the book actually has eight chapters, and five of these deal with Benedict's theory of society and culture. They are a substantial contribution to anthropological thought and philosophy, and a major statement of one variant of the Classic approach to Culture. Margaret Caffrey, Benedict's biographer, has provided a synthesis of Benedict's theoretical perspective in a somewhat overblown presentation which uses a number of short sentences culled from *Patterns* (Caffrey 1989: 208–13). These give a somewhat misleading impression of Benedict's ideas, making them sound more abstract than they are. But *Patterns of Culture* does have a distinctive point of view and did have a powerful impact on popular and professional thinking. As Caffrey notes, it became a "catalyst" for the culture and personality field, and was the original chef d'oeuvre of the configurationist "school" in ethnology. There are those who think—although not always with approval—that it was the most influential work ever produced in the English language by an anthropologist.

Now, the premier, and most frequently cited, thesis of the book was the notion of cultural relativity, expressed in several ways, but all based on the theme of "selection" of particular and/or differing patterns of behavior by different "cultures." The principal units of analysis, then, are partitive cultures. Mankind is divided into these units; each unit has its own song and dance; and none is "better" than another. There is no need to elaborate on the available criticisms of this approach: the relativist view may be methodologically sound as a rule for the ethnologist to follow to avoid bias, but it makes little sense from the standpoint of problems of human existence, most of which are moral and which require judgements of good and bad, evil and benevolent. Obviously Benedict felt that the anthropologist had no business making such judgements about the peoples she studies, because she felt that judgements like this are always based on prejudices derived from the judger's own culture.

But at the same time Benedict was in effect urging her readers to examine their own cultures to see if the ways of life of other peoples might provide a lesson for domestic change and reform. By featuring highly competitive behavior on the Northwest Coast, and interpersonal hostility among the Dobu, she was suggesting that Americans might think twice about their own similar proclivities. But Benedict never goes all the way. She implies that such comparisons can teach a moral lesson, but she could not make this point openly because to have done so would have contradicted her relativistic premise that all cultures are equally "good," or more accurately, that there are no pronounced "goods" or "bads" in the interpretation of human cultures. But clearly she believed that some cultural behavior is better, less conflictful, or more adaptive than others.

A related theme, and one especially articulated by Caffrey (1989: 211) concerns Benedict's interest in order and symmetry in cultures—which properties she denied were universal. Benedict's acceptance of "dissonance," (to quote Caffrey) is not always easy to observe, because Benedict's portraits of the three cultures are so carefully and logically presented that they give an impression of consistency. She simply didn't deal openly with conflict and dissidence, even though she acknowledged their presence. But the trouble was that she was using the *culture* as the unit of analysis—not individuals, and it is individuals who oppose, resist, fight or dissent—not cultures. The reader views the three cultures from the standpoint of the analyst, not from the point of view of the culture bearers. Caffrey loads the dice somewhat: she introduces the fashionable term "chaos," in order to state that Benedict tried to present a balanced picture of dissonance—Chaos—*plus* order and control. This, Caffrey suggests, constitutes "a new world view" (ibid.: 211). A more familiar word for it is optimism: Benedict was a humanist, pure and simple: she accepted the bitter with the better in human nature—culture—and along with her avoidance of moral values, was unable to view the human adventure as irrevocably biased to one side or the other. It was, in her view, more or less homeostatic (although she could not use the term since it did not exist when she was active): man has divine as well as luciferian tendencies, and on the whole, this works out as a more or less balanced process. Anthropology was reluctant to present the sinister without affirming that the beneficent will ultimately balance it off. Maybe so—but as a practical matter, gratification is easier than renunciation.

The fourth theme deals with the individual and his relationship to society. Not, as noted above, with respect to his appraisal of his culture, but rather in a technical sense, once again invoking the idea of homeostatic balance. The individual and society were not (necessarily?) antagonistic, but in some form of dialectical interaction—"mutual reinforcement" is the term used (Benedict 1934: 253). This, like other matters, was probably designed as a chiding note: American society, with its many antagonistic groups—labor versus management, sectarian tensions, rich versus poor, racial conflicts, and so on—were probably necessary from a humanistic standpoint, but they imposed social costs.

This tendency toward a theory of moral homeostasis is manifest in nearly every one of the theory chapters, and perhaps represents Benedict's chief contribution to anthropology. Paradoxically the insistence on the equality and value neutrality of cultures was a necessary postulate in order to build up a basis for such judgements. But the inner contradiction is inescapable: if human cultures are inherently *human*, that is, both good and bad, and if these elements are frequently out of balance, then is not this disharmony also characteristic of Culture? Is not man possibly incorrigible and unredeemable—at least, unpredictable? Benedict's relatively optimistic humanism did not allow her to confront the dilemma, and no anthropologist has, or can—given a basic "objective" approach to the study of man.

But Benedict knew something; she had discovered something, and one of her peers—A. L. Kroeber (1935)—acknowledged it in his famous favorable review of *Patterns*. Alexander Goldenweiser, however, was less favorable: ". . . what is taken to be a central theme in a native culture might prove to be but a conceptual device of the investigator" (1937: 803). Benedict, from one point of view, had discovered that the sole identification of anthropology—that is, ethnology and cultural anthropology—with the scientific tradition and method, was incomplete and possibly wrong-headed. So much of the data simply could not be bent into the formal shapes that science required, and scientific canons of proof were really not relevant for conveying the truth and value of human existence. Was she saying that science is all right in its place, as in, for example, bioanthropology and possibly some aspects of linguistics and certainly social phenomena rooted in demography? But *culture*—that is another story.

From the standpoint of the most influential trend in cultural anthropology in the 1990s, one must say that Benedict has had the last word. As the principal innovator of humanistic-literary approaches, she won the battle, since cultural anthropology—as distinct from social anthropology—has become, to a considerable degree, a branch of literary analysis.

Because Benedict's standing rests almost entirely on *Patterns*, hardly anyone reads its precursor: "Psychological Types in the Cultures of the Southwest" (1928). This paper is in some respects more revealing of the underpinnings of her cultural-patternist-cum-personality approach than the chapter on the Pueblos in the book. On the first page of the article occurs this passage:

> There is in their [Pueblos] cultural attitudes and choices a difference in psychological type fundamentally to be distinguished from that of surrounding regions. It goes deeper than the presence or absence of ritualism; ritualism itself is of a fundamentally different character within this area, and without an understanding of this fundamental psychological set among the Pueblo peoples we must be baffled in our attempts to understand the cultural history of this region. (Benedict 1928: 572)

Three "fundamentals" in a single paragraph. They suggest the "fundamental" view of the Classic ethnologist: partitive cultures were all distinguishable one from another by distinctive behavior. Culture was the mark of distinction among human groups and communities—not politics, not subsistence, not adaptation to the physical environment, not language (although it might be part of culture, of course), not social organization (although it was hard to distinguish from culture, to be sure); and certainly not genes or phenotype.

There follows a paragraph on the Nietzschean concepts of Appollonian and Dionysian, and here we learn why the Pueblos are so "fundamentally" distinguishable from tribes in the region: they are *Appollonian*, whereas the rest of the population is Dionysian. So cultures not only have distinctive behavior patterns, but they fall into distinctive *types*, and never the twain shall meet—which of course is not really what she meant, because Benedict knew that all human groups have basic similarities. But she was trying to dramatize the differences; or really, by separating the distinctive characteristics into polar types she was simply making the behaviors that defined the differences dramatically emphatic. A purely literary device—exaggeration for the sake of making something clear to the reader. Easily done: just find the available and relevant typologies in literature, especially those in the German romantic tradition. The fact that the Navaho had picked up a lot of the "fundamentally" different Pueblo ritual and "Appollonian" behavior, especially with respect to curing ceremonials, or the fact that the Pueblos also engaged in witchcraft and other anxiety-prone behavior, was probably not clearly realized by Benedict at the time of writing. But the problem is deeper than that: she simply picked out from the available data those behavioral traits that exemplified the types. And the fact that the ethnographers, including herself, had focussed on these traits, meant that to some extent she loaded the dice. Don't we all.

The paper continues with descriptions of the ritual behavior of the Dionysian, that is, non-Pueblo peoples of the Southwest, emphasizing their frenzy, use of drugs, ecstasies, orgies, torture, and so on. But Benedict does not mention that such behaviors were prevalent in these more or less nomadic Plains-based societies, whose members came together only infrequently on an annual round (which by the way was almost as rigorously observed as any routine in Pueblo society). The Pueblos, on the other hand, were penned up in their villages, working hard to raise crops in the desert, and exercising daily surveillance over behavior in order to keep the peace. The settlement-subsistence pattern, as it would be called in the late Classic and post-Classic, was as much the cause of the behavior patterns as anything else. So the difficulties with the patternist approach was simply that without some understanding of the way humans react or adapt to circumstances—environmental and domiciliary—one is left with a mystery: why these "fundamentally" distinctive or different ways of life are characteristic of relatively isolated—vicinally isolated—small populations. The answers, of course, lie ultimately in the nature of the human mind and behavioral potentialities.

Actually, Benedict does acknowledge a number of "Dionysian" rituals which did take hold in Pueblo culture: "filth eating"; clowning; the "isolated case" in Zuñi of ritual fornication on the part of priestesses; and the scalp dance. Benedict also acknowledges the witch, but declares that witchcraft is interpreted differently: its power can be laid aside, that is, there is no such thing as "a witch," but witch *power*. Well, maybe. Later ethnography gave a different picture (see chapter 8 for further discussion).

Tribal patterns aside, Benedict demonstrated her method and her insights in her 1946 book, *Chrysanthemum and the Sword*. The book emanated from a War Department-sponsored research project designed to supply the Army with studies of character and culture of the enemy countries. But the resulting book was a long way from a government manual: it was a startling and highly original treatise on a national character—in fact, it was the first such attempt by an anthropologist, and it was the first in a whole train of studies, most of them done by Margaret Mead and her disciples. (Mead always felt a certain envy of and competitiveness with Benedict, despite her public approbation and declarations of indebtedness.) Benedict's book not only demonstrated that the configurationist approach could be used in analyzing the culture of a modern national society, but it also cemented Benedict's status as a unique and imaginative anthropologist. She did the research for the book by interviewing *issei* (Japanese people born in Japan, who migrated to the United States or Hawaii) and others in the relocation camps, and then taking the data back to Washington where she worked it up.

The book explored the Japanese cultural ethos, or configuration, by focussing on the overarching theme of interpersonal relations and the distinctive values that supported the system. These all had their background in the Tokugawa feudal system, which lasted until the 1870s, and was incompletely liquidated in the nationalization and modernization of the country. The book was a startling demonstration of how an informal, but organized social substructure could shape national-level institutions and attitudes. The remarkable thing was that while Japanese scholars knew most of what Benedict described, they had not been able to conceptualize and systemize it. They spotted some errors, but the amazing thing was that she got it all so right. (Details of the reaction of Japanese scholars can be found in the Supplement.) The book was required reading for all of us in the Japan Occupation, and we acquired reflected prestige among the Japanese as members of the same society or profession that produced such a brilliant interpreter of their unique culture.

Margaret Mead and the Anthropological Ego

No anthropologist could equal her for sheer chutzpa and nerve: she was a shameless self-promoter; self-appointed national sales agent for the discipline of anthropology; scourge of various Classic-era anthropologists and their picayune quarrels and preoccupations; a friend and tireless mentor of bright young anthropologists (especially those who acknowledged her ascendancy and who were willing to work for her); a self-appointed scientist among scientists (she became President of the American Association for the Advancement of Science during her last decade; but it took her longer to gain the presidency of the American Anthropological Association); a friend and devotee of Ruth Benedict; and perhaps above all, a political liberal but one with strong libert*arian* tendencies. When youths started taking drugs, she did not openly criticize, but in women's mass-circulation magazines and on countless soapboxes, preached tolerance and ways to divert their attention to needs which could be satisfied otherwise. And she could admit she had been wrong: when the peril of lactose intolerance in certain populations was discovered and publicized, she confessed that she, along with others, had been pushing the consumption of milk by everyone as the perfect food, and obviously *that* was going to have to be more carefully handled. If breast-feeding was advocated by feminists, she spoke up with the ethnological evidence on breast-feeding in tribal societies. She was a cautious feminist—not on the Benedict model, which drifted toward the idea of the nurturing and aesthetically superior woman—but sociologically and ideologically: women deserve a better break, look at what I have accomplished!

Her Oceanic books, along with Benedict's *Patterns of Culture*, were for a decade the apotheosis of ethnology for the literate public. Mead was close to the neo-Freudians, and so her work tended to merge with the burgeoning popularity of Freud in the 1930s and 1940s. These early field studies and subsequent investigations like *Balinese Character* (Bateson and Mead 1942) were bound up with her personal life: husbands, divorces, partnerships, promotions, excursions into advocacy. Advocacy was her life: she promoted causes—especially if she could find something in anthropology to justify her position. She was the consummate public anthropologist of the era—a kind of analogue to Ralph Nader, about whom, by the way, she once said to me that she envied his ability to swim in the murky waters of modern life and its problems.

She took no pronounced positions on the dichotomizing issues of the inner discipline: science or humanities; rigorous method or impressionism; culture or society; functionalism versus historicism; science versus history. But when Leslie White and others tried to revive evolutionism in the early 1950s she promptly published a book converting all of her old Oceanic data into evolutionary propositions (Mead 1964). She was all things to all anthropologists. It is possible to give her almost any kind of intellectual status one wishes, by selecting passages from her professional and popular writings.

So what, precisely, was her role and her influence? Her public role is easy to describe: First and foremost was her advocacy of the discipline and her conviction that anthropology had something the world needed and could use. This certainly instilled confidence in young anthropologists. I can recall going to social events when I was a graduate student and young professional and when questioned, admitting I was an anthropologist, to be met immediately by eager questions about Margaret Mead. She *was* professional identity: and while sometimes it was embarrassing to have to say that one had doubts about her probity with respect to research, her name and persona always opened up a line of conversation. And of course her example was especially important for young women anthropologists. She probably indirectly recruited a whole generation of female members of the discipline.

Her intellectual and scholarly influence is much more difficult to assess. She was a typical Classic era anthropologist insofar as her primary terms of reference were cultural. Anthropology for her was equivalent to the study of Culture and culture*s*: this is what distinguished it from other social sciences. Sometimes she gave the impression that she invented the concept. But her idea of Culture was certainly not Kroeber's or Linton's, although she regularly used the standard-brand Classic rhetoric in her popular writings. Her basic conception was much closer to Benedict's, but it went beyond in the sense that culture for Mead was a matter of *personal* discovery. She felt culture, breathed it, or as Roy Menninger remarked (as quoted in Jane Howard's biography of Mead),

> I never thought that facts were particularly important to Margaret. She didn't *need* facts. She could pick up patterns, observations, trends without them . . . she could put A and Q and X together in a way that nobody would have thought of. . . . (Howard 1984: 429)

In Menninger's and Howard's views, I suspect, this is offered as a compliment, an appreciation of her brilliance and of the *verstehen*-anthropologist approach. But to the scientist-anthropologists, the approach was anathema, and it led eventually to distrust of her accuracy and contempt for her egocentrism—and ultimately to Derek Freeman's (1983) acidulous polemic. But whatever one may think of it, the talent was genuine, and there is no question that the good ethnologist should have some of it—perhaps so long as he or she is able to subject it to a certain amount of intellectual discipline.

The criticism began to pile up, and the famous Balinese expedition was acknowledged by Mead in writing and public addresses as her response to the critics who said that they could not trust her reportage because they didn't know how she got the material. So off she and Gregory Bateson, her then-husband, went with cameras, to photograph every step of their interviews and observations. *Balinese Character* is some kind of masterpiece, but like all of Mead's productions, it is hard to evaluate despite the abundant photographic evidence. Because she used neo-Freudian concepts to interpret what she described and took pictures of, the critics had another field day: she tended to guide her interests and her camera by psychocultural concepts, not by the attitudes and ideas of the Balinese themselves.

The story of Bateson's and Mead's selection of Bali for their *pièce de résistance* of childhood and character formation is told in Jane Howard's biography of Mead (1984: 189–200). Summarizing, Bali represented the kind of culture that the late- Classic-era anthropologists dreamed about: substantial, multicultural, with many traditions intermingled, yet autonomous and integral, full of exotic rituals and strange behaviors. In short, Bali had experienced an environment of relative isolation over a long time that produced what used to be called "primitive culture"—only Bali was far from "primitive" since it had a synthesis of great traditions: Hindu, Buddhist, a little Chinese, and increasingly, international urbanism and tourism.

The section "Autocosmic Play" (Bateson and Mead 1942: 131–143, and photographic plates 38–44) illustrates the basic approach of the project: a dozen or so photographs, taken with 35 mm. Leica equipment, appear on a page, with a text describing the photos and their meaning on the facing page. The "Autocosmic" section contains plates illustrating Autocosmic Symbols: The Baby; Genital Manipulation; Autocosmic Toys; Autocosmic Symbols on Strings (toddlers pulling toys and small live animals on strings); Bird on a String (more of same); Cockfighting (men holding roosters to fight as penis symbols?); Audiences and Autocosmic Symbols (children and adults handling various objects in various situations). Now, the authors seem to regard handling of any object live or dead, animate or inanimate, as (potential?) examples of "autocosmic play," which in turn is somewhat ambiguously defined as "genital symbolism." The Balinese have the "autocosmic type;" i.e., "some object in the outside world is identified as an extension of own body" (ibid.: 131). The authors also note that the "vast majority" of these symbols represent male genitals, and the "most important" of all these symbols is "the baby." In other words, babies, toddlers, young children in Balinese culture are supposed to represent male genitals? This is putting it a bit bluntly, and I am sure Bateson and Mead would have objected on the grounds that symbols are not reality, and the Balinese do not *really* think their children are male genitals. But what is the reader to make of this kind of neo-Freudian rhetoric, and how can he tell that the Balinese themselves do or do not make such symbolic connections? The book has only ten pages of general ethnography, and the plate captions do not provide detailed material taken from structured interviews in which attempts were made to link up the interpretive explanations of the photos with actual attitudes of Balinese respondents. The problem, in greater or lesser degree, extends through the entire book, so the authors did not do what Mead had hoped they would: by the use of photographs, demonstrate the soundness of neo-Freudian interpretive theory (the "autocosmic" idea came from Eric H. Erikson, a neo-Freudian psychiatrist and researcher, whose own books on childhood and adult behavior among American Indian groups usually had a commonsense plausibility and relationship to reality issues).

My own feeling is that Mead's chief contribution to anthropology was imagination and verve: she had the courage to go places and interpret what she found in novel and imaginative ways. But as one who worked for or with her for a brief period (on wartime food-habits research, see Bennett and Passin 1943), and participated with her over the years in a variety of public scholarly affairs, I feel that her lasting or most significant role was what Jane Howard (1984: 389) calls "citizen philosopher." A third of her life span was devoted to this kind of activity, and while it is hard to separate her public and professional personas, my feeling is that she was happiest when telling other people, with enormous conviction, what is, what ought to be, and what will be if you make it so. I listened to her sound off one night in the early 1950s, when I and two students drove her from Columbus, Ohio, to Bloomington, Indiana, for an anthropology meeting. She talked non-stop the entire trip; it was midnight or so when we took off, and dawn was stirring when we arrived. The students were sound asleep. Mead was still telling us all what was what in the world, in the world of Man, and in Anthropology as the sun begun to come through the windshield.

There has always been a question of how influential anthropology has been in recent Western thought. Anthropologists have, of course, assumed that whatever the influence might be, it would be good. The idea of scientific truth about race—the concept of culture—tolerance and value neutrality—the revelation of human diversity—these and other shibboleths of the discipline were advertised as an unmitigated gain to modern civilization. Some doubts arose when value neutrality was accused of breeding immorality; when racial hatred was perceived to stem from political and economic causes and not biological ignorance.

In her last, furious "citizen philosopher" decade, Margaret Mead used "culture" as her keyword. Anthropology had invented culture—she seemed to imply—and by using the concept it was possible to diagnose the condition of humanity in the latter quarter of the twentieth century. But in the heat of public debate and education, a subtle change had taken place in the way she defined or represented culture. To her it had come to mean "bad habits," obsessions, and behavioral tendencies dangerous to happiness and well being. In sum, anything that, if altered, would leave mankind—or at least Americans—in an improved state. And her remedies were based on recommendations to return to former ways, or at least to control the tendencies with a mixture of individual forbearance and regulatory institutions. "Anthropology," while appearing in almost every sentence, had seemingly dissolved into the rhetoric of a liberal social stance, usually carefully hedged. However, my feeling is that Mead was beginning to realize that the modern age, with its distrust of orthodoxy and institutional rigor, was making a transition to a world of disorder, in which anthropology just might be one of the causes, or at least a symptom. But aside from these larger implications, her own changing practical conception of culture suggested that once one directs his attention to real-life, contemporary issues in human behavior, the concept of culture begins to dissolve into a form of intellectual commentary. And at any rate, she was more successful than any other anthropologist in using anthropological information in her diagnoses of contemporary culture.

While most anthropologists at the height of the Classic era were insisting that humans were—at least to a very large extent, "creatures of their culture"—philosophers and liberal ideologists were insisting that all change, progress, or significant spiritual adventures of the human species originate in the behavior of people who *resist* their culture—who stand against it and innovate. Anthropologists were also interested in change, and acknowledged that it does take place in human affairs, but they had no satisfactory theory to account for it. This was a consequence of the ethnological concentration on tribal societies: those small, isolated, ecologically adapted, low-energy-producing human groups whose survival depended on maintaining the status quo—at least until someone or some natural force came along and forced a transition to a new state of affairs.

One modern world historian—Filipe Fernandez-Armesto—has seen sufficient importance in the anthropological saga to discuss its relationship to civilizational change in his *Millennium: A History of the Last Thousand Years* (1995). There Margaret Mead is on page 484, in her outrageous printed skirt and insect-bitten legs, frizzed hair, talking to her lovely informant Fa'amotu on Samoa. The point, of course, is cultural relativity, and the passage is the conclusion of a chapter with the title, "Graveyard of Certainty." The topic of Fernandez-Armesto's chapter is the possible decline of the West, and in his view, cultural anthropology finds a place alongside Sigmund Freud, Oswald Spengler, and other people who broke the frame of the present and destroyed the confidence that the world of the nineteenth and early twentieth century was the only possible true world.

Fernandez-Armesto's concluding paragraphs:

> After long exclusion, the noble savage reappeared among anthropologists drawn back to the Pacific like the lovestruck mariners of the eighteenth century. Perhaps the most influential of all anthropological books was Margaret Mead's *Coming of Age in Samoa*, published in 1928 and based on fieldwork with pubescent girls in a sexually unrepressive society. Whether the paradise depicted was real or imagined has been much debated by critics. The image, however, was seductive, of an uncompetitive world, creatively fertilized by freedom, protected from the agonizing restraints and inhibitions which psychoanalysts were busy uncovering in Western cities and suburbs. The extent of the influence imputed, if not attained, can be

inferred from the ferocity with which the work was attacked during a reaction, soon after Mead's death in 1976, against the social and educational nostrums which in the meantime had reshaped Western adolescence: uncompetitive schooling, rod-sparing discipline, and cheap contraception.

Mead had certainly been an advocate of and lobbyist for these innovations, though the implication that her scholarly work helped to lubricate their flow, rather than reflecting a permissive *zeitgeist*, may have been exaggerated. She was accused of falsifying evidence, projecting a spinster's frustrated fantasies onto her interviewees, and importing into Samoa the hang-ups and hedonism of twenties America. The status of her reputation is still a matter of doubt. Her story shows how cultural relativism drags moral relativism in its wake. If what is wrong for one society can be right for another, then what is wrong for one generation can be right for the next. If Western educationists could learn from the wisdom of Samoan adolescents, what right or hope had the white masters of dying nineteenth-century empires? In a world without barbarians and "savages," where the differences between "primitive cultures" and "advanced civilizations" were reformulated, in value-free language, as "elementary and complex structures," no such empire could survive. Where all peoples had their collateral share of earthly bliss, invidious distinctions withered. (Fernandez-Armesto 1995:485)

Supplement: A Note on the Critique of Benedict's *Chrysanthemum and the Sword* by Japanese Scholars[2]

Benedict's War Department-sponsored book was a tour de force: no one had ever attempted to reduce a great national society to a single cultural expression—and above all, to do it without a single visit to the country concerned. The book was brought to Japan early in the Occupation—it was part of the baggage of nearly every Occupationaire, including mine—and was translated and published by 1948—by 1952 it had gone through eight editions. And this occurred during a period of intense national self-examination and social reform, and the fact that the book had been written by an American—one of the Occupiers who "democratized" Japan—made it all the more intriguing. When I came back to Ohio State University in 1952, after a turn in the Occupation, I found a Japanese education research student who had been recruited by an Ohio State professor while consulting in Japan in 1949. This was Michio Nagai, who later received his doctorate at Ohio State in educational philosophy and who eventually wound up as a

---

[2]This is my 1996 summary of the article by J. W. Bennett and M. Nagai, "Echoes: Reactions to American Anthropology: The Japanese Critique of Benedict's *Chrysanthemum and the Sword*," *American Anthropologist*, vol. 55, pp. 404-11 (1953).

Minister of Education in a 1960s national government and an editor and writer for the *Asahi Shimbun* (Japan's equivalent of the *New York Times*). Michio and I translated a series of scholarly appraisals of the Benedict book. Only one of the fifteen writers we found was a professional anthropologist—the remainder were sociologists, philosophers, or scholarly pundits. The lone anthropologist was Prof. Kunio Yanagida, sometimes called the "Boas of Japanese anthropology," and whose career included the writing of essays rather resembling the subjective culture-patternist work of Benedict, but dealing with indigenous Japanese traditions.

While all of the fifteen commentators found highly favorable aspects in the book, most had some criticisms as well; and one of the fifteen was quite negative. The favorable criticisms centered on features of the book which reminded the Japanese of their methodological shortcomings due to the long period of militarist isolation, when social science was more or less taboo in Japanese universities. Many of the features of Benedict's operation in the War Department which produced the book, methods of which were taken for granted by Americans, were seen by the Japanese as novel and needed; e.g., collective ownership of data in team projects; rational planning of research; coding and filing of data; and the development of a common conceptual language. (Our division in the Occupation had as one of its missions training Japanese social scientists in such methods). The most favorably received aspect of Benedict's book was its theoretical approach (although there were, as we shall see, some criticism of this as well). This mainly concerned Benedict's desire to find in Japanese culture a central principle or a relational value system; then to construct a conceptual terminology from this; finally, to apply the concepts to further interpretations of Japanese behavior and ideas. This approach, known, of course, as the configurationist school in American anthropology, was also a vaguely defined goal in traditional Japanese folklore and humanistic studies. It was something of a shock to find that this approach had been highly developed by the rational, materialistic Americans!

The criticisms centered on many of the same issues that American critics of the configurationist-patternist approach were concerned about. Most of these criticisms were pronounced by Japanese social scientists who had managed to "catch up" with modern trends during the Occupation period (some of these were people who had received our training and advice in our Public Opinion and Sociological Research Division). For example, one critic was concerned over the ambiguity of Benedict's conception of "Japanese culture" or "the Japanese." In other words, in direct contradiction to humanistic Japanese commentators who approved such holistic ambiguity, the critics condemned it as vague and misleading. One critic felt that Benedict, without being aware, had really focussed on the fascist-militarist, ex-samurai class, residues of which still believed in these "feudal" patterns of social relationships. However, a social psychologist, Hiroshi Minami, felt that the concept of "Japan" or "Japaneseness" in Benedict's book was really an ideal type and referred to no particular class or group. This critic also echoed certain American criticisms (usually from sociologists) of Benedict's work as challenging but also methodologically tricky.

Criticisms were voiced about the ambiguity of the concept of culture—as used by Benedict and in American anthropology generally. The sociologists in the panel of commentators were critical of the holistic conception of national culture when, in fact, the Japanese were divided into various classes and groups, like any urban-industrial society. Other criticisms centered on the tendency in Benedict to use "culture" as a causal concept, implying that it determined behavior. Professor Kunio Yanagida—the anthropologist whose work probably most closely resembled Benedict's, was concerned that there was an implication in the book that the "culture patterns" perceived by Benedict seemed to be "permanently attached to a nation or a race," and were not modified by time or social change.

Others were quite critical about the way Benedict used her data. Some felt she should have treated the data statistically, since there was no indication in the book of the frequency with which certain behaviors or ideas actually occurred in Japanese social life. Perhaps the most vociferous criticism of her use of data—mostly obtained in interviews with older Japanese living in the United States—was that she really had listened to propaganda emanating from reactionary Japanese and accepted it as truth. Such criticism came, of course, from "democratized" Japanese scholars.

Finally, there was criticism of Benedict's use of child-rearing data as a device for explaining the form of certain adult behavior patterns or cultural patterns in general. These criticisms, as with the others, were similar to those voiced by American social scientists who distrusted patternist methodology even while admiring the imagination that so often lay behind it.

Several of the critics, like Takekoshi Kawashima, a distinguished sociologist of law, recommended alternative approaches. Most would support a series of studies using some of Benedict's findings as hypotheses, but examining the extent to which these were manifest in different institutions and social groups. Attitude surveys were mentioned as an ideal approach (and it is interesting to note that shortly after these criticisms were written, several Japanese attitude survey institutes did collaborate on a series of national-sample surveys to do exactly this—surveys which have continued to be run in subsequent decades—making Japan, as of the 1990s, probably the best monitored national culture on earth).

Others spoke for studies of particular features like the family, in light of the fact that such features showed different amounts of modernization or change. The family, in particular, had probably changed less than other aspects of social life, according to one of the critics, and was therefore probably more responsible for some of the traditional, "feudal" patterns spotted by Benedict than other things. In other words, Benedict's findings were a pastiche of behavior patterns with different temporal significance—but with all of them undergoing change in the "new Japan."

Literature Cited in the Essay and the Supplement

Bateson, Gregory and Margaret Mead. 1942. *Balinese Character: A Photographic Analysis*. New York: Publications of the New York Academy Science, vol. 2.

Benedict, Ruth. 1928. "Psychological Types in the Culture of the Southwest." Proceedings of the Twenty-third International Congress of Americanists: 572–81.

———. 1934. *Patterns of Culture*. Boston: Houghton-Mifflin.

———. 1946. *Chrysanthemum and the Sword*. Boston: Houghton-Mifflin.

Bennett, John W. and Herbert Passin. 1943. "Social Process and Dietary Change" in *The Problem of Changing Food Habits*, edited by M. Mead. National Reseach Council bulletin 108, Washington, DC.

Caffrey, Margaret M. 1989. *Ruth Benedict: Stranger in This Land*. Austin, TX: University of Texas Press.Fernandez-Armesto, Filipe. 1995. *Millennium*. London: Bantam Press.

Freeman, Derek. 1983. *Margaret Mead and Samoa: The Making and Unmaking of an Anthropological Myth*. Cambridge, MA: Harvard University Press.

Goldenweiser, Alexander A. 1937. "Review of Benedict's *Patterns of Culture*." *American Sociological Review* 2: 802–4.

Howard, Jane. 1984. *Margaret Mead: A Life*. New York: Simon and Schuster.

Kroeber, A. L. 1935. "Review of Benedict's *Patterns of Culture.*" *American Anthropologist* 37: 689–90.
Mead, Margaret. 1928. *Coming of Age in Samoa: A Psychological Study of Primitive Youth for Western Civilisation.* New York: W. Morrow.
———. 1964. *Continuities in Cultural Evolution.* New Haven, CT: Yale University Press.

14

Populist Anthropology: Robert Lowie, Marvin Harris, and Clyde Kluckhohn

Introduction

This essay is based on the assumption that the way anthropologists present themselves and their knowledge to the reading public can tell us something about the intellectual foundation of their discipline. I have selected three works covering a period from early Classic to post-Classic eras: Robert Lowie's *Are We Civilized?* (1929), Clyde Kluckhohn's *Mirror for Man* (1949), and Marvin Harris's *Our Kind* (1989). However, I shall not discuss them in strict chronological order. I will compare the Lowie and Harris books first, then present Kluckhohn's volume as a "mirror" for the first two. Other books of similar nature will be discussed in context.[1]

Books on anthropology designed to inform and entertain the public (or at least the better educated segment) are nothing new, although the strict disciplinary venue of such works dates from the last quarter of the nineteenth century. During that period, the discipline—mainly inspired by the intense popular interest in Darwinian ideas—developed confidence in the educative potential of the converging fields of anthropology. This faith in the social value of the discipline and its knowledge leads me to use the term "populist" rather than "popular." For a moment or two I toyed with a neologism, *poparist*, but discarded it because it seemed to refer to Vatican personnel. However, readers are welcome to use it without charge.

Written in 1995–96 for this volume.

I am convinced that populist tracts have had considerable influence in and outside of the discipline. I know that in my own case I was drawn into anthropology—or at least archaeology—by my reading of Robert J. Casey's *Four Faces of Siva*, a 1929 work of ethnological travel-journalism dealing with Angkor Wat and the Khmer Civilization. There is a fine line between a thoroughgoing populist book and standard texts or monographic volumes. A. L. Kroeber's *Anthropology* (1923) was designed as a college textbook, but it was read by many laymen since it contained the only full-dress account of all the fields of knowledge in the general discipline. It was the first encyclopedic textbook—the ancestor of such works as Herskovits (1948) or Beals and Hoijer (1953).

Herodotus's *Historiae* (1987) is usually taken as the earliest populist literature on human culture, a work consisting mainly of anecdotes and narratives about the peoples and cultures of the ancient world, selected in order to present a contrast to the civilizations of the northern shore of the Mediterranean. Later, Pliny the Elder (1855–57) produced volumes of anecdotes and stories of curious customs, fabulous beasts, and human troglodytes. By the Renaissance, more serious scholarly descriptive accounts of foreign cultures began to appear, like Peter Martyr d'Anghera's resumes of travellers' and ship captains' reports on indigenous cultures (MacNutt 1912). These writings gradually developed into the scholarly ethnological compilations of the eighteenth and nineteenth centuries, done largely for classificatory interests, in order to illustrate the breadth and variety of human cultures and also to demonstrate historical change and progress. And in 1872, one Winwood Reade, a British writer and naturalist, published *The Martyrdom of Man*, which sounds like something from the Middle Ages but what is in reality a Herodotus-style account of culture history in the Old World, classified into the major categories of "religion," "war," "liberty," and "intellect"—in some ways a precursor of Lowie's *Are We Civilized?* The curious title was selected by Reade since the era was characterized by religious dogma and controversy, with public lectures and meetings on obscure doctrinal subjects. Since Reade wrote about the seamy side of human existence, he chose to present the theme in doctrinal language—"martyrdom" referred to the imprisoning of human creativity and intellect in marrow-minded dogma.

Franz Boas's *Anthropology and Modern Life* (appearing in 1928, a year before Lowie's book) dealt mainly with race prejudice and other ideological hang-ups of the age which anthropology had a professional stake in refuting. On the whole, however, the book was rather dull, and omitted much of the sprightly and unique data anthropology had to offer a curious reader—precisely the materials that Lowie (and Harris) provide.

Lowie's *Are We Civilized?*

Robert Lowie published *Are We Civilized?* in 1929 during the early Classic period when American anthropology and ethnology had a single main idea: *Culture*. The definition of Culture used by the disciplines consisted principally of the descriptive findings of ethnologists, and for U. S. anthropology, this meant Indian reservations or "tribes," as they were called in the ubiquitous "ethnographic present" rhetoric. The dimensions of the concept were based on a classification of artifacts and customs which were used to create tables of contents for ethnographic monographs and the catalogs and labels of museum exhibits.

In his chapter 1, Lowie describes his frame of reference and his basic objectives: to demonstrate that people share ". . . (the) comfortable delusion that our way of doing things is the only sensible . . . one . . . ." (Lowie 1929: 3). "Each group has somehow developed its peculiar style of thought and behavior and thrives on adding to its quips and cranks" (ibid.: 4). "Somehow" was probably an attempt at using colloquial language but it is significant that Classic era anthropology had no acceptable theory of the *origins* of culture, since they had no theory of human social behavior, other than the assertion that humans were better endowed mentally than the apes and had more "complex" behavior. There were vague ideas about how traits or patterns might emerge in the course of social interaction, but the basic problem was not emergence or origins—that smacked of "evolutionism" and that had been refuted by Franz Boas once and for all.

Lowie continues: ". . . all we have to do is place him (any human) in a new setting and he at once follows new rules" (ibid.: 4). Does he? Equally often he is miserable and refuses to adapt—especially if there are political values associated with the old ways. And of course Lowie's insouciance—the implication that people instantly adapt—is another giveaway concerning the absence of a coherent or sophisticated (even by 1920s psychological standards) theory of behavior. Lowie, and most of his early-Classic colleagues, felt that adaptation was possible and immediate because humans were rational beings—although, and paradoxically, anthropologists loved to emphasize nonrational elements in ethnographic cultures. However, their confidence in an ultimate human rationality was documented by the historical record of cultural transmission and acculturation, as, for example, exemplified in the remarkable spread of certain basic customs and artifacts among the groups of various origins who entered the Great Plains of North America (e.g.: the Sun Dance—see chapter 7). But there was little attempt to find out how this transmission worked: how learning took place at different speeds in different situations; why the opposite of learning new ways—resistance to them—was perhaps as common historically as the opposite (eventually this led to the interest in "acculturation"—a typical middle-Classic attempt at dealing with complex historical-change causational problems but still adhering to rather simplistic culture concepts (see Herskovits et al. 1938). Lowie did make some attempt to explain the transmission of cultural elements from the old to the young: "Of course there are scores of things chimpanzees hand down to their progeny, but it is by a different mechanism altogether" (Lowie 1929: 5). Altogether? I suppose Lowie was thinking of language here, but since much basic learning by human infants is done without language, perhaps the chimp methods are not so different, at least in the early months.

On page five he concludes with the definition: "Anything and everything a man thus acquires from his social group is called a part of its 'culture.'" Everything? How about ideas and habits of brief or passing duration? Does it include language? How about a borrowed item—when does it become part of the local culture, or is it ever a part, and in whose minds? Of course these questions were in Lowie's mind also, but probably he ignored them because he was writing a popular work. On the other hand, the academic anthropology of the period really had no good answers to such questions.

Lowie, like all of his colleagues, was preoccupied with the unity-diversity problem: while acknowledging the "universals," he asked, "Certainly the enormous variation of culture in time and space calls for some explanation" (p. 6). But he gives it none—other than to talk about invention and so on. But the real issue is the phrase, "enormous variation," since this implies Lowie's famous (or infamous) "shreds and patches" idea.[2] He was convinced that diversity and variation were the true marks of culture, but unlike Benedict, who emphasized the differences between "whole cultures," Lowie stressed individual traits and trait complexes. He said that the historical record presents us with "a thousand intriguing puzzles."

One of the main themes of all of the earlier populist tracts in anthropology was the refutation of the idea of superior and inferior human races—a refutation which had its equivocal side since anthropologists continued to hold to a classification of races which put the various types and subtypes in what could appear to be watertight categories. In Boas's 1928 "Modern Life" book, 59 out of the total 197 pages (I exclude the last chapter on "modern civilization" because it does not deal with anthropological knowledge directly) were devoted to race and racial types. The racial issue was the main thing (geographical determinism a somewhat distant second) that anthropologists had sufficient knowledge of, or at least convictions about, to make some definitive value judgements about public prejudices and beliefs about race. (So much for the "value-free science" of the Classic era!) Anyway, Lowie, on the other hand, deals with race in only one chapter out of nine, because he was primarily concerned not with "modern life" or "our kind," but with *Culture*. The book is, therefore, to quote the paper jacket blurb (which by some miracle has survived on my copy, which I bought as a senior in high school) "An Entertaining Anecdotal Book by a Famous Anthropologist."

Now, as to the anecdotes themselves: they are presented as factual and absolute—no qualifications, or hardly any. These anecdotes pertain to cultural forms and customs drawn from tribes, nations, or civilizations other than the Western. Lowie assumed that Western civilization was something comparable to a whole, integrated culture. The book contains no such concept as "Oriental civilization" or "Roman civilization," and anecdotal material drawn from earlier or non-Western civilizations are put on the same level with material drawn from the simplest tribal source. In other words, the anecdotes contain disparate cultural traits without regard for their developmental status or level of literacy. Culture is culture. There is no evidence that Lowie was implying that the non-Western materials were inferior or less rational than the Western. On the contrary, he was mainly concerned to show that all cultures and civilizations are composed of mixtures of traits at varying levels of rationality. For example, with reference to our individualistic way of eating: "Not so among the Hopi. Here everybody gathers around a big vessel and dips his wafer bread into the common pottage" (pp. 47–8). No information on whether an individual Hopi, eating at a local restaurant, did the same! But this is what you get when you view culture as a smorgasbord of traits: variation and diversity is the spice of human existence.

The chapter headings on the whole provide an index of the Classic era's conception of basic categories. Here they are, from chapter 5 through 22: food; food etiquette; fire and cooking; domestic animals and plants; housing; dress and fashion; crafts and industries; travel and transportation; sex and marriage; the family; clan and state; prestige and etiquette; education; writing; art; religion; hygiene and medicine; science. Actually this is a different, more detailed version of the 1920s "universal pattern," popularized in anthropology by Clark Wissler (1923). Such lists have been extensively criticized, but in fact they are useful, once you accept the fact that no one language—English or any other—can completely accurately render the universals in human behavior and experience. This is the grand unity-diversity thematic in Classic anthropology: Culture is diverse, but has a kind of unity—the commonality of categories—even if it is difficult to express it without creating problems of cultural or linguistic distortion of a complex reality.

Harris's *Our Kind*

While Marvin Harris uses the word "culture" often enough, he simply takes the concept for granted, in contrast to Lowie's presentation of culture as a thing, a discovery, a clue to the nature of the human species. Part of the first paragraph of Harris's preface reads: "And do you wonder as much as I what part of the human condition is in the genes and what part is in our cultural heritage . . . (Harris 1989: ix). No more specific statement about the nature of Culture occurs anywhere in the book, so far as I could see: no entry on "Culture, concept of" or the equivalent appears in the index. We might accept this as prima facie evidence that anthropologists, between 1929 and 1989, had completed their task of demonstrating the existence of Culture—or at least the validity of the concept. This saves Harris a lot of space, and he can devote it to culture content and low-level theory. And there is a lot of both in this book—far more than Lowie, and understandably so, considering the accumulation of knowledge in general anthropology since the 1920s.

Whereas Lowie had eighteen chapters of substantive material, Harris has no less than seventy-five, although most of these are very short, often echoes or continuations of each other. If we condense chapters more or less dealing with the same topic, we get fewer; for example, thirteen or so chapters dealing with aspects of food can be collapsed into about five. This proliferation of short chapters dealing with manifold topics is a reflection of Harris's personal style in part, but it is also *the consequence of the way Classic era anthropological dialog developed since the 1920s, as information began accumulating, and its interpretations became controversial.* For example, the chapter entitled "Game Wars" (chapters are not numbered) begins, "The problem of getting enough animal fats and proteins seems to be the underlying cause of the Yanomami's intense warfare and male supremacist complex" (ibid.: 310). And so on: the complex Yanomami controversy and other facets of the nutritional-diet-cultural patterns discussion with respect to various tribal groups is presented in a series of chapters, the titles of which define the issues: e.g., "Knapper, Butcher, Scavenger, Hunter"; "Primitive Languages?"; "Meat, Nuts, and Cannibals"; and "Are Men More Aggressive than Women?"

That is, in the 1920s cultural accumulation was expressed in terms of single traits or complexes treated as integral units, but by the 1970s the emphasis had shifted toward the attempt to find causal links between phenomena. However, the same descriptive-comparative methodology prevailed: by examining the situation in Tribe A, or possibly also Tribe B, it would be possible to achieve a general theoretical proposition about the human condition. To some anthropologists this was futile since each case is one of response to particular situations, and hence contextual diversity is endless. The effort was especially questionable since there was no agreement among anthropologists on the numerical significance of the evidence: precisely how many instances of the same case would be needed to establish a generalization? Anthropologists then and now rarely ask the question, partly because no one knows how to find the number, and partly because everyone knows that it is basically a matter of situational variation. Intellectual difficulties traceable to the linear-causal method of scientific generalization have always been apparent and recently criticized in anthropology, but never really resolved. In this sense, Lowie and Harris have much in common despite the differences in outlook and databases.

Harris's well-known "cultural materialism" (Harris 1979) suffuses the book, of course, and this is a bias he acknowledges and defends. And it does create an old-fashioned flavor to his writing. For example: "I propose, in brief, that bands and villages make war because they find themselves in competition for resources such as soils, forests, and game upon which their food supply depends" (Harris 1989: 296). This sweeping generalization may apply to some cases, but not the numerous other instances in which war between local groups is a kind of recurrent ritual combat; or other cases in which it is "political," that is, the rivalry between "big men;" and so on. Even if the generalization could be found to encompass a majority of cases, it simply cannot explain them all. The rhetoric: "I propose that so-and-so make war *because* . . ."—is the root of the problem. This kind of linear explanation was a specialty of the nineteenth century pre-Classic era anthropologists, and which Boas and his students attacked—with mixed success, since the logic continued to appear in their own ethnological writings. If Harris had said, "Some groups make war because . . . and others, because . . . ." He would have been on safer ground. However, in other passages Harris takes the idea of situational variability as a key to both diversity and unity. In one of his mini-chapters entitled "Was There Life Before Chiefs?" he argues that the simplicity of power hierarchies and leadership systems in tribal entities was due largely to the small populations, "so that the bonding of reciprocal exchange could hold people together" (ibid.: 344). Here the causal sequence is complex: the phenomenon—simple power structure—is caused by small population, which in turn creates "reciprocal exchange bonding." That is, in the presence of two factors—small population and reciprocal exchange—power structures tend to be simple. Although one might argue that there are missing variables which appear in many instances: for example, *paranoia*, which released in a small group, can result in various forms of projected hostility, and thence to complex and rigorous authoritarian controls. But this type of processual, multi-factorial analysis is not Harris's style—and of course it was not Lowie's either. The difference is that anthropology by Harris's time of writing had progressed to the point where such analysis was *necessary*, whereas Lowie need not have been concerned with it. And to do him justice, Harris *is* aware of it, and uses it occasionally, but in the main he sticks to an old-fashioned, classic, limited-factor approach. Is this the effect of attempting to write a "popular" book? Or is it simply Harris's inimitable style? Was it in 1989 early Classic anthropology's last hurrah?

Actually on closer inspection Harris seems to be shooting at a particular issue: the tendency to assume that a dominant or statistically prevalent form of social behavior is inherent, "natural," and therefore universal. For example, ". . . let me hear no more of our kind's natural necessity to form hierarchical groups . . ." (ibid.: 35). This is followed by a statement which notes that if we had observed human existence in, say, the Paleolithic, the "natural" tendency of the species would have been diagnosed as egalitarian. When Harris wrote *Our Kind*, ethological generalization was in the news, and its refutation by sociocultural anthropologists was *de rigueur*. Possibly so—but Harris slips into the single-factor explanation mode himself from time to time.

Harris's tendency to replicate some of the intellectual methods of the nineteenth century anthropologists in his desire to achieve large-scale, attractive generalizations is also echoed in his desire to return anthropology to the level of generalizing historical science: "Rather than produce endlessly diverging varieties of cultures, cultural evolution has resulted in massive parallel and convergent trends" (ibid.: 494). Now, the "endlessly diverging" bit is of course aimed at Classic era anthropologists who emphasized cultural differences in their effort to counter the claims and methods of the evolutionary anthropologists. Leslie White, a late-Classic figure with early-Classic and pre-Classic instincts, attempted to revive the evolutionary mode of thinking—which was to find sweeping historical generalizations in the belief that culture is basically a natural phenomenon with scientific regularities (White 1945). Harris, like White, had a strong materialistic or "neo-Marxist" bent, and therefore shared a view of history as a lawful, regular process.

But of course the evolutionists continually stumbled over the persistent disorder and variability of the historical record. Their search for *invariant* processes was doomed to ambiguity and few of them had a clear conception of statistical probability, stochastic progression, or chaotic regularity, where recurrent or mutually influential phenomena are so hidden within long-cyclical or permutational multiple factors that only computerized analysis can crack the pattern. This is what Culture is all about—yes, there are some recurrent regularities, but their recurrence may be limited to a very few cases; or, the similarity between cases may be largely a matter of linguistic rhetoric. Culture is like weather: the same phenomena keep recurring, but the order of appearances and the relationships of one to another is extremely difficult to predict or explain (the nature of human behavior!).

So, Lowie divided his book into grand cultural categories filled with anecdotes, and Harris divided his into boiled-down versions of controversies. Presumably post-Classic anthropologists no longer consider all cultures to be divided into grand topics of religion, food, or education, because such terms are derived from our civilization and therefore may misrepresent the meanings and uses of particular phenomena. Lowie had a *single* chapter, "Religion"; Harris deals with the topic in no less than thirteen of his mini-chapters, and has *no* general chapter on "religion." The term "religion" appears in the titles of three of the minis: "Why We Became Religious," "Killing Religions," "Nonkilling Religions" (twice), and there is also a chapter on "Beliefs and Disbeliefs." There is no doubt that Harris assumes the existence of things called "belief" and "religion," but he breaks them up into analytical contexts. Lowie has no formal definition of religion, but on the first page of the chapter he says that "What the savage prizes as sacred is the *supernatural power* linked with the inanimate object" (ibid.: 214), and the rest of the chapter makes it clear that this is his baseline definition of religion. His effort is to show (1) that our "civilized religion" is on a different level than the primitive, and that ours is also based on a "moral principle" rather than magic, power, and so forth, but (2) in line with his book title, he also provides examples of the "primitive" forms of religion occurring in our "civilization"; for instance, good luck charms, rural witchcraft, and spirits of all kinds. Harris's chapters on other topics are full of segmental items of religious or magical practice, in contexts like chiefdom, food, political power, reproductive control, and so on.

What has been lost or gained in the progression from Lowie to Harris on, say, the "religion" issue? Information, without doubt, has been gained on the various functions of "religious" practices in human societies. Both Lowie and Harris possess a general category of "Religion," though Harris avoids saying so. In other words, the accumulation of information has not eliminated the category—merely made its definition indirect. The reader of Harris seeking a formal concept or definition of religion will be disappointed. While the Lowie chapter is weak on the multifarious roles "religion" plays in human society, it does give the reader a useful general definition. Therefore Lowie wins the argument, if the populist anthropologist is supposed to educate readers in the general similarities among symbolic conceptions of reality in human societies. But both writers fail to offer a useful theory of similarities and differences. Functional explanations didn't really exist for Lowie; Harris was more or less hostile to them.

One fault or error in both approaches is the inability or failure to use a concept of *adaptive behavior*. Harris tries to avoid adaptation because, as he announced in an early paper (1960) it is really a form of functional analysis, and Harris distrusted functionalism. So out went the baby with the bathwater. Lowie could have used adaptation and deepened his explanation of the analogies and similarities in "primitive" and "civilized" cultures. Harris could have deepened *his* analysis by using adaptation and functional explanations where they are relevant. He tends to do so anyway in his exposition of controversial issues, but he avoids use of the terminology. Harris's index has just one entry to "adaptation," referring to human biological adaptation to climate; "functional" has no entry.

Kluckhohn's *Mirror for Man*

Now: how does Kluckhohn's 1949 book compare to the Lowie and Harris books? It is shorter, containing only ten chapters. The first six chapters cover Queer Customs, Potsherds, Skulls, Race, Gift of Tongues, Anthropologists at Work, an eighth chapter entitled "Personality in Culture—The Individual and the Group," plus two chapters on anthropology and modern life. The culture/personality chapter covers a topic barely alluded to by Lowie, since the personality-and-culture subdivision of anthropology did not exist for him (although there existed a forerunner, Brinton's 1902 book on the application of Kraepelin's psychiatric concepts to ethnology—but it is doubtful if Lowie had seen it). Harris, likewise, omits culture/personality because by the 1980s it had largely been absorbed by other approaches, or assimilated as empirical generalizations in some of the controversies he explores. Moreover there is an "applied" note running through the entire Kluckhohn volume which is absent in Lowie and underplayed in Harris: and signalled in Kluckhohn's subtitle "The Relation of Anthropology to Modern Life." Kluckhohn's view of the discipline is fundamentally different from Lowie's conception of anthropology as an independent discipline, gathering information about the human species. Kluckhohn viewed anthropology as one social science among several, and above all, a field intimately concerned with the real world: that is, his first sentence reads: "Anthropology provides a scientific basis for dealing with the crucial dilemmas of the world today: how can peoples of different appearance, mutually unintelligible languages, and dissimilar ways of life get along peaceably together" (Kluckhohn 1949: 1). The implication is that to do so is difficult, and on the basis of what has happened since 1949, Kluckhohn's implied pessimism is relevant. Of the three books, only Kluckhohn's was committed to relevant endeavor—suggesting that for him the only real justification for anthropology was its ability to make contributions to the human condition.

Lowie believed that culture is the distinctive human trait and its manifestations vary, but all are more or less equally effective in providing a guide for survival for their human bearers. Therefore, "civilization" is to some extent a myth, and no manifestation of culture should be considered to be "higher" or "lower" than another. Harris has one theme: his pet theoretical bias of "materialism," which appears to mean that the central issue in human existence is the search for subsistence and gratification. Kluckhohn's central thesis is ideological:

> . . . anthropology . . . has explored the gamut of human variability and can best answer the questions: what common ground is there between human beings of all tribes and nations? What differences exist? what is their source? how deep-going are they? (ibid.: 2)

Perhaps this is not really so different from Lowie's objective, and while Kluckhohn's data is far superior to Lowie's, and his sophisticated social science approach transcends Lowie's enthusiastic descriptive naïveté, the two books on this issue are closer than either is to the Harris volume.)

That means also that Kluckhohn is constantly preoccupied with a sociology-of-knowledge question: how does anthropology come to know these things?" For example, with regard to archaeological method:

> By extending in time as well as in space the comparisons that can be made as to how different peoples have solved or failed to solve their problems, the chances for testing scientifically certain theories about human nature and the course of human progress is much improved. (ibid.: 51)

Or, in the chapter on "tongues,"

Because anthropological linguists have usually been trained as ethnologists and have often done general field work, they have tended less than other students of language to isolate speech from the total life of the people. (ibid.: 148)

The reader thus is not simply fed information—as he is in the Harris compendium—but is told how the information has been assembled. This, of course, reflects the growing self-consciousness of anthropology as a discipline—a marked characteristic of the late Classic era.

While Lowie's book is dominated by a notion of Culture as a universal phenomenon which determines the behavior of humans; and Harris simply ignores Culture as a concept, perhaps taking it for granted and so not bothering to define it—the Kluckhohn book devotes major space to a discussion of Culture, viewing it as not only anthropology's innermost concept, but also as the discipline's distinctive contribution to our understanding of the human species. Kluckhohn stood on the threshold of a more worldly and sophisticated anthropological social science; still, he possessed the heritage of the early-Classic depictive tradition as, on the whole, represented by Lowie.

Thus, instead of using such terms as "culture traits"—assimilating behavioral content into the culturalogical abstraction—Kluckhohn's primary reference points were behavioral, social, or environmental:

> Only when we find out just how men who have had different upbringings, who come from different physical stocks, who speak different languages, who live under different physical conditions, meet their problems, can we be sure as to what all human beings have in common? (ibid.: 9)

> Nonliterate societies represent the end results of many different experiments carried out by nature. (ibid.: 15)

> . . . culture is not a disembodied force. It is created and transmitted by people. (ibid.: 22)

But a tendency toward reification remains:

> Culture produces needs as well as provides a means of fulfilling them. (ibid.: 26)

Kluckhohn also viewed Culture as a largely descriptive term, and in this mode he considers that "patterning" is the key to the scientific analysis of culture. That is, regularity or habituated behavior is the essence of the problem, and therefore it is "possible to predict a good many actions of any person who shares that culture" (ibid.: 38). This is typical late-Classic anthropology—having one's Culture cake, but also diminishing its phenomenology.

However, the entire discussion is pointed toward practical and ideological matters:

> If we understand our own culture and that of others, the political climate can be changed in a surprisingly short time in this narrow contemporary world providing men are wise enough and articulate enough and energetic enough. (ibid.: 44)

This was written just after World War II, in the ideological climate that produced the United Nations and other postwar innovations. It was an era of hope and optimism: that knowledge of and contacts between cultures and nations would produce tolerance and understanding. This was an era of cultural mixing: movement across international boundaries by countless refugees, college students, and travelers. Kluckhohn viewed anthropology as an indispensable aid in understanding these movements and their consequences—the same enthusiasm and confidence in anthropology manifested in Ralph Linton's 1945 venture, *The Science of Man in the World Crisis*. And like Linton, Kluckhohn freely acknowledged that anthropology, while possessing a key concept for the task, cannot do it alone—"Present day anthropology, then, cannot pretend to be the whole study of man . . ." (ibid.: 1). And thus Kluckhohn's book is transitional in another sense: its writer was to a considerable extent the first interdisciplinary anthropologist—and certainly one who sought to coax the discipline out of its preoccupation with tribal people (ibid.: 9). Lowie's book presents anthropology as a form of entertainment and education for the public; Harris sees it as a series of intellectual puzzles; but Kluckhohn was concerned with an inquiry into the nature of the human species and its destiny. Kluckhohn was, after all, one of the founders of applied anthropology, although he always worried about the ethical aspects of intervention.

Lowie, Harris, and Kluckhohn on the Modern Human Condition

I mentioned earlier that whatever their theoretical views, each of the three populist writers concluded his book with a relatively pessimistic statement on the state of human society.

Lowie ends his with two chapters, entitled "Science" and "Progress."

The first of these is quite remarkable—a foretaste of Thomas Kuhn's *The Structure of Scientific Revolutions* (1962) insofar as Lowie states flatly that "science is a part of culture" (Lowie 1929: 270), and then proceeds to demonstrate how scientists have repeatedly reflected the biases of their time in selecting or rejecting topics for research, or succumbing to the cultural and even racial prejudices of the period:

> The intellectual caliber of scientists was put to test by the European war [i.e., World War I]. As a class they failed miserably. The same men who had prated fervently at international congresses about the cosmopolitanism of science turned jingoes with the declaration of war. (ibid.: 278)

The chapter includes excoriating passages concerning such events as Galton's use of heredity as a way of analyzing superiority and inferiority; Italian professors who refused to check Galileo's findings for fear of offending the Church; and British and French physicists who derided their German colleagues in spite of their knowledge of the triumphs of German science. The language of this chapter reveals intense feeling, and it is not hard to imagine why: Lowie was in many ways German to the core—yet he was also a liberal American scholar, and perhaps this chapter was his way of defending his German heritage against the extreme jingoism of World War I Imperial Germany, and U.S. postwar jingoism. He also had hopes of making money with a popular work (as he tells us in a passage from his autobiography[3]). So there were undoubtedly personal issues at stake, aside from his desire to show that scientists were as biased as any other culture bearer—which of course means they were nonrational at least part of the time. And this, of course, appears to contradict the implied idea of culture as a rational construct.

His chapter on "Progress" opens with these sentences:

> Is the long-distance view of civilization depressing? Well, what could be expected? Life is grim. The savage who believes in sinister forces lowering on every side expresses everyday experience more accurately than the philosophers of optimism. (ibid.: 291)

Since "culture is a part of reality" it mirrors the grimmer side of human existence: "A German scientist aptly said that man developed when conditions were ripe for his being, but *before* the conditions for his *well*-being." So "human societies can exist with a minimum of rational adaptation." And, "As if Life were not an inexhaustible source of ills, man gratuitously adds to the load" (all quotes, ibid.: 291). So Lowie's search for the answer to his question, *Are We Civilized?*, is essentially—to paraphrase—no more than any savage. In fact, he concludes "We are still savages. But the word loses its sting when we recall what savages have achieved" (ibid.: 294). In other words, humans manifest similar abilities and triumphs at all levels of cultural development—and the good and bad is mixed in all cultures. The outlook for Man is not encouraging but it is not all bad—and anthropology can help us decide. Because of all the social disciplines, it thinks in spans of thousands of years, and so there is time for improvement.

Harris's views (as stated in two very brief closing pieces) are not really dissimilar, but obviously they reflect a different time and place: World War II; the cold war; plus refugees, nationalist revolutions, and environmental disasters. Harris, like Lowie, is aware of the nonrational nature of human activities and outcomes—"unconscious form of consciousness" he calls it (Harris 1989: 495), meaning by this that the final or decisive outcomes of human ventures often, or usually, differ from the objectives. He says, "The Twentieth century seems a veritable cornucopia of unintended, undesirable, and unanticipated changes" (ibid.: 495). (This is probably consistent with his materialistic views: humans seek gratification segmentally, and the consequences are rarely foreseen.)

Harris mentions the dangers of nuclear war; the predatory nature of the national state; the need for a way of "maintaining law and order on a global basis" (ibid.: 500); and the necessity of understanding the limits of natural resources. Who could disagree? But one wonders what most of the book really has to do with these noble and necessitous aims? Food habits, rituals, gender roles, genes, fossils, tribal subsistence, child rearing, and all the rest of the late-Classic or post-Classic inventory of favorite topics and whipping horses seem to have little to do with what Harris seems to feel are the really important issues. And much the same can be said of Lowie: he seems much more concerned about the fate of mankind than about the myriad customs anecdotalized in the book. Are anthropologists students of culture or of mankind? Do their understandings transcend their databases?

Now for Kluckhohn's views. In line with the general emphasis on practicality in the book as a whole, Kluckhohn gives us far more meat than either Lowie or Harris: two long chapters, one, "An Anthropologist Looks at the United States," and a final one, "An Anthropologist Looks at the World." The first of these is a contribution similar to Margaret Mead's *And Keep your Powder Dry* (1943): descriptive analysis of the major cultural patterns of American life and history. However, a critical note comes at the end, when Kluckhohn shows concern over the need for greater personal responsibility for the state of society, in order to avoid the collapse of democratic liberalism.[4] America gave the world the gift of freedom and a sociopolitical system that guarantees it, and while belief in this system is prevalent, such beliefs and confidence cannot be expected to continue indefinitely. For, as Kluckhohn the anthropologist points out, national moods and anxieties are by no means determined completely by Culture. Thus, his insights into the modern world in this case drive a basic critique of the Classic anthropological faith in cultural determination. There are loopholes in the determinist process: unanticipated things happen, people rebel against culture, freedom can lead to irresponsibility.

Kluckhohn's final chapter opens with some heretical remarks about applied anthropology:

> It is one thing to be able to make some useful predictions as to what is likely to happen . . . It is quite another thing to interfere, willfully to introduce new complications into an already tortuous social maze. (Kluckhohn 1949: 263)

Kluckhohn is generally supportive but skeptical of anthropology's ability to make sense of the larger world of history and politics and economics within which anthropologists are not really trained. "Present anthropology has recognizable limits. There is a wide gap between program and accomplishment" (ibid.: 264). But at the same time, anthropology does have insights into human thoughtways, and the need for "common purposes" (ibid.: 266). Anthropology is based on the notion that certain human experiences and behaviors are universal, and that the differences between peoples always need to be qualified by this awareness of commonality. While not all cultures may be equally palatable, respect and tolerance of these ways is necessary to keep the peace. Here Kluckhohn is once again articulating post-World War II intercultural optimism. One wonders what he might have said in the 1990s period when intercultural contact seemed to lead everywhere to hostility and confrontation.

He concludes the chapter with a plea for faith, for something like a new universal religion which is based on the true "absolutes" (ibid.: 282) found in human experience, rather than on the idiosyncratic images and symbols of a particular culture-bound faith. He visualized anthropology as playing a role in this effort to find a universal guidance system, and makes a plea (probably based on his work at the time in the Harvard Values Project) for a search for "absolute" values—although he seems to be skeptical of its outcome. More than absolutism, search should focus on attitudes of tolerance and acknowledgment of divergence in values. This, he feels is the anthropological message: "the world with all its variousness can still be one in its allegiance to the elementary common purpose shared by all peoples" (ibid.: 289). But surely Kluckhohn knew, as we certainly do now, that the "elementary common purposes" are defined differently by classes and cultures and religions, and that it is quite likely that in the last analysis, Culture is one name for divisiveness in human affairs—a process which cannot be terminated—only perennially confronted.

These arguments from the three books illustrate the perils of drawing conclusions about the larger human condition from historical perspectives of particular times. None of the three authors commented on the real roots of the human problem: our inability to control the basic biosocial forces which drive the species and its environmental adaptations. It is becoming more apparent daily that a growing, largely uncontrolled human population and an equally uncontrolled technology, are menaces not only to other species and to the Earth, but also to humanity. Kluckhohn comes closest: he recognizes the evils of excessive nationalism (and well he might, having lived through the era of fascism). And nationalism, combined with population increase, leads to expansion at the expense of others, to refugees, to ethnic cleansing, and to other horrors of our times. Harris noted environmental problems, predatory nationalism, and also the great threat of nuclear war, but is curiously silent on the biosocial forces leading toward overpopulation and ethnic hostilities. While Lowie lived too early to see these dangers, one suspects he would have, on the example of his passionate and despairing chapter on "Science." A Teutonic humanist, aware of the dark forces in German culture, Lowie was equipped intellectually to know the dangers lurking in the inability of *Homo sapiens* to control his desires and lusts.

Notes

1. Related aspects of the problem of popular appeal can be found in chapter 9, an earlier essay on ethnological method.
2. "To that planless hodge-podge, that thing of shreds and patches called civilization . . . " (Lowie 1947: 441). The quote originally appeared in the first, 1920 edition of *Primitive Society*, and reprinted without change in the 1947 edition. However, Lowie's preface to the 1947 edition also contains the following:

> The sentence in which civilization is called "that thing of shreds and patches" had no bearing on anthropological theory. It was written in a period of disillusionment after World War I, a sentiment very intelligible at the present moment. I was casting about for something derogatory to say about *our* [sic] civilization, and as an admirer of Gilbert and Sullivan naturally bethought myself of the phrase. . . . (pp. xi–x)

As we have noted, this same post-World War I disillusionment surfaces in the last chapters of *Are We Civilized?* Given his self confessed disillusion, perhaps the entire book can be interpreted as a disguised indictment of Western civilization as equivalent to primitive cultures.

3. Lowie has left us with a candid and informative account of the *Are We Civilized?* writing project which is worth reproducing *in toto*:

> *Are We Civilized?*—Since my experience at the American Museum of Natural History, which discharged me with a two years' notice, I intensely resented the idea of dependence on institutions. Before the depression set in, a number of writers had made money by writing popular books. I was confident of my ability to do likewise and once more felt the urge to appear as an *Aufklärer*. The result was *Are We Civilized?*, which Alfred Harcourt published in 1929. He was very enthusiastic about the manuscript, but for some reason lost all interest after publication, so that there was a minimum of advertising, and the sales remained relatively low. Incidently, the pessimism that disturbed some readers has since been amply justified by subsequent events in Europe. For years the book remained out of print. In 1937 a teacher in Hunter College, where it was used for collateral reading, persuaded Harcourt to reprint it in a cheap edition [the one JWB bought]. The first half year about one thousand copies were sold, but since then—with secondhand ones becoming available—the annual sales have dropped to half that figure. However, the book continues to sell in small quantities.
>
> A characteristic feature of the book—apart from its critique of the Nordic myth—is the critical attitude toward scientists themselves as subject to irrational impulses. As compared with my earlier writings, it shows a more intensive concern with the culture history of Europe. I utilized especially Alfred Franklin's volumes on France and T. F. Troels-Lund's work on Scandinavia. The style was certainly at the opposite pole from the ponderousness of *Primitive Society*. The reception of this book varied, especially among anthropologists. Boas, surprisingly, told me it was a very good book; Elsie Clews Parsons approved of this inculcation of the comparative method with modern examples; and several younger colleagues found the examples fresh and in part piquant. Berthold Laufer's review in the *American Anthropologist* was all I could have wished in my wildest dreams: "It is at once the production of mature scholar-

ship coupled with wide reading and keen thinking, and more than that—it is the book of a man of culture and a philosopher who has seen and observed much of life and who has his own ideas about men, things, and events. Besides, he is an eminent teacher, and he is amply endowed with the faculty which makes the real scholar, but which is growing rarer and rarer among modern scholars—the faculty of thinking objectively, without bias, without newspaper and mob psychology. . . . As an introduction into modern anthropological thought, as a guide into the workshop of a clear-minded and honest thinker, this book is excellent . . ."

However, A. M. Tozzer wrote me the book, although perhaps useful for "pepping up" introductory courses, was not equal to my previous books—as though its aim were at all comparable! Others, like Leslie Spier, thought it a waste of time to write such a book; and Radin was scornful on general principles, not being on particularly good terms with me at the moment.

In any case, the book did not put me in a more secure financial position, and altogether I doubt whether it netted me five hundred dollars over the expenses for typing. (Lowie 1959: 136–7)

4. Reminiscent of a major issue in Tocqueville's *Democracy in America*. See the analysis of Tocqueville's exposition in various editions of the book, in Jardin. (1988: 266–70)

Literature Cited

Beals, Ralph L. and Harry Hoijer. 1953. *An Introduction to Anthropology*. New York: Macmillan.

Boas, Franz. 1928. *Anthropology and Modern Life*. New York: W. W. Norton & Co.

Brinton, Daniel G. 1902. *The Basis of Social Relations: A Study in Ethnic Psychology*. New York: G.P. Putnam's Sons.

Casey, Robert J. 1929. *Four Faces of Siva: The Detective Story of a Vanished Race*. London: G.G. Harrap.

Harris, Marvin. 1960. "Adaptation in Biological and Cultural Science." *Transactions of the New York Academy of Sciences*, series 2, 23(1): 59–65.

———. 1979. *Cultural Materialism: The Struggle for a Science of Culture*. New York: Random House.

———. 1989. *Our Kind*. New York: Harper & Row.

Herodotus. 1987. *Historiae*. Leipzig: Teubner.

Herskovits, Melville J. 1948. *Man and His Works: The Science of Cultural Anthropology*. New York: Alfred A. Knopf.

Herskovits, Melville J., et al. 1938. *Acculturation: The Study of Culture Contact*. New York: J.J. Augustin.

Jardin, André. 1988. *Tocqueville: A Biography*. New York: Farrar, Straus and Giroux.

Kluckhohn, Clyde. 1949. *Mirror for Man*. New York: McGraw-Hill.

Kroeber, A. L. 1923. *Anthropology*. New York: Harcourt, Brace & Co.

Kuhn, Thomas S. 1962. *The Structure of Scientific Revolutions*. Chicago: University of Chicago Press.

Linton, Ralph. 1945. *The Science of Man in the World Crisis*. New York: Columbia University Press.

Lowie, Robert H. 1929. *Are We Civilized?* New York: Harcourt, Brace & Co.

———. [1920]1947. *Primitive Society*. 2d ed. New York: Liveright Publishing.

———. 1959. *Robert H. Lowie, Ethnologist: A Personal Record.* Berkeley: University of California Press.

MacNutt, Francis Augustus. 1912. *De Orbe Novo: The Eight Decades of Peter Martyr d'Anghera.* Translated from the Latin with notes and introduction, 2 vols. New York: G.P. Putnam's Sons.

Mead, Margaret. 1943. *And Keep Your Powder Dry.* New York: William Morrow & Co.

Pliny, the Elder. 1855–57. *The Natural History of Pliny.* London: H.G. Bohn.

Reade, William Winwood. [1872]1968. *The Martyrdom of Man.* Reprinted with an introduction by Michael Foot. London: Pemberton, in association with Barrie & Rockliff.

White, Leslie A. 1945. "History, Evolutionism, and Functionalism: Three Types of Interpretation of Culture." *Southwestern Journal of Anthropology* 1.

Wissler, Clark. 1923. "The Universal Pattern," chapter 5 in *Man and Culture*, by C. Wissler, pp. 73–98. New York: Thomas Y. Crowell.

15

Epilogue: A Philosophical Voice at the End of the Classic Era: Pierre Teilhard de Chardin

Introduction

Anthropology lies among and between the social sciences, biology, aesthetics, historical studies, and philosophy. But while anthropologists may identify with one or more of these fields, they never quite fully affiliate with any one. This uncertainty accounts for triumphs as well as failures. For cultural anthropology the former are best represented by the descriptive ethnology of tribal peoples: the latter in the attempt to substitute the concept of culture for a philosophical or synoptic view of Humanity and its role on Earth.

I have emphasized the relativism, pluralism, secularism, and moral ambiguity of Classic anthropology, and the consequent unwillingness to engage in predictions or treatises on the Nature of Man. Considering the breadth of interests in the discipline, and its desire to see humanity whole—the scientific "study of Man"—one can understand the relativism and secularism, and since the discipline of philosophy until recently was devoted to a search for Truth or the Nature of Reality, it bordered on religion and morality. Thus, anthropology fell into the crack between its larger objective and its chosen methodology. However, the empirical ingredients for a cross-cultural philosophy of the human enterprise were present in ethnological treatises and various attempts at theorizing about culture as a common human phenomenon.

Consider the following passage from the very first paragraph of Julian Huxley's introduction to Père Teilhard de Chardin's classic work, *The Phenomenon of Man* (1955–59). Describing the general theme of the book, Huxley notes that the author achieves

> a threefold synthesis—of the material and physical world with the world of mind and spirit; of the past with the future; and of variety with unity, the many with the one. He achieves this by examining every fact and every subject of his investigation *sub specie evolutionis*, with reference to its development in time and to its evolutionary position. Conversely, his is able to envisage the whole of knowable reality not as a static mechanism but as a process. In consequence, he is driven to search for human significance in relation to . . . that . . . process. (Huxley 1959: II)

This paragraph also seems to describe the aims and objectives, and to some extent, the generalized findings, of Classic anthropology in all its subdivisions: archaeology, paleontology, culturology, language, the study of religion, and so on. Yet the Classic anthropological effort was professionally devoid of philosophical meaning or at least formal synthesis. It fell to others, either on the margins of anthropology, like Père Teilhard—or members of other disciplines like psychology or history, who extracted meaning from anthropological data. David Bidney, a trained philosopher, undertook to examine the concept of culture and its associated concerns under the label, "theoretical anthropology" (1953): "theory" in this case implying pure ratiocination based on the findings of the discipline. But this sort of speculative anthropo-philosophy (or, as Bidney called it, "meta-anthropology") has a long history: there was the medieval Islamic philosopher Ibn Khaldun, and the Renaissance scholar Giambattista Vico, both of whom could be considered anthropological philosophers. Immanuel Kant wrote *Anthropology from a Pragmatic Perspective* (1798); and Alexander Pope, in his long poetic disquisition, *An Essay on Man* (various editions) used anthropological along with literary and historical material to philosophize about the moral behavior and social nature of humanity. In our time, an American literary analyst, Roy Harvey Pearce, published *Savagism and Civilization* (1988, rev. ed.), a more or less philosophical commentary on the intersection of European civilization and American Indian tribal peoples. Novelists working with ethnological themes have often emphasized the moral ambiguity of colonialism and ethnology. There are other examples but all of them do not add up to a "school" or even a tradition. These writings had considerable moral content: the inconsistencies and contradictions of the good and the bad in human nature; and the unpredictability and multidimensional variety of human existence were seen as the source of irresolvable moral and ethical dilemmas and were viewed as appropriate topics for religious but not scientific discourse.

So, anthropology has certainly influenced the field of philosophical and literary commentary on human behavior and society, but has not made much of a disciplinary contribution, nor has it felt it should. In my undergraduate and graduate education in anthropology, not one reading list, and not one professor (not even Robert Redfield, who had more of a moral conscience than most Classic anthropologists) recommended reading any books in the brief list above and others like them. This was simply 'not anthropology.' And when in seminars someone read a term paper commenting on such meta-anthropological literature, it usually was with reference to whether the writer got his facts straight. We simply were not interested in the validity or moral rightness of the ideas.

Pierre Teilhard de Chardin's Contribution to the Cause

There is one significant modern anthropologically informed philosophical disquisition on the nature of humanity and that is Teilhard de Chardin's *The Phenomenon of Man* (1955–59)—a heavily criticized but nevertheless neglected work produced at the end of the Classic era. Teilhard defined the basic consequence of "Culture" (using the term for the moment as a descriptive, partially normative term for civilization or the increasing sophistication of humans as to the nature of the universe and human society). The consequence is anxiety: "the men of today are particularly uneasy, more so than at any other moment of history" (1955–59: 288). That is, the effects of Culture were not all good, and there was a price to pay for success: not only in the destruction of the physical environment, but in the nature of Man himself. Père Teilhard felt that increasing "complexity" introduces more problems than humans can solve, because the solution to one problem creates new ones (i.e., the negative side of "adaptation").

But Teilhard went beyond this complexity issue in pointing out that Man's understanding of the nature of evolution had introduced anxiety about the immensity of the universe: humans, isolated on their little world, face out into the universe with the frustration born of ignorance. Where is God, now that we have an inkling of the vastness and unlimited vacuity of space? But the anxiety of space is only part of the story: equally important is the uncertainty over the "suitable outcome," as Teilhard called it: will evolution prosper, and will Man benefit from it, or is it heading for disaster: a crowded and fractious planet with its despoiled resources, and the increasingly deadly competition for the residue?

And even more anxiety-producing is the possibility that thought itself can become the source of the fall of Man: that, as Teilhard put it, "the elements of the world should refuse to serve the world—because they think . . ." (ibid.: 230). Disgust, alienation, despair that the future is irredeemable and therefore possibly a refusal to keep the machine going. The dilemma is simply that while *thought*—the ability to anticipate the future and build toward it—is responsible for the human triumphs, it is also responsible for destructive impulses and outcomes. Therefore the human situation is a stand-off, forks in the road, and nothing to tell us which one to choose: back toward the pre-human past or forward with thought and "progress"? All this sounds like pop-philosophy, but the dilemmas are real, and create a crucial fork in the road for anthropology as well. Shall the discipline move toward philosophy and morality, or shall it continue the increasingly frustrating and ambiguous scientific "study of man"? The evolution of anthropology, like the evolution of Man, has brought us to this point. Anthropology helped to create history, and now history challenges the value and continuity of the discipline.

About half the pages in *The Phenomenon of Man* are devoted to topics which would normally appear in elementary or general textbooks of geology and anthropology, dealing with the history of the Earth and Life. These set the stage for Man, and with his appearance, cosmic or general evolution took a new turn. The nature of this turn is the great mystery:

> [Man is] the most mysterious and disconcerting of all the objects yet met by science. . . . anthropology in its turn does its best to explain the structure of the human body and some of its physiological mechanisms. But when these features are put together, the portrait manifestly falls short of the reality. (ibid.: 163)

This is Teilhard's basic position: that *there is something about humanity which science cannot determine or resolve*. Since Teilhard was a member of the Church, it is tempting to say that he is making a plea for the Spirit—something that God created within, for Man that no other living form possesses. And this interpretation of the passage is strengthened by a later chapter in which Christianity is singled out as something special in the general evolutionary process. However, a more general interpretation is simply that neither anthropology nor any other scientific field can really *explain* Man the way a zoologist or animal psychologist can explain felines and canines. Humans are genetically but a few small steps from the anthropoidea, yet they are also "completely different." Man's willfulness, his creativity, his constant remolding of the universe around him, simply defies simple explanation (unless, of course, some of the 1990s studies of the neural system and the brain begin to bear fruit). To my own mind, the great mystery is not *why* Man does these things, but what their ultimate consequences might be for the Earth and the Universe. These questions are, upon close reading of *The Phenomenon of Man*, the ones that Teilhard was ultimately concerned with. They are questions from the borderlands of science, religion, and philosophy. The issues are by no means new—Western medieval scholars were preoccupied by them, and in the great Oriental universal religions the questions of transcendence of the human species and its paradoxical consciousness was a central puzzle.

Anyway, Père Teilhard's favored answer to the question of human uniqueness is simply that the species possesses a capacity no other living form has—*reflection*: "the power acquired by a consciousness to turn in upon itself" (ibid.: 165). In slightly different terms, this is the process of *reflexivity*, which can also be viewed as the basic property of language and culture: Culture can define and change itself—although—I think Teilhard was right in casting the capacity in a psychological context. Of course, reflection is only half of the story: as I have argued elsewhere (Bennett 1976, reprinted 1993–96), *anticipation*—the ability to define a future state of affairs and then work toward its accomplishment—is the other half. But perhaps reflection *contains* anticipation, and certainly it can be argued that both are manifestations of something more basic—the ability to think linguistically: to find *names* for time, being, the self, the material world, and the immaterial, and then to reify these and use them in equations—and finally, to link them up—or discover their contradictions.

From this standpoint, Teilhard believed that Man is a kind of current culminating point in the evolution of Life. Evolution for him was a "primary psychical transformation"; that is, in this formulation, psychology would become the master science of change, and Man's role is to carry the development of consciousness and sequential, linguistic, reflexive thought further than any other organism. Stated this way, it would seem that there is no mystery—just a natural process. But this glib solution to the human situation did not satisfy Père Teilhard any more than it satisfies any inquiring mind. In the gap between a common sense explanation of the Human phenomenon like this one, and the questions one wants answered about Man, is where philosophy and religion dwell.

With Man, then, occurred a "change of state" (ibid.: 169)—not a simple quantitative shift or addition, but some kind of quantum jump: from the materialist standpoint, a jump created by an increase in quantity (the 1990s keyword would be neurons and their hookups). Père Teilhard acknowledged the duality of the explanations:

> Those who adopt the spiritual explanation are right when they defend vehemently a certain transcendence of Man over the rest of nature. But neither are the materialists wrong when they maintain that man is just one further term in a series of animal forms. (ibid.: 169)

This view has always been part of anthropology. Paraphrased, it would be something like this: human behavior is a simple quantitative extension of capacities found in the mammalian order, and especially among the Primates, and while the extension has major consequences, which can be interpreted by religious belief, we do not find it necessary to take that step. Anthropology, as a student of religion, is in no position to deny its importance—but its dilemma is its inability to accept religious-derived spiritual or metaphysical explanations of the phenomena of human culture.

Then comes Teilhard's key term: *hominization*. Or, in Classic anthropological terms: the evolution of culture. Here again we note that the phenomena that anthropology considers to be material changes or characteristics of culture, become, for Père Teilhard, major events in evolution; for instance, in a discussion of what the anthropologist would simply call cultural accumulation, Teilhard notes that ". . . *something* (even in the absence of any measurable variation of brain or cranium), irreversibly accumulates . . . and is transmitted . . . down the course of ages (ibid.: 178, emphasis original). This is another mystery: that change, accumulation, increasing complexity, can occur without any material or biological alteration in the species producing it. Or can it? Some of the new theories and research on the brain might suggest that accumulating knowledge does make a difference in the complexity of the neuronic linkages. But still Teilhard has a point, and one that anthropologists have probably not done enough thinking about. "Culture accumulates" we say _ but then we qualify the statement by saying "not always," or "selectively." But what is apparent is that this accumulation is a new phenomenon in Nature—Nature as we earthlings know it, at any rate.

But Teilhard's ideas also represent the limitations and shortcomings of a global philosophy of Man and culture. While the expansion of the noosphere, the increase of complexity, and the coming together of humans in a universal mind is certainly taking place, it has done so—especially in the years since Père Teilhard wrote his book, with *technology*: in particular, the technology of Marshall MacLuhan's global village: advanced electronic communication devices. The latest of these, the Internet, has as many possibilities for the extension of human evil as human good. In other words, the evolutionary process of mind that Teilhard and others perceived works not by some benevolent osmosis, but by the manipulations of people who control the machines, and who have their own objectives and desires. In the United States in the 1990s, this means the telephone companies, the advertisers, and anyone else who wants to make a buck out of listeners and viewers. In other words, the noosphere is increasingly governed by institutions and organizations—assemblages of people and machines pursuing particular objectives which *may or may not* serve morality, benevolence, or genuine human needs.

If Culture exists, or if the concept has any meaning at all, it is with respect to human purpose, and purpose can work for the benefit or disbenefit of anyone who seeks it—a shaman who manipulates his patients for enhancing his own power; the technocrat who wants to know all he can about his customers; or the politician who seeks control over his constituency with the help of opinion polls.

The chief value, its seems to me, of *The Phenomenon of Man* is its recasting of the simplistic language of the anthropological concept of culture into larger philosophical terms, and the synthesis of the root ideas of the discipline—evolution, cultural process and dynamics, Man's relationship to other animals, and so on. But in the last analysis, Teilhard tended to do what most anthropologists and anthropologically inclined commentators on the human condition have been doing for decades or even centuries: *celebrate* Man and his accomplishments—but not really to face up to the consequences of their long-range significance for the Earth. It is rather sad, perhaps, that Père Teilhard did not experience the latter-day effects of burgeoning population, environmental deterioration, and the communications revolution. Hominization is a good idea, but the price one may have to pay is increased *control*, and that can mean authoritarian politics.

Père Teilhard manifests a sense of wonder throughout the book. His title, "The *Phenomenon* of Man" suggests two things: (1) Man is a "phenomenon"—in the sense of a perpetual wonder in the universe, a unique thing; and (2) Man can be treated as a single entity because his mind and behavior prevented transpeciation or evolutionary radiation. Paleontological evidence suggests continual convergence, or even reconvergence after minor differentiation due to temporary demographic isolation. Hence we can speak in the singular—Man—or as the Classic era anthropologists did, Culture. Every philosopher or theologian in the past thousand years has tried to find a single word or label for the human phenomenon—even while acknowledging the diversity of habitat and outlook among the groups of this single species: the "unity and diversity" theme that late-Classic anthropologists liked to talk about.

But this dual condition *evolved*: it was not born *de novo*. As Teilhard notes, "Man comes silently into the world" (ibid.: 186); that is, without speech as an infant; and more generally, without culture. And the early millennia provide us with archaeological data on simple, rather uniform culture: stone tools, fire, etc., with only rare evidence of spiritual matters or objective thought processes. *Hominization* then is a process which takes place in the individual as he matures; and in the species as it proceeds down the slope of time. The species seems to tolerate a degree of diversity, but movement and communication tends to homogenize the content. This, in the last analysis, was the "wonder" that Teilhard senses, and which irrevocably gives rise to the mystery of precisely who we are and where we are going, and how we should be viewed by science, philosophy, and religion.

Père Teilhard also discusses the idea of *progress*. Trite and deceptive as the concept may be in an era of technological barbarism, in general terms it represents the inner dynamo of the human species. Père Teilhard deals with it in his discussion of the "organic crisis in evolution," or, "something is developing in the world by means of us, perhaps at our expense" (ibid.: 230). Teilhard never comes out openly and says what it is, but the implications are fairly clear: technology run amok, war, violence, and of course deterioration of the physical environment—although as noted, this latter was not felt as a major issue at the time Teilhard did his writing. He then seems to define Progress normatively: a way to reinforce the good in Man by trying for a *balance* in human achievements—to avoid letting one or more sector to run away with the ball. Overspecialization is one of the characteristics of hominization, but it has both desirable and dangerous consequences—and this, it seems to me, is the final lesson. Man is a multidimensional creature, and this is his fate as well as his glory. And anthropology must direct its attention to this larger problem of which "Culture" is nothing more than a catchword summarizing the bitter with the better. Yes indeed, there really is a *human nature*, despite the cultural diversity the Classic-era anthropologists loved to describe. This nature is the propensity to drive ahead, to accumulate, to seek mastery, and hopefully, to repair the inevitable damage.

The most controversial aspect of Père Teilhard's philosophy was his religious optimism over the future of mankind: the idea of a unified *noosphere* or world mentality, which also would represent a further step in cosmic evolution. Evolution, for Teilhard, the zoologist and paleontologist, was the master process and concept, and human evolution represented a new step in this cosmic process insofar as mankind was progressively capable of greater and greater coordination, cooperation, and integration. Behind this argument lay an attempt to introduce Christianity by insisting that the emerging unified noosphere was the outcome of Christian thought. Even Julian Huxley in his enthusiastic introduction to the book, refused to follow Teilhard Chardin into this attempt to bring religion into the argument, or to "personify the nonpersonal elements of reality" (Huxley 1959: 19). And in the cold light of the 1990s, there are serious empirical objections to this optimistic treatment of the human future: the increasing violence, disintegration of political units, and excessive ethnic separatism. As noted, the World Wide Web and the Internet do seem to represent something akin to Teilhard's emerging pan-human integration, although the contents of these communication devices reflect and implement the intense pluralism and relativism of the times. The picture is decidedly mixed.

The Phenomenon of Man was treated gingerly by anthropologist reviewers, who saw it either as a religious tract—"after all" Père

Teilhard was a clergyman—or, as a disquisition of dubious philosophical significance from a paleontologist (and one who had accepted Piltdown as real!). However, the basic difficulties with the acceptance of Teilhard's work probably centered on his essentially religious identity. Anthropologists have always had trouble with religion: they are students of all religions, and since religions are based on absolute values, it was necessary to see them all as equal, and avoid all implications of preference for one or another. No other issue in the ethnological glossary was so demanding of a relativistic approach.

But this attitude also prevented measuring differences between religions with respect to crucial values concerning human survival. Faiths that required bodily sacrifice, ritual murder, slaughter of the enemy, dacoity, or other aggressive acts promoting the glory of gods and the spirits were reported on without clear or detailed analysis of what the consequences might have been for living populations. The issues were similar to the witchcraft problem we discussed in chapter 9. It seems clear enough that anthropologists cannot afford to become apologists for any particular religion, but there must be a middle way: an approach in which the adaptive consequences of various religions—and moral values (see Hatch 1983)—are compared. The issue is probably largely moot, now that tribal and other exotic and minority religions have been waning, becoming absorbed into the larger universal faiths. And the latter in recent decades have certainly shown more strength and sanctioning power than would have been guessed in the 1930s, when secularism seemed to have won the day.

And Teilhard, for all of his religious conscience, also seemed to suggest another kind of middle way, in which religious ideas are translated into philosophical propositions, and explored both in terms of their logical fit and also with reference to scientific evidence bearing on their beliefs. Most important is the idea that *religion matters*—something that anthropologists often seemed to forget. Relativism—whatever its merits as a vehicle for tolerance and objectivity—tends to breed irreverence, indifference, even contempt. Philosophy tells us that humans need belief in order to make the world comprehensible. Anthropologists have always known this, of course, but often acted as if they did not. There is nothing so personally liberating as relativism, but it can produce antisocial attitudes, or more congenially stated, alienation.

Literature Cited

Bennett, John W. 1976. "Anticipation, Adaptation, and the Concept of Culture in Anthropology." *Science* 192: 847–53. Edited version published 1993–96 in *Human Ecology As Human Behavior* by J. W. Bennett. New Brunswick, NJ: Transaction Publishers.

Bidney, David. 1953. *Theoretical Anthropology.* New York: Columbia University Press.

Hatch, Elvin. 1983. *Culture and Morality: The Relativity of Values in Anthropology.* New York: Columbia University Press.

Huxley, Julian. [1959] 1975. "Introduction," *The Phenomenon of Man* by Teilhard de Chardin. New York: Harper Colophon.

Pearce, Roy Harvey. 1988. *Savagism and Civilization: A Study of the Indian and the American Mind.* Berkeley: University of California Press. Rev. ed. of *The Savages of America* (1953).

Teilhard de Chardin, Pierre. 1955–59. *The Phenomenon of Man.* Originally published in French as *Le Phénomène Humain* (1955) by Editions du Seuil, Paris. First published in English in 1959 by Wm. Collins Sons and Co., London. English translation by Bernard Wall. New York: Harper Colophon (1975).

Some Afterwords

Q: Did "Classic Anthropology" survive into the "Post-Classic" (whatever that may be)?

Anthropologist No. 1: Of course it "survives"—it never died. We are still doing research on tribal cultures, and theorizing about the nature of culture and social organization.

Anthropologist No. 2: Nah. It is dead as a dodo. Cultural anthropology sold out to a bunch of literary critics, and tribals are about all gone—or have become ethnic politicos or cultural revivalists—or both. Anthropology lost its soul with its subject matter.

Anthropologist No. 3: Well, yes, in the sense that the basic eclecticism—the theoretical hallmark of the discipline—still exists. Anthropologists have no choice but to be eclectic, since the discipline has no real intellectual core.

Anthropologist No. 4: It pooped out in the '60s or '70s because I think anthropologists missed the boat—several boats. They were unable to accept modern life—and human behavior—as generic topics, and they didn't award prestige to anthropologists who did—or to those in the applied fields, for that matter. Other people, like social psychologists or the new culture historians, have taken over topics that anthropologists should have dominated. The only real post-Classic success was work on peasants.

Anthropologist No. 5: This nutty discipline will survive so long as universities and foundations finance it. And its major significance is pedagogical because Classic anthropology collected a lot of good stuff. Them were the days.

Anthropologist No. 6: Well, parts of the discipline seem stronger than ever—particularly human paleontology—if, that is really part of anthropology. Archeology also does well. But the whole ethnological sector is moribund or fanciful; or chasing little propositions which are really a matter of private quarrels based on inadequate samples. I call it "buzzward ethnology."

Index of Names

I have included names of persons whose works and ideas are given special attention. That is, if a name is associated only with a particular bibliographic item it was not included in this index. Those anthropologists—"principal players"—whose works are given extended treatment can be observed on the basis of the very large number of page citations for them. (Incidentally, all of these "principal players" are deceased.)

Index of Principal Topics